LIBERATION THEOLOGY

AN INTRODUCTORY READER

LIBERATION THEOLOGY

AN INTRODUCTORY READER

Edited by
Curt Cadorette
Marie Giblin
Marilyn J. Legge
Mary Hembrow Snyder

ORBIS BOOKS

Maryknoll, New York 10545

Third Printing, October 1994

The Catholic Foreign Mission Society of America (Maryknoll) recruits and trains people for overseas missionary service. Through Orbis Books, Maryknoll aims to foster the international dialogue that is essential to mission. The books published, however, reflect the opinions of their authors and are not meant to represent the official position of the society.

Published by Orbis Books, Maryknoll, NY 10545-0308

The texts included in this volume are taken and in some cases adapted from previous Orbis publications, with the exception of "Defining Women-Church" by Mary E. Hunt, © Women's Alliance for Theology, Ethics and Ritual, 8035 13th St., Suites 1 & 3, Silver Spring, Maryland 20910.

The publisher wishes also to acknowledge the cooperation of SCM Press, which published British editions of Robert Schreiter, ed., *Faces of Jesus in Africa*, Chung Hyung Kyung, *Struggle To Be the Sun Again*, and Gustavo Gutiérrez, *A Theology of Liberation*; and Geoffrey Chapman, British publisher of Jean-Marc Éla, *My Faith as an African*.

Manufactured in the United States of America

Library of Congress Cataloging-in-Publication Data

Liberation theology : an introductory reader / edited by Curt
Cadorette ... [et al.]
   p. cm.
  Includes bibliographical references and index.
  ISBN 0-88344-801-7 (pbk.)
  1. Liberation theology. 2. Theology, Doctrinal. I. Cadorette,
Curt, 1948- .
BT83.57.L489 1992
230'.046 – dc20
                                    92-15666
                                       CIP

Contents

III. The Church in Solidarity: Liberation Ecclesiology

IV. Spirituality and Liberation

Preface

We live in a world that is both interconnected and divided. As we approach the third millennium, social and economic barriers that have divided human beings for centuries are melting away. In Europe, many nations are moving toward a federation that could not have been imagined a few decades ago. We are witnesses to the increased communications across continents facilitated by satellites, mass media, fax machines. Some would even speak of the globalization of human consciousness. That we are developing the technical means for achieving a global community can be a source of hope.

At the same time, however, we know that we live in a world still divided. Too many women and men lack the essentials of life: food, shelter, means of livelihood, channels for participation in shaping their own future. Discrimination rages on—against women, peoples of color, the poor. Our moral sensibilities are offended by the presence of homeless beggars on the streets of the United States and Europe and by the presence of starving African children on our television screens. All of this makes us wonder if contemporary civilization is going backward instead of forward.

Much in Western culture would have us turn aside from the questions these contradictions pose. "Eat, drink, shop, be sexy" is the message of advertising. Don't ask questions, don't worry; be happy!

Nevertheless, as Christians we can't help but stop and ask questions. Why these divisions? Where do they come from? What light does our Christian faith throw on the conflicts rending our world? How can we work to end them and promote a more just and peaceful human community? Christian churches have long struggled with these questions. But now there is a new element. Christian communities among the poor and the oppressed have joined this reflection, adding a perspective that is different from that of those who share in the benefits of power and prosperity. The viewpoints of these communities can help us better understand what is going on in the real world of the poor. What is more, theological writing that emerges from such communities helps us encounter God in a new way with profound implications for the way we understand our faith and live our lives. For these communities, the gospel is a powerful source of hope, not only for Christians, but for the world at large. It is out of these communities that there has emerged a new way of doing theology that has deeply challenged the universal church. It has come to be known as the theology of liberation.

Liberation theology is a diverse movement within the global Christian community. Its unifying principle is a passionate concern for the poor and oppressed and a commitment to living the gospel in ways that link everyday life with its transcendent foundation—God's love and concern for all human beings. The essays that follow offer an introduction to liberation theology through a selection of writings by a wide cross-section of theologians from around the world. The complexity of the material varies. While some essays are relatively concrete others are more theoretical.

We will explore liberation theology from four angles. In the first part we will analyze the way liberation theologians understand the larger world and their task within it as Christian thinkers. This section corresponds to the traditional category of theological method. The second part will deal with the subject of christology, the way liberation theologians approach the person and ministry of Jesus. The third part concerns ecclesiology, the identity and mission of the church or Christian community. Finally, we will examine the way liberation theologians understand contemporary discipleship or spirituality. Each of these parts begins with an introductory essay, written by one of the editors. These initial discussions are meant to clarify key ideas and concepts that will surface in the material that follows. Each part concludes with questions for further study or reflection. Finally, a glossary of theological terms has been included at the end of the book.

Whether the book is read for academic, pastoral, or personal reasons, we hope that readers will find it a convenient and stimulating collection of theological essays. Our hope, however, is that these texts do more than stir new thoughts. Ideally, reflection leads to action. The reader may not agree with everything that follows. It is to be hoped, however, that many will not disagree with the premise, so central to liberation theology, that faith is made real in action on behalf of other human beings, particularly those who are poor and oppressed.

LIBERATION THEOLOGY

AN INTRODUCTORY READER

PART I

LIBERATION THEOLOGY: CONTEXT AND METHOD

Introduction

CURT CADORETTE

THEOLOGY AND THE SEARCH FOR MEANING

As we come to the end of the twentieth century, most people in the developed world lead lives that are far more secure and comfortable than those of their grandparents. At first sight, it might seem that we have solved most of our problems as human beings. Despite our sophistication and wealth, however, there are large numbers of people who find a meaningful life elusive. Unfortunately, none of our material possessions can really tell us who we are or how to live our lives. Even more disturbing is the large number of people in the developing world who die unnecessarily from hunger, disease, and oppression. We have taken immense scientific strides forward but only faltering steps in achieving a just and authentic human community.

We cannot expect science and technology to solve our problems and answer our questions about the meaning of life. They are marvelous tools for understanding and dealing with the material world, but tell us little or nothing about why it exists and how we should live in it. To answer those questions we need a vision, a transcendent understanding of ourselves that goes beyond the present moment and material world. The majority of people reach a transcendent understanding of themselves through the medium of religion. Over the centuries human beings have developed insightful religious traditions. All share a concern with the question of transcendence, but each understands and articulates it in different ways. What makes

Christianity unique is its belief that Jesus of Nazareth, a first-century Palestinian Jew, articulated a transcendent vision of life of unparalleled incisiveness. He was able to do so because he embodied or incarnated the divine itself. He was a revelation of God in human form. Twenty centuries of reflection on God's presence in Jesus by his followers has produced a rich body of wisdom that we call Christian theology.

Christian theology is much more than a collection of texts. It is actually an on-going attempt to understand and respond to God's presence in history. There are serious presuppositions behind this statement. The most obvious is that Christians understand revelation as something that takes place in history. In other words, we find the meaning of life in the world, not outside of it. We also find it in relationship to our fellow men and women. For this reason, our particular historical context and the material conditions of our lives assume special importance in shaping our self-understanding and approach to God. The fact of being male or female, rich or poor, is not some insignificant biographical detail, but a matter of great consequence. Another result of Christianity's concern with history is that revelation is understood as an on-going event, not a static, once-and-for-all phenomenon. The Christian tradition perceives Jesus as an all-important revelation of God's presence in history. Christians, however, live in a changing world. This means that their belief in Jesus as God's incarnation must be expressed in ways that make sense in a given historical situation.

In the late twentieth century, Christians face a unique theological challenge. By the use of science and technology we have achieved remarkable material progress. We have also produced sprawling slums, the specter of nuclear war, and possible ecological catastrophe caused by global warming. What does it mean to believe in God in a world where the rich oppress the poor, men denigrate women, and human beings with white skin consider themselves superior to people of color? What do Christians have to say about these injustices? What is the relationship between their beliefs, their daily lives, and the suffering that afflicts millions of human beings? These are serious questions that go to the heart of the Christian message.

One of the tasks of the theologian is to make a correlation between revelation and history, always keeping in mind that while they are related, they are not the same thing. To confuse one with the other is to risk turning a particular historical moment into an idol. Thus, we end up worshipping ourselves, with terrible consequences. Christians must relate to their world dialectically, neither condemning nor accepting it too quickly. Achieving this balance is a perennial task that is crucial to the credibility and survival of the Christian community. It requires systematic analysis and study. In other words, it requires theology and theologians, the thinking members of the Christian community charged with articulating their faith in an intelligible way.

CHRISTIANITY AND THE WESTERN WORLD: A THUMBNAIL
SKETCH

For more than a thousand years Catholic Christianity shaped the self-understanding of people in the West. From the reign of Constantine until the decline of the medieval world, most Europeans thought that there was only one legitimate way of understanding life and God—theirs. This monolithic perspective began to break apart in the sixteenth century when Luther and other reformers challenged the power of institutional Catholicism and the theological presuppositions behind it. Suddenly there were many ways of understanding and living the Christian faith. Tragically, however, Christians began to kill each other in large numbers because of theological differences. This led to an inevitable reaction against the churches, Protestant and Catholic, on the part of many educated Europeans. This anti-church sentiment is best exemplified by the thinkers of the Enlightenment, an eighteenth-century intellectual movement that produced many of the values that underpin our social and political world today.

The leaders of the Enlightenment saw reason, not religion, as the best way to answer people's questions about the meaning of life. They were convinced that human rationality, working with the sciences, could eventually create an ideal world. They tolerated religion as a social convention, but rejected any role for the institutional church in the new social order they advocated. There is much to admire in the Enlightenment. The notion of the individual as a person with inherent rights that the state must uphold and protect took shape during this period. Pluralism and tolerance of social difference became legal principles. At the same time, some Enlightenment figures put such stress on individual autonomy that they underemphasized the collective nature of society. They also suffered from an exaggerated confidence in the ability of scientific rationality to solve human problems.

From the eighteenth until the twentieth century a futile battle was waged in the West between religion and rationality. Caught between two hostile parties, people were often forced to choose between belief and non-belief, religion and modern social freedoms, as if there were no middle ground. This intense dualism began to diminish in the late nineteenth and early twentieth centuries. Protestant theologians were the first to stick their heads out of the trenches and come to the conclusion that many modern values could be reconciled with Christian belief. In certain theological faculties in northern Europe and North America a tradition known as liberalism developed. Its proponents accepted the validity of the Enlightenment and the modern state it helped develop. They also stressed the legitimacy of theology as an academic discipline and the reasonableness of Christianity as a religious system. They were intent on making Christianity a moral force again in Western culture, especially among the educated and affluent members of society, many of whom had lost contact with the institutional church or were non-believers. In Catholic circles it would take more time to declare a truce between the church and modernity. Still reeling from the Reformation and the attack on its power by Enlightenment thinkers, the Catholic church would remain a defensive bastion until the 1960s.

Protestant liberalism suffered major setbacks as the twentieth century moved forward. The mindless slaughter of the First World War, and the horror of Nazi death camps a generation later, pointed to basic flaws in modern values. Gruesome historical events called into question the liberal assumption that Europe and North America were Christian parts of the world. By the mid-point of the twentieth century self-doubt replaced self-confidence as the dominant mood of many people in the West. Both Christianity and rationality seemed to have failed when they were most needed. In response to this pervasive crisis of faith, theologians began to rethink the role of Christianity in society. Although they recognized that much of modernity was good, they also realized that certain of its presuppositions demanded criticism. The exaggerated individualism and materialism of the twentieth century were clearly related to the fragmentation and violence of the times.

Finally shaking off its defensiveness, the Catholic church addressed the crisis and challenge of modernity during the Second Vatican Council, held from 1962 until 1965. During this meeting an international body of bishops and theologians, from many cultures and every continent, tried to refashion their church as a prophetic force capable of satisfying people's thirst for a life-giving vision. After decades of negativity toward modernity, the bishops tried to understand it in a more balanced way, assessing both its positive and negative qualities. In documents like *Lumen Gentium* and *Gaudium et Spes*, the bishops called on Catholic Christians to live the gospel more seriously and carry its message to secular society in a more productive way. They looked for a resurgence of Christian faith that would replace the self-doubt and skepticism that afflicted so many people in the developed world.

When the Council ended a massive effort was undertaken to implement its insights in the Catholic community. In few parts of the world did this campaign achieve greater success than in Latin America. The people of this largely Catholic continent had experienced profound social and economic changes in the 1960s that prompted serious questions about the relationship between their faith and the societies in which they lived. The Council's call to take the world seriously and forge a more just social order was welcome news for Latin American Catholics. Long associated with social and political conservatism, members of the church moved to the vanguard of intellectual and social activism. The Council's mandate would be carried out by a new generation of energetic theologians. They would create a theology faithful to the letter and spirit of Vatican II while going beyond its sometimes limited, European perspective.

THE BIRTH OF LIBERATION THEOLOGY

In the late 1950s a number of gifted Latin American priests were sent to Europe for training. When they arrived they found the theological scene in a state of transition. Despite some opposition from conservative elements in the hierarchy, theologians like Teilhard de Chardin and Karl Rahner were exploring the relationship between modernity and Christian belief. Gradually their views gained wide acceptance in the church and influenced the discussion and documents of the Council itself.

Priests like Gustavo Gutiérrez from Peru and Juan Luis Segundo from Uruguay found themselves caught up in a rare moment of theological excitement. A lively dialogue going on in Europe between theologians and social theorists also fired their imaginations. Pitted at each other's throats for decades, certain social scientists had begun to discover the more progressive side of Christianity while theologians had come to appreciate better the social scientists' analysis of modernity. Latin American theologians began to study Marx and Freud as well as Augustine and Aquinas. They returned to their countries with new theological ideas and a solid grasp of sociology, psychology, economics, and political theory. They were well equipped to respond to Vatican II's call for a renewed, socially committed Christian community.

When this new generation of theologians returned from Europe they realized that much of what they learned had to be translated to fit their context. In the 1960s Europeans had achieved a high level of economic affluence and political stability. Many Latin American countries, however, had sunk into unprecedented levels of poverty and political violence. As much as they were committed to the theology and vision of Vatican II, the young theologians realized that its message was directed to an audience different from their own. Vatican II tried to address the question of the church's role in developed societies afflicted by a crisis of meaning. Latin America's problems, however, had little to do with belief or the pros and cons of the Enlightenment. The vast majority of Latin Americans were Christians and few even knew about the Enlightenment. The problem in Latin America, as well as in Africa and Asia, was dehumanization. How could anyone talk about God when millions of human beings had been turned into "non-persons" by economic exploitation and political repression?

In 1968 the bishops of Latin America assembled in Medellín, Colombia to develop a pastoral strategy for implementing Vatican II in their continent. The document they issued, shaped by theologians like Gutiérrez and Segundo, called for a radical transformation of the Latin American church, along with the sociopolitical structures of the continent. Soon after Medellín Gustavo Gutiérrez published *A Theology of Liberation* in which he insisted that Christians commit themselves to the liberation of the poor and oppressed. The title of this book would soon be applied to a larger theological and pastoral movement in the global church that began to take shape in the late 1960s.

For Gutiérrez the poverty and injustice inflicted on millions of women and men in the developing world was a scandal that demanded redress. But for Gutiérrez liberation entailed more than economic and political justice. He acknowledged also a transcendent or spiritual dimension to the struggle for liberation. Social systems that deprived people of bread and freedom also deprived them of their God-given dignity. It numbed them to their own worth and beauty. If Christians believed in an incarnate God revealed in history they had to do something about the impoverished human beings around them. If they did not their talk about God would be meaningless.

For the first time in Christian theological history the question of the poor, the "non-persons" in the developing world, became the focal point of discussion. Traditional European debates between conservatives and liberals about modernity were not the real issue in Latin America. The question was how impoverished and oppressed people in the developing world fit into the Christian community. What did the institutional church, its social teachings, and the Bible have to say to them? Was the Christian community in the developed world willing to listen and respond to these people?

Gutiérrez's ideas and writings quickly gained a readership in other parts of the world, particularly in developing nations afflicted with problems similar to Latin America's. He is sometimes known as "the father of liberation theology," but the title is not entirely accurate. At the same time that he was writing James Cone, an African-American theologian, was spelling out a powerful theology of Black liberation in the United States. Cone's ideas were published slightly before Gutiérrez's and were remarkable for their vigor and intellectual incisiveness. Cone provided the Christian community with a powerful service by pointing to the suffering and oppression of minority people in developed countries and the dismal record of the Christian churches in confronting the racism in their midst. Cone's ideas would be useful in turn to African theologians, especially those in South Africa who were confronting the evils of *apartheid*.

LIBERATION THEOLOGY: ITS CONCERNS AND CHARACTERISTICS

As liberation theology emerged as a coherent movement it became clear that its proponents, despite geographic and cultural differences, faced a common oppressive reality that challenged their Christian beliefs. As liberation theologians looked over their social and economic environments they saw that the affluence and freedoms of the industrial world were confined to a small percentage of people in the northern hemisphere. They began to charge that this disparity was actually a result of the way modern economic and political systems worked. It was symptomatic of an economic and political order that exploited a majority for the sake of a privileged minority.

The first phase of liberation theology, roughly until the 1970s, focused heavily on the relationship between faith and socioeconomic issues. To overcome the suffering around them, liberation theologians first had to understand its causes. Since capitalism was the dominant mode of production throughout the world, linking developed and developing countries, it was important to understand its economic and political characteristics. Because a great deal of analysis of the capitalist system had been done by Marxist social theorists, liberation theologians selectively employed their insights. Few liberation theologians, however, were naive about the limitations of Marxism, or any particular method of social analysis. Economics and sociology were helpful in explaining how societies worked, but could not entirely explain the poverty and oppression of the developing world. A more fundamental explanation, and one familiar in theological language, was the reality of sin. Simply put, much of the developing world's suffering was the result of sinful behavior on the part of powerful, developed nations. Many people in developed countries considered the developing world simply as a source of cheap raw materials and labor.

It was obvious that a solution to this pervasive injustice would require more than economic or political action. It demanded a change of heart. The solution liberation theologians offered for the poverty and oppression around them was Christianity lived in a radical way. Without rejecting modernity, they pointed to the individualism and materialism of people in the developed world as manifestations of sin, of a disordered worldview that caused others to suffer. At the same time, they called on the victims of exploitation in the developing world, particularly members of the Christian community, to overcome their passivity and act as the "voice of the voiceless" in the struggle for justice. The concern of liberation theologians was to formulate an explanation of Christian faith that took into consideration the experience and hopes of the poor and oppressed.

In the texts that follow, the reader will come across a term that is dear to most liberation theologians—*praxis*. Its precise meaning varies from one author to another, but essentially praxis implies action informed by reflection. Liberation theologians see praxis, especially what they call liberative praxis, as the principal task of the Christian community in the world today. The believing community cannot counsel patience when children die of malnutrition or people are murdered because they merely ask for a just wage. In such situations the Christian community must act. Liberative praxis, however, is more than a knee-jerk reaction to injustice. It flows from the community's understanding of itself as a gathering of Jesus' disciples called to embody his vision of God. The community does not exist for its own sake, but for the sake of all women and men, whether Christian or not. It serves them by working for justice and freedom. It also serves them by providing a setting in which human beings can enjoy each other, worship

God, and achieve spiritual depth. The life of the community is itself a type of liberative praxis. It is an example of living freedom and just relationships made possible by faith.

Praxis is ultimately an expression of the Christian community's commitment to the world and faith in the gospel's power to transform life in a positive way. These factors make the praxis of the Christian community different from the activities of a political party or social movement. Political and social actions are indispensable components in the process of liberation. For the Christian, however, the ultimate purpose of liberation is the material *and* spiritual redemption of human beings from suffering and sin. Liberation theologians constantly stress that the poor are not powerless. As Gustavo Gutiérrez has pointed out, the developing world is made up of "poor but believing" people. To the extent that they believe in each other and the God who gave them life, they have enormous strength.

Liberation theologians have occasionally been accused by some of their critics of treating the poor and history romantically. Liberation theologians, however, see a side to history academics in developed countries rarely discover. They see innumerable instances in history when poor but believing people have maintained their self-respect, solidarity, and hope for the future. The fact that many contemporary Christians are committed to the liberation of their societies, despite all sorts of repression, speaks of an enigmatic power that Gutiérrez has called "the power of the poor in history." This power is a thread that liberation theologians see running through the complex fiber of history, giving it coherence and a transcendent purpose visible to people of faith.

Most of the essays in this anthology contain quotations from scripture, both Hebrew and Christian. It will be clear that liberation theologians, both Catholic and Protestant, rely heavily on the Bible. They see it as a source of revelation that provides insight into the meaning of life and the significance of contemporary events. The Hebrews' escape from slavery in Egypt and Jesus' preaching of the Beatitudes are paradigmatic stories and sayings that reveal the true purpose of human existence. For liberation theologians, the Bible has a unifying theme and purpose, despite its historical and literary complexity. It narrates how human beings come to perceive God in their midst. The God of the Bible is made manifest on Sinai and in the person of Jesus. But this same God is also present in the poor and oppressed, and in all people of good will. In a world characterized by exploitation and violence, the person who believes in the God of the Bible will inevitably be involved in the struggle for justice, much like the great figures of the Hebrew and Christian scriptures.

Liberation theologians approach the Bible as a source of continuing revelation rather than as a collection of ancient writings. In some ways, the Exodus is still going on and the Beatitudes are still being preached. In almost every base Christian community, the Bible is the central book used to help its members understand their faith and task in the world. By reading and discussing the texts they come to realize that their struggle for justice is part of God's plan for creation. They see a correlation between the Hebrews in bondage, Jesus' preaching, and themselves. This awareness gives them a sense of dignity and confidence they often have never had. The Bible, then, is a key tool in raising people's consciousness and helping them chart an effective course of action in society.

Apart from the Bible, liberation theologians are also sensitive to the importance of Christian tradition. It makes us aware of the pains and joys, failures and successes of the Christian community throughout its complex and varied history. It links the Christian people together with symbols and stories that are the heritage of every member of the church. Liberation theologians have come to appreciate tradition as a life-giving force whose power is often manifest in cultural and artistic activity. In the slums of South Africa and Indian villages of Guatemala they have heard songs and seen dances that celebrate the pains and joys of ordinary human beings. In base Christian communities, the poor and oppressed celebrate what has been called the "underside of history." They remember and act out the lives of their predecessors in faith, simple but courageous people whose names are not mentioned in history books. They celebrate what the German theologian Johann Metz has called the "dangerous memories" of the Christian people. Liberation theologians point to the subversive nature of these memories. The history of the poor and oppressed is marked by victimization, but not total acquiescence to injustice. Of course, many people are overwhelmed by situations beyond their control and become fatalistic or passive. Nonetheless, there is also a tradition of resistance that speaks of a vibrant vision of life that negates the effects of injustice. Workers organize unions and women in slums muster their meager resources to create soup kitchens because they have faith and hope.

What liberation theologians have attempted to do in their varied ways is to insure Christianity's continued vitality and significance in today's world. Living among the poor and oppressed, they have seen just how powerful and positive their faith can be. Their writings try to capture the promise of this faith for the sake of the entire Christian community, and a world that desperately needs liberation from injustice and sin. What is liberating and revolutionary about Christianity is that it recognizes every human being as a child of God, something we too often forget in our modern, materialistic world. Many of the poor and oppressed, however, have not forgotten. It is they, and their tenacious faith, that call us to conversion and the affirmation of our own transcendence. If liberation theologians are correct, it may be the poor and oppressed who help save modernity from its own destructive impulses. In their struggle for justice many of them have achieved a profound understanding of life that liberation theologians see as an integral part of God's redemptive plan.

In many respects, the liberation theologians whose essays follow in this section on theological method are no different from their colleagues in other parts of the world. They spend a great deal of their time studying, reading, and writing like theologians and pastoral agents anywhere. Like them, they constantly try to make correlations between the revelation found in scripture and tradition, and the experience of Christian people. Liberation theologians, nevertheless, have distinguishing marks that set them apart from most of their peers in the developed world. Because they are so committed to the poor and oppressed you will sense a pathos in their writing that is rarely found in European or North American theology. When a feeling, thinking person is surrounded by suffering and violence, it is impossible to be dispassionate. Liberation theologians, however, do not engage in shrill diatribes. Their work is the product of deep thought and years of experience. While the essays that follow may be difficult to accept or understand, they are far from unreasonable. Justice for the poor and political rights for the oppressed are not unreasonable demands. What is unreasonable is their denial. What liberation theologians ask from their fellow Christians is a reasoned, passionate commitment to their fellow men and women as a sign of faith.

A PREVIEW OF OUR TEXTS

In the first reading for this section, Clodovis Boff, a Brazilian priest, tells of his experience working with rubber-gatherers in the Amazon. A theology professor who usually teaches in the city, he has gone to the jungle to visit base Christian communities. The Brazilian church has invested tremendous time and energy in the last thirty years in creating local lay groups or communities. These small groups serve as a forum in which ordinary people can come together and talk about their faith, discuss issues of local concern, and support each other on a material and spiritual level. The rubber-gatherers Boff is visiting are poor. Many of them are descendants of Indians and are consequently looked down on by white Brazilians. Very few of them can read or write since they have no formal education. The rubber-gathering families are often exploited by middlemen who pay them very little for the latex they collect. The situation Boff encounters is bleak since this pattern of poverty and abuse is well established. Understandably, he asks himself if he can really accomplish anything positive by visiting these people.

Boff realizes that he cannot perform miracles. He alone cannot change the lives of the people he will visit. At the same time, he is guardedly optimistic about the possibility of change. As Boff points out, the purpose of his visit is to start a "subjective revolution" in which these rubber-gatherers will come to realize that they have a right to a fuller, more human life. While Boff is among these people he comes to an important insight. The rubber-gatherers' concern for each other, their efforts to organize themselves, and their continuing hope in the future point to a God who is already in their midst. As Boff points out, the rubber-gatherers have obvious deficiencies. They are victims of poverty who live in a culture of backwardness. Yet in simple ways, especially through their small Christian communities, they are trying to challenge the people and social forces that make them poor. In the journal of his experience, *Feet-on-the-Ground Theology,* Boff is taught a powerful lesson by the people he has come to teach. He realizes that God is present in the lives of very ordinary people. Ultimately, their world is a source of revelation and his theology must reflect what he sees and experiences in the Brazilian Amazon.

The next essay was written by Tissa Balasuriya, a theologian from Sri Lanka. Balasuriya raises the question of context and its relationship to theology. It is important to understand that theologians are influenced by their social and intellectual environment. There really is no such thing as a timeless truth or "contextless" insight. The theology of Thomas Aquinas reflected his medieval, monastic setting and used the philosophy of Aristotle to make sense out of the world. Likewise, Karl Rahner's theology was shaped by the concerns of twentieth century Europeans and employed concepts drawn from existentialist philosophy. Both Aquinas and Rahner were superb theologians, many of whose insights have abiding validity. We must keep in mind, however, that they were male clerics who lived all of their sheltered lives in Europe. Consequently, many of their ideas make little sense to people from a different culture and intellectual tradition. Christians in Asia have a different set of experiences and a different approach to reality. Balasuriya contends that Christianity has been too closely associated with the Western world. This connection limits the appeal of Christianity for most Asians and its effectiveness as a catalyst for humanization. What Balasuriya calls for is a new type of "globalized" theology that takes into consideration the experience of non-Westerners, Christians, and non-Christians alike.

The third essay on theological method explores the place of the Bible in liberation theology. It is entitled "The Use of the Bible in Christian Communities of the Common People" and was written by Carlos Mesters, a Dutch scripture scholar who has worked for decades among the poor of Brazil. As previously indicated, the Bible is the key document for liberation theologians, pastoral agents, and members of base communities. It is the foundation on which their faith is laid and the measuring rod by which their actions are gauged. As Mesters points out, hearing the word of God requires three things: the Bible, a believing community, and awareness of the larger world. When these three ingredients are blended together we begin to hear God's word in a clear way. If the Bible just sits on a bookshelf it is merely a collection of texts written by people long ago. When, however, the members of a believing community begin to read the Bible and reflect on it in light of their own lives it assumes a deeper significance. A type of conversation is initiated between ancient and modern believers that turns the Bible into a source of revelation. The word of God is not merely a set of phrases. It is much more. It is an evolving experience of the deeper meaning of life that is constantly happening in people's lives and history.

More than half of the poor and oppressed people in the world today are women. Clearly, however, women do not make up half the leadership of any country. Nor do women exercise half the leadership in the Christian churches, although they almost always represent more than half of its active membership. What we see everywhere, even in the Christian churches, is a phenomenon known as sexism. In many societies women are doubly victimized. They are poor as well as women. Many women, however, are doubly strong. Rather than giving in to poverty and oppression they resist. Throughout the world today women are assuming leadership roles in the struggle for justice. This is even taking place in the Christian community, although more slowly because of resistance from certain males intent on maintaining their privileged place in the church hierarchy. The next article we will examine was written by Ivone Gebara. She and women from Asia, Africa, North America, and Europe are writing a feminist theology that adds a whole new dimension to the struggle for liberation.

Ivone Gebara writes from the north-east of Brazil, one of the poorest sections of her country. She is surrounded by women who are struggling to survive. Their lives are bleak and often short. Many are abused by their husbands and bosses. In the north-east of Brazil, *machismo* is still a powerful force. Yet many of these women tenaciously hang on to their hope for a better life. They reject the presuppositions behind *machismo* — their supposed inferiority and the supposed rights of men to oppress them. What Ivone Gebara sees around her is a revolution, what she calls an "irruption of history." More and more women are challenging the people and social values that oppress them. Feminist theologians like Gebara are trying to articulate women's experience of oppression and resistance. They are saying in unequivocal terms that any Christian community that does not take women's experience into account is necessarily distorted. Worse still, it may even be a source of oppression.

The final essay is by Jean-Marc Éla, a theologian from Cameroon, a country in West Africa that was colonized and exploited by both the English and French. Africa is rich in natural and human resources, but the continent's material wealth benefits very few Africans. The real beneficiaries are often non-Africans in the northern hemisphere who extract the continent's resources and keep almost all of the profits for themselves. Behind such economic violence and greed lies a none-too-subtle racism. Africans have often been deemed culturally backward and superstitious people who needed to be led into the twentieth century by better-educated foreigners. Éla condemns the so-called development of Africa by non-Africans while he calls on his people to recognize their own rich and dynamic cultural heritage as Africans. Like other liberation theologians, he sketches the outlines of a believing community capable of responding to the twenty-first century, in Africa and throughout the world.

1

In the Heart of the Endless Jungle

CLODOVIS BOFF

In this book I am going to be speaking of a missionary journey I undertook deep into the jungle in western Brazil, visiting rubber-gatherers and newly formed communities. This odyssey was both theological and spiritual, and certainly human.

Monday, August 1, 1983: Manoel Urbano

FROM THE METROPOLIS TO THE BUSH

I've come from the south of Brazil as fast as the wind. As usual, I've spent the first semester teaching theology at the Pontifical Catholic University in Rio, helping out in pastoral work in *favelas* [urban slums – ed.], and traveling to help with consultations here and there. And so, yesterday, Sunday, after the end of the big assembly of religious priests and sisters in Brazil, in which I took part, I took a plane to Rio Branco. And very early today, Monday, I've come along with some sisters and lay women in a pickup to the town of Manoel Urbano, in the state of Acre, on the banks of the Purus River.

I chose to travel the whole way in the back with Sister Otacília in order to get filled in on the general situation of the local church, to immerse myself in the sights of the vast landscape opening up before us, and to get my bearings in this new universe.

To shift from an urban center like Rio to these edges of the world always gives you a jolt – psychologically, spiritually, and culturally. At first it leaves you stunned, but as time passes it seasons you in both spirit and body.

These extracts are taken from Clodovis Boff's *Feet-on-the-Ground Theology: A Brazilian Journey* (Maryknoll, N.Y.: Orbis Books, 1987), pp. 3-22. Translated by Phillip Berryman.

Manoel Urbano is a small town, with little more than a hundred families. Friday I'm going to set out from here on a trip with Sister Nieta to keep some commitments already made. I'll be in the jungle until the end of the month.

I'm quite worn out from the work that kept piling up toward the end of my time in the south, my theological period, so I want to see if I can rest a bit both physically and mentally before facing this new period, my pastoral period.

Tuesday, August 2: Still in Manoel Urbano

FAITH AND THE TRANSFIGURATION OF THE WORLD

These days I make it a point to take part in the life and work of the community of the Sisters of St. Joseph who are responsible for this vast region: Sister Otacília, Sister Nieta, and Sister Teresinha.

At morning prayer we were reflecting together on the gospel of the day: Peter walking on the water (Matt. 14:22-36). There's no doubt that of itself faith is not a *force* for *transforming* the *structures* of the world. Faith is rather a *light* that *transfigures* the *meaning* of the world. True, this light is also an energy that is brought to bear on world structures and can change them. Nevertheless, faith doesn't directly change the *form* of things or events. What faith changes is their *figure*. It is not trans-form-ation but trans-figure-ation. It is a *meta-noia,* a subjective revolution, a transformation of the spirit, and it is active in the world.

The world of the believer is not the same as the world of the unbeliever (paraphrasing Wittgenstein: "The world of the happy man . . ."). Thus the world of Francis of Assisi was different, infinitely far removed, from the world of Pietro Bernadone, his father. What's different is the perspective, the vision or the conception, not the external, objective, or physical makeup of things.

Revolution, in the full sense, involves both structure and meaning, world and spirit, existence and consciousness, *physis* and *pistis.*

And so the big question is how to fit together truth and reality, and the ideal and the real, meaning and system, kingdom of God and society. That is what God calls humans to do—and it is also what God promises.

Wednesday, August 3: Still in Manoel Urbano

CHRIST STILL MOVES THROUGHOUT THE WORLD

At Mass tonight, with the whole town present, we reflected on the gospel of the day: the Canaanite woman (Matt. 15:21-28). Today Christ continues to roam to the ends of the earth—participants said—in order to find those who are abandoned or shunted aside. And to find all the persons who are here, and even more those who live in the jungle along the rivers or in the "centers" ("center" here means deep in the jungle, as opposed to "the edge" or "the road"). The Messiah is going to come to visit them, to save them, to liberate them, to bring them the kingdom, which is life, joy, hope, justice, and peace.

I apply all this to myself, for my own consolation, because every time I come from the "marvelous south" up to these remote areas, I'm always overwhelmed by a strange, and no doubt false, feeling that it is all useless, even absurd.

Besides, I recall the gospel passage, "When that day comes, many will plead with me, 'Lord, Lord, have we not prophesied in your name? Have we not exorcised demons by its power? Did we not do many miracles in your name as well?' Then I will declare to them solemnly, I never knew you. Out of my sight, you evildoers!" (Matt. 7:22-23).

That's the most important thing. Not big gestures that attract public notice, but rather humility, fidelity to the Lord of the kingdom in everyday practice. And you should engage in political action or any kind of revolution with the same naturalness and simplicity with which you set the table or weed the garden.

No scene in the film *Gandhi* impressed me more than the one where he's meeting with the great leaders of India, discussing with them the all-important question of the liberation of the people, and he sees a child pulling along a little goat with its left leg injured. Gandhi gets up, breaks off the discussion, and goes over to treat the animal with mud from a nearby pond.

If politics does not take as its supreme value the creation, preservation, and increase of life—and fullness of life—it loses all its meaning.

The Kingdom Is of the Poor and Oppressed—and of Children

Today I spent the afternoon giving children a ride on the back of a bike, riding around on the quiet streets of Manoel Urbano. There were more than twenty of them, waiting for their turn and running alongside the bike through the dusty streets, noisy and happy. These children are dreamlike in their beauty, with their brown hair and Indian features.

Does this have any liberating significance? None at all, it would seem. But it's enough that it's significant in human terms. Isn't that enough for it to deserve our wholehearted attention?

Children are graciousness itself. They are the living expression of receiving, of accepting the kingdom, which is always a gift. In that sense they are the symbol of the highest and noblest activity the spirit is capable of.

The kingdom is to be found here, in children. Indeed, is there more kingdom present when you give a conference to a hundred important adults than when you entertain a half dozen children by riding them around on a bicycle?

True, there's no need to set one thing against another. It would be more beautiful if speakers could give a conference like they give kids a bike ride. With the same freedom and simplicity. Like someone who's a "useless servant." That is perhaps the only way that political practice will not end up being a new kind of "justification by works," something Paul so thoroughly condemned, as had Jesus of Nazareth before him.

Thursday, August 4: Still in Manoel Urbano

JESUS' MESSIANISM—THE MESSIANISM OF THE POOR

Today's gospel, which we meditated on this morning in our own community and discussed with the people in the evening, speaks of how the Messiah must suffer and be rejected and then enter into glory (Matt. 16:13-23). This passage helps us understand how the liberation of this world takes place within the course of history. For if the "messianic people" (Vatican II, Constitution on the Church, #9) liberates, it does so on the basis of its poverty. The Liberator in history is not Napoleon, but the poor person. It is the suffering Servant, as corporate figure of the chosen people, who liberates the world from suffering. That is what Daniel 7 sees in the "son of man" (v. 13), that he represents a people made up of those who have been defeated (v. 21). Second Isaiah sees in the "servant of Yahweh" a symbol of the people, "the one despised, whom the nations abhor, the slave of rulers" (49:7).

The way things go for the eschatological or definitive Messiah is also instructive for understanding the way things go for the messiah in history: the people of the oppressed.

Peter's problem—and he is "Satan," "stumbling block," filled with the "thoughts of men," which run counter to those of God—continues to be the problem of those with common sense, those who are "carnal" and "alienated." But there is more to it.

Observing the population of this little town and evaluating its potential for acting in history, one is overwhelmed by the same doubt Peter had. It makes you want to laugh and ask yourself: What can this lead to? Or: Can anything good come out of this Nazareth (cf. John 1:46)?

Even if the prospects of what can be done in history are obviously quite limited, things are not that way when it comes to "God's thoughts." The standard of real political effectiveness is not the only thing that counts, nor even the main thing. In any case, it isn't absolute at all. It is relative to human beings and their concrete history.

As a final note, didn't today's saint, the Curé of Ars, have a well-known saying, "A single soul is enough of a parish for a priest"? The scope of liberation. . . .

Saturday, August 6: A Settlement Called Roçado

FORCED MARCH

My legs and feet are aching. We went from Manoel Urbano to a little place called Deposito on foot all the way. That was perhaps forty kilometers. That was the day before yesterday, our first day of traveling.

Next, we came here from Deposito, seven more hours. We left at 7 A.M. and got here after 2 P.M. We only stopped for a little more than a half hour to have lunch at Parana, a settlement on the way.

This is too much for the first couple days, especially for someone like me who has to begin with a trip like this. Yesterday, when we got to where we were going, after greeting the owners of the house — shy, as these folks always are — I couldn't hold out any more: I threw myself on the floor and stayed there like a corpse, with a terrific pain in my legs. I had a horrible swelling on my left leg near my groin and I was limping along the road. I grabbed a stick on the side of the trail and made it my staff. By leaning on it, I could take the weight off my left leg.

Dona Joana, the lay leader, told me, "Father, go take a swim in the river — you'll feel refreshed." I answered jokingly, "You can bury me here; I'm not going to budge." But I ended up going.

That night when I lay down in the hammock, my legs were so tired and sore I couldn't sleep. I would stretch them out or curl up, but I couldn't get relief and go to sleep. I said to Sister Nieta, "Sister, unless I feel better when I get up tomorrow, I don't know how I'll be able to keep going." "But Father," she answered, "the word is out to everyone in the area, and they're expecting us. . . . Don't do this now." I would have to keep going, even if I had to ride on the back of an animal, like an ox or donkey. I massaged my legs to loosen up the stiff muscles, and I finally got to sleep.

Very early in the morning, it got bitterly cold, as it always does at this time of year. I couldn't stay warm even with the two blankets I had brought. Besides that, you could hear a poor child with whooping cough, coughing away as though it were about to stop breathing and die. It was enough to tear your heart . . . and keep you awake. All I could do was wait for daybreak and get up. . . .

Lay Leaders: Of the Same Stock as the People

The lay leader in Roçado is *Seu* Maia. He is illiterate, as is everyone else in the community. There had been a young woman who could read the gospel, but she had moved away. The inhabitants don't come together often, only to pray the rosary during a novena to honor a saint.

Right now *Seu* Maia is away. He caught his foot in an animal trap and he went to the city for treatment. He's not dirt poor: he has a big enough house and a few head of cattle.

Dona Joana, on the other hand, the leader in Deposito, is something else. A lively woman, she can read well and is a driving force in her community. She told me that on Holy Thursday she had organized, in addition to everything else, a community meal, using homemade wine, in memory of the Last Supper of Jesus.

Nieta and I are quite taken with *Dona* Joana and the low-key but serious way she gets things done.

Sister Otacília said *Dona* Joana had lost two teenage children, one right after the other. It was the kind of thing that could drive you crazy. In fact, that's what happened to her husband: he lost his mind from so much suffering. He went to the city and was downing one drink after another. He wandered around the streets, out of contact, unaware of what he was doing. But with the help of friends and the community he eventually overcame the grief brought on by the tragedy.

In the deep gaze and sad smile of this couple you could see traces of all these terrible torments. Only God knows how much they have suffered. They themselves don't say anything. They don't show how much they've suffered. They bleed and weep alone, facing a savage environment, and a society that is even more savage. Who is concerned about what they feel? Perhaps only the "Mystery of our faith" (1 Tim. 2:16), the One who "will wipe every tear from their eyes" (Rev. 7:17).

Sunday, August 7: São Romão Rubber Plantation

OPPRESSION IN THE JUNGLE: A LONELY CRY OF SUFFERING

Seven families live here in São Romão. Their houses are clustered around the shed (a warehouse for merchandise and rubber) and the "big house" for the manager. The owner of this plantation is the mayor of Manoel Urbano, and his brother Raimundinho is the manager.

There are more than twenty rubber-gatherers who work on the mayor's plantation and they have to sell the rubber they get in exchange for other goods. Until recently, he even paid some money for the rubber, but now he pays only in goods, and according to a price that he himself sets. "That's the law laid down by the mayor," a worker tells me.

The worst of it is that the warehouse very, very often doesn't even have basic goods: there's no salt, sugar, milk, kerosene, and so forth. A whole year goes by with no new supplies. So the rubber-gatherer has a hard time. The result: hunger.

Injustice is unleashed here in the bush. Here the law of the jungle holds for animals and also for human beings. The managers or traders set the price for everything: both for products like rubber and the goods they furnish. That way they profit both buying and selling.

But the workers' greatest complaint isn't that they're exploited, but that there isn't enough merchandise, especially basic goods, like milk for children, cooking oil, and so forth. But they think well of *Seu* Raimundinho, the manager, the mayor's brother. They blame his boss, the mayor, saying he has "no concern for the people." When you first hear about this you find it revolting. It's a demonstration of how far cynicism can go.

In other places workers have gotten out from the claws of the company store or of the trader's supply boat by organizing a consumer cooperative. That's what they've done in Icuriã.

Nature and Society against Human Beings

It's impressive to see the hard natural conditions in which the jungle inhabitants live: their houses, their trails and canals, their food, transportation, and so forth. They sit on the ground, together with animals and insects: dogs, cats, parakeets, roaches, spiders, mosquitos, and so forth. Often they don't have a table or even a chair. Is that from their Indian heritage? Their features carry clear Indian traces.

There are very tiny black mosquitos that don't buzz, but they bite you on the arms, feet, neck, and head, leaving a pink swollen spot with a bright red point in the middle. Arms and legs here are full of black dots, left from bites after they dry up.

As if this unpleasant side of nature weren't enough, human beings exploit other human beings. . . .

The Lowly Are Worth Any Effort

"What am I doing here?" That's the feeling I'm obsessed with and it mortifies the *homo carnalis* we all have inside us.

The truth is that it was for the "weak," for those who are last in this world, for all of them, that Christ died (cf. Rom. 14:5). If that's so, then anything done for them is worth the effort. If the least of all were worth the blood of the Messiah, the Son of God, aren't they worth our effort?

I'm beginning to appreciate how much sacrifice there is in the life of pastoral workers here: priests, sisters, and lay persons who labor in areas as harsh as this one. These missionaries are spoken of sometimes with respect, sometimes with scorn, and almost always in ignorance.

Obviously a person doesn't get involved in this kind of life for any sort of pleasure or personal interest. There has to be motivation that is beyond any question or criticism. It is in the realm of Mystery.

Yes, the missionary is impelled by the same Mystery of God that holds the monk fascinated. Only here the orientation to Mystery takes a different tack: urgency rather than fascination, work rather than contemplation, *liberatio* rather than *vacatio.*

Nevertheless, it is ever the same Mystery: always painful, crucifying, but always liberating as well. For God is inscrutable, unfathomable. "God's thoughts are not our thoughts," says Isaiah. Otherwise, how explain the contradictions in life that are here so scandalously obvious? Why does the panther have to chase and rip innocent deer apart in order to eat and live? And why does the manager have to pressure the rubber-gatherers to produce so much, even if it means squeezing them with hunger, and keeping them without supplies? In other words, why this huge contradiction between God, Mystery of everything good and of infinite love, and the reality of both nature and of human history? Job seems to have felt this contradiction with particular force (12:6-12).

It is between these two terms of the contradiction that we must set human freedom and responsibility, including the possibility of sin (as well as the possibility of faith and grace). Without the category of sin, including "original sin" in particular, there is no way of coming to grips with the contradiction between such a God and such a world. The fact of sin provides a theoretical foundation for the mystery of salvation *through the cross.* In fact, without sin, salvation—as the fullness of humankind and of the world—wouldn't be resurrection from the dead, but the self-generated flowering of the movement and history of the world.

Furthermore, the idea of sin is the basis for the imperative of liberation: "underlying all those situations where humankind is humiliated, enslaved, abandoned, and made an object of contempt"—as a famous Jewish writer of the last century put it. He was only echoing biblical language: "When the Egyptians maltreated and oppressed us, imposing hard labor upon us, we cried to the Lord ... and he heard our cry and saw our affliction, our toil and our oppression" (Deut. 26:6-7). Or Mary of Nazareth: "He has deposed the mighty from their thrones and raised the lowly to high places" (Luke 1:52).

The Gospel Way of Looking at Things

Looking at the Brazilians of the bush country and their living conditions doesn't lead to enchantment or ecstasy. It doesn't move you to poetry but to indignation and anger. That's why you need conversion and faith in order to look at the people clearsightedly and justly. The gospel way of looking at things passes by way of the death of a "human, all too human" way. It is a paschal way of looking, a view "according to the Spirit," and no longer "according to the flesh" (2 Cor. 5:16).

I'm thinking about the children who come forward to be baptized. Who is even aware of them in this world? How much do they weigh on the scale of history? And yet, in baptism we say they are sons and daughters of God—

and given preference precisely insofar as they are ignored. Such enormous greatness! — but *in mysterio*.

To believe in this is already to move into the perspective of the divine vision: seeing the disadvantaged as God does, seeing them in the surest and truest way possible.

The Lord's Supper in the Heart of the Jungle

Today, late in the afternoon, we celebrated Sunday Mass. The sun was setting as we began. It occurred to me that it was just at this hour that Jesus held his last repast with his disciples, and that his command, "Do this . . . ," was echoing two thousand years later here in the middle of the largest forest in the world.

The community had arranged itself in the afternoon shade, stretching along behind some lemon trees. The participants, about thirty of them, sat on benches, on tree stumps, or even on the ground, around the supper table.

While Sister Nieta was teaching the hymns, I prepared myself to hear confessions. Five adults came forward. The confessions were good and valid. Three were confessing for the first time — and they made their first communion during that Mass.

The Mass was unconstrained, focused on essentials. After all, it's not at all appropriate to insist on the letter of the law or the official ritual in a situation where nothing is official.

Everything went quite well. The community discussed who could take the place of the leader, *Dona* Raimundinha, who was going to move to the city. They singled out Nonato — a young man who can read, sings well, and is very dedicated to the people. We had a ceremony of handing over the New Testament to him, as a sign of investiture and blessing.

By the end of the celebration, you could see the evening star prominent in a soothing pink sky. And the community gave thanks in its spontaneous prayer after communion.

Wednesday, August 10: A Settlement Named Porongaba

HUNTING AND *IMBIARA*

Yesterday we came to the community of Neném Ponte, after going through Centrinho.

A little after our arrival, *Seu* João Paulo, the head of the house, took his gun and went hunting. His nephew, with another youngster, also went hunting in the jungle, but in another direction.

The reason: tomorrow several families will be coming for the get-together, with baptisms and weddings, and the hosts have to "lay out a spread." The jungle is the rubber-gatherer's reservoir: a kind of market, shop, and refrigerator all rolled into one.

I learned from João Paulo's children that the term "hunting" is used with regard to deer, boars, tapirs—that is, large animals; getting monkeys and birds isn't called hunting but *imbiara*.

Night has fallen and I'm in my hammock. In the rose-colored west Venus is smiling, and directly above there is a new moon, shaped like a thin fingernail.

Collaborative Reading

We asked the villagers if they had known we were going to arrive. They said they did. But in order to decipher the letter sent to tell them that we were coming, a group of them got together. It took a collaborative effort. After more than an hour of struggling, all of them huddling around the piece of paper, they managed to understand the main point, more or less. "But there was a lot we didn't get," said a woman, who recounted that strange battle to us. They had agreed to wait for the boatman who was due that evening so he could "read out the rest of the letter."

Poor souls! Someone has to come up with some kind of communication not in writing, something pictorial, for those whose culture does not include writing. To send letters to a group of illiterate persons is, at the very least, a sign of pedagogical carelessness.

Stumbling into a Blessing

My left foot is all swollen up. Yesterday I took a nasty fall, coming from Neném Ponte to São Francisco. I had only sandals on (because they had told us the road was clear) and I banged up my little toe.

Last night, in the Centrinho rubber plantation, they suggested I put on an ointment, but in the morning my foot was more swollen than ever. That was undoubtedly from the long walk during the day.

Dona Maria prayed over my bruised foot, making a blessing over the red area. She rhythmically traced repeated signs of the cross, silently pronouncing a secret prayer. I only saw her lips moving.

Then it was my turn to get into the act. She asked me to bless some saints' pictures she had gotten in the city. Why not? I was happy to bless them. Then she asked me to bless the right foot of her mother, *Dona* Eline, a lay leader. Her foot was really one whole wound. She could only drag herself around the house, but she was going to the hospital soon.

In any case, it was a chance for different religious procedures to mesh together. Our pastoral practice is unaware of, and hence overlooks, the religious resources of the people. But whoever ignores the people is in turn ignored. Bourdieu says the priest tends to consider the natural healer and witch doctor as his rival. But why does it have to be that way? Couldn't this element of the people's religion be taken up into what is a true ministry of the church—ministry to the sick?

Walk and Sing!

Last night in Centrinho we had a baptism ceremony with lots of feeling and participation. Only three families live there, but there were four baptisms.

We had arrived around four in the afternoon, after having gotten caught in some rain along the road. I led the way, singing anything that came into my mind to keep up our spirits as we were walking and to get my mind off the rain and how tired I was. We had been walking since 7:30 A.M. "Walk and sing!" was St. Augustine's recommendation.

After refreshing ourselves at a spring, as is our customary ritual whenever we arrive at a settlement, I put up my hammock and flopped into it. I was numb with exhaustion, and my left foot was all swollen. After just fifteen minutes, they called us to eat.

We were served three kinds of meat from the jungle: spider monkey, squirrel monkey, and deer. We had brought the deer ourselves from São Romão, provided by *Dona* Raimundinha. That was in order to make sure we had something to eat when we reached our destination.

I thought to myself: So much meat! But this is how it is in the bush: they put everything they have on the table. If they have a lot, they put a lot; if they have only a little, they put a little. Why save things? Besides, *how* could you save things? If you have to, later on you can go into the jungle and hunt.

We ate sitting on the floor of the hut.

Night Baptism on the Hill

Around 8 P.M. everyone was gathered in the meeting room, about twelve persons. While Sister was taking down the names for baptism and marriage, I was speaking with Manoel, *Dona* Maria's husband, asking if he would be willing to be a leader and take charge of the community meetings, because *Dona* Eline was going into the hospital. He said he would and that he would go for the training session in Manoel Urbano from the 25th to the 28th of that month. I took his word for it.

At 8:30 we started the marriage ceremony. The two young couples, whose four children were to be baptized, were in a very good mood. They sang and prayed with unusual enthusiasm. They even inspired me in the celebration.

For the baptism we formed a procession toward the creek that was about three hundred meters from the house. That's where they go to get water, wash clothes, and bathe.

At the head of the procession someone carried a huge torch made of *sernambi* sticks. The others came behind with candles and lanterns. As we went we sang "The People of God Wandered in the Desert." It was a miniature reproduction of Israel's march through the desert, with a column of fire leading the way.

When we got to the creek, after a litany composed of a series of "we renounce," "we promise," and "we believe," closely linked to the everyday life of the community, we baptized the children. I cupped the water in my hands and, as I repeated the baptismal formula and poured the water, the adults in the creekbed held out their right hand over the child being baptized and made the sign of the cross, paralleling the words of the minister. Then one of the mothers on the other side of the creek bent down and laid the head of her child in the water, so it could receive the bath of new life. As we went from one baptism to another, everyone kept singing. And the torch of *sernambi* wood stood over the gully, lighting up the waters, the faces of those present, and the trunks of the closest trees, making them stand out against the darkness.

We returned to the house singing, "Our joy is to know that one day this whole people will be freed." In the meeting area we finished the celebration, almost two hours after it had begun. No one was tired or had even noticed the time pass. We were all full of emotion and joy. A holy and unforgettable moment!

"Now whenever anyone goes by the spring and goes there to bathe, they will remember the baptism of our children. Later on we're going to tell them about it, when they can understand," one of the mothers told me. Memory made present, like the Old Testament memorials.

And so, when the children were baptized, their world was also being baptized. The creek became an abiding sacrament.

Daytime Baptism by a Spring

The day before yesterday, in a settlement named Santa Maria, in the jurisdiction of Nením Ponte, we carried out a similar baptism, except that it was during the day. We went to the nearest spring, and in the shade of towering trees we baptized two children out in the open (the gospel we read spoke of how Jesus saw the "heavens opened" at his own baptism . . .). For over two hours we waited for a third child, but the family never came.

Nením Ponte is the name of the hamlet and the name of its lay leader. (Was he its founder?) The community is not well integrated, and Nením knew why: he had married a second time. So when I spoke, I stressed that a person's past is redeemed to the extent that the person is living well in the present and is moving forward. Faith in the forgiveness of sins tells us that the past is always absolvable and that no human life is beyond recovery.

It really seemed stupid to me to expect Nením to send away his present wife, with whom he has lived for five years and by whom he has two children, and to return to his first wife; besides, she's living with another man. The church is church, not synagogue. The gospel is gospel, not Torah; not a *dys-euangelion,* as Barth would say.

We went back home by night with *sernambi* torches. *Seu* Neném Ponte went ahead with one torch and I came at the end with another. The darkness of the bush is absolute night.

That was the first time I'd walked in the jungle at night. It's a unique musical performance. On top of the loud croaking of frogs comes the chirping of hosts of crickets, and the mysterious and varied song of night birds.

Seu Neném's two little children came along with us, one in its mother's arms, the other on its father's back. This one was amazingly bright, and I wondered how the jungle could produce such a child.

The Rubber-Gatherers' Mental Horizons

Life in the jungle might be said to take place outside history. It's like an eternal present, without a differentiated past and auguring the same kind of future. It's something like the experience Carlo Levi describes in his famous memoirs, *Christ Stopped at Eboli.*

The horizons of the jungle denizens are limited to nearby settlements, the rubber plantation, the animals and insects, Manoel Urbano (which here they call by its old name, Castelo), and little else. What goes on around here? Nothing that even deserves mention in our mass media.

Eliene, a very sharp eleven-year-old girl, was telling me stories, things that I found quite incredible, but for her were eminently believable. There's one about a soul of a *caboclo,* mulatto, that comes out of its grave to devour humans; there are faces that pass by in the night as though they were going off to fetch water; there are apparitions that shout like nighthawks. . . . In short, a world where the imagination takes over and masters reality. Or better, where the violence of reality takes over and masters human beings and their imagination.

Although this region is one of the most remote outposts for our state and our church, that doesn't mean it stands utterly outside our ongoing process in history and outside the social system we live under — capitalism. Production relationships are still quite obviously precapitalist; in fact they're semifeudal and slavelike. They constitute a precapitalist enclave within the capitalist system and serve that system. Capitalist patterns haven't penetrated this far yet, although that's what's happening more and more all over Amazonia. But they've got to be knocking at the door, for it's clear that the (semifeudal) rubber plantation system is coming apart.

Although all this is real in the life of the rubber-gatherers, it's not yet something they've consciously thought about. Hence their level of politicization, vis-à-vis a system they can perceive only on the outer fringes of their life, is zero.

Extending the Church through the Bush

During our long hikes from one community to another we talk a lot — about everything and everybody.

On our way back to Centrinho yesterday, Nieta, Nonato (our guide and the new lay leader in São Romão), and I were discussing the possibility of lay leaders in the jungle being ministers of baptism. There sprang up a hypothetical notion — actually quite remote — that certain more mature communities might celebrate the Lord's Supper in their own way and with their own means: bread made from *macaxeira* (millet), wine made from the fruit of *açaí* or *patoá* (palmlike trees), and so forth. All this of course in concordance with the church.

The pastoral life of our church has to be decentralized. Religious responsibilities have to be "popularized" in its ministries. In short, the grass roots must become involved in the church's being and doing.

In principle, there don't seem to be any serious reasons for holding up the church's "hinterlandization" — that is, against its really extending itself into the jungle, so that the elements of the local church would be more and more able to stand on their own.

Of course, this would require preparation of individuals and the creation of new structures. The idea alone isn't enough. But the idea has to be raised, the possibility has to be opened, in order to get on to making it a reality.

Thursday, August 11: Still in Porongaba

THE FOREST PEOPLE

I watch the children. They spend their time rolling around the house on the floor, with animals all around, their faces dirty and their bodies grimy and dotted with mosquito bites. They all eat sitting on the ground with plates and food all around. They sit surrounded by dogs and cats, monkeys and other animals. The animals get what's left over, or else it's thrown out into the yard where the rest of the animals — ducks, chickens, pigs, etc. — gather around and fight over the scraps. It's an ecological community.

It's not unusual for two or three persons to eat from the same plate, as was done in the ancient world. As Joseph, Mary, and Jesus must have done. Sometimes the one sharing is a dog, as I saw today: the baby was giving the animal a spoonful of mush and then taking one for himself. And they kept on that way, taking turns.

When you ask a question that would be obvious for us, like, "Why did so-and-so die?," they say, "Of a fever," or "It was a childhood disease," or "It was a woman's disease." And that ends the matter. And you don't know any more than you did before you asked.

Life in the bush is brutalizing. The horizons of awareness remain very limited. Forced to confront a series of problems, these brothers and sisters of ours assume an air of closed impenetrability, and their faces take on a severe and rough look that reminds you of the wild face of the jungle itself. This is just a part of the truth, however.

The other side of the coin is that the rubber-gatherer possesses a deep humanity. There's nothing of the emptiness and flabbiness you can see in the great ones of this world. Here everything is truth, pure and hard — with the hardness found at the center of certain trees and the pit of certain fruits.

There's a strong sense of honesty. There's a similar sense of hospitality, courage, respect for the other person, etc. Sure, that's partly because the conditions of life aren't very developed (because of the prohibitions existing in their society) but it's also because the human quality of life is very high.

There's no comparison between how basic the human life of these rubber-gatherers is and how futile and frivolous bourgeois life is, as it comes out, for example, in novels. Here life is more truly life, the human being more human, and God more God.

Friday, August 12: Still in Porongaba

COMMUNITY MEETING

Throughout the day families kept arriving in groups. They came from far away. Some came more than five hours on foot, the women carrying children in a sling and the men bringing along another child, perhaps asleep, with a piece of burlap that served as both blanket and hammock. They came single file, sweating like animals, giving off a strong, pungent smell. After a few words, they went off to bathe and swim. They stayed there the rest of the day in conversation. When the priest or sister visits, it's a holiday.

Last night, when the meeting began, the place was full. There were fifty persons or more.

I began by proposing to them something I'd discussed with Nieta. Because they live far apart with no church community and no one who can read, they could get together as families and say the rosary. The family would then function as their community, the rosary as their gospel, and the father or mother as the lay leader.

I tried to explain to them how they could pray the rosary. But it was useless. They simply couldn't hold onto five mysteries in a row. So it occurred to me to suggest that they replace the mystery with any intention at all. They seemed to understand and to commit themselves to getting together in families to pray the rosary on Sundays.

But I'm not at all sure they'll do it: when we prayed the Our Father and Hail Mary together, I could see that they were mumbling along rather than really saying the words. They don't even know how to make the sign of the cross correctly.

Perhaps our pastoral work overlooks these simple and basic things in our faith, things the old style of catechism was very careful about, even to the point of formalism, but which retained what is essential in the gospel message. Starting with the sign of the cross, you could get to the central christological mysteries, and starting with the Our Father, all of Christian ethics.

Two important aspects of the rosary, among others, are that it is a prayer of the people, because it is easy and rhythmic, and that it is connected to the gospel, both through the prayers that make it up (Our Father, Hail Mary, and Glory Be) and through its mysteries — a summary of the core events in the New Testament.

True, in order to get beyond formalism, this prayer would have to make room for variation and creativity: with intentions, reading or calling to mind the Bible, etc.

But all that sort of thing is still just a band-aid or a crutch, because nothing can replace living contact with the word of God, and its dynamic confrontation with reality. Base Christian Communities are based on that method. But how can you do that in this kind of situation? . . .

Friday, August 12: A Settlement Named São Pedro

POVERTY AND MISERY

On the way here from Porongaba we went through two settlements: Descanso and Boa Fé. They were an hour and a half apart, at a rubber-gatherer's pace — that is, moving along the path with huge strides.

I've just bathed in some stagnant water that smelled bad, down by the riverside here in São Pedro. In the summer, as we are now, many of these channels dry up; there's some water left standing here and there.

I asked *Dona* Maria José, who has a family, for some water. It tasted like dishwater. "Sorry, the water's a bit rancid," the poor woman apologized. Then she offered me some coffee in a fruit can cut in half. It didn't taste like anything — it was just a black liquid.

Three families live in this settlement. All are of Amerindian descent and all are related. One was "his son" and another was "her son." One of them was Daniel, fifteen years old, who had been in Porongaba. Together with his partner, who was still a young girl, he was living nearby — where his mother could keep her eye on him. The other one, Antônio, thirteen years old, had brought us here. He went ahead with a gun. On the way he killed a *macaco zogue* and then a *guariba* (two kinds of monkey) for the evening meal. It's not much meat but it's enough to make a broth to eat with flour. That's what we did. That was it: there wasn't any other food.

Besides, eating is something that doesn't take a lot of time here. You get to a settlement, and unless there's something else, you take some flour, mix it with eggs or fish, or simply with salt or sugar (with sugar it becomes *jacuba)* and there's your lunch. If it's not nourishing, at least it fools your stomach. That's what we ate yesterday, when we went through Boa Fé, and tonight when we got here. No wonder that once on an earlier trip through these parts, Father João Pedro fainted with hunger as he got to a settlement.

There's no question that poverty is the result of exploitation or marginalization. But it goes hand in hand with backwardness or an undeveloped state of things.

I look around the house to see if I can find any fruit, because everything grows around here: pineapple, avocado, banana, papaya, guava, cashews, and so forth. No luck. Folks here plant hardly any fruit, just pineapples and bananas.

Poverty isn't just something economic; it's also cultural. It's a matter of awareness. Overcoming it involves a learning process and techniques. The "developmentalists" have a portion of the truth. It's not enough just to blame the bosses or the government.

Being here, I realize how true it is that there is a distinction between misery and poverty. Charles Péguy proposed that distinction and it's now becoming common. Leon Bloy defined the difference very precisely when he said, "Misery is the lack of what is necessary; poverty is the lack of what is superfluous." The one is a mutilation; the other a virtue.

The Greatness of the Faith Stands by Itself

I keep coming back to this question: How much political capital do these Brazilians have, in the sense of power for social change? They're spread out over the jungle, isolated by the very way they harvest rubber (spread throughout the forest) and utterly dependent on nature and on the trading post system. Under such conditions the influence they can bring to bear to change their life is minimal. So how can they be expected to change history?

Asking about how much political capital these persons have may not get to the deepest and most decisive aspect of their life, or of the work one might do here—as I see it. After all, why would anyone ruin their feet on these horrible trails (the one from São Francisco to Porongaba was terrible) unless it is simply to meet these rubber-gatherers whom society leaves abandoned, then announce to them the word of hope and liberation, pass on to their children the dignity of being children of God, and encourage them in their struggle for life and fullness of life, and bring them together in communities?

But what can all this lead to? It's really only *sub specie aeternitatis* that all this becomes comprehensible to us, not *sub specie historiae.* In other words, here there's no question of Marxism—here it's Christianity pure and hard.

True, those things aren't necessarily in opposition. But they don't necessarily go together either. There are cases—and this is one of them—
where faith and theology say what they have to say without any other
mediation. In other words, there is some work worth doing for reasons that
have to do just with the gospel, with no other considerations of a political
nature coming into play. If you were here for political reasons, you'd be a
real loser. I repeat: you have to have naked faith, the faith of the mystics.
Going through these forests is like going through the "dark night of politics." Faith has to withstand this test!

As I was coming here today, beating my way through the jungle trail, I
felt this in a very lively way: that faith is something irreducible, that the
greatness of the gospel stands on its own, that it is incommensurable, and
that its weight is something absolute. To reduce everything to politics and
to liberation within history means failing to realize the greatness, the dignity, and the excellence of divine realities. Resurrection, eternal life, the
forgiveness of sins, the absolute future of life and of history, *agape* between
humans—all that is what comes out of this point, manifesting all its meaning
and its power.

In our meetings with the communities in this area, this is basically what
we talk about, and it's what's most appropriate in the situation. Obviously,
the social implications of the faith always come up: community and justice
(I've always tried to sum up these implications in these two words). But we
have to recognize that we just make a quick run through this area and what
we have to say evaporates. That's because the horizon, both mental and
real, of those we're talking to soon narrows down again, as does their
understanding and interest.

Work Somewhere Else?

I think my practical experience here in Acre is reaching its limits. The
local church has formulated its line of work and is moving along. The
foundations for a local church with its own characteristics have been laid
and are now solidified. There's no longer a need for the kind of theological
service I provide. The theology course, now in its third year, is a sign that
this church is now capable of using its own brains. My own impression is
that we're reaching the limits of comprehension, that there is a kind of
saturation point. Maybe I should shift my area of practical work. Some
activity in an urban area or, better, on the outskirts of a city, would be fine.
In lower-class barrios with a working-class concentration, inspired Christians might feel the faith as a ferment in history, emphasizing its social
implications, because that's where the cutting edge of history is. We'll see.

Events are the vehicles God uses to move us along. *Fata volentem ducunt,
nolentem trahunt.* You go along, whether willingly or unwillingly.

2

Toward the Liberation of Theology
in Asia

TISSA BALASURIYA

THE SUBJECT OF THEOLOGY

Theology flows from a conscious reflection on the faith as lived in a given context. Its scientific systematization and critique can depend much on full-time professional theologians.

However, not only professional, scientifically trained theologians but also others more directly engaged in the effort to transform their lives and society motivated by the Christian faith can make valuable contributions to the elaboration of a theology relevant to our situations. In this, both groups need to listen to, learn from, and creatively challenge each other to an ever more faithful response to the demands of the teaching of Jesus Christ.

But there are inevitable problems in this collaboration process. Academic theologians in general do not usually question the social conditioning of their own theology, or the centuries of theological tradition that lie behind it. They are more mindful of the years of effort that have been put into their own training, and they can tend to be rather wary of a theology drawn from mere experience and reflection by "lay persons." They may even see the fallacies in such efforts, since "lay persons" who are not well versed in scripture may use sacred texts without understanding them in their original context.

On the other hand the "lay person" in theology may think that the academic theologians seldom—if ever—come to the heart of the matter, to the real gut issues of human existence, with regard to both interpersonal

From *Asia's Struggle for Full Humanity*, edited by Virginia Fabella (Maryknoll, N.Y.: Orbis Books, 1980), pp. 16-27.

relations and societal injustices. The committed "lay person" in theology thus suspects that the academic theologians may really be finding in their scientific method an escape from the exigencies of the gospel in the real circumstances of our time.

There is thus a need to build mutual confidence and respect among persons of these two levels of orientation in theology or Christian reflection and to learn to benefit from each other's expertise in their common endeavor towards a relevant theology. Committed persons from action groups can bring the sensitivity of lived experience and struggle, while professional or technical theologians can contribute a more scientific understanding, especially of the scriptures, in the light of advances in modern knowledge.

In all this we must have the widest ecumenical approach of openness to all others of different religions, Christian denominations, ideologies, and cultures. At the same time we must see ourselves and all others under the critical light of conscience, both individual and collective.

The formation of new attitudes is necessary if we are to contribute to the creation of a relevant theology in Asia. Rethinking our definition of "theologian" is necessary, but a prior necessity is to remove from our minds any fears we may have about theology or doing theology.

THE FEAR OF THEOLOGY

Most people tend to think that "theology" is something beyond their competence. They think of it as a highly sophisticated discipline or as demanding an ecclesiastical appointment for "doing theology" or as needing a direct communication line with God.

But the fact is that all of us do theology in some form or other, even if it be in negating the existence of a God. When we reflect on the meaning of our lives in relation to its ultimate values, its source, and destiny, we are theologizing. When we consider the good and bad of an action we are making a theological reflection. Our conscience, the inner light and voice within us places us before such values, and in relation to the deepest insights and instructions within us. Theology relates to the act of righteous living and reflection concerning it in relation to the light we receive from God in different ways. God can manifest himself (or herself) to us in many ways: e.g., by his revelations through other persons, or his voice within us, through events, through religious leaders, etc. The believer in God believes that God is in direct and indirect relationship to every person. This is the first source of our knowledge of and union with God. From it can flow the science or wisdom about God, or theology. Therefore in some way or other all believers in God are doing theology.

The professional science of theology relates to the systematic study of its sources in the Bible, in history, and in the present situation. Professional theology tries to make a systematic analysis of faith in God. It uses human reason and scientific skills in doing so. It presents an organized body of knowledge that tries to interpret belief in God and its consequences, in a scientific manner.

However, theology is also an art, in that it is to be lived in a given situation. Experiencing God in prayer and contemplation often gives a richer awareness of the divine than the scientific analysis of God in a theological study. Likewise active commitment in trying to live the message of Christ is a deep experience of the meaning of the gospel that cannot be attained by mere academic study.

While appreciating the role of the specialist in theology as a help to others, we can all reflect theologically and try to live our beliefs. We can also contribute to the development of a theology relevant to our times and situation. Liberation from the fear of doing "theology" is then a condition for our creative contribution to theological reflection.

TOWARD THE LIBERATION OF THEOLOGY IN ASIA

As we reflect from an Asian point of view on the Christian message and activities present and manifest today, we are struck by the extent to which they have been molded by the experience and interests of the Western peoples, especially of Europe and North America. While the Christian faith is presented as universal, valid for all times and meant for all peoples, the content of its dogma, moral teachings, and pastoral orientations has been largely related to the needs, concerns, and interests of the Western peoples. It is as if Christianity, having converted Europe, had in turn been made European.

A Methodological Problem

This raises a methodological problem for an approach to theology by non-Westerners, especially by Asians. If we do not accept the Euro-American worldview of history, geography, economics, technology, and culture, we find that many elements in the Christian teaching are not relevant to us. Many issues that have agitated the minds of Christians are not really our major concerns. They are peripheral to us; they are imports to Asia. A clear example is the division of Christianity into denominations and sects. These have been largely fashioned by European history and American concerns. They are not a central issue for us. Having first created the problem for believers in Christ, Western Christians then present us with an ecumenical movement and guidelines for contact between Christians: e.g., Roman Catholics and Anglicans. This is an example of the irrelevancies passed on to us. Europeans fought their politico-religious battles in the sixteenth century, and we as a result are divided into separate Christian churches today in Asia; plus we need their permission for greater communion among us.

A similar situation can be seen in attitudes toward other religions. Christians began by defining their self-importance in God's plan of salvation as expounded by them. "Outside the church, there is no salvation" was a theological axiom. Into this the so-called "pagans," "non-Christians," and "nonbelievers" had to be fitted. Christian theology opened itself to a less indecent consideration of the position of these "outsiders" only after the latter became politically independent and intolerant of the attitude of Christian missioners who wanted to save the pagans.

For us in Asia, though, the problem poses itself the other way round. As an Asian I cannot accept as divine and true any teaching which begins with the presupposition that all my ancestors for innumerable generations are eternally damned by God unless they had been baptized in or were related to one of the Christian institutional churches. It is no use beginning by burdening ourselves and God with such a vision and then trying to elaborate theories of how the "pagans" might have been related to the church even prior to the birth of Christ. Such theological gymnastics do not do honor to God or to us. God is surely not an unfair God; God is no acceptor of persons; God loves all. Theology must honestly respect these millions upon millions of my ancestors and future human beings, before I can accept theology as a true interpretation of revelation from a loving God, Father of all.

The problem poses itself for us, even if we do not accept the premise of "no salvation outside the church" and the theological method of poring over centuries of Christian writings. We get buried in a mass of irrelevancies on which we do not wish to waste our lives. In discussions with Westerners we spend time and energy (as I did in the early 1960s) trying to disabuse them of their holy convictions and learned prejudices. When I present to them the only view which they can accept, namely, that God is just and fair to all persons of all times and ages, they say, "Then of what use is the church?" or "Why should my uncle have gone to Indonesia as a missionary to save the natives?" Their point of departure is different.

For an Asian theology to evolve with genuine respect for the other religions there must be a fundamental change in the mental attitudes of Christians towards others. So long as we have an attitude of superiority and self-justification we cannot meet others in frank dialogue. We need to disabuse ourselves of many views and prejudices which we have held and harbored over generations. This means we have to rethink basically our "conversion mentality." We have to rid ourselves of a competitive mentality with regard to other religions; suspicions need to be replaced by warmth and a desire for understanding. In this manner our own theology must be requestioned; our reading of scripture undertaken with a universal vision of humankind. These things cannot be done with mere declarations and patchwork reforms; we need a total reorientation of mentalities and practices. We have to begin from other premises, such as: God loves all persons; all are called to his kingdom; this kingdom has to be understood in a manner consonant with the aspirations of all human beings.

We find a similar viewpoint on other issues, such as: the teaching and practice of international affairs, the right of colonization, capitalism and socialism, the relationship between church and politics, and local cultures and liturgy. Capitalism and colonialism were acceptable to the churches; socialism and communism were anathema to them irrespective of their impact on our people.

Thus we see that we cannot accept many of the conclusions, premises, and even issues which concern theology in the West as necessary, true, or relevant. We see further that these have, in many instances, been damaging to our own self-respect and creative inquiry. They have also been harmful to us economically, politically, and socially. They help domesticate our peoples. They inhibit meaningful theological reflection by Christians in Asia. For Asian Christians to be able to relate meaningfully to the aspirations of our people and the vast changes taking place in our countries we need a freeing of our theology from many categories imposed from abroad and by the past. For theology to be helpfully connected with struggle for liberation, theology itself needs to be liberated.

Culture-Bound

Theology in recent centuries has in fact been profoundly culture-bound in almost the totality of its human elaboration. It has been, at least implicitly, ethnocentric—meaning what concerns the West. It has been a handmaid of Western expansion; an ally, at least, in the centennial exploitation of the peoples of other continents by the North Americans. The combination of the "sacred" duty of civilizing, baptizing, and saving the pagans with the military, economic, political, and cultural domination by Europe over our countries has been disastrous for Christianity itself. It has not only made Christian theology unacceptable in many aspects to the rest of humankind, it has even dehumanized the content of theology and, as it were, culturally blindfolded theologians themselves.

These statements are made very briefly and badly in order to explain some of the reasons for the need of a liberation of theology, and hence also for a different methodology in theology. There is a need for a critique of the way in which theology is elaborated. We cannot assume that theology is not limited by the cultural limitations of those who have elaborated it. Naturally this will be said of our present work, and rightly so. Hence from the beginning it is accepted that what I can present is only a point of view, some aspects of the overall human problem. Similarly Euro-American theology has to be relativized in its human elements. It goes without saying that the substance of divine revelation meant for all is universally valid. The problem is to get to this core message without its human limitations; this concerns not only Asians but all others.

Church-Centered

Theology has been very largely church-centered. It has tended to equate the universal kingdom of God and the common good of humanity with the progress of the church. The church was regarded as so divine that all else was faulty and in need of submission to and remedying by the church. The church was in fact made an ultimate value. The church was regarded as the necessary vehicle of salvation, with many distinctions about belonging to it. The focus of interest of theology has been the life within the institutional church; and among Roman Catholics, very much dominated by the more powerful European churches, with their focus on the Church in Rome. A heavier accent was placed on this juridical belonging than on living a life of love and service.

Male Clerical

That the churches are so taken with themselves is due in part to the near monopoly of theology by the clergy, especially as teachers in seminaries and universities. Hence theological preoccupations have been very much those of persons within the church institution and administration, or dependent on them. Incidentally, in the Roman Catholic Church, they are almost all males and mainly celibates. Thus theology has given much attention to issues which concern adult, male, celibate clerics. Theologians have tended to read the Scriptures with culture-bound eyes. They naturally were inclined to find in revelation many texts which reinforced their power, self-importance, and indispensability even for God.

An obvious example of the blind spots in theological reflection concerns the rights of women. Here too the method seems to be to start by attributing all rights a priori to the males, beginning with the garden of Eden, and then let the women fight for their rights when they can. During the many centuries of male domination, churchmen—in particular those in the Roman Catholic Church—have placed God on the side of the dominating male. Whatever changes are accepted are still mere reforms and tranquilizers. Thus women are to be accepted as deaconesses, to be given functions such as the distribution of communion under exceptional circumstances. But there is no acceptance of the fundamental equality of men and women in the life of the church—and this in an age when there have been women heads of states including elected prime ministers. Real power in matters both spiritual and temporal within the church is kept in the hands of the males. The same is true of the laity-clergy relationship. The theology of marriage is such that it is considered a bar to certain positions within the Roman Catholic Church. These may be purely disciplinary norms, but they are also the reigning pattern of thought, in spite of the practice of the early church.

Theology is also adult-dominated. It is still rather unthinkable that youth could be theologians. A theologian is supposed to be someone who has spent many years in reading hoary volumes of the past, whereas the contribution which youth can make is essentially in their vitality, sense of justice, dynamism, freshness of approach, openness to the future, and preparedness to face risks. The whole apparatus of church life is adult-dominated. The higher the echelon of authority, the higher is the average age of those exercising it. Hence youth are practically excluded from an impact on the thought and action in the churches. Here too, as yet, even the most forward looking changes give youth only a subsidiary role. There is little acceptance that persons of eighteen to twenty-five or thirty years of age can be mature human beings capable of making a significant contribution to the community, precisely as youth.

Capitalistic

In its social orientation theology has for many centuries been procapitalist. Theology and church action have been influenced by the class composition of church personnel. The lifestyle of most theologians has been within the framework of Western capitalism and benefiting from it. This is also true of church leaders, particularly in the higher echelons. Hence, consciously or unconsciously, they do not deal with issues that threaten their interests and positions. Thus theology has had little to do with the condition of the working class. It has been rather unrelated to the issues which concern the peasantry, who form the bulk of the people in the poorer countries of the world.

Where theology or church social teachings were concerned with these issues, the remedies proposed were in the nature of palliatives rather than of a fundamental reform of the social structure itself. Economic power was to remain with the owners of capital, with a certain softening of the exploitative process through sedatives such as recreational facilities for workers, labor laws, profit sharing, diffusion of shares, workers' councils, and trade unions. These are good in themselves; but there was no intention of fundamentally altering the social system so that the benefits of work would accrue principally to the workers themselves. There was to be no basic change of the social order to end exploitation of one person by another. The practical impact of the church was even more conservative than the official church teachings.

Another wide area of theological blindness, up to recent years, has been concerning Communist regimes. Our problem is that the church first condemns them, but now that the rest of the world is coming to a co-existence with the Soviet Union, Eastern Europe, and China, Christian thinkers are beginning to open their eyes. Even here, openness to China is still only beginning. On the other hand, Communist regimes have not harmed Asians in the same manner as Western imperialistic capitalist ones have done over the past four to five centuries. Hence we find it rather awkward to begin our theological search with the attributing of positive values to our known enemy and negative ones to Communist regimes which have been to some extent the liberators of Asian peoples. Once again culture-bound preferences of the West pass for Christian theological positions with, of course, many references to the recent teachings of churchmen. There is here an implicit identification of the interests of the world order dominated by the West with the good of all humankind and the cause of God himself. Asians are thus in a dilemma which is more profound than the assimilation of Christianity with its Western languages, rituals, and even culture and mentality.

A similar evaluation can be made of the thinking among church leaders concerning development, justice, and peace. Development within the present world order, with the technology of the West and its financial and economic institutions, is thought to be normal. At most, it is thought that some adjustments have to be made. As yet the churches have not opted for a world system other than the prevailing capitalist, Western-dominated one. As within society, the remedies suggested are palliatives—except for one or two references in Pope Paul's encyclical *Populorum progressio.* The churches recommend reforms within the world system such as economic cooperation through "aid," commodity agreements, reform of the currency, reduction of the arms race, and peace. These are good things in themselves, but utterly inadequate to transform the system in which 80 percent of the population of the world has only 20 percent of the resources. Poverty thus continues in the midst of plenty. Peace is understood as the preservation of the present world order.

Yet from an Asian point of view totally different approaches are necessary. We need a revolutionary change in the world system. Revolutionary does not mean necessarily violent. It does mean a radical and rapid change in the world system; the change has to be not merely marginal, or quantitative, but rather throughout the whole system and qualitative. The world is meant for all humanity; and a qualitative change in the relationships among peoples and resources is required to ensure basic human rights to all persons in the world. The churches lack a theology that is revolutionary in the content of change advocated—be it within countries or among nations. In this sense, while the world requires revolutionary changes, theology is still fundamentally conservative, capitalist, and pro-Western.

Lack of a Socio-Economic Analysis

There are other characteristics of the theology of recent centuries that are gradually being questioned all over the world and yet are still prevalent as the major orientations of Christian thinking. Thus analysis of society has not been accepted and incorporated as a basic element in theological reflection. Theology tends to be deduced directly from the scriptural sources and church traditions. Since there is an absence of the data of the world, it is influenced more by the prejudices, myths, and preoccupations of the theologizers. This is a further point of methodology that needs to be remedied radically if there is to be any worthwhile consensus in the churches concerning Christian action in society. The absence of socio-political power analysis makes the churches complacent about the consequences of the dominance of some over others, especially of the Western powers and the local elites in Asian countries. They even become implicit legitimizers of such domination. Since a good deal of theological thinking is individualistic in orientation, the social aspects of the kingdom of God, sin, conversion, and salvation are neglected. Sometimes these social aspects are considered merely human, humanitarian, horizontal, and natural as if they were not related to the spiritual, to God. Here too the basic presuppositions have to be overhauled if we are to meet the aspirations of modern human beings, and be honest to reality with its absurdities, such as immense poverty in the midst of unprecedented affluence.

Absence of Action-Orientation

Closely related to this is the absence of action-orientation in theology. When theology is only theoretical, it fails to take into account the exigencies of the real situation, and of the effort to change it. It is only in action that the many discussions of a problem become clear. When action is absent from reflection, the thought tends to be sterile; and hence, in fact, status quo-oriented and conservative. It is possible to elaborate theology merely academically, but with little relevance to the actual conjuncture of events and forces as they develop in the world. An action-oriented theology, on the other hand, would have to assess the forces operative in a situation, think of goals, strategies, and tactics, of timing, and groupings of persons. All these require skills different from those of the merely academic theologians. It will also have to develop a different spirituality, including active participation in social change even in conflictual situations.

The church has been action-oriented, even though theology may have been speculative. But this action has been church-centered in its missionary approach, and conservative in its social impact. We need a theology that is more human-centered, and oriented towards justice in society. This requires an option in favor of the oppressed. Such a theology would also be more God-centered, as God is present and active in human history. There has been a neglect of the dynamic nature of the kingdom of God being realized through history.

A theology that is action-oriented must take into account the time dimension. Timing is of the essence of the matter. The pace of events has to be an input for decision making. Today it is not much use to condemn the old colonialism (except Macao, Hong Kong, etc.). Today we have to deal with new colonialism and new forms of exploitation as in some nations in Asia and in Czechoslovakia. The church has had a knack for siding with the prevailing oppressors, but then trying to make up with the liberators, once these are successful. This is opportunism. Prophetic timing is to be with the oppressed in their struggles—while they are engaged in them.

Such a theology would be one which would be continually in process rather than static. It would have to meet the problems posed by a fast-changing world. A theology that is action-oriented would be largely lay— unlike at present; the ministerial clergy, as such, would not necessarily be leaders in such a theology requiring the skills of socio-political analysis, decision making, and risk bearing. The youth too would have a significant role in the growth of such a theology, for youth are more present where the action is than are the adults, especially the aging academics and clerics. It would also be a theology that is concerned with real issues and events as they occur in time and in different places and environments. Hence theology would be more practical than merely speculative.

Action orientation will mean that theology is to be concerned with strategies of action. Theology over the past few centuries has been concerned largely with intra-church strategies and methods: conversion to Christianity, fight against personal sin, spiritual combat within oneself and inside cloisters, ecclesiastical sanctions and controls, rewards and punishments. Today action is very much in the field of public life. Hence the conjuncture of events, forces, and obstacles has to be evaluated, different strategies weighed and adopted. Risk taking in these areas is quite a different phenomenon from the risks inside cloisters.

The spirituality of conflict situations requires a different evaluation of virtues and of progress in the spiritual search. Ascetical practice and mystical experience can and will have to evolve within such a context of a struggle against the sinfulness of socio-political structures and consequent sacrifice and joy. All these elements are only beginning to be brought into Christian theology. They are essential elements for the building of the kingdom of God in our world.

These considerations together point to the need for a new orientation in theology, a fundamental break from a theology which was, in fact, the ideological support for the Western hegemony of the world, for capitalist domination over the poor, and for adult, male clerical domination within the church which was in the service of the prevailing world order. We need a theology and an action that will help rid the world of the enormous injustices that are a planetary evil. Theology must counteract this global madness masquerading as civilization blessed by God.

HOW CAN ASIAN CHRISTIANS HELP SUCH A REORIENTATION?

Some of the approaches required are already being developed in the "political theology" in Europe, the practical action-oriented theology in North America, and especially in the theology of liberation in Latin America. We can help in broadening this reflection by relating to Asia more consciously. This will not only widen the scope of these approaches but also intensify the issues. The Asian contribution can include a certain understanding of the human person which the Asian religions and philosophical traditions can contribute, as well as a sharpening of the strategies due to the demands of the Asian revolutionary processes. In this sense, our reflection relates to the tradition of Western theology at the point which it has reached today in the more future-oriented thinkers and persons in the "movement" for freedom and justice in the world.

Yet if we wish to try to meet the problems faced by Asian reality or the Asian religions, we cannot begin with a consideration of the issues that are dealt with in traditional European theology. For this unnecessarily involves us in a mass of less relevant material that merely takes up time and energy and mystifies the issues. The major thrust for us cannot come from the Euro-American worldview. We have to think about how we view the world from our context.

We have to take a fresh look at the central core of the Christian message. This requires a direct return to the sources of revelation, especially to the person of Jesus Christ in the gospels. In this too we have to bypass many less relevant debates and get as much as possible to the core of his message. We even have to purify our minds of merely Christendom-centered theologies which have missed the universality of Jesus Christ. We need a deeper awareness of the historical Jesus of Nazareth. We have to ask ourselves how we understand the Gospels today in our times. Here again modern Euro-American thought can help us, but we need to go further than they have gone hitherto.

Another point of departure has to be a socio-economic and political reflection on the world of our times, and on the Asian scene. This can be a partial view—one aspect of a contribution to a theological inquiry. We should try to relate reflections to the basic yearnings of the human person for freedom and personal fulfillment.

Fulfillment and liberation struggles are being sought in Asian countries at different levels and with different means. Persons seek meaning and peoples want a chance to be, and be themselves. In sincerely relating to this Asian quest for full humanity, Asian Christians can evolve a theology relevant to our aspirations, needs, and struggles.

A consideration of the situation of the church in Asia can help us see what its impact in Asia has been in the past. From a reassessment of this position in the light of our understanding of Christ and the Christian mission in the world we can see what directions the church should take in Asia and elsewhere—at least in relation to the Asian problems.

The overall considerations indicate to us that a fundamental reorientation of the thinking of Christians is required to meet the challenges of our times. It requires a liberation of our own thought processes to know the issues and respond to them. What we need amounts to a veritable cultural revolution within the church, including its theology.

3

The Use of the Bible in Christian Communities of the Common People

CARLOS MESTERS

PRELIMINARY OBSERVATIONS

The Bible is very important in the life and growth of grassroots communities. But its importance must be put in the right place. It's something like the motor of an automobile. Generally the motor is under the hood, out of sight. It is not the steering wheel. The history of the use of the Bible in grassroots communities is a bit like the history of car motors. Way back when the first cars came out, the motor was huge. It was quite obvious and made a lot of noise. It also wasted a lot of gasoline and left little room for passengers. Today the motors are getting smaller and smaller. They are more powerful, but they are also quieter and better hidden. There's a lot more leg room and luggage room in the car. Much the same is true about the Bible and its function in the life of Christian communities. The Bible is supposed to start things off, to get them going; but it is not the steering wheel. You have to use it correctly. You can't expect it to do what it is not meant to do.

Perhaps what I am going to say to you may seem a trifle optimistic. If so, it is something like the optimism of a farmer watching the grain surface above ground. A storm may come later and wipe out the whole crop. But there is room for optimism, and it's good to be optimistic.

INTRODUCING THE ISSUE: THREE BASIC SITUATIONS

First Situation

In Brazil there are many groups meeting to focus on the Bible. In this case the motivating occasion for the group is some pious exercise or special

From *The Challenge of Basic Christian Communities,* Sergio Torres and John Eagleson, eds. (Maryknoll, N.Y.: Orbis Books, 1981), pp. 197-210. Translated by John Drury.

event: a feast day, a novena, a brotherhood week, or what have you. The people meet on the parish level. There is no real community context involved. The word of God is the only thing that brings them together. They want to reflect on God's word and put it into practice.

Second Situation

In Brazil some groups are meeting within a broader context. They are meeting on the level of the community and its life. I once went to give a course to the people in such a community. In the evening the people got together to organize the course and establish basic guidelines. In such groups you generally get questions such as these: "How do you explain the Apocalypse? What does the serpent stand for? What about the fight between David and Goliath?"

The questions, you see, are limited to the Bible as such. No hint of their own concerns, no hint of real-life problems, no hint of reality, no hint of problems dealing with the economic, social, and political life. Even though they are meeting as a community, the real-life problems of the people are not brought up.

Third Situation

To introduce the third situation, I am going to tell you a typical story about my experience in this area. I was invited to give a course in Ceará, in northeast Brazil. The group was made up of about ninety farmers from the backlands and the riverbanks. Most of them couldn't read. In the evening we met to get things organized. They asked me about a dozen basic questions, but these are the ones I remember:

1. What about these community activities we are engaged in? Are they just the priest's idea? Are they communism? Or do they come from the word of God?

2. What about our fight for land? (Most of them had no land. But they had plenty of problems and fights on their hands.) What about our labor struggles and our attempts to learn something about politics? What does the word of God have to say about all that?

3. What about the gospel message? Does it have to do just with prayer, or is it something more than that?

4. The other day, in a place where there was a big fight going on between the landlord and his tenants, this priest came, said Mass, and explained the gospel in a way that made the landlord right. Then the local priest of the parish read the same gospel and explained it in a way that made the tenant farmers right. So who really is right?

5. The landlord gives catechism lessons that teach subservience and bondage. In our community we have a catechetics of liberation, and the landlord persecutes us for it. So how do we settle the matter and figure it all out? We want to know whether the Bible is on our side or not!

Here we have three basic situations. In the first situation the group involved comes together solely for the sake of discussing the Bible; the Bible is the only thing that unites them and they stick to it. In the second situation the people focus on the Bible, too, but they come together as a community. In the third situation we have a community of people meeting around the Bible who inject concrete reality and their own situation into the discussion. Their struggle as a people enters the picture. So we can formulate the basic picture of Figure 1.

We find three elements in the common people's interpretation of the Bible: the Bible itself, the community, and reality (i.e., the real-life situation of the people and the surrounding world). With these three elements they seek to hear what the word of God is saying. And for them the word of God is not just the Bible. The word of God is within reality and it can be discovered there with the help of the Bible. When one of the three elements is missing, however, interpretation of the Bible makes no progress and enters into crisis. The Bible loses its function.

When the three elements are present and enter the process of interpretation, then you get the situation that I encountered when I gave a course in Ceará. The people asked me to tell them the stories of Abraham, Moses, Jeremiah, and Jesus. That is what I did. But in their group discussions and full meetings, the Bible disappeared. They hardly ever talked about the Bible. Instead they talked about real life and their concrete struggles. So at the nightly review the local priest asked them what they had learned that day. They quickly got to talking about real life. No one said anything about the Bible. Ye gods, I thought to myself, where did I go wrong? This is supposed to be a course on the Bible and all they talk about is real life. Should I feel upset and frustrated, or should I be satisfied? Well, I decided to take it easy and feel satisfied because the Bible had achieved its purpose. Like salt, it had disappeared into the pot and spiced the whole meal.

Figure 1

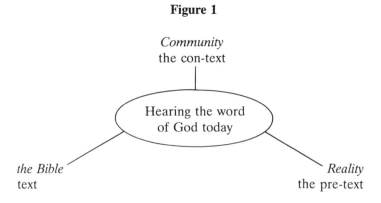

It's like what happens when you take a sponge and dip it in a little bowl of water. The water is soaked up and disappears inside the sponge. At the end of the nightly review the people were asked what they had learned from the biblical explanations. They squeezed the sponge a bit and let a few drops of water out. I could see that the sponge was filled with water. At the final ceremony for the week, which lasted four hours, they squeezed the sponge completely and everything inside came out. I realized that when the three elements are integrated — Bible, community, real-life situation — then the word of God becomes a reinforcement, a stimulus for hope and courage. Bit by bit it helps people to overcome their fears.

Conclusions

1. When the community takes shape on the basis of the real-life problems of the people, then the discovery of the Bible is an enormous reinforcement.

2. When the community takes shape only around the reading of the Bible, then it faces a crisis as soon as it must move on to social and political issues.

3. When the group closes itself up in the letter of the biblical text and does not bring in the life of the community or the reality of the people's struggles, then it has no future and will eventually die.

4. These three factors or situations characterize the use of the Bible by the common people and reveal the complexity involved. The three situations can be successive stages in a single ongoing process, or they can be antagonistic situations that obstruct and exclude each other. It all depends on how the process is conducted.

5. It doesn't matter much where you start. You can start with the Bible, or with the given community, or with the real-life situation of the people and their problems. The important thing is to do all you can to include all three factors.

SOME OBSTACLES AND HOW THE PEOPLE
ARE SURMOUNTING THEM

It is not always easy to integrate all three factors in the interpretation of the Bible. There are many obstacles along the way that the people are trying to surmount in various ways.

Many Don't Know How To Read

Many people don't know how to read, and the Bible is a book! Sometimes no one in the group knows how to read. They are inventing ways to get around this problem. They are using song and story, pictures and little plays. They are thus making up their own version of the "Bible of the poor."

Thanks to songs, for example, many people who have never read the Bible know almost every story in it.

Slavish Literalism

Another obstacle is slavery to the letter or fundamentalism. This usually occurs when the Bible is read in dissociation from a real-life community and concrete situation. The circle closes and the letter becomes a source of further oppression rather than of liberation.

The Bible is ambiguous. It can be a force for liberation or a force for oppression. If it is treated like a finished monument that cannot be touched, that must be taken literally as it is, then it will be an oppressive force.

Three things can help to overcome this obstacle. The first is the good sense of the people. In one community composed of blacks and other farmers the people were reading the Old Testament text that forbade the eating of pork. The people raised the question: "What is God telling us today through this text?" Their conclusion was: "Through this text God today is ordering us to eat the flesh of pork." How did they arrive at such a contrary conclusion? They explained: "God is concerned first and foremost with life and health. In those times eating the flesh of pork was very dangerous to people's health. It was prohibited in God's name because people's lives had to be protected. Today we know how to take care of pork meat, and the only thing we have to feed our children are the piglets in our yards. So in this text God is bidding us to eat the flesh of pork."

A second thing of great importance in breaking through enslavement to the letter is the ongoing action of a local church that takes sides with the poor. The ongoing movement of the church in this direction is helping to ensure that questions focused exclusively on the letter of the biblical text gradually give way to others. Literalist questions are falling from the tree like dry leaves to make room for new buds. The larger complex of a local church that sides with the poor and joins their fight for justice is very important in correctly channeling the people's interpretation of the Bible.

The third thing has to do with the various devices of a fairly simple kind. For example, we can show people that many of the things we talk about in words cannot be taken literally. Symbolism is an integral part of human language. In many instances the first step toward liberation comes for people when they realize that they need not always take the biblical text literally. They discover that "the letter kills, the Spirit gives life." This realization unlocks the lid and lets new creativity out.

The Conception of Time

Another problem or obstacle is the people's conception of time. Often folks will ask questions like these: "Did Abraham come before or after Jesus Christ? Did David live before or after Cabral discovered America?

Was it Jesus Christ who created the world?" Such questions may seem to indicate a great deal of confusion to us, but I think not. Apart from a certain amount of ignorance about the content of the Bible, I don't think it is a matter of confusion at all. Instead it is an expression of their circular conception of time. In such a conception you don't know exactly what comes at the beginning and what comes at the end. A simple explanation will not suffice to change this view of time, because it is a cultural problem rather than a problem of mere ignorance. In their minds the people simply don't have a peg on which to hang a concept of linear time.

How do we help them to overcome this obstacle? How do we unroll the carpet of time in their consciousness? Perhaps the best way we can help is to help them discover their own ongoing journey in their lives today. We can help them to recover the memory of their own history, of struggles lost and forgotten. We can help them to begin to recount their own history. In Goiás a group of farmworkers was asked: "How did the Bible come about?" An old farmer gave this reply: "I know. It was something like this. Suppose fifty years from now someone asks how our community arose. The people will reply: In the beginning there was nothing here. . . ." Thanks to his own concrete journey in life, the old farmworker perceived that the Bible had arisen from narrative accounts, from stories people told to others about their history. He realized that the Bible was the collective memory that gave a people its identity.

Dependence on Informational Knowledge and the Learned Expert

You often hear people say something like this: "I don't know anything. You or Father should do the talking. You're the ones who know things. We folks don't know anything." In the past we members of the clergy expropriated the Bible and got a monopoly on its interpretation. We took the Bible out of the hands of the common people, locked it with a key, and then threw the key away. But the people have found the key and are beginning again to interpret the Bible. And they are using the only tool they have at hand: their own lives, experiences, and struggles.

Biblical exegetes, using their heads and their studies, can come fairly close to Abraham; but their feet are a long way from Abraham. The common people are very close to Abraham with their feet. They are living the same sort of situation. Their life process is of the same nature and they can identify with him. When they read his history in the Bible, it becomes a mirror for them. They look in that mirror, see their own faces, and say: "We are Abraham!" In a real sense they are reading their own history, and this becomes a source of much inspiration and encouragement. One time a farmworker said this to me: "Now I get it. We are Abraham, and if he got there then we will too!" From the history of Abraham he and his people are drawing the motives for their courage today.

Now here is where the danger comes in. Some teacher or learned expert may come along. It might be a pastoral minister, a catechist, or an exegete. This expert may arrive with his or her more learned and sophisticated approach and once again expropriate the gains won by the people. Once again they grow silent and dependent in the presence of the teacher or expert. Our method is logical. It involves a reasoning process, a careful line of argument. We say it is scientific. When the people get together to interpret the Bible, they do not proceed by logical reasoning but by the association of ideas. One person says one thing; somebody else says another thing. We tend to think this approach has little value, but actually it is just as scientific as our approach! What approach do psychoanalysts use when they settle their patients into a chair or couch? They use the free association of ideas. And this method is actually better than our "logical" method. Our method is one for teaching information; the other is one for helping people to discover things themselves.

Lack of Tact on the Part of Pastoral Agents

Another obstacle that crops up at times is the lack of tact on the part of pastoral workers among the people. They are in a hurry and have no patience. They ride roughshod over some of the natural resistance that people have to our interpretations of the Bible. One time a nun went to give a course on the Old Testament. Halfway through she had to close down the course because no one was showing up. The people said: "Sister is destroying the Bible!" A certain priest offered an explanation of the Exodus. Many people never came back. "He is putting an end to miracles," they complained.

Meddling with the faith of the people is very serious business. You must have deep respect and a delicate touch. You must try to feel as they would and intuit their possible reaction to what you are going to say. The people should be allowed to grow from the soil of their own faith and their own character. They should not be dragged along by our aggressive questions.

Erudite Language

Another obstacle is erudite language, abstruse words. We talk a difficult idiom, and the language of translations is difficult. Today, thank God, various efforts are being made to translate the Bible into more popular terms. Nothing could be more desirable. People now feel that they are getting the point at least. The first and most basic requirement is that people talk in such a way that their listeners can understand them. It sounds simple enough, but often it is very hard to do.

Another important point is that we must not lose the poetry of the Bible. We must not reduce it to concepts. The Bible is full of poetry, and poetry is more than a matter of words. It is the whole way of seeing and grasping life.

From Confrontation to Practical Ecumenism

Another problem crops up on the grassroots level with "fundamentalist" groups. They head for people's homes with the Bible in their hands and make it clear that they have the only right answer. This leads to a defensive reaction and sectarian apologetics. It is hard to foster any ecumenism around the Bible in such an atmosphere.

In some areas, however, practical biblical ecumenism is growing from other starting points. Roman Catholics and Protestants are meeting each other and working together in labor unions, in fights for land ownership, and in other real-life struggles. Gradually other sectarian issues are taking a back seat to practical ecumenism.

CHARACTERISTICS OF THE PEOPLE'S INTERPRETATION OF THE BIBLE

In a sense we can say that the tabernacle of the church is to be found where the people come together around the word of God. That could be called the church's "holy of holies." Remember that no one was allowed to enter the holy of holies except the high priest, and he was allowed in only once a year! In this holy of holies no one is master—except God and the people. It is there that the Holy Spirit is at work; and where the Spirit is at work, there is freedom. The deepest and ultimate roots of the freedom sought by all are to be found there, in those small community groups where the people meet around the word of God. One song in Ceará has this line: "It is the tabernacle of the people. Don't anyone touch it!" Certain characteristics are surfacing in this tabernacle, and I should like to point them out here.

The things I am going to mention now are not fully developed and widespread. They are more like the first traces of dawn in the night sky. We are dipping our finger into the batter to savor how the cake will taste when it is baked and ready. The following characteristics are just beginning to surface here and there in the ongoing journey of various communities. I think they are very important.

The Scope of the Biblical Message

In the eyes of the common people the word of God, the gospel message, is much broader than just the text itself. The gospel message is a bit of everything: Bible, community, reality. For the common people the word of God is not just in the Bible; it is also in the community and in their real-life situation. The function of the Bible, read in a community context, is to help them to discover where God is calling them in the hubbub of real life. It is as if the word of God were hidden within history, within their struggles. When they discover it, it is big news. It's like a light flicking on in their brains. When one leper in Acre made this discovery, he exclaimed: "I have been raised from the dead!" He used the idea of resurrection to express the discovery he had made.

Theologians say that reality is a *locus theologicus.* The common people say: "God speaks, mixed into things." A tinker defined the church this way: "The church is us exchanging ideas with each other to discover the idea of the Holy Spirit in the people." If it hadn't come from Antonio Pascal, I would have said it came from St. Augustine. But it came from Antonio Pascal. It is us exchanging ideas with each other to discover the idea of the Holy Spirit in the people. Not in the church, in the people!

So you see, when they read the Bible, basically they are not trying to interpret the Bible; they are trying to interpret life with the help of the Bible. They are altering the whole business. They are shifting the axis of interpretation.

The Unity of Creation and Salvation

The common people are recovering the unity or oneness of creation and salvation, which is certainly true in the Bible itself. The Bible doesn't begin with Abraham. It begins with creation. Abraham is not called to form some group apart. Abraham is called to recover for all peoples the blessing lost by the sin of Adam. This is the oneness between life and faith, between transforming (political) activity and evangelization, that the people are concretely achieving in their praxis.

The Reappropriation of the Bible

The Bible was taken out of the people's hands. Now they are taking it back. They are expropriating the expropriators: "It is our book! It was written for us!" It had always been "Father's book," it seemed. Now it is the people's book again.

That gives them a new way of seeing, new eyes. They feel at home with the Bible and they begin to link it with their lives. So we get something very interesting. They are mixing life in with the Bible, and the Bible in with life. One helps them to interpret the other. And often the Bible is what starts them developing a more critical awareness of reality. They say, for example: "*We* are Abraham! *We* are in Egypt! *We* are in bondage! *We* are David!" With the biblical data they begin to reflect on their real-life situation. The process gradually prompts them to seek a more objective knowledge of reality and to look for a more suitable tool of analysis elsewhere. But it is often the word of God that starts them moving.

The rediscovery of the Bible as "our book" gives rise to a sense of commitment and a militancy that can overcome the world. Once they discover that God is with them in their struggles, no one can really stop them or deter them. One farmworker from Goiás concluded a letter this way: "When the time comes for me to bear my witness, I will do so without any fear of dying." That is the kind of strength that is surfacing. A sort of resurrection is taking place, as I suggested earlier.

We who have always had the Bible in hand find it difficult to imagine and comprehend the sense of novelty, the gratitude, the joy and the commitment that goes with their reading of the Bible. But that is why these people generally read the Bible in the context of some liturgical celebration. Their reading is a prayer exercise. Rarely will you find a group that reads the Bible simply for better understanding. Almost always their reading is associated with reflection on God present here and now, and hence with prayer. They live in a spirit of gratefulness for God's gift.

History as a Mirror

Another characteristic I hinted at already is the fact that the Bible is not just history for the people; it is also a mirror. Once upon a time we used to talk about the Bible as "letter" and "symbol." Today we might do well to talk about it as "history" and "mirror." The common people are using it as a mirror to comprehend their own lives as a people.

We who study a great deal have a lot more trouble trying to grasp the point of images and symbols. If we want to get a handle on symbolic language, we have to go through a whole process of "demythologizing." We have to go through a long process of study to get the point of the symbol. To us images are opaque glasses; we can't see through them at all. To see at all, we have to punch out the glass and smash it. To the common people in Brazil, an image or symbol is a pair of glasses with a little dust or frost on it. They just wipe them a bit and everything is as clear as day.

I don't think we pay enough attention to this educational item. We are awfully "Europeanized" in our training. Take the question of the historicity of a text. I think you have to approach it very differently, or worry about it differently, when you are dealing with ordinary people. Very often pastoral workers are talking about the Bible and they ask questions like these: "Did that really happen? Did Jesus walk on top of the water? Were there only five loaves and two fishes?" They think that this is the most important problem that the people have with the text in front of them. I don't think so. Once, in Goiás, we read the passage in the New Testament (Acts 17:19) where an angel of the Lord came and freed the apostles from jail. The pastoral worker asked his people: "Who was the angel?" One of the women present gave this answer: "Oh, I know. When Bishop Dom Pedro Casaldáliga was attacked in his house and the police surrounded it with machine guns, no one could get in or out and no one knew what was going on exactly. So this little girl sneaked in without being seen, got a little message from

Pedro, ran to the airport, and hitched a ride to Goiana where the bishops were meeting. They got the message, set up a big fuss, and Dom Pedro was set free. So that little girl was the angel of the Lord. And it's really the same sort of thing."

The people don't always take things literally. They are far smarter than you would think. Our question simply will have to take more account of the way that ordinary people understand history. They are far more capable of understanding symbols than we assume.

DISLOCATIONS

When there are only five persons in a room, then each one can be pretty much at ease. When fifty more persons enter the room, then the original five find themselves a bit crowded and some moving around has to take place. Well, the common people have entered the precincts of biblical interpretation and they are causing much shifting and dislocation.

A *Shift in Standpoint*

First of all, the Bible itself has shifted its place and moved to the side of the poor. One could almost say that it has changed its class status. This is important. The place where the people read the Bible is a different place. We read the Bible something like the wealthy car owner who looks out over the top of his car and sees a nice chrome finish. The common people read the Bible something like the mechanic under the car who looks up and sees a very different view of the same car.

The common people are discovering things in the Bible that other readers don't find. At one session we were reading the following text: "I have heard the cries of my people." A woman who worked in a factory offered this commentary: "The Bible does not say that God has heard the praying of the people. It says that God has heard the cries of his people. I don't mean that people shouldn't pray. I mean that people should imitate God. Very often we work to get people to go to church and pray first; and only then will we pay heed to their cries." You just won't find that sort of interpretation in books.

The Bible has changed its place, and the place where the common people read the Bible is different. It is the place where one can appreciate the real import of Jesus' remark: "I thank thee, Father . . . that thou has hidden these things from the wise and understanding and revealed them to babes; yea, Father, for such was thy gracious will" (Matt. 11:25–26). If you take sides with the poor, you will discern things in the Bible that an exegete does not see. All of us have a slight blind spot that prevents us from seeing certain things.

From Biblical Text to Real Life

Another shift mentioned earlier has to do with the fact that the word of God has moved in a certain sense from the Bible to real life. It is in the Bible but it is also in real life—especially in real life. So we come to the following conclusion: the Bible is not the one and only history of salvation; it is a kind of "model experience." Every single people has *its own* history of salvation.

Clement of Alexandria said: "God saved the Jews in a Jewish way, the barbarians in a barbarian way." We could go on to say: "God saves Brazilians in a Brazilian way, blacks in a black way, Indians in an Indian way, Nicaraguans in a Nicaraguan way, and so on." Each people has its own unique history. Within that history it must discover the presence of God the Liberator who journeys by its side. The scope of this particular dislocation is most important.

From Meaning in Itself to Meaning for Us

Another dislocation is to be found in the fact that emphasis is not placed on the text's meaning in itself but rather on the meaning the text has for the people reading it. At the start people tend to draw any and every sort of meaning, however well or ill founded, from the text. Only gradually, as they proceed on their course in life, do they begin to develop an interest in the historical import and intrinsic meaning of the text. It is at this point that they can benefit greatly from a study of the material conditions of the people in biblical times: that is, their religious, political, and socio-economic situation. But they do so in order to give a better grounding to the text's meaning "for us." In this framework scientific exegesis can reclaim its proper role and function, placing itself in the service of the biblical text's meaning "for us."

From Abstract Understanding to a Community Sense

The common people are doing something else very important. They are reintroducing faith, community, and historical reality into the process of interpretation. When we studied the Bible back in the seminary in the old days, we didn't have to live as a real community or really know much about reality. We didn't even have to have faith. All we needed was enough brains to understand Greek and Hebrew and to follow the professor's line of reasoning.

Now the common people are helping us to realize that without faith, community, and reality we cannot possibly discover the meaning that God has put in that ancient tome for us today. Thus the common people are recovering something very important: the *sensus ecclesiae* ("sense of the church"). The community is the resonance chamber; the text is a violin string. When the people pluck the string (the biblical text), it resonates in the community and out comes the music. And that music sets the people dancing and singing. The community of faith is like a big pot in which Bible and community are cooked just right until they become one tasty dish.

From Neutrality to Taking Sides

The common people are also eliminating the alleged "neutrality" of scholarly exegesis. No such neutrality is possible. Technology is not neutral, and neither is exegesis.

Clearing up Overly Spiritualized Concepts

The common people are giving us a clearer picture of concepts that have been excessively spiritualized. Let me give just one example. Pope Paul VI once delivered an address in which he warned priests not to become overly preoccupied with material things. He urged them to show greater concern for spiritual things. One farmworker in Goiás had this comment: "Yes, the pope is quite right. Many priests concern themselves only with material things, such as building a church or decorating it. They forget spiritual things, such as food for the people!"

That is what the people are doing with such notions as grace, salvation, sin, and so forth. They are dusting them off and showing us that these notions have to do with solid, concrete realities of life.

Putting the Bible in Its Proper Place

Finally, the common people are putting the Bible in its proper place, the place where God intended it to be. They are putting it in second place. Life takes first place! In so doing, the people are showing us the enormous importance of the Bible and, at the same time, its relative value — relative to life.

PROBLEMS, CHALLENGES, REQUIREMENTS

There are many problems, difficulties, and failings associated with the interpretation of the Bible by the common people. But every good tree has a strong, solid limb that can be pruned when the time comes. The point is that its roots are okay. The common people are reading and interpreting the Bible as a new book that speaks to them here and now. And this basic view of the Bible is the view that the church fathers of the past had when they interpreted the Bible.

Here I simply want to enumerate a few further points that need greater attention.

1. There is the danger of subjectivistic interpretation. This can be com-

bated in two ways: by more objective grounding in the literal sense of the Bible and by reading the Bible in community.

2. It is possible to read the Bible solely to find in it a confirmation of one's own ideas. In this case the biblical text loses its critical function. Community-based reading and interpretation help to overcome this tendentious use of the Bible. In addition, people must have a little humility and a little signal-light in their brains that calls them up short when they are tempted to absolutize their own ideas.

3. People may lack a critical sense in reading and interpreting the biblical text. They may be tempted to take the ancient text and apply it mechanically to today, without paying any serious attention to the difference in historical context.

4. The above three points underline the proper and necessary function of scientific exegesis. Exegesis is being called upon to concern itself, not with the question it raises, but with the questions that the common people are raising. In many cases the exegete is like the person who had studied salt and knew all its chemical properties but didn't know how to cook it. The common people don't know the properties of salt well, but they do know how to season a meal.

5. We need biblical interpretation that will reveal the material living conditions of the people in the Bible. We need a materialist reading and interpretation of the Bible, but not a narrow and confined reading. It must be broad and full.

6. We urgently need to give impetus to ecumenism on the grassroots level. It is a hard and challenging task, but a beginning has been made here and there.

7. The Bible is a book derived from a rural environment. Today we live in an urban environment. Rereading the Bible today here in São Paulo, in this urban reality, presents no easy task of interpretation.

8. There is the matter of revolutionary effectiveness and gratitude for the Father's gift. This is another matter that needs further exploration.

9. Criticism can be derived from the word of God to foster transforming action.

4

Women Doing Theology in Latin America

IVONE GEBARA

The expression "women doing theology" is new, as is the explication of what the expression means. Previously, there was never any mention of sexual difference with regard to those who wrote theology, since it was obvious that the task was something proper to men. Today it would seem that the matter is no longer obvious, and the gender of the authors must be specified. Gender is understood not only as a biological difference prior even to birth, but especially as a cultural dimension, that is, as a stance or an aspect that affects the production of other cultural values, of other kinds of human interrelationship and other ways of thinking.

The fact that women have entered the world of economic production and, more broadly, into politics and culture and the consequences for change in society and in the various churches deserves deeper reflection on its own. Such a deepening would go beyond the scope of our contribution, since right now we have another aim.

I am going to devote my attention especially to the question of the task of theology, emphasizing some points of reflection on what has already been said, and I shall continue my reflection beyond issues that are properly theological.

WHAT CHARACTERIZES THE WAY WOMEN DO THEOLOGY?

In order to sketch a response to this question, we must first explain what we understand today by the theological activity of women. I should make it clear that my starting point is the situation in northeastern Brazil. Placing myself at that starting point is crucially important, since it conditions my

From *Through Her Eyes: Women's Theology from Latin America*, edited by Elsa Tamez (Mary-knoll, N.Y.: Orbis Books, 1986), pp. 37-48. Translated by Phillip Berryman.

reflection as a woman out of a particular socioeconomic, political, and cultural situation. This situation shapes my being and my acting, my seeing and my feeling, my speech and my silence.

To speak or write from northeast Brazil is to situate myself in a region where misery and exploitation take on extremely dehumanizing forms and where most of the people, and especially women, are its victims. This region is the victim of internal and external contradictions of the capitalist system and is marked by various kinds of contrasts: (a) by economic and social contrasts: a few largescale property-owners, most people landless, very high unemployment; (b) by political contrasts: power of the "colonels" — sugar-mill owners, industrialists, and politicians — alongside the lack of decision-making power on the part of millions of people in the northeast; (c) by cultural contrasts: utilization of popular culture to serve the dominant culture, machismo, and subjection of women.

As we know well, these contrasts entail enormous social consequences, reducing most of the people to subhuman living conditions. It is out of this situation, which sustains my being and my reflection, that I can speak of women's theology. I recognize that I am a woman who lives in privileged conditions, conditions that give me enough space to reflect, to speak, and even to write. I speak of the woman that I am myself, and of others, the poor women of my region, in an effort to move over into their world on the basis of my option for our liberation, as well as on the basis of our common human condition as women.

As I see it, the theological task is multiple and varied. There is nothing new about such a statement. What may be new is the fact of explicating it from the starting point of the situation of women. Hence, I speak of different theological tasks.

Shared Experiences

There is a way of doing theology that starts with shared experience from oral transmission, from the simple fact of sharing life. I believe this way of doing theology is what is most representative of the popular milieus. Many women are especially gifted with a deep intuition about human life and are able to counsel, to intuit problems, to express them, to give support, to propose solutions, and to confirm the faith of many people. They explain biblical passages on the basis of their experience and respond to doctrinal questions by simplifying them and setting them on the level of existential reality. Some of these women are illiterate. That would pose problems for a more academic doing of theology, but it does not hinder the exercise of this ministry. This activity is sapiential; it springs from life, and life is its reference point. It is received as a gift from God and handed on as a gift.

Discourse dealing with the important issues in life is the heart of every theology. God's life is related to the life of humankind, and the life of humankind is related to God. All subsequent systematizing, all thematizing, all connecting of ideas, is vitally linked to this most basic aspect. . . .

Doing Theology from Daily Life

The theological activity of women who teach in theology departments and institutes is a ministry not limited just to courses but involves advising the various groups and movements in the Christian churches. Above and beyond the academic theological formation, which both men and women receive in higher institutions of learning where men are the majority, there is something quite special in the way that women do theology. The elements of everyday life are very intertwined with their speaking about God. When women's experience is expressed in a church whose tradition is machistic, the other side of human experience returns to theological discourse: the side of the person who gives birth, nurses, nourishes, of the person who for centuries has remained silent with regard to anything having to do with theology. Now she begins to express her experience of God, in another manner, a manner that does not demand that reason alone be regarded as the single and universal mediation of theological discourse. This way of doing theology includes what is vital, utilizing mediations that can help to express what has been experienced, without exhausting it, a discourse that leads to the awareness that there is always something more, something that words cannot express.

What is vital cannot be expressed through formal mediations. It can be done only through those mediations that are proper to a sapiential discourse in which relationships with others express the diversity and complexity of human situations and challenges. Theological speech is expressed in the kind of prophecy that denounces the present, in songs of hope, in lament, in the form of counsel. It is as though the aim were to bridge the gap between speech and reality, the distance that the formal and idealist discourse of religion has imposed on us for a long time. It is as though we were discovering, very powerfully and starting from our own situation, the mystery of the incarnation of the divine in the human, not just because "we have been told," but because we experience it in the confines of our lives as women.

The experience of this theological activity is still in its early stages. In Brazil there are not many published works to confirm it and make it known. There is only what I regard as most basic and prior to theological elaboration: faith and its expression based on an encounter with the experience of the oppression of women as an experience of the oppression of the poor. This expression has been more oral and more direct, and has proved to be effective.

At this point, I am limiting myself to taking note of this kind of activity. Further on, I shall seek to explain some characteristics, intuitions, and efforts involved in this activity.

HISTORIC CONTEXTS

The different theological activities spelled out above take place on different levels and in different situations, characterized by various kinds of conditionings. At this point, I propose that we reflect on some "historic contexts" and some characteristics that, I think, are proper to women doing theology in Latin America during these last few years.

Irruption of History into Women's Lives

When we speak of the irruption of history into the lives of women — and especially the theological expression of their faith — we do not mean the entrance of women into history; they have always been present. What we have in mind is something qualitatively different and new, that is, the irruption of historic consciousness into the lives of millions and millions of women, leading them to the liberation struggle by means of an active participation in different fronts from which they had previously been absent. It is as though a strong wind had begun to blow, opening eyes and loosening tongues, shifting stances, enabling arms to reach out to new embraces and hands to take up other tools, impelling feet to take other steps, raising the voice so its song and its lament might be heard. Woman begins to take her place as agent of history. The fact is that with her activity and new stance toward what happens in life, a new awareness is clearly coming into being. Participation in labor unions, neighborhood movements, mothers' groups, and pastoral leadership all manifest a change in the consciousness and in the role women play today. Entering into history in fact means becoming aware of history, entering into a broader meaning, in which women are also creators or increasingly want to be forgers of history.

Discovering Causality within Women's Experience

In connection with history, one can speak of the causality of things. The condition of women is the result of an evolution: it has been different, and it can be different. Their present state can be partly explained on the basis of historic causes. The discovery of the causes of the oppression of the poor and, among them, of the oppression of women, has changed women's understanding of themselves as persons individually and corporately. Woman is not marked for an unchangeable fate, nor is she the object of alien wills that shape her existence. Despite the conditions inherent in human existence, she can conquer spaces in which to express her word and her being. This new historic moment of hers is pregnant with future, a moment that announces a Good News that is both present and yet to be lived in its fullness.

It is worth noting that the discovery of causality within women's experience bears the characteristic marks of the particular way in which they perceive and approach the problems of life. No one single cause is absolutized but, rather, the causes are multiple. This way of looking at matters is obedient to their perception, as women, in its complexity, diversity, and mystery.

Entering the Labor Force

The fact that more and more women are entering the world of paid labor, and the world of work and struggle for survival, has awakened them to struggle in other areas where human destiny is also at stake.

Entering the labor force has changed the expression of women's faith. From their previous horizon of home and family, women have opened out to a broader reality. God is no longer one who addresses a world limited to the activities of home and family; God becomes the one who addresses socioeconomic and political challenges in the new militancy of Latin American women. The image of God is no longer that of the father to whom one owes submission; rather, God is basically the image of what is most human in woman and man, seeking expression and liberation. A working woman said, "God is the force that won't allow me to surrender to the will of those who oppress my people."

Women's entry into the struggle of the world of paid labor has thus brought about a change in the way they relate. Obviously, this is not the only factor, but it seems important to remind ourselves of it, since it tends to be forgotten or left as a purely accidental aspect within a traditionalist or reactionary theological vision.

CHARACTERISTICS OF FEMINIST THEOLOGICAL ACTIVITY IN LATIN AMERICA

Living Realities and Theological Elaboration

Feminist theological expression always starts from what has been lived, from what is experienced in the present. Consequently it rejects an abstract type of language about life and those matters deeply affecting human relationship. That is why there is a growing effort to clear the field of old theological concepts in order to discover what vital realities they correspond to, and to what extent they really do so. Living realities are the takeoff point for theological elaboration; they are rational symbols that arose in a particular period, the product of a series of conditions, and they were able to bring together rationally certain experiences of reality. It is urgent that we get to know them and discover their meaning for today, and for our history. In their theological work, women seek to retrieve existential realities, to let them speak freely, to allow them to become reorganized on the basis of our context today, and only subsequently to connect them to a prior tradition.

This way of proceeding represents an attempt to restore to theological language its capacity for touching some vital centers of human existence. In other words, to some extent this procedure means returning the poetic dimension of human life to theology, since the deepest meaning in the human being is expressed only through analogy; mystery is voiced only in poetry, and what is gratuitous is expressed only through symbols.

Purely rational concepts do not take into account the meaning, desire, flavor, pleasure, pain, and mystery of existence. Given their own history, women are bolder in questioning concepts, and they have a creative curiosity that opens new paths and allows new understandings. This new mode makes possible a kind of theological creation in community. That is, the new formulation gathers a broader number of experiences and is not narrowed to a formulation or a text with individual "authorship."

This is a "new way" of expressing something after it has been heard, lived, and felt many times and in many ways, so that people recognize themselves when they hear it spelled out, and they feel invited to a deeper reflection on the questions that life poses. It is their own issues that they see reflected on, questioned, or clarified so that the reflection proposed touches most deeply the questions and doubts present in the lives of millions of people.

Re-creating Tradition

In women's theological discourse, the theological tradition shared by the different churches does not function as a legitimizing justification that we need only to go on repeating. If we do repeat, it is because that is what today's situation demands, because it does touch the roots of our existence, because to some extent it responds to the problems that ongoing history sets before us. In this sense, what is normative is primarily the present, what calls out today; tradition is viewed in terms of the present. Thus the tradition of Christian communities in the past is continually re-created, and one may even speak of fidelity to that tradition to the extent that both today and yesterday are faithful to the Spirit of God manifest in history and demanding absolute respect for life. The past is not only information, but enlightenment, teaching, and witness for the present to the extent that it relates to the question of being human.

Human Complexities

The theological work of women reflects an ability to view life as the locus of the simultaneous experience of oppression and liberation, of grace and lack of grace. Such perception encompasses what is plural, what is different, what is other. Although this way of looking is not the exclusive property of women, we must say that it is found to an extraordinary extent among women. In popular struggles, in which women have played a very important role, this ability to grasp in a more unified way the oppositions and contradictions, the contrasts and differences as inherent in human life, has been a characteristic feature of the way in which women live and express their faith. Such behavior enables them to avoid taking dogmatic and exclusive stances, and to perceive or intuit the real complexity of what is human.

The Tapestry of Human Life

In addition to these factors or characteristics of the theological work of women, we cannot fail to recall the inestimable contribution of the social sciences — anthropology, psychology, and different theories about language — as elements that have been changing, directly or indirectly, women's understanding of themselves. These same elements have contributed to the emancipation of women's power in the social dimension of human relations and in the way these relations are organized.

All these contributions form part of the tapestry woven by women expressing and reflecting human life as this century ends. The threads, colors, flowers, and other designs — all taken together, interconnected, and linked to each other — are forming the embroidery of life while the artists themselves are beginning to appear, to show their faces in public, to demand respect and appreciation. It is also worth noting that the international women's movement, in its expressions and organizations, has played a role in opening up the oppressed situation of Brazilian women so they could be aware of the situation of women in different areas of the world.

The persistence of women in the struggle for life and the restoration of justice have been linked together and lived out as expressions of faith, as the presence of God in the struggles of history. Many women see in these developments the expression of their desire to struggle for a more human world, in which certain values presently dormant may be aroused, where people can accept affection, where life may triumph over the powers of death.

Basic Ecclesial Communities

Finally, I want to take particular note of the work of women in basic ecclesial communities. No doubt this work has been present throughout this reflection, but I can not avoid dealing with it more fully at this point, before concluding my thoughts. I am not going to describe what women do in basic ecclesial communities. That would fill a long essay, and besides it is well known to all of us.

I would simply like to emphasize how their active role is prefiguring within the Christian churches a new way of organizing ministries. Even though these ministries are not sanctioned by church officials, they are recognized by the poorest, those to whom this service is especially directed. The new element in this service is found in the way it responds to a certain number of the community's vital needs and in the fear that it is generating in those who are in charge of the churches and who are gradually losing their former prestige. Women's ministry is shaking up men's ministry, challenging their practice and the exercise of their authority. This is taking place, not because of some decision taken by women to make it happen, but because of the nature and quality of their service and of the new social role that they are winning in the world. To the extent that women actively move onstage in the churches, their organizations, institutions, and expressions must be revised to meet the challenges continually posed by today's world.

In Conclusion: My Hope for the Future

Theological formulations that are extremely machistic, privileges of power over what is sacred, and the need for male legitimation for things to "happen" in the churches are beginning to be affected by the clashes that hint of the future. Such a statement in no way intends to replace the "masculine" model with the "feminine" one but to anticipate a new synthesis in which the dialectic present in human existence can take place, without destroying any of its vital elements.

This is my hope: The day will come when all people, lifting their eyes, will see the earth shining with brotherhood and sisterhood, mutual appreciation, true complementarity. . . .

Men and women will dwell in their houses; men and women will eat the same bread, drink the same wine, and dance together in the brightly lit square, celebrating the bonds uniting all humanity.

5

The Granary Is Empty

JEAN-MARC ÉLA

It seems that drought and famine have become an African scourge. Pictures of its victims, African children with swollen bellies and skeletal limbs, are projected throughout the world by the media. Public opinion, teams of researchers, and many different organizations are mobilized, while the Food and Agriculture Organization cries out in alarm over the seriousness of food shortages. Paradoxically, these same shortages have fed vast markets during the last fifteen years, and the industry of misery prospers!

Christians are celebrating the Eucharist while entire populations are vulnerable to the weapon of grain, and condemned to live on imported food products. Is the question of food essential to our faith? Of course! The Eucharist is not even imaginable without the fruits of the earth produced by peasants, who bring together agriculture and the celebration of the history of salvation. But can our Eucharist be called Christian if it abandons countless young people to their sad fate in regions where "the other half of the world is dying"? How can we truly be nourished by the body of Jesus Christ, while a minority is satiated, and yet each year millions of people have no food and face an empty granary? We cannot help but associate the table of the altar with the "table of the Magnificat" as did Anselme Sanon, a theologian from the Sahel.[1] Our practice of the Christian faith faces a major challenge from African men and women who agonize over where their next meal is coming from.

Our churches today expose us to the dangers of atheism each time we celebrate the Eucharist in areas where no one is working to create conditions that would allow hungry people to feed themselves. The peasants in

From *My Faith as an African* (Maryknoll, N.Y.: Orbis Books, 1988), pp. 87-101. Translated by John Pairman Brown and Susan Perry.

the village of Tokombéré in northern Cameroon showed us how they have been prevented from feeding their families. Before they began their Easter celebration, they recalled the events that marked their life during the year, and then they ended with a recitation of the Passion of Jesus. Bouba, the leader of the community, began:

> The farm supervisor, the chief of the district, and the sub-prefect called us all together. They told us, "Now you will pull up all the millet that you have grown in order to plant cotton." While they watched, we began to pull up our millet. Lifting our arms to heaven, each person held the stalks of millet with one hand and said, "My God, you can see that I am not the one who is doing it; my God, it's not me."

In order to understand the meaning of this gesture, we must remember that for the people of northern Cameroon, and in particular the Kirdi, millet is a gift from God. According to their tradition, it was God who told them to "Dig up the mountain and cultivate millet." Millet means life; custom forbids pulling it up. So, in this act, the peasants called God to witness that they had no part in the action. "My God, it is not me." We must remember all the elements of the scene: the millet, the peasants, the agents of the government, the administration, and above all, the invocation to God. Bouba finishes, "This is the suffering that Jesus carried for us; it was our sorrows that he bore."

"AFRICA STRANGLED": THE PEASANTS

The drama of the Kirdi is shared by millions of African peasants who ask only to live. "We know that we are peasants, we do not want to be like the city people, the rich! We just want to live better!" This disclosure by an old man appears in a film shot by Frères des Hommes in Piala, a village in Burkina Faso. The bush people in a village lost in the immensity of the Sahel are torn between famine and "here today, gone tomorrow" development schemes. They are prisoners in a system devised elsewhere for the interests of others. These attempts at "rural modernization" actually seem to enlarge the cities and shantytowns, and endanger the productive base of the society that lies in the villages. But what else can we expect? After all, the development of these projects matches the interests of foreign capital and its "watchdogs." The axis of the African economy, from their point of view, is producing cotton, coffee, peanuts, palm oil, sugar, cocoa, and rubber.

Multinational corporations and banks have invaded a diversity of situations and political systems in Africa, and strangle the peasant men and women who comprise the majority of its people. Almost everywhere throughout the black continent, the various forms of coercive apparatus of the multinationals guarantee optimal conditions for the over-exploitation of human labor and natural resources. Although the capitalist-oriented economies dominate our societies and profit from them, it is not clear that they actually improve the lot of the African masses. René Dumont has shown how bureaucratic minorities squander foreign aid, while they exploit the peasants and ruin their land and soil.[2] And Julius Nyerere testified to the emergence of a privileged élite whose scandalous lifestyle feeds off the over-exploitation of village laborers: "The countryside produces, the city consumes."

Today the constraints of international trade have become overwhelming. African governments and social authorities, however, do have a certain freedom of initiative and action. And yet, using a surplus of export crops to extend its authority, the state seems to have allowed the growth of a managerial élite and supported a political-administrative class that oppresses the peasant masses.

While the specter of hunger and death prowls our continent, certain peasants continually say that "independence is the business of the sons of the Whites." They feel that this black minority has restored the use of a model of development for African villages that is based on exploitation. Unemployment (which has begun to affect even university graduates), malnutrition, and torture are outcomes of this control held over all of black Africa. We have been permanently reduced, it seems, to a situation where poverty and oppression surround a few islands of affluence. A multitude of the oppressed are up against an élite that always tends to reinforce its position of power by setting up a system whose results are clear. Millions of expelled citizens have been uprooted from their backgrounds and families, and become refugees in other countries.

Others live in "interior exile" within their own countries where small stirrings of opposition are nipped in the bud by repression and intimidation.

The reality of Africa — after it has been stripped of its folklore — demands attention. Twenty years of independence have not brought development, but rather developed underdevelopment. The situation becomes more serious when the state itself is the instrument of repression. It is important to understand the relationship in Africa between the government and the people. There is little effective participation of the people in public affairs, and the masses have practically no way of controlling government power, but only of applauding its use. Did God really plan that our continent be a land of oppression, poverty, and injustice? As black Africa becomes increasingly impoverished, must we close the door on hope?

THE CONFRONTATION OF CULTURES AND THE IRRUPTION OF THE POOR

For more than twenty years, black priests, pastors and theologians, bush catechists and urban intellectuals, an ever-increasing number of bishops, and foreign missionaries have discussed the advent of African Christianity. The event of Pentecost makes it clear that the gospel should be lived and translated into all languages. But who has the right to impose a foreign style of living on other people? Because Christianity has failed to speak about God in a relevant manner, independent churches and sects have proliferated. We must rethink our basic faith because it has failed to enter genuinely into African life and root itself there, and because its claim to universality has been destroyed. As we bring Christianity face to face with the African reality, we must rethink God.

For some years we have reflected about our Christian faith in the context of the confrontation of cultures. If the future of Christianity lies within Africa (and many signs seem to indicate this is true), the irruption of the poor must challenge our faith as Africans. Soon the church will no longer be able to pass by "the man who fell among robbers." Our African society is sick in this same way with corruption and injustice; it is consumed by bitterness, and threatened by the clutches of famine whose very appearance strangles the whole of life. Fear paralyzes energy and initiative. People lacking the power of speech back away from their own history. They do not react to the failures of the public authorities or to the powerlessness of the parasitic middle class.

But there is a sign of hope in the ferment of small communities committed to the poor and the downtrodden. These communities' experience of the Christian faith goes beyond all those acts and rituals that are included in the indigenization of Christianity: initiation rites, the world of the invisible, the cult of ancestors, and the importance of sacrifices.

Evangelizing people shaped by a certain culture must go hand in hand with their struggle for development in all aspects of their lives. Hence, the work of our faith must be understood in reference to the overall situation in Africa today. We must deal with down-to-earth questions, and get back to ground level where the Kingdom of God is built day by day. For the hope for a new world that is built in the framework of justice, peace, and freedom is the heart of the Christian message. We must get involved in this experience and use it as our starting-point for a radical critique of all that is happening before our eyes. This is the only source of energy that will impel us to interpret Christian responsibilities in the current context of black Africa.

The irruption of the poor throughout the countries of the Third World is radically changing the mission of the church. Religious communities, pastoral workers, and lay movements are shifting their focus. New questions are being asked of theological reflection, pastoral practice, and spiritual life in many different places where the church is getting out of its traditional rut, and being born again from the dominated and exploited people. The poor and oppressed are reclaiming the Word of God and changing the structures of a world that is incompatible with God's plan. Working through historical dynamics, the poor are called by the gospel to ask hard questions and to become participants with the power to change their own living conditions.

This is all happening at a moment when the strength of the gospel is being discovered in the midst of the plundering of the Third World, the destruction of its cultures, and its relegation to a simple source of raw materials for the dominant industrial countries. This is a momentous experience of faith. Solidarity is now the business of the poor themselves, as they learn to be together in a village or a slum and work to solve their own problems and to share their life and their struggles—everything that comprises their essence and their deepest hopes. The most striking development is their will to make common cause in a dynamic directed to create a different society.

Nascent Christian communities are being built around a sharing of initiatives and projects so they can go beyond the impasses posed by development. In this way, the practice of the gospel is much closer to the reality of Africa, which today is a vast battlefield of multinational interests closely tied to life in the villages and the slums. By working in communities, people are able to come together to take charge of economic, social, and practical realities: the use of money, privately owned dispensaries, grain banks, methods of drilling wells, and so forth. We should ask ourselves if these actions of small communities aren't the best response to the impasses reached in many countries.

One thing that is clear is that the African church is still waiting to hear strong voices denounce corruption, torture, exploitation, and the oppression of the masses by a minority. Communities forming today throughout Africa will certainly make it clear that injustice and famine result above all from the acceptance of the current model of development—a model imposed on the peasants since independence. The extreme misery of the countryside and the outlying urban areas is the direct effect of a whole system of domination that forces peasants to grow cotton and other export crops even though they feed no one.

A MINISTRY OF THE GRANARY

What use is there in mobilizing communities unless the goal is to shelter peasants from the weapon of food? Peasant families are crushed by requirements to produce peanuts, cocoa, or cotton. That is why I deliberately chose a "ministry of the granary." African agriculture has been disrupted by its emphasis on capital. Today the question of food must again become the center of daily life—starting from an African culture that is based on granaries, and the dynamics of the revelation as it is read in Genesis through Matthew. In times of famine, God wills that humanity should be fed (Gen. 42:1-2, 43:1-2), and in the end God totally identifies with the hungry (Matt. 25:35-42).

Because the God of the gospel is revealed as the God who brings life, our faith requires us to reject any system that produces empty granaries — signs of famine and death. The message and the work of Jesus denounce exploitation of peasants, and demand new forms of relationships where people can organize themselves so that no one is deprived of the needed ration of millet. How can we speak of the Lord of Life, knowing full well that famine is the messenger of death? A look at village life in Africa today shows that it is no longer just the elderly who are near death; now children are dying of malnutrition. Is this an action of God? Does God will it? Would this still happen if people organized themselves in working groups so they could have enough food all year round? Such a project demands a clear understanding of the place of the granary in village life, of concerns for children, the relationships between men and women, the whole question of health care, and, of course, the importance of land.

The overall organizing process requires a series of mutually complementary actions. Primary-school students are taught to become the eyes of their village. After this type of training, one student observed during a discussion that, "Because they have taken away our fields, there is no place left to grow millet." Literacy training for adults is also an integral part of this project. Over a period of several weeks, groups of men and women learn to read and write using texts that show they cannot eat cotton. The newly literate can then send news to members of their family who have gone to the city, and tell them what happens in the village after a bad harvest. Their messages describe what is going on in the village, the need to speak out, the centers of decision-making, and the various groups engaged in different activities: educators, doctors, rural organizers, those in charge of agriculture, government representatives. These messages might include reflection on the theme that feeding people is a political problem.

This "ministry of the granary" has led me to a better understanding of the mechanisms operative in the cotton-growing region of northern Cameroon — the economic choices available, the strategies of the state-owned corporations, speculation in millet, and administrative corruption. (In the process, I became somewhat suspicious of the information services, which would hide the real misery of the peasants if it served their purposes.) When I worked in youth camps deep in the mountains, I glimpsed how hope could be born again in the hearts of the poor when students from secondary schools or grammar schools returned to the villages to be with the peasants, live with them, and talk with them. The students seriously questioned the practices of the communities, and challenged a system that creates hunger and yet makes "the rich richer and the poor poorer." Each year these people have less to eat, and wonder if they will continue to live so poorly, or perhaps not live at all. How can they be helped to take responsibility for eliminating the causes of famine and death so as to live the life of justice and mutual help described in the gospel? I finally realized that it is in the community itself where we experience the power of the Lord, and can celebrate God through signs of our faith.

My ministry in the north was motivated by a challenge made to me more than ten years ago by a wise old man. One evening I was in a village in the north intending to bring the Word of God to the people. Some young people had announced my arrival, saying "This is the son of Baba Simon, who is coming here to talk about God." Shortly after I began, this old man interrupted me: "Once upon a time God talked to people, but now he has fallen silent, and he has left us prey to hunger, sickness, and death."

Communities controlled by hunger and slavery *can* recover their true dignity through a peasant reading of the Bible. It can lead them to a path of liberation that will show each of them the secret of their existence and a reason for living. I feel this is what is at stake today in the searching and experimenting going on in Africa where the Spirit is working to build a church from the struggles of peasants. Today God is again speaking to the Kirdi. God's message is revealed when peasants gather together, hear anew the gospel, and recite it by heart. God speaks through their efforts to take charge of their own lives in communities that show an understanding of themselves and work for their own evangelization.

I could cite a whole series of testimonies to show this is true but I need only recall these words of a leader at a community meeting:

In the beginning, children and adults came to hear the Word of God. Somebody asked, "Why are we different? Why are we so poor?" When we heard the story of Adam and Eve, people said to themselves, "We are the ones driven out of the garden to settle here in the mountains." We went on reflecting together, trying to understand why we were so unfortunate and poor. We saw that we didn't have any water. What could we do? We sunk a well. The villagers helped us lay down the pipes and we saw the results. That was an idea that came from people working together.

Then we looked at the problem of health care. We put some people in charge and set up a health committee. We taxed ourselves to buy the basic medicines and have a small dispensary. Even though the parents of the school children had never gone to school themselves, they formed a self-help committee to help each other buy what their children needed. In other words, they organized themselves. Now they cultivate one field in common and have a person in charge and a treasurer.

The young people spoke in their turn. They said, "To get money we must go to the city." Then we reflected together, "Is this really the only way? What can we do right here?" Some young people started to sell peanuts so they could make a living while staying in the village. Women began to knit clothing and manufacture peanut oil. For us, the community means people who reflect together to see why their life is different and to find a new outlook.

There is no doubt that this experience gives hope to people who seek to live and have a future. In this particular village, the millet granary became the axis of church activity. During the long months of the dry season, communities and villages were unified around land, water and millet. All this helped people go beyond the usual dead-ends of development, which is nothing other than a destructive integration into the world market, creating a socio-political and economic situation where growing cotton for export benefits only the traditional leaders, the ranks of the administration, the dignitaries of the government party, and the multinational corporations.

This experience gives an insight into the potential force the Word of God can have when it is liberated from its yokes, as Vincent Cosmao says.[3] The poor have a way of backing us into a corner where we must make a choice, and then they use the Bible to show us that we must adopt a relevant pastoral program. They show us how disturbing the Word of God is — faced with injustices in villages and slums, excessive interest payments, arbitrary fines, detention without trial, forced labor in the fields of the chief, customary rents, the pulling-up of millet to grow cotton, and so on. In the face of all these problems, these efforts I describe are modest — not at all spectacular; but they are small steps toward living better.

Given the extent of corruption on all levels, it is very difficult to find a way out of our maze. Our countries are considered secure — a sort of fiscal paradise — for foreign investors. Soccer is the only subject one dares to discuss in total freedom. But within these new communities, people discover each other and the socio-economic conflicts that entrap them. People are speaking up and utilizing the energies of a heretofore paralyzed Africa. When these communities analyze their own difficulties, they discover the great anxieties of Africa today: growing inequities, the continuing deterioration of living conditions, and an increasing dependence on other countries.

An analysis in the heart of village communities of the causes of misery reveals the muted speech of the most exploited people in our society. Today basic communities liberate peasants to speak out in villages that have been pulled apart by the production of export crops, and whose authority has been replaced by the government's propaganda apparatus of radio, television, and the party press. Peasants who want to grow millet denounce this blind alley of development geared to outside interests as the prime cause of dependence and the cause of a series of inequities and misery. The current model of development is part of what can certainly be called a "vulgar ideology of development" — a plan that licenses whatever is used to starve a people, under the pretext of accumulating foreign exchange for the profit of a club of the affluent.

POPULAR RESISTANCE AND CREATIVITY

While official and unofficial organs of the state continue to impose their model of development, the communities that we have been trying to form here and now insist that we also listen to what is *not* being said in official speeches in order to understand what is going on in the heart of the African bush. These new communities are identifying the cultural elements that would support a process of change, and they are looking for people who can motivate the villages. The communities are planning a form of development that keeps our actions and research today open to the alternative of a different future.

In this way, starting from the gospel, Africa is becoming reconciled with itself. Capital does not have to be king in all the areas where the single-crop economies of cocoa, peanuts, tea, or coffee have disrupted African agriculture. There are often isolated areas within the interior of countries where the people display their ability to resist and to be creative. Colonial history is peppered with stories of the suppression of peasant revolts. Historians tend to omit the stifled cries of an entire people who have been exploited repeatedly throughout centuries, in spite of the variations in the type of domination and in their resistance to it. Ever since the time African societies were first destructured by foreign trade, they have never stopped struggling to escape from its domination. This resistance is part of the memory of traditional Africa. But how can we draw on this source of popular knowledge and energy that has been neglected for so long, in order to devise and re-create conditions for survival today? This is the question presented to Africa today by the poor who are taking responsibility themselves and working in communities to change their living conditions.

We already have a rich base of reflection to help us rethink the problems of health care, education, famine, and dependence, and their real alternatives. As communities grasp the Word of God, they require the Christian churches to re-examine their practices of faith in dealing with problems that arise in the villages and slums. In the end, this "ministry of the granary" brings us back to a radical demand: that we live our faith in solidarity with the poor and the exploited in our societies.

The growth of inequalities of every sort, the degradation of the African peasantry, repression, dependence, including dependence on foreign interests, imperialism with all its legacies and its ideological apparatus challenge African Christians. Under the influence of our mother-churches, our faith has long been committed to a strategy of aid, based on a reading of Matthew 25:31-46 that emphasizes charity. Today we must move on to a strategy of liberation as we follow the crucified one of Golgotha who confronted everything that did not conform to God's plan. Today, as yesterday, we encounter the living God when and where God hears the cry of the poor and remembers the covenant. If we view the Eucharist itself as a sign of mutual exchange and as a political act, we must turn away from a world that prevents us from sharing. The Eucharist celebrates and anticipates that relationship of communion among human beings willed by God. It calls us to question radically all structures of injustice throughout the world.

A whole life is at stake as soon as we define faith in terms of a ministry that gets its hands dirty. Every manifestation of our faith today takes place in a world of domination and injustice. Can we remain untouched? Or must we live with our people? In what way? How can we feel ourselves genuinely involved in this situation? We can no longer think in terms of a commitment by those who call themselves pure — those people who have experienced a personal conversion and are now like foreigners, trying to convert others so as to lift them out of this sinful world.

Our faith can no longer be described simply and exclusively in terms of the Roman setting. Rome risks marginalizing the problems of the Third World because it is caught up in its preoccupations with what we may aptly call a three-dimensional universe centered on the doctrine of sin, the sacraments, and grace. The churches of the Third World have other concerns, other preoccupations, other objectives: to see their people free themselves from oppression, from slavery, poverty, and hunger.

This is the liberating commitment to our people that we celebrate in our communities. God transforms us while transforming the world, through the provocative power of the gospel. The heart of our faith is to discover in Christ that God who frees and transforms life in solidarity with human beings, and this must happen in a world where God speaks to us and summons us by the facts of injustice and by every situation of misery.

One thing is very clear to me: faith is at work among the poor in every place when we begin with our own cross, and are called to confess Jesus crucified. Remember the words of the leader Bouba: "It is our sufferings that Jesus bears, our sorrow that Jesus carries." These were his words after his entire village was forced to pull up their millet and plant cotton to increase the prosperity of the multinational corporations and the governing minorities.

THE CROSS OF THE THIRD WORLD

If we view the cross of Jesus Christ as the cross of the Third World, the very existence of the Third World shows us what sin is and how it is structured in history. The Third World carries within itself the hidden Christ. It is the historic body of Jesus Christ today.

We must go and rediscover Christ in the slums, in places of misery and domination, among the majority of the poor and the oppressed people. It is the Third World that allows the church to make salvation in Jesus Christ visible. How do we say "I believe in God" in a community where Christians are organizing to resist a society structured in injustice and corruption? And this is the question asked of our faith today in most of the countries of our continent. Our choice is simple: either we choose to work with the agents of change to create a world habitable for all, or we choose not to work with them. If we choose to be agents of liberation, how do we talk about God?

In the modern West until now, it has seemed that any discussion in which God is the subject is socially insignificant. Theology continues to be practiced even though many people accept as an unavoidable cultural axiom that it is impossible to have any meaningful language dealing with God. Thus theology is in crisis in a world where atheism has somehow become a social necessity.[4] For some time, the Christianity of special devotions and confraternities has disincarnated the faith, leading from passivity to resignation in the face of misery and injustice. To speak of God afresh today, in a post-atheistic world, perhaps the church and theology should take up those questions coming from the periphery, from the margins.

What God do the people of the West believe in? What is the Good News for those who live in dominating societies? The answer is simple: "Join the front of resistance formed by all who are rising up against the forms of exploitation and domination!" As Nyerere pointed out, we are entering a time of challenge when the church must grasp the opportunity to identify itself with the poor of God. This is what is happening when we can no longer neglect those sectors of our societies where the question of food is a question of the relation of God to his people (Matt. 25:37).

Christians should consider the failure of decades of development to date, and design a model of life that leaves room in our daily work for whatever may create a different future. Otherwise we are setting aside our century and our historical role, and irrevocably contributing to the coming of death. Death is already appearing here and there in the turns of daily life, as it does wherever cotton drives away millet.

In the painful march of the peoples of the Third World toward the victory of life, perhaps Christians should remember that the God of Life has lifted up the poor and fed the hungry. Today that God calls us to struggle for justice and right. Then we shall be able to sing the Magnificat, not in Latin, but in deeds, wherever faith is lived among the poor. We shall be able to sing the Magnificat in the slums, in the villages, in the streets — wherever we are — because the truth of God is fully engaged both in the countries of hunger and in the dominating societies.

If we wish to put the Christianity of museums behind us and restore to the gospel all its relevance, we must recognize that the question of God is being presented to the churches whenever famine and oppression are incompatible with God's plan for humanity and the world.

How can we not hear the frightening words of an African writer? Cheikh Hamidou Kane writes in *Ambiguous Adventure:*

> For a long time God's worshippers ruled the world. Did they do it in accordance with God's law? I do not know. I have learned that in the country of the Whites, the revolt against poverty and misery is not distinguished from the revolt against God. They say that the movement is spreading, and that soon, in the world that same cry against poverty will drown out the voice of the muezzins. What must have been the misbehavior of those who believe in God if, at the end of

their reign over the world, the name of God should arouse the resentment of the starving?[5]

To believe today is a matter of faithfulness to the God of hope, who went out from himself to place himself at the side of human beings as they struggle to stand up erect in the image of the Risen One. Such a faith requires a fresh re-reading of revelation.

NOTES

1. Anselme Tatianma Sanon, "Dimensions anthropologiques de l'Eucharistie," in *La Documentation Catholique* 78 (19 July 1981): 721-728.

2. René Dumont, *False Start in Africa* (New York: Praeger, 1966). Translated by André Deutsch Ltd. from *L'Afrique noire est mal partie* (Paris: Seuil, 1962).

3. Vincent Cosmao, *Changing the World* (Maryknoll, NY: Orbis, 1984).

4. Claude Geffre, "Non-Metaphysical Theology" in *A New Age in Theology* (New York: Paulist, 1974).

5. Cheikh Hamidou Kane, *Ambiguous Adventure* (London: Heinemann, 1972; NY: Walker & Co., 1963), p. 11.

Questions for Discussion

1. In his travels in the Brazilian jungle, Clodovis Boff experiences what he calls a "culture of backwardness" that afflicts the poor and oppressed. What does he mean by this term? Do you see a "culture of backwardness" in your own society? What do you think Christians should do about it?

2. How does your context and environment shape the way you see the world? In what ways is your viewpoint about life Western? Do you accept Balasuriya's contention that Christianity is too Western? What would a "globalized" version of Christianity look like?

3. Compare and contrast the way the Bible is used by base Christian communities in Brazil with the way it is employed in most North American and European churches. Where do you think the Bible will have the greatest impact on people's lives?

4. Why do you think women have not assumed positions of real leadership in the Christian churches? What do you think would happen if they did? Do you want them to?

5. Jean-Marc Éla asserts that the way some people live their Christian lives pushes others toward atheism. What does he mean? Why do so many people "opt out" of organized religion? What should believing people do about this?

PART II

JESUS CHRIST
IN LIBERATION THEOLOGIES

Introduction

MARIE GIBLIN

UNDERSTANDING OUR IMAGES OF JESUS

Each of us has images of Jesus in our imaginations. These images are like snapshots that we hold in our memories. Some come from traditional sources such as prayers, creeds, the Bible. Others come from more varied sources: parents and grandparents, religion books and teachers, films, artistic representations. What images do you have of Jesus? He may be redeemer, savior, Son of God, compassionate healer, imaginative teacher of parables, a man who loves children. For others the snapshots may include the Good Shepherd or the crucified and risen Lord. Some may remember Jesus' words in the Sermon on the Mount or remember him in terms of John's Gospel as "the way, the truth, and the light." Some may have formed negative images of Jesus as weak, passive, or moralizing. For others Jesus may seem too vague or too ethereal to be of interest.

In this section we will consider interpretations of Jesus from the perspective of liberation theology. The readings that follow will present images of Jesus Christ that have developed out of the experience of Christian communities struggling for justice. These communities exist around the world. The ones represented here are made up of African, Asian, Latin American, and African-American men and women. Their depictions of Jesus may be surprising or a bit shocking. It is important to keep in mind that they are writing from the experience of being impoverished, marginalized, and disregarded by the powerful. They want to know what Jesus has to say to their situations. On the one hand, they are aware that religion has sometimes been used to distract them from their pain by holding out promise of a better life hereafter. On the other hand, they know that Jesus' life, death, and resurrection have long been a source of hope for their communities and so they want to explore what meaning Jesus holds for them today. Their explorations are a search for ever-fresh relationship and communion with Jesus Christ that will inspire Christians to bring new life and hope to their own situations, just as Jesus brought new life and hope to the people of Palestine twenty centuries ago.

The images we have of Jesus foster different faith stances. Some images may lead to an active justice-seeking faith, others may stress loving interpersonal relations, some may stress Jesus as a personal companion or savior. No image of Jesus stands alone. His person is too complex and rich just as no snapshot can capture all the depth and beauty of any person. What kind of images have Christians had of Jesus through history? What images of Jesus are being used by communities who are struggling for economic, political, and social liberation? Are these images faithful to the biblical Jesus? What are the important elements of liberation christology? Do different contexts in Africa, Asia, Latin America, and among African Americans produce different emphases? These are the questions we will take up in this introductory essay.

IMAGES OF JESUS: FROM THE EARLY CHURCH TO COLONIALISM

The New Testament itself is filled with images of Jesus. He is the Lamb of God, the New Moses, the servant who suffers unjustly, the miracle worker, the vine, the one who sits down for meals with outcasts and prostitutes, the one whom some contemporaries characterized as "a glutton and a drunkard, a friend of tax collectors and sinners" (Mt 11:19; Lk 7:34).

The variety of titles that began to be associated with Jesus, during the formation of the New Testament from early apostolic preaching and various oral traditions, show how Christians were searching for ways to express the significance of Jesus Christ. They turned to titles such as Son of God, Messiah (Christ), the Word (*Logos*) of God, and Lord (*Kyrios*). All of these images and titles for Jesus were influenced by the particular contexts of the New Testament writers, whether Palestinian Jewish, Hellenistic Jewish, or Hellenistic non-Jewish communities. Each highlights the most meaningful image of Jesus *for them*. All of the various images and titles are the beginnings of theological reflection that have continued down the centuries even to our own day. This reflection is on-going because all Christians need to answer the question for their own context: "Who do you say that I am?" (Mk 8:29).

In the second century, the focus of reflection shifted from what Jesus *did* to who he *was* in his very being. Biblical images of Jesus Christ as exalted to "God's right hand" evoked questions about his relationship to

God. Was Jesus of Nazareth actually a divine spirit just posing temporarily in a body? Was Jesus an ordinary human being? Was Jesus somehow both human and divine? Such questions were debated against the background of Hellenistic philosophy. Different groups of believers had conflicting answers to the same questions. The most difficult issues were resolved in church councils between the fourth and seventh centuries. The most important of these were the Council of Nicaea in 325 that defined Jesus Christ as consubstantial (of one substance) with the Father and the Council of Chalcedon in 451 that declared Christ as having two natures, one divine and one human, which come together in one person. Christian thinking evolved on the one hand to say that the Savior had to be God in order to save. On the other hand the Savior had to share our humanity if our human nature were to be redeemed.

With Chalcedon, both the denial of Christ's humanity as well as the denial of his divinity were equally rejected. However, many people found it difficult to move away from images of Jesus that represented him as other-worldly. While both Jesus' humanity and divinity were officially affirmed, in practice many subsequent interpretations strongly emphasized the divinity of Christ and gave little credit to his humanity. Jesus' social context and his human relationships received little attention except as examples to demonstrate his divinity. This divine Jesus was depicted as hovering above the conflicts of his time, which, in comparison, appeared relatively unimportant compared with the eternal realm from which he had come and to which he witnessed. In Catholic tradition this tendency remained strong even until Vatican II.

Despite this overall tendency to emphasize Jesus' divinity, images of Jesus in every age have reflected the spirit of that age, its longings and its troubles, the experience and special interests of those who elaborate its theology. In the Middle Ages, Jesus was imaged as a monk by monks, as a bridegroom by mystics, as one who cares for the poor by Francis of Assisi. In a world of scholars and universities of the thirteenth century, Thomas Aquinas attributed to Jesus superhuman knowledge since, as he saw it, divinity must include the perfection of all-knowing. The reformers in the sixteenth century criticized theology for being too speculative. The focus, they thought, should be on what Christ does for us, the fact that he saves us from our sinfulness.

The Jesus Christ brought to Latin America in the sixteenth century by Spanish and Portuguese conquerors had many faces. Two were predominant: the suffering, conquered Christ who encouraged resignation among the indigenous peoples, and the "celestial monarch" — the Christ in majesty and power with whom the conquerors identified their royal patrons and themselves. It was only the exceptional figure like Bartolomé de Las Casas of Mexico who turned the imaging process around and saw in the exploited Indians "Jesus Christ, our God, scourged and afflicted and crucified, not once, but millions of times." It is his recognition of Christ in those who suffer unjustly that liberation theologians bring again to the fore.

JESUS IN WESTERN THEOLOGY FROM THE NINETEENTH CENTURY TO THE 1970s

By the nineteenth century, Western culture was marked by a growing historical consciousness—the realization that societies, institutions, and even thought develop over time. Scholars began to return to original sources to investigate the development of theology and the history of the church. Theology had also been affected by the philosopher Kant's "turn to the subject"—giving greater attention to the human subject and to human experience as a basis of knowing. Christology was affected as Protestant biblical scholars turned their attention to Jesus and attempted to establish the historical facts of his life and ministry. These efforts resulted in what came to be called the "Quest for the Historical Jesus," and led to the writing of "biographies" of Jesus that had wide appeal. They were later criticized as portraying a model of Jesus who mirrored and legitimized nineteenth-century European cultural values. Other theologians criticized this trend, seeking to demonstrate how deeply immersed were Jesus and his early followers in the world of first-century Judaism. This led finally to pessimism about scholars' ability to retrieve the historical Jesus out from under the New Testament's overlay of first-century Christian belief. In the early twentieth century the quest was abandoned.

Since the 1950s, however, both Catholic and Protestants renewed scholarly efforts often referred to as the "New Quest for the Historical Jesus." This time the task was not to arrive at a history or biography of Jesus, but to use historical skills to better understand the context and meaning of Jesus within his own times. This new effort brought new images of Jesus to the fore. They emerged from reflection on Jesus' life, ministry, relationships, teachings, suffering, and death. Advocates of this approach have tried to take seriously Jesus' historical context as described in the New Testament and as it emerges from historical and archeological studies.

The New Testament scholar Joachim Jeremias (1900-1979) was a very important figure in the new quest. Through detailed but beautiful studies of the texts, this German exegete developed the work of earlier scholars on the priority of the theme of the Reign of God within Jesus' preaching. He also highlighted Jesus' insistence that the Reign of God is for sinners, the poor, those considered outcasts, and those who did not "count," especially women and children. But Jeremias did not carry through his insight in terms of the poor and oppressed of the contemporary world, as liberation theologians later would. Instead, Jeremias focused on what appeared to him as the ultimate gift of the Reign of God. For Jeremias, the coming of God's reign meant *forgiveness* and the central image of Jesus was the One who brings forgiveness. This emphasis reflected Jeremias' Lutheran tradition, with its stress on the need for redemption from sin. The effect was to keep the message of the Reign of God as a *spiritual* message that concerns our relationship with God.

From the same post-war German context came the Catholic systematic theologian Karl Rahner (1904-1984) who rose to prominence in the 1960s during and after Vatican Council II. Rahner imaged Jesus not as the perfect man in terms of the Greek ideal of perfection (as the medieval theologians had), but in terms of a man who experienced his own limitations and growth in human knowledge and one who exercised real freedom. For Rahner, humans are best depicted as radically open and longing for the Absolute (even though they may not realize what or who they are longing for). God fills this longing so there is a unity between God and the human person. In Jesus this unity was most profound. In Jesus we learn that in accepting our humanity, with its risks, limitations, anxieties and inevitable death, we open ourselves to the fullness of God's grace. Rahner's gift was to see the depth of everyday life with its choices, its joys, and its worries, as part of the redemptive process. Liberation theology would later build on this insight to see the depth of everyday struggles for human rights and political freedom, as factors that directly affect the way Christians understand salvation.

The German Catholic theologian Johann Baptist Metz (1928-) was a student of Rahner. Metz appreciated Rahner's insights, but in a book called *Theology of the World* he criticized Rahner's theology as "privatized" for giving but a shadowy existence to the sociopolitical reality in which people live. The gospel message was taken as a word addressed to the person, God's self-communication, not as a promise given to humankind, to society. In contrast, Metz saw the cross of Jesus not as a challenge confronted in the intimacy of the personal heart, but outside, in public, the result, in the case of Jesus, of conflict with the religious and political powers of his time.

According to Metz, theology must become eschatology, that is, reflection on those ultimate realities promised for the future, yet which are rooted in the present. Salvation cannot be privatized because it includes the eschatological promises of biblical tradition: liberty, peace, justice, reconciliation. Salvation by Jesus sets us in a critical, liberating relationship to the social world and its historical processes. We are not left waiting for the Reign of God, but rather God's promises move us to be co-workers in forming it now. Metz wanted to bring to the foreground the critical and liberating power that Christianity can have in history and society. He urged Christians to give more attention to what was happening in society, and not just to existential questions, personal issues, and personal salvation. Indeed, he said that a person's existential condition cannot be understood apart from its social context.

Metz was writing in the period just following Vatican II. He shared the same intellectual climate as those theologians from Latin America, Asia, and Africa who had come to Europe to study. But when those theologians went home they met situations unlike anything that Metz encountered in Europe. The need to address the poverty and oppression of their people led them further along the road of a critical theology that required a new methodology. Christians in oppressed situations together with their theologians began to do theology in a new way, reflected in the first section of this volume. Inevitably, these reflections turned to the figure of Jesus, the Liberator.

What Jesus Christ, liberator, will mean, however, depends on the contexts of the various liberation theologies. First, let us explore the elements that liberation christologies share in common; then we will explore the way that varied contexts make a difference.

FIVE IMPORTANT POINTS OF LIBERATION CHRISTOLOGY

1. *God and Jesus are not neutral.* It is a central claim of liberation christology that the God of the Bible is the God of life and liberation. The biblical story is one centered on God's liberation of a people from slavery. The history of salvation gives special attention to justice and to the poor of the community: widows, orphans, the stranger, those in debt. All of the essays that follow will highlight the recurring biblical theme of a God who takes the side of the poor and the oppressed, a God whose purpose for history is the coming of justice and right.

God in the Bible is "father of orphans, defender of widows," the one who "gives the lonely a permanent home, makes prisoners happy by setting them free" (Ps 68). There is a special, reciprocal relationship between God and the poor. When we, in turn, respond to the poor, we are involved in what Jean-Marc Éla, one of our authors, calls a conspiracy. By actively taking God's side, we conspire against the sources of injustice that afflict the poor. Many liberation theologians point to Matthew 25 ("for when I was hungry you gave me food . . .") to ground this relationship in biblical teaching. The Hebrew Bible communicates again and again that being faithful to God includes working to establish justice. This kind of practical faithfulness is true holiness and is the condition for authentic worship. The opposite of knowing and loving God is to act unjustly and oppress others.

Just as God is not neutral, neither is Jesus. Jesus' religious and social milieu was marked by hunger, sickness, and oppression, and Jesus addressed his message to the poor, the sick, and the oppressed. He chose to create his community among them despite the criticism to which he was subjected. He fearlessly confronted those who oppressed and despised the poor, regardless of who they were. By choosing to favor those whom some considered "the dregs of the world," Jesus revealed the scandal of biblical faith — that God takes the side of the poor, the defenseless, the humiliated.

2. *What was of ultimate importance for Jesus was that the Reign of God is at hand.* What was ultimate for Jesus was not himself, not the church, and not God apart from God's relation to human beings and history. Rather,

it was that God is actively establishing a reign of justice for the poor in history.

Jesus, along with the Jewish people, had inherited a whole tradition about kingship which had evolved over Israel's history. In Jesus' time the people were intensely waiting for the coming of the Reign of God, but there were different ideas about how and when this event would come about. Some people, particularly the Pharisees, thought that by living in complete fidelity to the Law of Moses they could hasten the arrival of the final days. Every aspect of the Law assumed tremendous importance for them. Others believed that they should actively struggle against the non-Jewish oppressors, particularly the Roman Empire, in order to hasten the coming of the kingdom. Later, in 66 C.E., a group of this kind called the Zealots would lead a revolt against Roman domination. Jesus rejected both positions, although he seems to have had contact with both groups. What Jesus did was to point to the prophetic tradition found in the Hebrew Bible. That tradition stressed that the coming of the Reign of God means the establishment in history of God's will for justice and right with regard to the poor. In order to prepare themselves for it, people should take up the defense of the poor and act in solidarity with them. While Jesus saw the Reign of God as a divine gift, not yet here in its fullness, he anticipated it and fostered it in his life and his relationships.

3. *Jesus' life was in the service of the Reign of God.* In Luke's Gospel Jesus chose to read in the synagogue at Nazareth this passage from Isaiah:

> The spirit of the Lord has been given to me,
> for he has anointed me.
> He has sent me to bring the good news to the poor,
> to proclaim liberty to captives
> and to the blind new sight,
> to set the downtrodden free,
> to proclaim the Lord's year of favor.

He then added: "This text is being fulfilled today even as you listen" (Lk 4:16-21). This was Jesus' proclamation by word. His proclamation by deed was his identification with and compassion for those who suffered. It was not simply a consoling approach, giving people hope for some distant future. Rather, it was transformative. Jesus took liberating and transforming action through his miracles and his exorcisms. He broke down barriers among people by forming community, sharing at meals with outcasts, encouraging women followers, defending prostitutes, respecting and reaching out to Samaritans, lepers, and the handicapped—all considered at that time to be sinners.

From this perspective we can see that the new image of Jesus within this christology, Jesus Christ the liberator, is an active and engaging one.

4. *The cross was the historical consequence of Jesus' life.* The activity and

teachings of Jesus were threatening to those who held religious and political power in Israel. His message of freedom from oppressive interpretations of the Mosaic Law and his announcement of justice and community for the oppressed were easily recognized as dangerous. They were disruptive of the fragile status-quo of an occupied country with its tenuous balance between oppressors, collaborators, patriots, and unhappy masses. Jesus was a reformer of his own Jewish tradition and a critic of rule by the powerful who treated themselves as gods and the people as objects to be lorded over.

Jesus' death has always been of great importance for Christians. But very often the focus has been on Jesus' suffering and death and on its meaning in terms of forgiveness of sin and righting the injured relationship between humanity and God: Jesus died for our salvation. In looking at his death abstractly, however, we lose the historical context of his death. He did not simply die. Jesus was executed as a political subversive who proclaimed the rule of God on this earth as above the rule of the empire. Because he was faithful to his vision of the Reign of God, especially through his ministry and relationships with the poor, Jesus was crucified. He paid the full price for standing with the oppressed in a situation of conflict. Seen in this way, Jesus' death challenges us to ask where we stand in our own world—what we believe in and those with whom we side in the conflicts going on around us. Likewise, the resurrection becomes the vindication of Jesus' activity and the promise that injustice will not have the final word.

5. *The salvation/liberation that Jesus announces is not simply a gift which we passively receive.* Rather, salvation/liberation is a process in which we become engaged. It has several levels:

a) the level of the limited political-economic-social liberations in which greater justice is achieved;

b) the level of personal transformation and historical actions in which people stop blaming their fate and take responsibility for their own destiny and the construction of a new kind of society;

c) the level of liberation from sin (the root of all injustice) and communion with God.

The coming of the Reign of God in its fullness will be a gift, but our activity here and now of bringing about love and justice proclaims the future fulfillment of God's Reign and impels us further toward communion. So we are challenged to become involved in bringing about social change, even if we know that we will not be able to achieve total justice or perfect community. What we are able to accomplish points to the promises of God that will one day be fulfilled.

A PREVIEW OF OUR TEXTS

The first reading in this section is by Leonardo Boff, a Brazilian Franciscan. In his short essay, "How Can We Know Christ?," Boff describes some of the characteristics of Latin American christology. He points to the change in the order of importance given to various elements in christology, for example the primacy given to living in accord with the gospel (ortho-praxis) over correct thinking about Christ (orthodoxy).

The second reading in this section, "Christology and an African Wom-an's Experience" is by Anne Nasimiyu-Wasike, a Kenyan woman theolo-gian. She considers Jesus' relations with women in the gospel stories and the contemporary relationships that African women experience with Christ in their everyday lives. Nasimiyu-Wasike stresses that christology in African women's experience has to be based on a holistic view of life that will let Christ permeate all of life in every corner of the village and in all relation-ships. In this reading, the importance of social and cultural context as a basis for christology is evident.

The third reading is from Central America and is called "Jesus and the Kingdom of God: Significance and Ultimate Objectives of His Life and Mission." It is written by a Spanish-born Jesuit priest, Jon Sobrino, who has lived for many years in El Salvador. Sobrino lived with six Jesuit priests who, along with their cook and her daughter, were murdered in November 1989 by members of the army of El Salvador. Sobrino himself is still alive since he was away at the time of the attack on the Jesuit residence at the University of Central America in San Salvador. More than 70,000 assassi-nations have taken place in El Salvador over the past ten years. Most of the victims have been workers and peasants associated with political parties, labor unions, student organizations, and Christian communities. In El Sal-vador, being involved with any progressive social or religious group means risking one's life. To even question the way things are can result in torture and death. It is for writing and teaching ideas like those in our selection, "Jesus and the Kingdom of God," that the Jesuits were attacked and killed. Sobrino's writing emerges from this violent context. He sees Jesus as living out "the kingdom at hand" and he challenges us to seek out how we can serve the coming of the Reign of God concretely in solidarity with the majority of the world's peoples who are poor and oppressed.

The fourth article, "Who Is Jesus for Asian Women?," is by Chung Hyun Kyung, a Korean woman theologian. Chung consciously writes her article as representing the collective work of Asian Christian women. The context for Chung is Asia, the continent in which Christians are a tiny minority.

Her context is also that of Asian women's struggle against patriarchal cultures in which they are considered inferior to men and their subservience is sanctioned by social traditions. Chung presents some traditional images of Jesus and explains how they have been transformed by Asian women's praxis and reflection. She also deals with emerging christological images: Jesus as mother, as shaman, and as a priest of *han*. *Han* is a Korean word which describes the feelings of indignation, oppression, grief, and suffering which have resulted from centuries of occupation and division. There are many images of Jesus briefly outlined in this essay. They come from Asian culture, from native Korean religions, and from women's struggles for full humanity. They show a transformation of christology that leads to creativity and diversity. As with much feminist theology, both Chung's and Anne Nasimiyu-Wasike's work reveal how women's theology often communicates women's experience concretely and personally. Both these women's essays should be read not only as representing an African and Asian context, but women's context. Feminist re-imaging of Jesus has only just begun and is a task for all Christian women who are struggling for their own identity in a male-dominated church.

The fifth and last essay in this section is by one of the originators of Black Theology in the United States, James Cone. It is entitled "Jesus Christ in Black Theology" and was first published in 1970. The essay was written at a moment in history when the Black Power movement was having its greatest impact on African-American religious thought. Cone later described how young black ministers like himself were torn during that time. Like Black Muslim leader Malcolm X, they could not deny the depth of white racism and their anger at its perpetrators. On the other hand, they had a profound loyalty to the Christian, nonviolent message of Martin Luther King, Jr. Black Theology is the effort to confront the evils of racism and consider the struggle for black liberation in light of the Christian message.

In his essay in this volume, Cone wants to present an image of Jesus that is faithful to the Bible and to relate that image to the struggle of African Americans. Cone proposes the image of a black Christ as the most appropriate one today. If Jesus identified with the oppressed in his own time, would he not be black in America today? The question is not whether Jesus was actually black, although in today's terms he was certainly a person of color, a Near Eastern Semite. But what is more important is the recognition that Jesus aligned himself with and was present to the oppressed of his time. If he lived in North America, Europe, or Australia today, he would identify himself with and live among people of color. The struggle of black people and other people of color to gain their rightful place in society is Jesus' contemporary struggle.

Cone admits today that the tone of his writing twenty years ago may have blocked dialogue. His early writings were often impassioned and angry. Nevertheless, his essay belongs in our collection since it brings the challenge of liberation christology closer to home for those of us who live in the northern hemisphere by focusing on the painful issue of our own racism.

Jesus' identification with the oppressed and the despised, and his commitment to bring about change by acting out the values of the Reign of God, is the primary insight of liberation christology. If this is so, are we able to see the presence of Jesus and his challenge to us from ghettos, housing projects, and other impoverished areas in our own country? Can we see Jesus present among migrant workers, guest workers, new immigrants who speak different languages and come from different cultures?

A final word should be said about whether liberation theologians are romanticizing the poor and oppressed. These theologians do not claim that the poor are morally better, but that God and Jesus take their side because they are suffering unjustly. It is the unnecessary suffering and the injustice involved that give them special importance in the eyes of God and the Christian community. This tells us something very important about the love and compassion of God and of the savior Christians call Jesus of Nazareth.

6

How Can We Know Christ?

LEONARDO BOFF

TOWARD A CHRISTOLOGY IN LATIN AMERICA

We cannot simply speak *about* Jesus as we would speak about other objects. We can only speak *with him as starting point,* as people touched by the significance of his reality. We come to him with that which we are and have, inserted into an unavoidable socio-historical context. We see with our eyes the figure of Christ and reread the sacred texts that speak of him and had him as starting point. Consequently, a christology thought out and vitally tested in Latin America must have characteristics of its own. . . . Our sky possesses different stars that form different figures of the zodiac by which we orient ourselves in the adventures of faith and of life. Here are a few characteristics of such a christology.

The Primacy of the Anthropological Element over the Ecclesiastical

The special focus in Latin America is not so much the church but the human person that it should help, raise up, and humanize. In Latin American theological thought, there reigns an accentuated ecclesiological skepticism: Here the church reproduced models and structures imported from Europe. Very little creativity was allowed the faith that, lived and tested in our milieu, could have expressed itself naturally and with greater liberty within structures having peculiarly Latin American characteristics. The general horizon was one that dogmatically interpreted canon law and juridically interpreted dogma. This basically impeded healthy attempts to create a

From *Jesus Christ Liberator* (Maryknoll, N.Y.: Orbis Books, 1978), pp. 43-48. Translated by Patrick Hughes.

new incarnation of the church outside of the inherited traditional framework of a Greco-Roman understanding of the world.

The future of the Catholic church, given the diminution of the European population, is undeniably in Latin America. It is in the more anthropological vision, in the new human being being elaborated here, that we can gather elements to nourish a new, renewed Christian reflection. What are the great expectations among the people to which the faith can address itself, announcing the joyful news? We must be aware of the connection between question and answer if we want to offer a reflection that will heal reality where it hurts.

The Primacy of the Utopian Element over the Factual

The determining element in the Latin American person is not the past (our past is a European past, one of colonization) but the future. Herein lies the activating function of the utopian element. Utopia ought not to be understood as a synonym for illusion and flight from present reality. As recent studies in philosophy and theology have revealed, utopia is born in the springs of hope. It is responsible for models that seek a perfecting of our reality, models that do not allow the social process to stagnate nor society ideologically to absolutize itself, models that maintain society permanently open to ever increasing transformation. Faith promises and demonstrates as realized in Christ a utopia that consists in a world totally reconciled, a world that is the fulfillment of what we are creating here on earth with feeling and love. Our work in the construction of a more fraternal and humanized world is theologically relevant: It builds and slowly anticipates the definitive world promised and demonstrated as possible by Jesus Christ.

The Primacy of the Critical Element over the Dogmatic

The general tendency of people, and in particular of institutions is to stagnate in an existential arrangement that was successful during a specific period. Then there emerge the mechanisms of self-defense and the dogmatic mentality that fears and represses every kind of criticism that looks to the proper functioning of all institutions and to that continuous opening to the future that a society ought always protect at the risk of losing the rhythm of history. This explains the primacy of the critical element in Latin American theological reflection. Many ecclesiastical traditions and ecclesial institutions were functional at one time but today have become obsolete. They are centers of a conservatism that locks the door to a dialogue between faith and the world, the church and society. Criticism refines and purifies the core of the Christian experience so that it can be made incarnate within the historical experience we are living.

The Primacy of the Social over the Personal

Latin American society is most afflicted by the problem of the marginalization of immense portions of the population. The question cannot be posed merely within the dimensions of a personal conversion. There are structural evils that transcend individual ones. The church is, whether it likes it or not, involved in a context that transcends it. What will be its function? Shall it be oil or sand within the social mechanism? On the other hand, it ought not to create its own little world within the great world. It ought to participate, *critically,* in the global upsurge of liberation that Latin American society is undergoing. Like Jesus, it ought to give special attention to the nobodies and those without a voice. It ought to accentuate particularly the secular and liberating dimensions contained in the message of Christ. It should emphasize the future that he promises for this world, a world in which the future kingdom is growing between the wheat and the cockle, not for a few privileged people, but for all.

The Primacy of Orthopraxis over Orthodoxy

The weakness in the classical christology of the manuals resides precisely in that wherein it considers itself to be strong: its theological-philosophical systematization. It did not lead to an ethic and a comportment that was typically Christian. The fundamental theme of the Synoptic Gospels, on following Christ, has been poorly thematized and translated into concrete attitudes. Orthodoxy, that is, correct thinking about Christ, occupied primacy over orthopraxis, correct acting in the light of Christ.

It was also for this reason that, although the church preached Christ the liberator, it generally was not the church that liberated or supported liberation movements. Not rarely the church has left active, participating Christians as complete orphans. This has resulted in recent years in the continuous exodus from the church of the best minds and most active forces. We know nevertheless that for Christ and for the primitive church the essential did not consist in the reduction of the message of Christ to systematic categories of intellectual comprehension but in creating new habits of acting and living in the world. This praxiological moment of the message of Christ is especially perceptible in Latin American theological reflection.

CONCLUSION: BEGINNING WITH JESUS CHRIST, TO SPEAK IN SILENCE

In our christological study we will try to reflect with Jesus Christ as the starting point and within the wide horizon opened up in the above pages. We can no longer be scientifically ingenuous and acritical. Whether we wish it or not, we are inheritors of the christological discussions of the last decades, though the questions will be framed within our Latin American horizons. What we say here with words about Christ and his message is nothing compared with that which faith discerns and gratefully embraces.

"Concerning things that we cannot speak of," commanded Wittgenstein, "we ought to be silent." Nevertheless, we ought to speak of Jesus Christ, not with a view to defining him but rather ourselves, not the mystery but our position when confronted with the mystery. Every scholar of Jesus Christ has the experience witnessed by the ardent mystic St. John of the Cross: "There is much concerning Christ that can be made more profound, since he is such an abundant mine with many caverns full of rich veins, and no matter how much we tunnel we never arrive at the end, nor does it ever run out; on the contrary, we go on finding in each cavern new veins and new riches, here and there, as St. Paul witnessed when he said of the same Christ: 'In Christ all the jewels of wisdom and knowledge are hidden'" (Col. 2:3).

7

Christology and an African Woman's Experience

ANNE NASIMIYU-WASIKE

INTRODUCTION

Christology, according to the *Oxford Dictionary of the Christian Church*, is the external expression of God and also the manifestation of God in time. Jesus Christ appeared on earth in history and summed up humanity in himself. Christ is the focus of Christian faith; thus christology is the most understandable symbol of redemption in Christian theology. As Rosemary Radford Ruether says, "Christology is a place where we envision the redemption from all sin and evil. It is a symbol which encompasses our vision of our authentic humanity and the fulfilled hopes of all human persons."[1]

From the beginning of Christianity, critical reflection on christology has occupied many Christian theologians. Unfortunately, most written theology until about twenty-five years ago was written by men and from a male perspective. The female perspective was left unarticulated. The theology on the person of Jesus tended to be much more philosophical and abstract than that of the existential Jesus of the Gospels who calls people as individuals and as a community to authentic human existence. Although Christian women of every century have reflected on the person of Jesus and on their relationship to him, much of their christology remains unwritten. Only a few African women have ventured into writing down their reflection on Christ-Event and their experience of Christ. Therefore, in order for a thorough investigation on christology and the African woman's experience to be carried out, some oral interviews have to be part of the study.

From *Faces of Jesus in Africa*, edited by Robert J. Schreiter (Maryknoll, N.Y.: Orbis Books, 1991), pp. 70-81.

AFRICAN WOMEN'S EXPERIENCE

The ways in which the life experience of women in Africa differ are numerous. On a national level, for example, there are cultural, physical, environmental, political, and economic variations between and within nations.[2] The diversity is even much more pronounced on a personal level, where the lifestyles vary according to poor or rich, single or married, with no children or with ten children, with husband present or absent, participating in domestic or commercial career, traditional or modern, rural or urban, at peace or at war, of social chaos or order, with a family system that is patriarchal or matriarchal, with opportunities for education and self-direction or not. These are some of the differences (and they may seem mind-boggling), but African women together with their African brothers suffer hunger and thirst continuously. Their main struggles are against the forces which rob them of control over their destiny and which do not enable them to fulfil their God-given potential.

African women in communion with their sisters in third-world countries are struggling for the bare necessities. Their lives are full of severe hardships. They work hard carrying heavy burdens such as firewood; fetching water from faraway rivers and wells; planting, weeding, and harvesting crops; caring for children; grinding corn and preparing food. The women in rural sectors, especially those who take on the status of rural educated, tend to work for long hours. Besides fulfilling the duties expected of them as women, they also do eight hours of work in their professional fields (nursing or teaching). They work an average of sixteen hours a day.[3] The main concerns of these women are physical needs: food, water, clothing, shelter, medicine for themselves and their children and education for their children.

There are also some cultural hardships that African women experience. In African ethnic groups, there are taboos which restrict women. For example, a woman should not talk when men are having a conversation. Women are not taken seriously, and at times their intelligence is belittled by men. They are customarily looked upon solely as childbearers and servers and often cruelly oppressed when they have failed in childbearing or when their child dies.[4] Despite their nurturing, maintaining, and serving life for the survival of human communities, women are always marginalized and given an inferior status.

In their oppression, African women have learned tolerance; they fatalistically accept the given conditions. They try to integrate all their experiences so that they appreciate the wholeness of life. The rural pastoralist or agriculturalist woman stands at the center of the life of the clan. She is the matrix that holds the whole society together. She gives birth to life, maintains it, and continues to nurture it. Her understanding of the universe and her empirical participation in this universe are imbued with religion.

This makes life a profoundly religious phenomenon.⁵ This religious background is what shapes the African woman's experience of Christ.

The supernatural is a presence which is felt in every village, and it claims every new life. The African woman believes that there is an indissoluble union between the supernatural and her everyday life, and she seeks to harmonize these elements in her life. For an African woman, Jesus is the person who enables her to combine her authentic inner experience of the divine with her effort to harmonize her life with this divine.

Six women were interviewed about women's experiences in relation to Jesus. Two were from a rural setting, two were religious women, and two were university lecturers. This sampling is very limited and obviously not an exhaustive inquiry. The question put before them was: Who is Jesus Christ in your life? Their answers were:

"Jesus is my strength. He is the one who enables and empowers me to carry on my every day work. He helps me to be able to cope with the hardships I face daily" (P. Nalyanya, 1989).

"Jesus is my savior. I live in an area where there are so many witches and evil forces that people have had to sell their property and gone in search of safer places. I believe that Jesus is a victorious Lord who conquered all evil spiritual forces and brought them under control. I am confident that Jesus protects me and watches over me so that no evil may come near me and my family. I continue to live here because Jesus' power is over us" (S. Nafula, 1988).

"Jesus Christ is my hope, and He gives me courage to be. He makes everything meaningful when in my everyday living, I try to make my existence original and creative. In my everyday activities I try to enter into communion with all people who are my fellow pilgrims in search of God, God who is the horizon of final meaning and who gives us our true identity. In God we meet Jesus who reveals to us our true identity and empowers us to participate in the on-going process of creation" (A. J. Namwolo, 1989).

"Jesus Christ is my savior, my model, my helper, my teacher, my everything and my God. His teachings guide my life, and usually I feel very guilty when I fail to follow His example" (A. Kubai, 1989).

"Jesus is my closest friend, who gives me light when everything about me is dark. From the Scriptures I know that He understands me as I am when I am faced with misunderstandings and misjudgments. Jesus accepts all women and men as equals; in Him there is no discrimination. He uplifts me as He does the whole of humanity. He is my everything" (E. Egesa, 1989).

"Jesus is the core of my life; He is my helper, my comforter, my refuge and my closest friend. He is kind and generous and shares in my sorrows when I am in trouble. He teaches me to be tolerant and understanding towards the weakness of others" (L. Wanja, 1989).

In these African women's statements of their acts of faith in Jesus, several factors emerge: first of all, their Christian concepts of Jesus which they have learned from their catechism; second, their holistic view of life, where Jesus affects their whole life; third, their belief in the reality of witches and evil powers from which Jesus has to save them; and finally, their courage to be, to suffer, and to endure hardships with the hope that soon all this will be over and everything will be restored to wholeness in Jesus Christ.

JESUS AND WOMEN IN THE GOSPELS

In order to relate current African women's experience to Jesus Christ, one has to briefly look at the Gospels. In the Gospels Jesus' attitude towards women is very clearly documented. Jesus bears the message of liberation for all, especially for the disadvantaged. In the Jewish society women were given inferior status,[6] but Jesus esteemed them and gave them equal status to men. The original relationship between women and men first established by God at creation was restored in Jesus Christ.

A few examples from Jesus' life will suffice in illustrating his attitude towards women and what he teaches with regard to them. Nowhere in Christ's life do we find him distinguishing between women and men as children of God. There is a startling contrast between Jesus' approach to women and the Jewish and Roman approaches to them during his time. As Sister Magnus McGrath observes: "By the regard he shows to women, by the treatment he gives them in word and act, by the purity and universality of his love and ministry, Jesus Christ erased all lines of superiority and inferiority between men and women and placed all on the same level."[7]

Jesus' attitude toward women is clearly reflected in miracle stories, parables, and discourses. All four Gospels portray Jesus in several incidents as showing concern for women, not just for their well-being but for their being as persons. He gave them their true worth and dignity. Jesus' approach to women was revolutionary. He treated women and men as equals; this was new, given the contemporary cultural view of his time.[8] There is a balanced way in which Jesus used women and men to illustrate his teachings. This approach was new, since the rabbinic parables carefully avoided women.[9] For example, in Matthew 13:31 and 13:33, Jesus compares the Kingdom of God first to a mustard seed which a man took and hid in his field and second, to the yeast a woman took and mixed in with three measures of flour. Woman's daily life experiences and man's daily life experiences are very important to Jesus. Both of them can be used to illustrate the meaning of the Kingdom of God which Jesus came to inaugurate. In

Luke 15:4 and 15:8 Jesus describes the love of God for the repentant sinner. First he compares this to a man with a hundred sheep who on losing one would leave the ninety-nine in the wilderness and go after the missing one till he finds it. Second, he compares it to a woman with ten drachmas, who, on losing one would light a lamp and sweep out the house and search thoroughly till she finds it. In Matthew 25:1 and 25:14 Jesus cautions his listeners on the necessity of being vigilant at all times. He compares the fulfillment of the kingdom of heaven to ten bridesmaids who took lamps and went to meet the bridegroom; then, to a man on his way abroad who summoned his servants and entrusted his property to them.

In the Gospels we find Jesus using stories of everyday life experiences of both women and men (ploughing, breadmaking, shepherding, grinding, and house-sweeping). The above examples illustrate God's joy over the salvation of a lost sinner, the need to persevere in prayer, and the necessity to be vigilant. In all these stories Jesus uses two examples in each case. He draws one instance from the women's experience and the other from the men's experience. Thus Jesus portrays that there is equality in the spiritual potential of women and men. Women and men are called to the same spiritual life, and there are no virtues demanded exclusively of women or of men.

In his teachings and relationships, Jesus recognized women as persons in their own right and disapproved of anything that discriminated against women. For example, Jesus explicitly rejected the Jewish law on adultery which penalized women but not men. In Matthew 5:28, Jesus says: "But I say to you that everyone who looks at a woman lustfully has already committed adultery with her in his heart." Again in Mark 10:11, Jesus declares, "The man who divorces his wife and marries another is guilty of adultery (against her)."

In the Jewish worldview, a woman was considered a constant danger to the man. Therefore, women were kept away from the public eye in order to protect men from this danger. It was believed, that if women and men came into social contact, lust was unavoidable.[10] Jesus dismissed this idea and called for recognition of women as persons in their own right and not as objects of men's sexual desire. It is important to recognize the rights and life of women and to accept them as people who can relate to men in other ways than sexually.[11] To affirm this reality, Jesus included women in the group of his disciples.

Adultery in the Jewish law was always a sin against the husband's property rights. But Jesus teaches that adultery could be committed by a man against his wife. This was indeed a new proclamation. It ushered in a recognition of man and woman as equal partners in the marital relationship. The wife is not an object to be dismissed at will but a partner whose rights must be respected. Both husband and wife are responsible in building and maintaining the relationship in marriage. Adultery can be committed against a husband as well as against a wife.[12]

Jesus viewed women as responsible persons who, like men, were sinners standing in need of God's mercy and forgiveness. When the woman caught as an adulterer was brought to Jesus, he challenged the hypocrisy of all those who brought her to him. He recognized the woman as a sinner in need of forgiveness and told her not to sin any more. Jesus charged the woman to be responsible for her life.

The account of the story of Jesus' conversation with the woman of Samaria portrays him as having crossed cultural boundaries. Jesus held conversation with a person who represents two suspect groups of people: first, Samaritans who were enemies of the Jewish people, and second, women who were of inferior status and dangerous to men's chastity according to the Jews. Jesus took the Samaritan woman seriously. He asked her questions and responded to her replies in order to help her understand the theological significance of their conversation.[13]

Jesus brings out two things in the woman of Samaria. First of all, she is a sinner in need of forgiveness and healing. Second, the woman is made to understand that she is responsible for her sins. Jesus recognizes this woman as an individual capable of spiritual discernment and with specific problems to be dealt with.[14] Jesus reveals profound theological truths to her. These truths concern the doctrine of grace, the standards of fitting service to God (John 4:24), and his own mission as Christ the Messiah.[15]

These few examples show how Jesus deeply respected women and inaugurated a startling new equality between women and men. He taught it to the apostles so that they could continue teaching this revolutionary doctrine after he was dead.[16]

If this is the new doctrine that Jesus left for his disciples, why is it that African women feel as if they are second-class disciples in the church? Why do they feel marginalized and not taken seriously? In order to answer these questions one has to briefly examine the tradition of the church which has formulated many declarations in the defence of its faith and which was brought to Africa by the western European missionaries. Early Christianity used the symbol *Logos* or *Word* to define that presence of God which was incarnate in Jesus Christ. The term *Logos* was adapted from the Hellenistic and Jewish traditions. Logos has a creational concept. It means the transcendent God coming forth into the immanence to found and create the world. Thus the Logos is the presence of God, the immanence of God, and the ground of creation. Early Christianity linked the Logos to Christ the Messiah in order to bridge the gap between creation and redemption and counteract the early gnostic beliefs.

The Word of God as revealed in Jesus Christ is the same God who created the world in the beginning. In Jesus Christ, we have the authentic ground of creation manifested in fulfilled form over against the alienation of creation from its true being.[17]

The term *Logos* was also linked to the rational principle of the human soul. Since rationality in Hellenistic and Jewish traditions was presumed to be nominatively male, all the theological references for defining Christ were defined in male-centered or androcentric ways. This reinforced the assumption that God was male; the male metaphors were seen as appropriate for God, and the female metaphors were inappropriate. The term *Logos* was all-inclusive for the divine identity for Christ and pointed the whole of humanity to the true foundation of its being, but the term was shadowed by the patriarchal cultural realities of the time. Therefore, Christ had to be male in order to reveal a male God, and this was taken literally. The male qualities were overemphasized in relation to God. Man was seen as the image of God whereas woman was seen only as an image of man, and it was through man that she was saved. These theological concepts about God and the Christ in relation to woman are the ones which shaped most of the great theologians' thinking throughout Christian history. For example, Thomas Aquinas, in all his sincerity, had this to say: "Woman is an occasional and incomplete being. . . . a misbegotten male. It is unchallengeable that woman is destined to live under man's influence and has no authority from her Lord."[18] Aquinas based his teachings on Aristotle's philosophy regarding woman's physical nature. Aristotle asserted that the female is a male which, for some accidental reason, did not attain its full development.[19] One wonders if this belief is not still being held in the church today. For example, when Pope John Paul II emphasized the ban on women's ordination, he called on the American bishops to support the dignity of women and "every legitimate freedom that is consonant with *their* human nature."[20] The fact that the Pope places *their* before human nature causes one to assume that women's human nature is somehow different from men's human nature.

The African church has inherited the misinterpretation of woman and her relation to God and Jesus from the European church. Therefore, the African woman, in addition to being under her cultural bondage and oppression, also experiences the socio-economic oppression of neo-colonialists in the church. According to missionaries, African women were not to be trusted. It was assumed that people from "hot countries are incapable of continence."[21] In Uganda no woman was allowed near the priest's house after 4:00 P.M.

As we saw at the beginning of this study, most African women spend sixteen to eighteen hours daily working to provide their families with food, shelter, water, clothing, medicine, and education. They have very little time to seriously reflect on their relationship with other people and with God. Nevertheless, these women believe that their lives are lived in union with God; their theology is not one which is written and articulated but one which is lived and practiced in everyday activities and experiences. A few African women are awakening to their dignity as human persons. This awakening brings them to the harsh reality that for centuries they have been excluded from the full dignity of human persons by their culture and by the patriarchal church. Their eyes are being opened to their societies' discrimination against women under the pretext of respect for traditions and culture, and their eyes are being opened to the patriarchal structure in the church which hinders the application of equal personhood and equal discipleship to women and men.

CHRISTOLOGY: A WOMAN'S REFLECTION

The African woman's experience calls for a christology that is based on a holistic view of life. She needs the Christ who affects the whole of her life, whose presence is felt in every corner of the village and who participates in everything and everybody's daily life. She needs the Christ who relates to God, the God who can be reached through the spirits and the living dead or through direct intercession. This God, the Christ, is the one who takes on the conditions of the African woman—the conditions of weakness, misery, injustice, and oppression.

In his own lifetime, Jesus rejected the androcentric culture of the Jewish people. His mission was countercultural. He gave special attention to the downtrodden and the marginalized of the society—the prostitutes, beggars, sinners, tax collectors, and ritually unclean. And most of these people were women.

Jesus Christ came to heal a broken humanity. He empowered and enabled the downtrodden of society to realize their dignity and worth as persons. He continues to empower and enable the African woman today so that she passes from unauthentic to authentic human existence, and so that she discovers her true identity of being made in the image and likeness of God.

There are several christological models that emerge, namely the eschatological, anthropological, liberational, and cosmological.[22] In the eschatological model, Christ is sent by God to an alienated world where the presence of God takes the shape of the Crucified One. Why does the One who is perfect and righteous have to suffer and die? This suffering and death was followed by the resurrection promises, which revealed God's ultimate victory over this world's alienating forces and which opened a future for a new humanity. In his suffering Christ took on the conditions of the African woman and conditions of the whole of humanity, and in his resurrection the African woman is called to participate in the restoration of harmony, equality, and inclusiveness in all human relationships in the family, society, and church.

The second christology model is the anthropological one. God calls us in Christ to a lifestyle that is dedicated to the love of neighbor and to a life which puts others first and gives them life. Jesus takes on the qualities of mother. He is a nurturer of life, especially that of the weak. The African woman's primary experience in relation to others is that of mother. This experience or reality is overemphasized to the extent that the African woman's social status depends entirely on it. Although giving birth and nurturing life is very important, women are not merely childbearers. They have other qualities which have for centuries been left untapped and which could help to establish mutual and inclusive human relationships in Africa and the world.

Jesus recognized women as responsible persons in their own right and took them seriously (Luke 11:27-28). Women were among Christ's followers and disciples (Luke 8:1-2). Jesus held theological discourses with women. He encouraged, taught, and held dialogues with them. This was the most revolutionary aspect of Jesus' approach to women, given the cultural context in which he lived.[23] Jesus today recognizes the African woman not just as a nurturer of life but as one who participates fully in the life of the church — as theological teacher, catechist, biblical interpreter, counsellor, and as one called to restore the church and humanity to the initial inclusive, holistic, and mutual relationships between women and men.

The third christological model for the African woman that arises in women's reflection is that of Christ the liberator. Jesus asks the African woman not to accept her hardships and pain fatalistically but to work at eliminating the sufferings and creating a better place for all. In her undertaking against the oppressive structures her struggles become God's struggles. It is then Christ who suffers in her and works in her to give birth to new and better human relationships. For the educated and privileged African woman whose load is lighter, she should identify herself with her disadvantaged sisters. These include petty traders who walk the city streets to find customers for their fruits and vegetables and are often harassed by the police; girls who are forced to drop out of school because their parents cannot afford to pay school fees; women who are forced to enter into polygamous unions because of economic reasons and cultural beliefs; and traditional rural women who are faced with all types of hardships and oppression. These women are always poor and hungry because they have to produce enough food to feed their families and sell the surplus in order to educate their children. In most cases, production remains the same while the number of children increases. In fact, agriculture is the pillar of the Kenyan economy and all national development efforts depend on it. Yet these rural women are hardly recognized. Their subsistence farming is not counted as a great contribution to the development of the nation; yet without it life in Kenya would stop.

Both women and men in rural life are still immersed in traditional beliefs and have fatalistic attitudes towards development. For example, among the Maasai the principles of quality and economic productivity are not the measures used to evaluate the people's wealth; rather, the number of wives and children and the number of cattle a man has constitute his wealth. In both traditional and modern rural life, women and their work are not given recognition despite their fundamental contribution towards national development. The petty traders, housegirls, and women in polygamous unions are a few of the categories of African women who are at the very top of the hierarchical scale of oppression. They are the paradigm of all the oppressed peoples of the world.

Jesus Christ is calling all women and men of good will to work for the liberation of all people. The identification with the poor, the oppressed, and the downtrodden can seem impracticable without the hope and assurance of Jesus Christ's cross and resurrection to affirm that it is God's own undertaking; we are called to fully participate in it.

The fourth christological model is that of Christ the cosmological restorer. In his letter to the Romans, Paul asserts, "We know that the whole creation has been groaning in travail together until now; and not only the creation but we ourselves, who have the first fruits of the spirit, groan inwardly as we wait for the adoption as (children), the redemption of our bodies" (Rom. 8:20-23). Paul affirms that there is no existential reality in this universe outside the influence of the redemption. Christ is the cosmological liberator who reconciles all things to God. The world is liberated because it participates in humankind's sin and redemption and because humanity dominates the world, humanity has united the world with its destiny.

The existential Jesus of the Gospels was sensitive to the harmony and beauty in nature. In Matthew 6:28-29, Jesus calls his disciples' attention to the harmony, form, and beauty found in the lilies which no human splendor could equal, even that of King Solomon. He was aware of the sufferings the people endured at the hostility of nature. He is also aware of and understands the suffering of Africans today. Drought, floods, and famine are harsh realities which have claimed millions of African people. Jesus, who in his time rebuked the winds and ordered harmony and tranquillity to be restored, could today restore peace and harmony to the African continent and to the world.

In Palestine Jesus came face to face with people suffering from various kinds of diseases of natural and spiritual disorders — epilepsy, paralysis, leprosy, hemorrhage, blindness, and demonic possession. Jesus restored those people to wholeness. As Peter says: "[Jesus] went about doing good and healing all who were oppressed by the devil for God was with Him" (Acts 10:38).

This brings us to another christological model which is much closer to the African reality and which speaks to many. That is the model of Christ the healer. Jesus attached great significance to exorcism and healing. In the Gospels, whenever Jesus healed individuals, it was both physical and spiritual, and it was the individual's initial faith which led to the healing. For example, in Jesus' cure of the paralytic, he says: "My son, your sins are forgiven. ... stand up, take your bed and go home" (Mark 2:5-11). And again in Matthew 9:27-29 Jesus restored the vision of the two blind men after they affirmed that they believed in the power possessed by Jesus. Jesus "touched their eyes, saying, 'According to your faith be it done to you.' "

Jesus inaugurated the restoration of individuals and societies to whole-ness and he invited the disciples to participate in this re-establishment. As Christians and as women who have seen the liberating power of Christ we have two functions to fulfill: first of all to witness to God's love and care for the universe; and second to give testimony to the continued human responsibility of creating a new world.

Jesus, just as African women today, believed in the existence of devils as beings endowed with intelligence and will.[24] Although the natural calam-ities and challenges of illnesses are understood differently today due to scientific advancement, African people still believe in evil spirits and demons as causes for many illnesses. African people are spiritually hungry and will always follow anybody who claims that he or she has the power to restore one to wholeness. We cannot rule out the possibility that today God is using individuals to heal the souls and bodies of those who are ill. One example is Mary Akatsa of Kenya who casts out demons and restores people to good health. This is an exceptional power, but it is a manifestation that humanity is participating in the fulfillment of the world.

CONCLUSION

This reflection is an attempt to give African women's experiences of Christ. Christ meets them in their own cultural, physical, environmental, political, and economic variations. For African women Jesus Christ is the victorious conqueror of all evil spiritual forces; He is the nurturer of life, and a totality of their being. Christ is the liberator of the sufferers, the restorer of all those who are broken, the giver of hope and the courage to be. Despite the threatening hardships encountered in women's daily lives, he is the one who calls all people forth to mutually participate in the creation of a better world for all.

NOTES

1. Rosemary Radford Ruether, "Christology and Feminism," lecture notes, Hiram College, Ohio, 1987.

2. Mary Burke, *Reaching for Justice: The Women's Movement* (Washington D.C.: Center of Concern, 1980), p. 95.

3. Beverly Lindsay, *Comparative Perspectives of Third World Women* (New York: Praeger Special Studies, 1980), p. 78.

4. Burke, p. 95.

5. John S. Mbiti, *African Religions and Philosophy* (New York: Praeger, 1970), p. 262.

6. Therese Souga, "The Christ-Event from the Viewpoint of African Women," in Virginia Fabella and Mercy Amba Oduyoye (eds.), *With Passion and Compassion: Third World Women Doing Theology* (Maryknoll, N.Y.: Orbis Books, 1988), p. 22.

7. Sister Albertus Magnus McGrath, *What a Modern Catholic Believes about Women* (Chicago: Thomas More Press, 1972), p. 17.

8. Mary Evans, *Woman in the Bible* (Exeter: The Paternoster Press, 1983), p. 45.

9. Ibid., p. 48.

10. Ibid., p. 45.

11. Ibid., p. 46.

12. Ibid., p. 47.

13. Evans, p. 52; McGrath, p. 21.

14. Evans, p. 52.

15. McGrath, p. 21.

16. Ibid., p. 20.

17. Ruether, ibid.

18. Thomas Aquinas, *Summa Theologica* I, q. 92, a.1; q. 99, a.2; q. 115, a.3 and 4.

19. Compare Sister Emma Therese Healy, *Woman According to Saint Bonaventure* (New York: Georgian Press, 1956), p. 10.

20. *Origins* 13: 14, 238.

21. Souga, p. 26.

22. Reginald Fuller and Pheme Perkins, 1983, pp. 137-57; Mercy Amba Oduyoye, *Hearing and Knowing* (Maryknoll, N.Y.: Orbis Books, 1986), p. 106.

23. Evans, p. 50.

24. Sebastian Kappen, *Jesus and Freedom* (Maryknoll, N.Y.: Orbis Books, 1977), p. 75.

8

Jesus and the Kingdom of God

JON SOBRINO

WHAT IS THE ULTIMATE FOR JESUS? A THEOLOGICAL PROBLEM

I open with this question of the "ultimate" for Jesus because the history of Christianity has given different answers to it and the diversity can cloud the simplicity of Jesus' answer. The *"ultimate"* can have the name of God, Christ, heaven, the church, grace, love, and so on; or, negatively, sin, hatred, condemnation, and so on. So complex a panorama can cloud the identification of what was really and truly ultimate for Jesus—that from which other ultimacies derive a Christian hierarchy.

As we seek what was really ultimate for Jesus, let us pose the problem theologically, and seek a reality that will be genuinely ultimate, that will impose itself as such, and that will preclude the temptation to replace it with something only seemingly ultimate. Since this search seeks to be critical and to keep account of what has come to pass as the ultimate for Jesus without really being so, I shall proceed dialectically, denying ultimacy to what does not have it in an absolute sense.

Jesus is not the ultimate for himself. Today this should be evident. On the plane of Jesus' consciousness it is clear that he did not preach himself.[1] Any attempt to make Jesus the absolutely ultimate breaks down in the face of the evidence of exegesis, and not only the historical Jesus, but the risen Christ as well.[2] The whole argumentation of modern indirect christology— the argumentation to show Jesus' peculiarity and his divine filiation—demonstrates that even christology can only be *relational,* not absolute. One can only understand Jesus as from something distinct from and greater than himself, and not as from something directly residing in himself.

From *Jesus in Latin America* (Maryknoll, N.Y.: Orbis Books, 1987) pp. 81-97. Translated by Robert R. Barr.

Jesus expels demons, and this is a sign of the novelty of his person. But this symbolizes not his own ultimacy but the approach of the kingdom of God (Luke 11:20). The antitheses of the Sermon on the Mount—"You have heard ... What I say to you is ..." (Matt. 5:21-47)—show forth the ultimacy of a new way of life. The radical following of Jesus is demanding (Mark 8:34-38). It is at the service of the ultimate salvation or condemnation of the human being. When Jesus says that no one should be ashamed either of him or of his words, the reason he gives is that otherwise the "Son of Man" (distinct from Jesus in Mark 8:38 and Luke 12:8) will be ashamed of them.

All of these statements are calculated to show that Jesus did not conceive of himself as the absolutely ultimate but rather in relation to something distinct from himself. Jesus does have a kind of ultimacy, as we shall see in the third part of this article. But in order to understand exactly in what his ultimacy consists, we must first understand his own ultimate pole of reference.

The ultimate for Jesus is not simply "God." Up to this point what has been said is fairly evident and commonly accepted. But this is not so with the next step: Jesus did not simply preach "God." "God" is not simply and absolutely Jesus' ultimate pole of reference. This seemingly shocking statement should, however, be evident, and theologians assert it by implication. Jesus preached the kingdom of God, not himself.[3] "The centre and framework of Jesus' preaching and mission was the approaching Kingdom of God."[4] Now, it is this implication that I wish to underscore. Theologians today agree that in order to name what was ultimate for Jesus one cannot simply cite "God," but must make a dual statement: God *and* kingdom, God *and* nearness, God *and* his will, God *and* motherhood/fatherhood, and so on.

Systematically, then, the ultimate for Jesus is God in relationship, rendered explicitly as kingdom with the history of human beings—God's nearness, will, parental love; or conversely, a history "according to God." But in order to state this clearly, and especially, keeping in mind the practical repercussions of ignoring the duality of the ultimate, it is appropriate to emphasize what is implicit in that ultimate: that it is not simply "God" that is the ultimate for Jesus. To state that God is would be equivalent to saying that what is ultimate for Jesus is not essentially related to history and that history is not essentially related to it.

The profound reason for which Jesus did not simply preach "God" is that Jesus is heir to a series of traditions according to which God is never God *in se*, but is always in relationship with history. Whether we take the exodus traditions, with their God who hears the cry of the oppressed and strikes a covenant with the people; or the prophetical traditions, with their God who seeks to establish right and justice; or the apocalyptic traditions, whose God seeks to renew reality eschatologically; or the sapiential traditions of a God who provides for creation; or the traditions of God's silence in the face of the world's wretchedness and sin—all of these traditions have one thing in common: God is not a God in and for God. God always stands in some type of relation to history. The concrete element of that relation will depend on the underlying theology of each respective tradition and hence will vary. But the formality of a God in relationship with history is in all Old Testament traditions. As a good Jew, then, Jesus cannot name the ultimate simply as "God." And if this causes a certain surprise, it is because Christianity has not sufficiently gotten beyond the Greek origins of much of its theology and has failed to assimilate—despite so many formal assertions to the contrary—its biblical origin.

Nor do the foregoing statements oppose—rather they confirm—the activity of Jesus that would most appear to have its correlate simply in "God": Jesus' prayer. We need only analyze the content of the two prayers that have been handed down to us to be convinced that in neither of them is the ultimate simply God. The correlates of the prayer of thanksgiving (Matt. 11:25-26) and of the prayer in the garden (Mark 14:32-42) are the realized will of God in history and the intended will of God for history. Jesus' prayer thereby appears, surely, as dialogue with God, but with God precisely as Father, and so against a broader horizon than that of the simple "Thou" of God—rather, in a context of God's parenthood, found or sought.[5]

All of this shows that the ultimate for Jesus is not simply "God," but God in concrete relation to history. Therefore any hermeneutical presupposition, conscious or unconscious, along the lines of a pure personalism is a serious obstacle to understanding what the kingdom of God was for Jesus.

The ultimate for Jesus is not the church or the kingdom of heaven. The reading of the gospels by the church customarily equated the kingdom of God with the "kingdom of heaven" and with the "church." Equivalence with the "kingdom of heaven" would mean that the kingdom of God is "heaven" in its absolutely transcendent version, in distinction from and in opposition to the realization of that ultimate in the history of human beings in any form. This misunderstanding arises from the expression found frequently in the Gospel of Matthew, "kingdom of heaven." But exegesis has clearly shown that Matthew's expression is a reverent circumlocution for the name of God. Reading "kingdom of God" as "church" would mean that the kingdom of God has a historical version, too, and that this is precisely what the church is. The calamitous consequences of this equivalency, and, positively, the correct relationship between church and kingdom of God, are treated in other places. Here suffice it to recall that, according to responsible biblical exegesis, the historical Jesus did not intend to found a church such as arose later in the New Testament, although he did desire the restoration of a remnant of Israel, faithful to the best traditions of his people.

The ultimate for Jesus is the kingdom of God. In this dialectical procedure — denying what is not absolutely ultimate for Jesus — we now come to the simple statement that the genuinely ultimate, that which gives meaning to Jesus' life, activity, and fate, is the kingdom of God. Even though it has not yet been made explicit what that kingdom would consist in for Jesus, certain systematic considerations of importance can help our understanding of what is to follow.

In Jesus, the ultimate is presented in a unity of transcendence and history. This unity, this oneness that necessitates a dual explanation, is due to the conception Jesus has of God as the God of the kingdom. The so-called vertical and horizontal dimensions, then, are equally "originary" in Jesus' relationship with the absolute. There is no longer any history but one, and its duality will not be adequately expressed as history of the "beyond" and history of the "amidst" (supernatural history and natural history), but will have to be expressed as history in the direction of the kingdom of God (history of grace) and history counter to the direction of the kingdom of God (history of sin).

No institution can lay claim to an absolute value that would threaten the absolute value of the kingdom of God. This is true not only factually, in that Jesus *de facto* did not intend the church concretely, nor did he equate the projects of the rabbis, Pharisees, Essenes, or Zealots with the kingdom of God.

This is true in principle as well, in that the values of the kingdom will be criteria of judgment upon any type of human configuration, religious or sociopolitical, that explicitly or implicitly seeks to put itself forth as the actual kingdom of God, although service to this kingdom will call for concrete configurations all through history.[6]

WHAT IS THE KINGDOM OF GOD FOR JESUS? A HISTORICAL PROBLEM

It is a well-established historical datum of the life of Jesus that he preached the kingdom of God. In this sense, the exordium of the Gospel of Mark, although it is only a theological summary, does make Jesus' ultimate horizon and its consequences explicit: "This is the time of fulfillment. The reign of God is at hand! Reform your lives and believe in the gospel!" (Mark 1:15).

In making this proclamation, Jesus continues that of John the Baptist (Matt. 3:1), whose disciple he probably was.[7] In this sense Jesus does not proclaim anything absolutely new, but summarizes the hopes and expectations of the best traditions of his people. Typical of Jesus is his concentration on this theme. "The per se traditional expectation of the kingdom of God to come is transformed in Jesus into the decisive, sole outlook."[8]

Now we are on the correct methodological track. From the Old Testament we learn the formal notion of the kingdom of God, and especially its content, addressees, and negation, in the prophetico-apocalyptic tradition.

From the New Testment, from the Synoptics, we learn what Jesus' concentration on the kingdom of God was. We learn what the kingdom basically was for Jesus, not only from what might be extracted from his notion of the kingdom, but also from *Jesus' actual life in the service of the kingdom.* This last statement is important, incidentally, for solving the difficulty proposed by Walter Kasper: "Jesus nowhere tells us in so many words *what* the Kingdom of God is. He only says that it is near."[9] In order adequately to deal with this difficulty we must consider not only what Jesus explicitly *says* about the kingdom, but what he *says and does* in the service of the kingdom.[10]

The reign of God in the traditions before Jesus. There frequently appears in the Old Testament a nomenclature of God as king, especially in the Psalms and in the liturgy. The nomenclature is not original with Israel. It existed throughout the ancient Near East. "In adopting the institution of the monarchy, originally foreign to them, Israel adopted its symbols as well, to express their belonging to the God who had saved them and made them his own."[11] But Israel historicized so many of the concepts of its milieu and the symbol of the king came to be applied to God — "eventually was used to set in relief his ability to intervene in history."[12]

Yahweh's historical intervention is seen in various ways in the stages of Israel's history. In the Mosaic times the reign of God is seen as a military and civil chieftaincy. In the time of the Judges it is seen as the exclusivity of the kingship of Yahweh — hence, for example, Gideon's refusal of the title of king. In the time of the monarchy, Yahweh's kingship becomes compatible with that of the human king of Israel — not without grave theological conflict — who becomes Yahweh's adopted child.

After the collapse of the monarchy, the national catastrophes, the exile and captivity, a new conception of God's reign springs up. Now it is seen as the future, and more attention is paid to the content of the kingdom as the prophets develop it. The apocalyptic approach universalizes that expectation, even to cosmic proportions, expressing it in a hope for a renewal of all reality, including the resurrection of the dead.

In Judaism, especially in the era in which Jesus appears, the reign of God is intensely awaited, and the nomenclature of the "kingdom of God" is revived. The most crucial question is how to await, how to hasten the coming of that kingdom. Will it be by fulfilling the prescriptions of the Law? By armed insurrection? By attention to signs from heaven?

The notion of the kingdom of God, the kingship of Yahweh, and so on, runs all through the history of the people of Israel in one form or another. But it is important to clarify the *formality* of this notion from the outset. As we know, the term "kingdom" suggests a series of spontaneous interpretations other than those that lie behind the original *malkūtā Yahweh.* The kingdom of God is not geographical, nor does it imply a static situation in which Yahweh is officially acknowledged as king. "Kingdom of God" has two key connotations: (1) God will rule through dynamic act;[13] and (2)

God's purpose will be to modify and establish a determinate order of things.[14] Both connotations are expressed in Psalm 96:13: "For he comes to rule the earth. He shall rule the world with justice and the peoples with his constancy."

What is important here, then, is that instead of speaking of "kingdom," one should refer to Yahweh's "reign"—what occurs when the one ruling the world is really Yahweh and no other power. Systematically, it is important to observe that the primary note of the kingdom of God is not the ascending movement of Yahweh's liturgical, orthodox, or official acknowledgment on the part of a particular people as king, and not another divinity; rather it is in the descending movement of a concrete historical reality: that the history of a determinate people be actually in conformity with what Yahweh wills. What is at stake, therefore, is that the kingdom of God comes to be historical reality and not just the profession of Yahweh as king.

The reign of God is the establishment of justice and right with regard to the poor. The prophetical period from which Jesus obtained his categories for understanding what the kingdom of God is, has a clear answer to the question of what happens when God reigns.[15] God is definitively a loving God. God is not condemnation but love. Yahweh therefore appears as a loving father (Hos. 11:1), faithful husband (Hos. 2:20), or consoling mother (Isa. 66:13). Yahweh has not abandoned the people. "Can a mother forget her infant, be without tenderness for the child of her womb? Even should she forget, I will never forget you" (Isa. 49:15). "I will be their God, and they shall be my people" (Jer. 31:33). This love of God's is seen as effective—capable of doing something novel. It is not only the interiorist declaration that the ultimate meaning of reality consists in love. It is also the declaration of a reality in conformity with God's love. The following passage from Isaiah on God's dream for this world will do better than a lengthy disquisition on the topic.

> Lo, I am about to create new heavens
>   and a new earth;
> The things of the past shall not be remembered
>   or come to mind.
> Instead, there shall always be rejoicing and happiness in what I
>   create;
> For I create Jerusalem to be a joy
>   and its people to be a delight;
> I will rejoice in Jerusalem
>   and exult in my people
> No longer shall the sound of weeping be heard there, or the
>   sound of crying;
> No longer shall there be in it
>   an infant who lives but a few days,
>   or an old man who does not round out his full lifetime;

He dies a mere youth who reaches but a hundred years,
  and he who fails of a hundred shall be thought accursed.

They shall live in the houses they build,
  and eat the fruit of the vineyards they plant;
They shall not build houses for others to live in,
  or plant for others to eat.
As the years of a tree, so the years of my people;
  and my chosen ones shall long enjoy
  the produce of their hands.
They shall not toil in vain,
  nor beget children for sudden destruction;
For a race blessed by the LORD
  are they and their offspring.
Before they call, I will answer;
  while they are yet speaking I will hearken to them
                                         [Isa. 65:17-24].

The prophet's dream proclaims the hope of good news, but not merely as conciliation. Rather it is proclaimed as reconciliation. The dream takes into account the current situation in history, a history dominated by sin, which is in formal opposition to hope. In its anathema against sinners, the dream observes *sub specie contrarii* what the hoped-for reconciliation ought to be: a world without oppression. This is why the prophets condemn those who "sell the just man for money, and the poor man for a pair of sandals"; who "trample the heads of the weak . . . and force the lowly out of the way" (Amos 2:6-7), "storing up in their castles what they have extorted and robbed" (Amos 3:10); who "oppress the weak and abuse the needy" (Amos 4:1); who "turn judgment to wormwood and cast justice to the ground" (Amos 5:7), who "hate him who reproves at the gate and abhor him who speaks the truth" (Amos 5:10), who have "trampled upon the weak and exacted of them levies of grain . . . oppressing the just, accepting bribes, repelling the needy at the gate" (Amos 5:11-12); who "hasten the reign of violence . . . lying upon beds of ivory, stretched comfortably on their couches" (Amos 6:3-4); who "trample upon the needy and destroy the poor of the land" (Amos 8:4); who build their houses without justice, who love bribes and look for gifts, who defend not the fatherless, "and the widow's plea does not reach them" as they are murderers (Isa. 1:21-23); who "join house to house and connect field with field, till no room remains, and [they] are left to dwell alone in the midst of the land" (Isa. 5:8); who "enact unjust statutes and who write oppressive decrees, depriving the needy of judgment and robbing [the Lord's] people's poor of their rights, making widows their plunder, and orphans their prey" (Isa. 10:1-2).

This list, taken from just two of the prophets, shows what they understand the kingdom of God *not* to be. The prophets speak not only of a world of limitation and natural misery, but of a world of historical misery originating in the oppression of some human beings by others. That world is the one that must be transformed and reconciled. Therefore the utopia of the kingdom is seen not only as the overcoming of misery (see the extended citation above from Isaiah 65), but as a world of reconciliation among human beings.

> Then the wolf shall be a guest of the lamb
>   and the leopard shall lie down with the kid;
> The calf and the young lion shall browse together,
>   with a little child to guide them.
> The cow and the bear shall be neighbors,
>   together their young shall rest;
>   the lion shall eat hay like the ox.
> The baby shall play by the cobra's den,
>   and the child lay his hand on the adder's lair.
> There shall be no harm or ruin on all my holy mountain;
>   for the earth shall be filled with knowledge of the LORD
>   as water covers the sea [Isa. 11:6-9; cf. 65:25].[16]

In that kingdom, the sorrows of war will give way to the joys of toil, for "they shall beat their swords into plowshares and their spears into pruning hooks" (Isa. 2:4). In that kingdom one may have true knowledge of God, which is nothing but the actualization of justice (Jer. 22:13-16; Hos. 4:1-2), and the true worship of God, not based on sacrifices, but on mercy and justice (Hos. 6:6, 8:13; Amos 5:21; Isa. 1:11-17).

This universal reconciliation, in the prophets as well as in the teaching of Jesus, has one basic and essential characteristic: the kingdom of God is for the poor. In the description of the sin that is the opposite of reconciliation we already have abundant testimony as to who are the ones oppressed by the antikingdom. Third Isaiah clearly declares:

> The Lord has anointed me; he has sent me to bring glad tidings to the lowly, to heal the brokenhearted, to proclaim liberty to captives and release to the prisoners, to announce a year of favor from the Lord [Isa. 61:1-2].

What the reign of God means for the prophets can be learned from the utopia they herald in the presence of the concrete historical reality of oppression, which is at once ignorance of the God of the kingdom and injustice to the poor. The reign of God, then, will be that situation in which human beings have genuine knowledge of God and establish right and justice toward the poor.[17] This is also the kernel of apocalyptic thought, garbed though it may be in other conceptual attire (resurrection of the dead, radical transformation of the ages). What is most profound in apocalyptic thought continues to be the expectation of God's justice in a world in which the innocent suffer and the unjust prosper.[18]

For Jesus, the kingdom of God "is at hand." With apocalyptic intensity, Jesus proclaims that the kingdom of God—what all have been waiting for—is at the very gates. The present world of misery has come to its end. Jesus seems to expect the irruption of this kingdom—God's definitive yes to history—during his own lifetime (Matt. 10:23; Mark 13:30, 9:1).

Unlike the Baptist, therefore, Jesus preaches the kingdom of God as good news. God sunders the divine symmetry: no longer is God equally near and far, equally just and merciful. Now God draws near in grace.

Of course this still gives us no information about what the kingdom of God will be in itself when it comes in plenitude, when the present world really comes to an end. The reason for this is simple: the end has not come, as Jesus acknowledges (Mark 13:32). The only thing that we can know of the kingdom of God in its intrinsic fullness is the *notion* that Jesus must have had and that we must gather from apocalyptic tradition.[19] What we know from Jesus is what the *reality* of a kingdom of God *at hand* consists of; and correlatively, *what Jesus does* in respect of this approach, how Jesus "corresponds" to the kingdom at hand. This observation seems to us to be important for knowing Jesus, as well as for understanding the relationship between church and kingdom of God. It will be of little avail to attempt to construct argumentation as to the correct behavior of the church from the ultimate realization of the kingdom of God. That ultimate realization is empirically unknowable. But it will avail much to observe the behavior of Jesus in the process of this kingdom's approach, for this process is our historical situation.

The kingdom of God is near for the poor. Joachim Jeremias writes:

> To say that Jesus proclaimed the dawn of the consummation of the world is not a complete description of his proclamation of the *basileia;* on the contrary, we have still to mention its most decisive feature. . . . The reign of God belongs to *the poor alone.*[20]

The kingdom of God is at hand because the good news is proclaimed to the poor (Matt. 11:5; Luke 4:18) and the kingdom of God is theirs (Luke 6:20). Thus we have a first important characterization of what it is for the kingdom of God to be "at hand." Since the absolute utopia is for the poor, it is to them that the kingdom is preached and proclaimed.

Jesus had two ways of describing the poor. According to the first way, the poor are sinners, publicans, prostitutes (Mark 2:6; Matt. 11:19, 21:32; Luke 15:1), the simple (Matt. 11:25), the little (Mark 9:2; Matt. 10:42, 18:10, 14), the least (Matt. 25:40-45), those who practice the despised professions (Matt. 21:31; Luke 18:11). The poor are the vilified, persons of low repute and esteem, the uncultured and ignorant, "whose *religious* ignorance and *moral* behavior stood in the way of their access to salvation, according to the convictions of the time."²¹ The poor are therefore society's *despised,* those lesser than others, and for them the prevailing piety proclaims not hope, but condemnation.

According to Jesus' second way of describing the poor, the poor are those in need in the spirit of Isaiah 61:1. The poor are those who suffer need, the hungry and thirsty, the naked, the foreigners, the sick and imprisoned, those who weep, those weighed down by a burden. The poor are therefore those who suffer some type of *real oppression.* The poor, to whom the good news of the kingdom is addressed, find themselves in some kind of misery and see themselves weighed down by a double burden: "They have to bear public contempt from men and, in addition, the hopelessness of ever gaining God's salvation."²²

When Jesus proclaims that the kingdom of God is at hand for the poor and not for the just (a piece of irony directed against the Pharisees, who set themselves forth as the just), he is making a first important statement on what it means for the kingdom of God to be at hand. He is saying that this approach of the kingdom is not generic and universal. It is "partial." It has a prioritarian addressee and at the same time a prioritarian locus for an understanding of how one "corresponds" to a kingdom of God that is at hand.

This way the kingdom has of being at hand produces scandal (Matt. 11:6): scandal that God would give hope to those who are deprived of it in the secular sphere, scandal that God would restore to dignity those from whom religious and sociopolitical society have wrenched it away, scandal that God would really be partisan love, mercy, and re-creator. Jesus' polemics against the Pharisees shows the importance of this scandal. It betrays the partiality of the "kingdom at hand." The Pharisees refuse to accept the approach of the kingdom precisely by reason of their own partiality. It would shatter the seeming equilibrium and justice of the law. Therefore they criticize a Jesus who eats with sinners and publicans (Mark 2:15-17) and heals a withered hand on the Sabbath (Mark 3:1-6). Therefore they criticize his disciples, who do not fast (Mark 2:18-22), who gather a handful of grain on the Sabbath (Mark 2:23-28), and who eat without washing their hands (Mark 7:1-7).

Jesus' polemics with the Pharisees is only superficially casuistic. It is not really legal prescriptions that are at stake, but God's partiality. The simplest conclusion to be drawn from this manner of the kingdom's approach is that persons ought to correspond to it by taking up the defense of the poor and acting in solidarity with them.²³ This is the "place to live" when the kingdom is at hand.

One corresponds with the approaching Kingdom of God in love and justice. But now we must ask whether the approach of the kingdom of God is exhausted for Jesus in the recovery of hope by the poor in knowing that they are loved by God, in knowing that they are actually God's favorite persons. If the answer were to be in the affirmative, the prophetical horizon sketched above would appear vain, since it depicts the poor not only as knowing something special about themselves, but as ceasing to be the oppressed of the secular sphere. We ask, therefore, whether, according to Jesus, the approach of the kingdom entails the surmounting of real misery and the transformation of society to the advantage of the poor. In order to answer this question, it seems most appropriate to observe in the concrete what Jesus says and does with respect to these problems in the time of a kingdom "at hand."

From this perspective, it is evident that Jesus' proclamation is not limited to God's scandalous, partisan love for the poor. It includes his quest to deliver the poor from their real misery. Here the important thing is to observe the *structure* of the liberation striven for by Jesus, without anachronistically looking to Jesus for the concrete mechanisms of liberation sought by so many Christians, and so rightly and so necessarily, today. At bottom, then, the problem is not the concrete mediations of Jesus' liberation. The problem is whether Jesus corresponded to the approach of the kingdom *only* by arousing a hope. Was it also through a determinate *praxis* objectively calculated to change the situation of the poor? Let us make some brief observations about this.

In the first place, Jesus' miracles and exorcism constituted a liberative activity. If we transport ourselves from the traditional christological concern to demonstrate Jesus' authority and power to the deeds themselves, then the miracles are not only prodigies and works of wonder, they are works *in favor* of the one in need. They constitute the transformation of an evil reality into a different reality, a good one.

In the second place, Jesus promoted solidarity among human beings not in generic and merely declaratory fashion, but by bringing his activity to bear on human beings' concrete historical situation. Jesus' concrete "placement" or status with his people, his efficacious acts and attitudes of solidarity show what he himself understood by solidarity. Jesus states that solidarity does not exist in his society, and then he moves toward those whom that society has ostracized. He defends prostitutes, he speaks with lepers and the ritually impure, he praises Samaritans, he permits ostracized women to follow him. These are positive actions of his, calculated to create a new collective awareness of what solidarity is, that it actually exists, and the partisan way in which it ought to develop. Jesus' meals with the poor have special importance for this point. Of course they are only symbolic. But symbols are effective. Correspondence with a kingdom of God "at hand" is had when human beings feel solidarity with one another around a common table. Jesus approaches the ostracized not only individually, but in their community, re-creating them as a social group through the materiality of the dining table.

In the third place, what, according to Jesus, is the impediment to the common table? Surely, sin; but sin not only as a closing up against a God who draws near in grace, but also sin as a rejection of the ideal of the kingdom as expressed in the prophets. The sin unmasked by Jesus in the shadow of the kingdom, as it were, is sin against the ultimate content of the kingdom. Jesus therefore denounces any action, attitude, or structure that keeps human beings divided into wolves and lambs, into oppressors and oppressed.

Jesus' anathemas are condemnations not only of individuals, but of groups and collectivities that through their power keep the poor in a state of oppression. They are anathemas of sin, sin against the kingdom. To the rich he says, "But woe to you rich, for your consolation is now" (Luke 6:24). He is not just threatening the rich with ultimate failure (Luke 12:16), or condemning them for leaving the solution of economic problems to God (Luke 12:31). First and foremost he is denouncing the unjust social situation. "For there can be no doubt: Jesus considers it an injustice that there are poor and rich. . . ."[24] That is an intolerable situation, even in the short time before the imminent arrival of the kingdom.[25] And the reason that Luke gives is that wealth is simply unjust (Luke 16:9), for it is the fruit of oppression. Therefore Jesus proposes another way of using wealth as the kingdom approaches—a way that will render it just: give it to the poor (Matt. 19:21; Mark 10:21; Luke 18:22).

The *priests,* who hold religious power, are accused by Jesus of having adulterated the meaning of the temple, transforming it into a den of thieves (Mark 11:15-17). Religious power has been converted into a means of profitmaking and thus of oppressing the weak. The *scribes,* who hold the intellectual power, are accused of laying heavy burdens upon others without lifting a finger themselves (Matt. 23:4), of preventing others from entering into the kingdom (Matt. 23:13), of having removed the key of knowledge and left others in ignorance (Luke 11:52), of devouring the living of widows on the pretext of having long prayers to recite (Mark 12:40). The *Pharisees,* who represent the power of exemplary holiness, are accused by Jesus of being blind guides (Matt. 23:24), and of having abandoned what is most basic in the law (Matt. 23:23). Jesus accuses the *rulers,* who hold political power, of governing with absolute power and of oppressing the masses (Matt. 20:25).

The denunciation of the sin of oppression is an action by Jesus in favor of the content of the kingdom now "at hand"; and the concrete identity of what is denounced enables us to appreciate as well the positive element in the proclamation of this kingdom. One corresponds to the kingdom of God by doing justice, by eliminating crass social discrepancies—by using power in a new manner, to the advantage of the poor.

Finally, Jesus himself lives and proposes the practice of love as the "law of life under the reign of God," as Joachim Jeremias phrases it.[26] I will not elaborate upon this theme at any length, but will make some brief observations on the reality of this love, not in its ultimate plenitude, but in the time in which the kingdom is at hand, as Jesus sees it. The first observation concerns the addressee of that love. Jesus' words about the final judgment leave no room for doubt: the prioritarian addressee of this love is anyone in need, and the need in question is surely made explicitly in Matthew 25:35-38. Further, we see that "my least brothers" (Matt. 25:40) has a universal extension not reducible to Jesus' disciples, but applicable to any human being in need. It is they who are the addressees of the kingdom; they are in the majority in society and are the fruit of society's oppression. So the love in question must be translated into the active word of justice.

The second observation concerns the agent of the practice of this love. The parable of the Good Samaritan admirably illustrates that true love is measured by the objectivity of what is done, not by the intention or a priori quality of the doer. The despised Samaritan lives the love that corresponds to the approach of the kingdom. He understands the locus of the praxis of love. Unlike the priest and the Levite, who make a detour so as not to meet up with the one in need (Luke 10:31-32), the Samaritan draws near (v. 34). Thus he becomes the victim's neighbor, and not the other way around, as Jesus notes (vv. 29, 36). And so my "neighbor . . . is not [the one] I find in my path, but rather [the one] in whose path I place myself."[27] The kingdom of God is at hand when men and women actively seek that efficacious love that will transform this world according to the ideal of the kingdom to come.

The third observation bears on the absolute element of that love as the way to correspond to the approach of the kingdom. Where there is love among human beings, seemingly so "horizontal" a love, we have the great paradox that God is approaching. We are familiar with the two passages concerned with the "great commandment" (Mark 12:28-34; Matt. 22:34-40; Luke 10:25-27) and with the superiority of the human being to the Sabbath (Mark 2:23-28; Luke 6:1-5). Both passages state that it is in love that human beings achieve their fulfillment, for it is in love that they correspond to the kingdom "at hand"—correspond to the love of God for human beings.[28]

We *respond* to the approach of the kingdom in the hope that God is at last "at hand" in grace and partisan love; but we ultimately and absolutely *correspond* to it by becoming like the reality of the God who is "at hand." In God's seeming self-forgetfulness, as God demands our love for other human beings, the kingdom comes near—a new world "according to God" is under way. Correlatively, in love for another human being, human beings are loved by God. In corresponding to God's loving reality they simultaneously correspond to God's love.

This is John's profound intuition. He deduces the demand of love for neighbor from one's awareness of being loved by God: "Beloved, if God has loved us so, we must have the same love for one another" (1 John 4:11). Luke's intuition is the same: "Be compassionate, as your Father is compassionate" (Luke 6:36).

Why is this of crucial importance for what was the real ultimate, the absolute, for Jesus? The biblical passages use generic language—like "love" and "compassion"—and therefore current mediations are always needed. But what is being asserted in these passages is that for Jesus the ultimate is *the realized will of God.* Therefore this absolute is not simply "God," and this in virtue of the very notion Jesus had of God. Jesus proclaims the irruption of the definitive kingdom of God, the work of God. In the meantime, in the time of the kingdom "at hand," he strives for a world according to God. Precisely because that God of his is love and not pure sovereign power, partisan, sides-taking justice for the poor, and not the universal moral law, because that God is not egocentric—for this reason, and not by reason of any secularist intention, God is the absolute only insofar as God's reality of being-love is actualized in this world.

Here is the theological kernel of what is meant by a kingdom of God "at hand." True this kernel is not simply to be deduced from the apocalyptical notion Jesus may have had. But it is to be deduced from seeing Jesus in *action*—preaching to the poor, forthrightly denouncing injustice and oppression, placing everything he has at the service of the approach of the kingdom, creating human solidarity from a point of departure in the poor, and staying faithful to that task even though the kingdom of God in its fullness did not come, and the kingdom "at hand" seemed tragically far-off in his death. What is ultimate for Jesus is not, when all is said and done, discoverable from his notions, but only from his life. The absolute for Jesus is what he *maintained in deed* as ultimate through his life, throughout his history and in spite of history: the service and love of the oppressed, in order to create a world in which right and justice will be established—a world worthy of the undying hope that, despite all, the kingdom of God is still at hand.

HOW DOES THE KINGDOM OF GOD COME TO BE AT HAND? AN ESCHATOLOGICAL PROBLEM

From what has been said thus far, I shall now explain what it means to say that the kingdom of God is eschatological. The eschatological character of the kingdom was rediscovered at the turn of the century by Johannes Weiss and Albert Schweitzer, and an earnest discussion on the part of scholars has continued from that day to this. The discussion bears on two points. First, while the kingdom must definitively have come with Jesus, either it has not yet come *in absoluto,* or—in Oscar Cullmann's formulation—it has "already" come, but "not yet." The question, then, is that of the *temporal nature of the kingdom.* The second point of discussion is whether the kingdom of God for Jesus is the pure work of God or also that of the activity of human beings. The question here, therefore, is that of the gratuity of the kingdom.

These discussions are crucial for explaining what Jesus really thought about the kingdom of God. I conclude this article by re-positing the eschatological problem from a systematic standpoint so that the theme "Jesus and the kingdom of God" may likewise be useful and normative for us.

It seems that Jesus thought of the eschatological coming of the kingdom as about to take place, in the near future, probably during or at the close of his life. The kingdom, then, was not fully present for him, but only "at hand." And yet Jesus preached it as something ultimate-and-present. He conceived of the kingdom as a gift of God. Nevertheless, he sought to foster it in a determinate manner throughout his life. However surely a point of departure in the mere notion that Jesus had of the kingdom of God leads us to the notional aporiae of eschatology—such as those of the reconciliation of present and future, or of gift and human task—if we begin instead from Jesus' real life, we gain a new approach to the eschatological.

From this viewpoint, what Jesus offers as eschatological and ultimate is a life in the shadow of God's kingdom. How the kingdom comes, what its element of gratuity is, what is historical about it and what transcendent—all of these questions are answered in the measure that Jesus' call is accepted: "If a man wishes to come after me, he must deny his very self, take up his cross, and follow in my steps" (Mark 8:34).

The following of Jesus is the primordial locus of all Christian theological epistemology and therefore of the understanding of eschatology as well. The *thought* tension between gift of God and human task dissolves in Jesus' discipleship, where grace is *experienced,* not only in new ears for hearing the good news, but also—and furthermore as fullness of grace—in new hands for fashioning a history itself at hand for the kingdom. The *thought* tension between the present and future of the kingdom is *experienced* as undying hope. In the *praxis* of love and justice one knows that the kingdom is at hand, is becoming present; and in conflictive *praxis* in the midst of the world's sin one maintains hope in God's future.

Jesus' discipleship does not furnish us with a response to the question "What is the fullness of the kingdom, and when will it come in that fullness?" Jesus' discipleship does offer us a place to ask these questions meaningfully. The ultimate reason for this is that this plenitude as reality can only be understood starting from and in historical reality. The continuity between plenitude and history is not to be found in thought. The following of Jesus provides, then, the living of a reality, the fashioning of a reality, of a kingdom "at hand," from which, at least in hope, an ultimate reality acquires meaning. That "God may be all in all" (1 Cor. 15:28) in the end is something that we can formulate only in serious, humble toil calculated to render God a little more present in our world today.

This is important for the church today in identifying its relationship to the kingdom of God. A routine repetition that "the church is not the kingdom of God but its servant" will not suffice—although it will be no small matter to be convinced of this. It will likewise be insufficient merely to recall that the Catholic Church must not walk alone but must collaborate with and learn from the other Christian churches and from all men and women of good will, who likewise objectively serve the approach of the kingdom and who even outstrip us.

The church must positively place itself in the locus from which its concrete task, to be realized in a determinate era, will be illuminated—the following of Jesus—and from there learn to evaluate its mission, not hastily appealing to the apocalyptic, to the unknown plenitude, and ignoring or undervaluing the historical present, but rather following the historical path of Jesus. The apocalyptic should be the ultimate horizon for the church today, too—but not at the price of ignoring the ultimacy of history. The mission of the church must be thought and accomplished not only from a point of departure in the kingdom of God, but from a point of departure in the kingdom of God *at hand.* This mission, then, today as in Jesus' time, takes on concrete, verifiable forms.

Because the eschatological existence available to the church is the following of Jesus and not a mere mechanical imitation of him, the church will have to learn how the kingdom of God "at hand" is served historically. Jesus will direct it along the proper channels: that God is greater than any historical configuration, even of the church; that, paradoxically, God is also smaller, for God's face appears in the least and the oppressed; that sin has concrete names in history, and takes flesh not only in the individual, but in society; that the praxis of love is the ultimate thing that can be accomplished; that this love must be really efficacious, really transformative, and therefore must reach not only the person as individual—one's spouse, one's relatives, one's friends—but society as such, the oppressed majorities—that is, that it must be justice; that the following and discipleship of Jesus is partisan, prioritizing the poor and oppressed; that one must be ready to change, as Jesus was, to be converted, to pass by way of a breach, a rupture, to "let God be God"; that one must be ready for surrender, for sacrifice, for persecution, for giving one's own life and not keeping it for oneself.

As it allows itself to be swept along the channel of discipleship, the church will gradually learn from within, by trial and error, which concrete mediations today bring God's kingdom near; what social, economic, and political systems render the kingdom-at-hand more illuminating; where the Spirit of Jesus is hovering, in the centers of power or the face of the oppressed; how to conceive and organize the church, from institutional steeples or popular foundations; which concrete sins call inexorably for denunciation; and so on.[29]

It is a simple matter, then, to pose the problem of the eschatology of the kingdom. All one need do is learn from Jesus how to live, how to be church, in the faith that the kingdom is at hand; and then, in the shadow of the approaching kingdom, how to go and transform human beings and society. The nearness of the kingdom is understood, without any tinge of false piety, in Jesus' nearness, in his discipleship and following. This is what is genuinely ultimate for the church, for here we grasp what was ultimate for Jesus.

I conclude these reflections with the words of the Salvadoran priest and martyr, Rutilio Grande, S.J., who grasped in Jesus' discipleship what he had to do, how he had to speak, because he *believed* that the kingdom of God was coming and because he *wanted* it to come to his *campesino* town of Aguilares.

The Lord God gave us a material world—like this material Mass, with its material cup that we raise in our toast to Christ the Lord. A material world for all, without borders. That's what Genesis says. I'm not the one saying it. "I'll buy half of El Salvador. Look at all my money. That'll give me the right to it." No! There's no "right" to talk about! "It's called right of purchase. I've got the right to buy half of El Salvador." No! That's denying God! There is no "right" against the masses of the people! A material world for all, then, without borders, without frontiers. A common table, with broad linens, a table for everybody, like this Eucharist. A chair for everybody. And a table setting for everybody. Christ had good reason to talk about his kingdom as a meal. He talked about meals a lot. And he celebrated one the night before his supreme sacrifice. Thirty-three years old, he celebrated a farewell meal with his closest friends. And he said that this was the great memorial of the redemption: a table shared in brotherhood, where all have their position and place. Love, the law code of the kingdom, is just one word, but it is the key word that sums up all of the codes of ethics of the human race, exalting them and presenting them in Jesus. This is the love of a communion of sisters and brothers that smashes and casts to the earth every sort of barrier and prejudice and that one day will overcome hatred itself.[30]

NOTES

1. Karl Rahner and Wilhelm Thüsing, *A New Christology*, trans. David Smith and Verdant Green (New York: Seabury, 1980); Hans Küng, *On Being a Christian*, trans. Edward Quinn (Garden City, N.Y.: Doubleday, 1976), p. 214; Leonardo Boff, *Jesus Christ Liberator: A Critical Christology for Our Time* (Maryknoll, N.Y.: Orbis, 1978), p. 63; Jon Sobrino, *Christology at the Crossroads: A Latin American Approach*, trans. John Drury (Maryknoll, N.Y.: Orbis, 1978), p. 41.

2. See Wilhelm Thüsing, "La imagen de Dios en el Nuevo Testamento," in *Dios como problema*, ed. Joseph Ratzinger (Madrid: Cristiandad, 1973), pp. 80-120.

3. See Rahner and Thüsing, *A New Christology*, p. 8.

4. Walter Kasper, *Jesus the Christ*, trans. Verdant Green (London: Burns & Oates; New York: Paulist, 1977), p. 72.

5. See Sobrino, *Christology at the Crossroads*, pp. 151-76.

6. By way of contrast with the insistence of so many first-world theologies on the eschatological reserve imposed by the absolute character of the kingdom, in Latin America the insistence is on the "mediating concretions of the kingdom," inasmuch as the latter "is not given in its totality, but in historical mediations, and

is realized at all levels of political, economic, social, and religious reality" (Leonardo Boff, "Salvación en Jesucristo y proceso de liberación," *Concilium* 96 [1974]: 385-87).

7. See Jürgen Becker, *Johannes der Täufer und Jesus von Nazareth* (Neukirchen/Vluyn: Neukirchener, 1972), pp. 12-15.

8. Wolfhart Pannenberg, "The Revelation of God in Jesus," in *Theology as History*, ed. James M. Robinson and John B. Cobb, Jr., New Frontiers in Theology: Discussions among Continental and American Theologians, vol. 3 (New York, Evanston, and London: Harper & Row, 1967), pp. 101-33.

9. Walter Kasper, *Jesus the Christ*, p. 72.

10. Walter Kasper, (*Jesus the Christ*, pp. 89-99) follows the same method, except that he does not sufficiently analyze Jesus' activity, especially in the aspect of its conflictuality, controversy, and praxis of efficacious, partisan, socio-political love. Kasper reduces the latter to a general love of God that in turn translates, likewise rather generically, into love, forgiveness, and mercy.

11. L. Armendáriz, "El 'Reino de Dios,' centro y mensaje de la vida de Jesús," *Sal Terrae* (May 1976): 364.

12. Ibid.

13. "Thus the reign of God is neither a spatial nor a static concept. It is a *dynamic* concept. It denotes the reign of God in action, in the first place as opposed to earthly monarchy, but then in contrast to all rule in heaven and on earth. Its chief characteristic is that God is realizing the ideal of the king of righteousness ... " (Joachim Jeremias, *New Testament Theology: The Proclamation of Jesus*, trans. John Bowden [New York: Scribner's, 1971], p. 98; italics in original).

14. "Whatever political dreams or indeed whatever fantastic expectations of the destruction or rebirth of the world were bound up with the hopes of the Jews, it is a fundamental part of these hopes that the spirit of resignation which banishes God to a misty place beyond our ideals and which accepts the idea that no change is possible in this world, is totally strange to it" (Günther Bornkamm, *Jesus of Nazareth*, trans. Irene and Fraser McLuskey [New York, Evanston, and London: Harper & Row, 1960], p. 65.

15. To be sure, Jesus moved in an apocalyptic atmosphere as far as the expectation of the imminence of the end and the transformation of reality is concerned. But his categories of *content*, of how the kingdom of God *draws near* and how one corresponds to its approach, are those of prophecy. Hence I detail the latter, however sketchily.

16. See José Porfirio Miranda, *Marx and the Bible*, trans. John Eagleson (Maryknoll, N.Y.: Orbis, 1974), pp. 77-108; J. Alonso Días, "Términos bíblicos de Justicia Social y traducción de equivalencia dinámica," *Estudios Eclesiásticos* (January-March 1976): 95-128.

17. Thus the age-old dream of the peoples will come to realization, a dream of genuine justice—justice because it is partisan justice. "Kingly righteousness ... was not primarily one of dispassionate adjudication, but of the protection which the king extends to the helpless, the weak and the poor, widows and orphans" (Joachim Jeremias, *New Testament Theology*, p. 98).

"When in human history the function of judge or of what later came to be called judge was conceived, it was exclusively to help those who because of their weakness could not defend themselves; the others did not need it. ... When the Bible speaks of Yahweh as "Judge" or of the Judgment whose subject is Yahweh, it has in mind precisely the meaning which we have seen for the root *špht*: to save the oppressed from injustice" (José Porfirio Miranda, *Marx and the Bible*, p. 114).

18. Although there is a discontinuity between the prophetical and apocalyptical traditions, a basic continuity obtains where the justice of God is concerned. " 'Resurrection of the dead' was not an anthropological or a soteriological symbol, but a way towards expressing belief in the righteousness of God. God is righteous. His righteousness will conquer" (Jürgen Moltmann, *The Crucified God: The Cross of Christ as the Foundation and Criticism of Christian Theology*, trans. R. A. Wilson and John Bowden, 2d ed. [New York, Evanston, San Francisco, London: Harper & Row, 1973], p. 174).

19. This notion is characterized especially by formal determinations: the sudden irruption of the kingdom, its attribute of universal judgment, its concealment and mystery in the present. See Günther Bornkamm, *Jesus of Nazareth*, pp. 64-81. This is why it seems so important not to center the occurrences of the kingdom's approach on apocalyptic *thinking*, but on what Jesus says and does in this "meantime," this interim.

20. Joachim Jeremias, *New Testament Theology*, pp. 108, 116; italics in original.

21. Ibid., p. 112; italics in the original.

22. Ibid., p. 113.

23. This is the ultimate explanation for the allegation of blasphemy directed against Jesus, for which he is sentenced to death. See Jürgen Moltmann, *The Crucified God*, pp. 128-35; Jon Sobrino, *Christology at the Crossroads*, pp. 204-9.

24. Oscar Cullmann, *Jesus and the Revolutionaries*, trans. Gareth Putnam (New York: Harper & Row, 1970), p. 27.

25. See ibid., p. 25.

26. Joachim Jeremias, *New Testament Theology*, pp. 212-13.

27. Gustavo Gutiérrez, *A Theology of Liberation: History, Politics and Salvation*, trans. Caridad Inda and John Eagleson (Maryknoll, N.Y.: Orbis, 1980), p. 198.

28. This is the ultimate explanation for the allegation of subversion that occasions Jesus' death, for he subverts a political order based on oppressive power. See Jürgen Moltmann, *The Crucified God*, pp. 136-45; Jon Sobrino, *Christology at the Crossroads*, pp. 209-15.

29. As discerned in history after the resurrection of Jesus. I have elaborated on this in "El seguimiento de Jesús como discernimiento cristiano" (*Concilium* [November 1978]: 521-29).

30. "Homilía con motivo de la expulsión del P. Mario Bernal" ("Homily on the Occasion of the Expulsion of Father Mario Bernal"), delivered in Apopa, February 13, 1977, as found in *Estudios Centroamericanos* 348-49 (1979):859.

9

Who Is Jesus for Asian Women?

CHUNG HYUN KYUNG

TRADITIONAL IMAGES

In order to express their experiences of Jesus, the majority of Asian women use the traditional titles that they received from missionaries. Since many Christian churches in Asia are still dominated by Western missionary theologies and androcentric interpretations of the Bible, some Asian women's theologies on the surface look similar to Western missionary or Asian male theologies. However, when we look closely at the Asian women's usage of the traditional titles of Jesus, we can find the emergence of new meaning out of the old language. The following are examples of traditional images of Jesus which have gone through the welding of meaning by the experiences of Asian women.

Jesus as Suffering Servant

The most prevailing image of Jesus among Asian women's theological expressions is the image of the suffering servant. Asian Christian women seem to feel most comfortable with this image of Jesus whether they are theologically conservative or progressive.

According to the "Summary Statement from the Theological Study Group of Christology,"[1] developed by the Asian Women's Theological Conference, Singapore, Asian Christian women from many different countries defined Jesus as "the prophetic messiah whose role is that of the suffering servant," the one who "offers himself as ransom for many." They claimed that "through his suffering messiahship, he creates a new humanity."[2]

Asian Christian women at the Singapore conference rejected such

From *Struggle To Be the Sun Again* (Maryknoll, N.Y.: 1990), pp. 53-75.

images of Jesus as "triumphal King" and "authoritative high priest."[3] They contended that these images of Jesus have "served to support a patriarchal religious consciousness in the Church and in theology."[4] Jesus became the Messiah through his suffering in service to others, not by his domination over others. Like Korean theologian Choi Man Ja, many Asian Christian women make connections between their humanity and Jesus' humanity through "suffering and obedience."[5] Because Asian women's life experience is filled with "suffering and obedience," it seems natural for Asian women to meet Jesus through the experience that is most familiar to them.

When Asian women live through the hardship of suffering and obedience their family, society, and culture inflict upon them, they need a language that can define the meaning of their experience. The image of a suffering Jesus enables Asian women to see meaning in their own suffering. Jesus suffered for others as Asian women suffer for their families and other community members. As Jesus' suffering was salvific, Asian women are beginning to view their own suffering as redemptive. They are making meaning out of their suffering through the stories of Jesus' life and death. As Jesus' suffering for others was life-giving, so Asian women's suffering is being viewed as a source of empowerment for themselves and for others whose experience is defined by oppression.

However, making meaning out of suffering is a dangerous business. It can be both a seed for liberation and an opium for the oppression of Asian women. These two conflicting possibilities shape Asian women's experience of encounter with Jesus.

Asian women have believed in Jesus *in spite of* many contradictory experiences they receive from their families, churches, and societies. Believing *in spite of* great contradictions is the only option for many Asian women who are seeking to be Christian. For example, their fathers are supposed to be the protectors, the ones who give Asian women safety in an oppressive world, providing food, shelter, and clothing. But too often Asian women are beaten by their fathers or sold into child marriage or prostitution. Asian women's husbands are supposed to love them, but frequently they batter their wives in the name of love and family harmony. Asian women's brothers are supposed to support and encourage them, but they instead often further their own higher educations by tacitly using their Asian sisters, ignoring the reality that their sisters are selling their bodies to pay for tuition. The promises of safety, love, and nurturing have not been fulfilled. Asian women have trusted their beloved men, but their men have often betrayed them. Yet Asian women still hope, still believe that, "Maybe someday, somewhere, somebody will love me and nurture me as I am." Is Jesus that somebody?

Some Asian women have found Jesus as the one who really loves and respects them as human beings with dignity, while the other men in their lives have betrayed them. At the Singapore conference, Komol Arayapraatep, a Christian woman from Thailand, shared her appreciation of Jesus:

We women are always very grateful to Jesus the Christ. It is because of him that we can see God's grace for women. God saw to it that women had a vital part in the life of Jesus the Christ from his birth to his death and resurrection.[6]

Yet the church's teachings about Jesus are very similar to what their fathers, husbands, and brothers say to Asian women, rather than what Jesus actually says to them in the gospels. The church tells Asian women:

Be obedient and patient as Jesus was to his heavenly father. He endured suffering and death on the cross. That is what good Christian women are supposed to do. When you go through all the suffering, you too, like Jesus, will have a resurrection someday in heaven. Remember, without the cross, there will be no resurrection; no pain, no gain. You must die first in order to live.[7]

This is a hard and confusing teaching for Asian women. They are asking, "Why should we die in order to gain Jesus' love? Can't we love Jesus while being fully alive?" For Asian women self-denial and love are always applied to women in the church as they are in the family. But why isn't this teaching applied to men?

Western colonialism and neo-colonialism have created an added burden to Asian women's belief in Jesus. When Western Christians brought Jesus to Asia, many also brought with them opium and guns.[8] They taught Asians the love of Jesus while they gave Asians the slow death of opium or the fast death of a bullet. When the soldiers of the United States of America raped Vietnamese women and children and killed many Vietnamese people with Agent Orange, guns, and bombs in the name of democracy, the people of the United States still sang, "God Bless America." Death and love are connected in missionary acts whether they are religious or secular.[9]

Some Asian women still choose Jesus in spite of these contradictory personal and political experiences. Why have they continued to choose Jesus over and over again? Where was Jesus when Asian women's bodies were battered, raped, and burned? What has he done to protect them from suffering? Who is Jesus for Asian women? Is he like his own father, who allowed his son to be killed by Roman colonial power and religious hierarchies even though he cried out for help? ("My God, my God, why have you forsaken me?") Is Jesus like one of those irresponsible, frustrated Asian men who promise their lover and wife love and "the good life" but then, after stealing the woman's heart and body, say: "I will come back soon with money and gifts. While I am away, take care of *my* children and old parents. Be loyal to me." Of course such men almost never come back to their hopelessly waiting lover and wife, leaving all the burdens of survival on her shoulders. Are Asian women stuck in the battered women's vicious cycle of passive dependency? In Jesus are they again choosing a male whom they again try to love in spite of his neglect and abandonment simply because they know of no other type of relationship with men?

Some brave Asian women proclaim a resounding no to this endlessly confusing love game defined by "in spite of." They say they love Jesus *because of* and not *in spite of* who he is. They refuse to accept old, familiar ways of relating to their loved ones, which were based on forced sacrifice by women. Rather, they choose *the respect* of self. Jesus is only good for these Asian women when he affirms, respects, and is actively present with them in their long and hard journey for liberation and wholeness. Asian women are discovering with much passion and compassion that Jesus takes sides with the silenced Asian women in his solidarity with all oppressed people. This Jesus is Asian women's new lover, comrade, and suffering servant.

One example of choosing Jesus *because of* is witnessed by a Filipino, Lydia Lascano, a community organizer for slum dwellers for more than ten years, who presented her experience of Jesus as a suffering servant actively present with Filipino women in their suffering and resistance.[10] She believes Jesus' suffering has two different moments. One is "passive" and the other is "active." She identifies poor Filipino women's suffering under colonialism, military dictatorship, and male domination with the suffering of Jesus. She quotes from Isaiah as an example of the passive moment of Jesus' suffering:

> He had no beauty, no majesty to draw our eyes, no grace to make us delight in him; his form, disfigured, lost all the likeness of a man. Without beauty, without majesty . . . a thing despised and rejected by men, a man of sorrows familiar with suffering (Is. 53:2-3 NEB).

Lascano sees that the humiliation and dehumanization of the suffering servant are the same as the core experience of Filipino women. Many Filipino women are "suffering passively without hope of freeing themselves" due to the overwhelming hardship of their day-to-day survival and the unawareness of the root causes of their oppression.[11] The suffering servant image of Jesus expresses well the reality that Filipino women are undergoing.[12] Jesus' passive moment of undergoing suffering is very important for poor Filipino women because they then can trust Jesus for his *lived* suffering. Jesus does not lecture or preach about suffering in the way the institutional church does. He knows women's suffering because he was the one who once suffered helplessly like them.

Lydia Lascano also identifies an active moment of Jesus' suffering which contrasts to the passive moment. The active moment of Jesus' suffering is "doing" and "accompanying" as acts of solidarity. For her, to accompany is to be beside and walk with someone.[13] Jesus is actively present in the Filipino women's struggle for liberation, accompanying them in their doing justice. For Filipino women Jesus is not a dispassionate observer of their struggle. Rather, Jesus is an active participant in their fight for justice. Another Filipino woman, Virginia Fabella, explains this accompanying and doing aspect of Jesus' suffering in this way: "Because he stood for all he taught and did, he consequently endured suffering at the hands of his captors as a continuation and overflow of his act of identification with his people who saw no clear end to their misery at the hand of the system."[14]

For Filipino women Jesus is neither a masochist who enjoys suffering, nor a father's boy who blindly does what he is told to do. On the contrary, Jesus is a compassionate man of integrity who identified himself with the oppressed. He "stood for all he taught and did" and took responsibility for the consequences of his choice even at the price of his life. This image of Jesus' suffering gives Asian women the wisdom to differentiate between the suffering imposed by an oppressor and the suffering that is the consequence of one's stand for justice and human dignity.

Korean theologian Choi Man Ja makes this liberative aspect of Jesus' suffering clear in her presentation on feminist Christology. She asks this question: "How do women who are in the situation of suffering under and obeying oppressive power, take on significance as suffering and obeying servants?"[15] Her answer is:

Suffering is not an end in itself, . . . it has definite social references of divine redemptive activity. Suffering exposes patriarchal evil. Jesus endures the yoke of the cross against the evil powers of this patriarchal world. This obedience is different from simple submission to the worldly authority.[16]

Another Korean women theologian, Park Soon Kyung, developed further the meaning of Jesus' servanthood. According to her, Jesus' servanthood changed the meaning of being a slave among the oppressed people. The yoke of slaves is proof of the world's injustice and witness to the desire for God's righteousness.[17] Therefore, servanthood is not mere submission or obedience. It is instead a powerful witness to evil and a challenge to the powers and the principalities of the world, especially male domination over women. This suffering servant who is undergoing passive suffering with powerless Asian women and who is also accompanying them in their struggle for liberation by doing liberation is the prophetic Messiah who creates a new humanity for oppressed Asian women. Through Jesus Christ, Asian women see new meaning in their suffering and service. They see life-giving aspects in their suffering and service that creates a new humanity for the people they serve.

Jesus as Lord

If the liberative dimension of the suffering servant image frees Asian women from imposed suffering and empowers them to accept suffering as a consequence of their own choice for liberation, the liberative dimension of the Lord image of Jesus frees Asian women from the false authority of the world over them and empowers them to claim true authority which springs from life-giving experiences.

Yet like the image of the suffering servant, the image of Lord also has been used against Asian women, perpetuating their submissive and oppressed status in Asian society and the church. Traditionally Asian women have not been the owners of themselves under mainline patriarchal culture. In the East Asian context where Confucianism was the dominant social and religious ideology, women have had to obey the men in their lives: fathers before marriage, husbands in marriage, and sons in widowhood. The Asian woman's man was her lord. In addition to Confucianism, feudalism and the emperor system did not give much space for the self-determination of women. Even though women could not actively participate in any public or political affairs, they did, of course, suffer from the results of the hierarchical social system (in such concrete ways as lack of food due to oppressive taxes).

Western colonialism used Jesus' image as Lord to justify political and economic domination over many Asian countries. Western missionaries tried to brainwash Asian people by identifying the Western colonizer's Lord Jesus with the Lord for Asians, claiming that the colonizer's Lord Jesus was ruler of the whole universe. Therefore to become a Christian meant obeying the Lord Jesus and the colonial power which brought him to Asia.

This ruler image of Lord Jesus became especially strong in countries like the Philippines which were colonized by Spain. The Spanish conquistadores put Lord Jesus over all the indigenous spirits in the Philippines and put their king over the tribal leadership of the Filipino people. In their recent research many Filipino women theologians have begun to name this lordship ideology of colonial Christianity and its impact on Filipino women's lives.[18] They demonstrate that the lordship ideology of colonial Christianity domesticated the vibrant pre-colonial Filipino women's self-understanding and power in the community.[19] Filipino women shared equally or with even more power than men in domestic and public life before Spanish colonialism. Filipino women were active members in local politics and economics. According to Mary John Mananzan's research, even some male scholars believe that Filipino society was based on a matriarchal culture before colonization.[20] This active image of the power of Filipino women was diminished as Christianity was spread along with the feudal ideology of the colonial power. The ideal image of the Filipino woman became one of passivity, submissiveness, obedience, and chastity.

Under this historical reality many Asian women who were seeking women's liberation and self-determination have become suspicious of the Lord image of Jesus. Yet they also see the liberative power of the image of Jesus as Lord of the poor and oppressed women in Asia. One of the most articulate voices who illustrate this point is Park Soon Kyung from Korea. She is fully aware of ruler ideology (*Herren Ideologie*) of the image of Jesus as Lord, but she asserts that the lordship of Jesus is "the exact opposite" of patriarchal lordship.[21] For her, the lordship of Jesus means the lordship of justice, which "judges the evil power of rulers in this world."[22] While patriarchal lordship of this world means the ruling power that oppresses people, lordship of Jesus means the power that liberates people. The concept of power and authority in Jesus' lordship is completely different from that in patriarchal lordship. Jesus' lordship is the lordship of the "creator and savior of human and nature."[23] The title *Kyrios* (Lord), which was the word for ruler in Hellenistic culture, transformed its meaning radically when it was used to name the power of Jesus. According to Park Soon Kyung, the lordship of Jesus which comes from God limits the lordship of the rulers in this world by showing the real meaning of lordship through Jesus' deeds and his eschatological vision. All lordship in this world "should return to its origin," which is God.[24] Therefore, all lordship in this world becomes "relativized" under the eschatological vision of Jesus. The lordship in this world should be "the means which serves the salvation of humankind" and to "the righteousness and providence of God."[25] Park says:

> The Lordship of Christ means that his Lordship is exact opposite of patriarchal Lordship and he eschatologically places the rule of the evil powers in this world under God's judgement. Jesus put a period to the power of patriarchal history by obeying to the righteousness of God as a male even to his death. His Lordship is the Lordship of the righteousness of God which is established by his suffering and death. This Lordship destroys the principality and power of the world and returns all the power and authority to God.[26]

Jesus' lordship, then, says no to patriarchal domination, freeing Asian women from false authority and empowering them to obey only God and not men.

Jesus as Immanuel (God-with-us)

Jesus, who became the Lord of the universe through his suffering and service for humanity, also shows Asian women God's presence among them. Many Asian women cherish the mystery of the incarnation through Jesus' person and work. "Both the human and divine nature of Jesus are important" for Asian women's identity and mission.[27] Their understanding of Jesus' humanity and divinity, however, is very different from that of Nicene-Chalcedonian theological definitions stressing the Son's relationship to the Father and the two natures of his person. Asian women's concern for the humanity and divinity of Jesus derives from their resistance to colonial, male domination in their churches and cultures. Two distinguished voices which articulate the meaning of incarnation (Logos becoming flesh in Jesus) come from India and Korea. Indian theologian Monica Melanchton and Korean theologian Lee Oo Chung, express the meaning of incarnation and Immanuel from their specific socio-political and religio-cultural contexts.

Monica Melanchton locates Jesus' divinity in his sinlessness, virgin birth, resurrection, and "the tremendous authority Jesus claimed and exercised."[28] She explains Jesus' divine power further:

> The thing that impressed the masses was that the teaching of Jesus was differentiated from that of the Scribes by its innate sense of authority. It was with this power vested in him that he performed exorcism, forgave sins, healed the sick and preached with authority. That any mere human could claim such authority and back it up with his actions is beyond the remotest possibility. Hence every New Testament book attributes deity/divinity to Jesus either by direct statement or by inference.[29]

But this Jesus also shares human finitude with us by "lying in the cradle, growing, learning, feeling the pangs of hunger, thirst, anxiety, doubt, grief, and finally death and burial."[30] For Melanchton, Jesus is a "representative"[31] of the reality of "God-with-us"(Immanuel). She claims, however, that the institutional church distorted Jesus' image by emphasizing his maleness rather than his humanity. Jesus' maleness became "a constitutive factor in deciding the place and role of women."[32] Jesus' maleness excluded women from full participation in the church. She emphasizes that through his incarnation Jesus becomes the representative of a new humanity, not only of men, who are just one-half of the human race, but of women too. Melanchton warns that emphasizing the maleness of Jesus is a pagan act.

> If we ascribe maleness to Jesus Christ, we are also committing the mistake of ascribing the pagan/Hindu notions of sexuality to our God who transcends this. The Church in India needs to recognize the personhood of Jesus Christ and the fact that Christ is the representative human being for all people including Indian women.[33]

For her, Jesus' humanity embraces all people. The Christian God transcends sexuality and therefore frees Indian women from the stereotypical role assignments in Indian culture. Jesus as the Immanuel (God-with-us) transforms Hindu culture.

In contrast to Melanchton, Lee Oo Chung shows how Korean culture transforms the meaning of Immanuel, incarnation, and the divinity and humanity of Jesus. Lee Oo Chung advocates a Christology from below in a Korean context. According to her the traditional concept of Korean gods in general is that "special persons having done special things in a lifetime, become gods after death."[34] There is a popular format for these special persons becoming gods:

1) The issue of noble family
2) Extraordinary birth
3) Extraordinary childhood
4) Becoming an orphan at an early age or facing other kinds of suffering
5) Being rescued from the situation or surviving by encountering foster parents
6) Facing a crisis again
7) Winning a victory by fighting and obtaining glory.[35]

The above format is often seen in the stories of heroes who became gods. However, interestingly enough, when the story is about heroines, it has similar steps up to the sixth stage but "in the end she wins victory to become a god by suffering, loving, being patient, and sacrificing instead of fighting."[36] There are many gods in Korea who ascended to the position of god from being human through his or her love, suffering, and sacrifice. Among them, the majority are female.[37]

In this cultural framework Christology from above (God become human) is difficult to understand for the ordinary masses of people (minjung), especially laborers. Conceptual and abstract images of God in Christian theology, such as "totally other," "unmovable mover," and "immutable, impassable, unchangeable God," do not make much sense to Korean people. Lee Oo Chung observes Korean people's understanding of Jesus:

> The doctrine of God's becoming a man is a hard proposition for them [Korean Minjung] to accept. However "A man becomes a god" is easy for them to understand. Jesus Christ as Messiah can be better understood in the image of historical Jesus who has loved his neighbors more than himself and for this great love he went through surmounting suffering and sacrifice to become the Messiah, the Savior of humankind. Whereas the theory which says that because Jesus was God he was Messiah does not appeal too much.[38]

Lee proposes a radical task of liberation for Korean Christian women: In order to fully "experience the mystery of doctrine of incarnation by choice," Korean women must get out of the imposed service role in the church and society. This is possible when Korean women "elevate our self-consciousness as high as in the realm of the divine."[39] This elevation of women's self-consciousness will be generated from women's "experience of real love of God, for our totality of being the body, mind, and soul, as an individual and as a social being."[40]

Korean women experience the mystery of incarnation and "God-with-us" by becoming like Jesus. Many Korean Christians in the movement claim that we should become "little Jesuses" in order to become true Christians. For many Korean women, Jesus is not the objectified divine being whom people must worship. Rather, Jesus is the one we relive through our lives. The meaning of Immanuel, then, has been changed through Korean mythological symbols and language from God-*with*-us to God-*among*-us, and finally to God-*is*-us in our struggle to reclaim our full humanity.

NEW EMERGING IMAGES

New images of Jesus have emerged from Asian women's movements for self-determination and liberation. The freer Asian women become from the patriarchal authorities of their family, church, and society, the more creative they become in naming their experience of Jesus Christ. Sometimes the images of Jesus are transformed to the degree that they show the radical discontinuity between the ones found in the Jewish and Christian culture and those from the Asian women's movement. Some Asian women have become confident enough in themselves to name the presence of Jesus Christ in their own culture, indigenous religions, and secular political movements, a Christological identity that is not directly connected in the traditional sense with Christianity. They use religio-political symbols and motifs from their movement in order to describe what Jesus means for them in today's Asia. This is a *Christological transformation* created out of Asian women's experiences as they struggle for full humanity. The old Christological paradigms are transformed, new meanings are achieved, and diverse images of Jesus Christ emerge. Asian women as meaning-makers jump into an unknown open future shaping a new Christianity out of their own experience that never before existed in history. The following are examples of new, emerging images of Jesus Christ derived from Asian women who believe in their historical lived experience more than imposed authority.

JESUS AS LIBERATOR, REVOLUTIONARY, AND POLITICAL MARTYR

Jesus Christ is portrayed as liberator in many writings of women from various Asian countries such as India, Indonesia, Korea, the Philippines, and Sri Lanka. The reason why Jesus as liberator is the most prominent new image among Asian women is a consequence of their historical situation. The liberation from colonialism, neo-colonialism, poverty, and military dictatorship, as well as from overarching patriarchy, has been the major aspiration of twentieth-century Asian women.

In the composite paper of the EATWOT [Ecumenical Association of Third World Theologians] Asian Women's Consultation, entitled "Women and the Christ Event," Jesus is defined as "the prototype of the real liberator."[41] They also claim that Jesus as liberator is evident "in the image of liberators in other non-christian religions and movements."[42] A participant at the consultation, Pauline Hensman, a woman theologian from Sri Lanka, described Jesus Christ as the one who "came with good news to the poor, oppressed and downtrodden" and through whom "humankind was released from servitude and alienation by those who dominated and oppressed them."[43] This image of Jesus Christ as liberator is made concrete as revolutionary or political martyr in the Filipino women's reflection on the Christ event presented at the same consultation. According to Lydia Lascano from the Philippines, Filipino women who participate in the people's struggle for liberation "live out with their lives the Christ event— Jesus' life, passion, death and resurrection leaving the mark of their womenhood in the Philippine liberation project, the project of God."[44]

Filipino women have suffered (under more than three hundred years of Spanish and American colonialism and military dictatorships) and have resisted in order to survive and reclaim their human dignity as a people. Filipino women find Christ's suffering, death and resurrection *in* the suffering, death, and resurrection of Filipino women themselves. They see revolutionary acts of Christ among "the militant protesting Filipino women who have taken up the struggle for themselves and for the rest of the Filipino nation."[45] In their organized action for liberation, Filipino women have been arrested, raped, tortured, imprisoned, and displaced from their homes. Many have even been killed in their struggle toward self-determination for their people. Their names are today remembered by women in protest movements. Some names include:

Lorena Barros, a freedom fighter; Filomena Asuncion, a deaconess who offered her life for the conscientization of peasants; Leticia Celestino, a factory worker shot in the picketlines while demanding for a just wage; Angelina Sayat, a freedom fighter who died while in the custody of the military; Puri Pedro, a Catechist who served the farmers, was tortured and killed while being treated in a hospital.[46]

In the death of those political martyrs for freedom is the death of Jesus. Unlike the women of Jerusalem in Jesus' time, women are not just comforting or shedding tears for Jesus on his way to the cross. Filipino women shed blood for their people. Sister Lascano explains the political martyrdom among Filipino women:

Today, the passion of Christ in the Filipino people is fashioning women disciples who would accompany the suffering Christ alive among the people, not merely to comfort and support but even to die with them. In the passion for social transformation, death takes on a new level of meaningfulness. . . . Today many Filipino women do not merely accompany Christ to Calvary as spectators. They carry the cross with him and undergo his passion in an act of identification with his suffering.[47]

The resurrection of Jesus comes alive in the resurrection of these martyrs. The Filipino women's resistance movement makes the spirit and vision of these martyrs come alive by persistent "organized action" and "active waiting and watching" for the future victory of the struggle.[48] When poor

Filipino women are awakened to see the root cause of their suffering in structural evils, they begin to claim for themselves land and rights as human beings. They utter in discovery, "We will also have our Exodus!"[49] And they take political action. This discovery has stirred hope in their hearts, believing that "the liberating God of the Exodus has become alive in the resurrected Christ, now alive among them as *the Bagong Kristo* (the New Christ)."[50]

Jesus as Mother, Woman, and Shaman

Many Asian women portray Jesus with the image of mother. They see Jesus as a compassionate one who feels the suffering of humanity deeply, suffers and weeps with them. Since Jesus' compassion is so deep, the mother image is the most appropriate one for Asian women to express their experience of Jesus' compassion. Hong Kong theologian Kwok Pui-lan explains this point in her essay "God weeps with our pain":

> Jesus cried out for Jerusalem. His sorrow was so deep Matthew had to use a "feminine metaphor" to describe what he actually felt: How often would I have gathered your children together as a hen gathers her brood under her wings (Matt. 23:37).[51]

Like a mother who laments over her dead son who died in the wars in Indochina, like many weeping Korean mothers whose sons and daughters were taken by the secret police, Jesus cried out for the pain of suffering humanity. Korean theologian Lee Oo Chung questions why Jesus suffered so keenly before his death.[52] Even Jesus says to the disciples: "The sorrow in my heart is so great that it almost crushes me. Stay here and keep watch." Jesus was not like one of those saints and heroes who died calmly and serenely. According to Lee, Jesus was different from those saints and heroes because they "bore only their own suffering while Jesus took on himself the pain and suffering of all his neighbors, even of all humankind."[53]

Like some of Jesus' disciples, people who were only interested in the expansion of their personal glory, honor, and power ("When you sit on your throne in your glorious kingdom, we want you to let us sit with you, one at your right and one at your left" — Mark 10:37) could not feel the pain of the suffering poor nor see the violence and evil of the oppressors.[54] Jesus was different from them in that he felt the pain of all humanity like a compassionate mother. Lee discovers the image of Jesus as a compassionate mother who really feels the hurt and pain of her child in Korean folklore:

> In the National Museum in Kyungju, Korea, capital of the ancient Silla Kingdom, is a beautiful bell. The Silla Kingdom at the time enjoyed peace, but the King, a devout Buddhist, wanted to protect

his people from foreign invasion. His advisors suggested that he build a huge temple bell to show the people's devotion to the Buddha.

A specialist in the art of bellmaking was commissioned. But despite his skill and care, he failed time and again to produce a bell with a beautiful sound. Finally, he went back to the council of religious leaders. After a long discussion, they concluded that the best way to give a beautiful tone to the bell was to sacrifice a pure young maiden.

Soldiers were sent to find and fetch such a young girl. Coming upon a poor mother in a farm village with her small daughter, they took the child away, while she cried out piteously: "Emille, Emille!" — "Mother! O Mother!" When the molten lead and iron were prepared, the little girl was thrown in. At last the bellmaker suceeded. The bell, called the Emille Bell, made a sound more beautiful than any other.

When it rang, most people praised the art that had produced such a beautiful sound. But whenever the mother whose child had been sacrificed heard it, her heart broke anew.[55]

For Lee, Jesus is like the little girl's mother. Jesus' heart breaks anew when he hears the cry of humanity. People who do not know the meaning of sacrifice enjoy the achievement based on other people's sacrifice. But people "who understand the sacrifice can feel the pain."[56] This image of Jesus shows Asian women that the redemption of humankind "has not come through those who are comfortable and unconcerned, but only through the One who shared the suffering of all humankind."[57]

This compassionate, sensitive mother image of Jesus was shared by the Indonesian theologian Marianne Katoppo. She illustrates her point by quoting a prayer of Anselm and a poem from the Indian poet Narayan Vaman Tilak:

> And thou, Jesus, sweet Lord, art Thou not also a mother?
> Truly, Thou art a mother, the mother of all mothers
> Who tasted death, in Thy desire to give life to Thy children
> — Anselm[58]

> Tenderest Mother-Guru mine,
> Saviour, where is love like thine?
> — Narayan Vaman Tilak[59]

This mother image of Jesus demolishes "the paternalistic, authoritarian and hierarchical patterns" in our life and builds the "maternal, compassionate, sensitive, bearing and upbearing" relationship among people.[60]

Some Asian women see Jesus Christ as a female figure in their specific historical situation. Two articulate voices on this position are found in Korea. Park Soon Kyung concluded her Christology at the gathering of the Korean Association of Women Theologians by saying that even though

Jesus has a male physical form, he is "a symbol of females and the oppressed" due to his identification with the one who hurts the most. Therefore, on a symbolic level, we may call Jesus the *"woman Messiah"* who is the liberator of the oppressed.[61] She claims justification for naming Jesus' humanity as female in the current historical situation because Christology needs to be liberated from the patriarchal church structure.

Choi Man Ja goes one step further by identifying Korean women's historical struggle for liberation with "the praxis of messiahship."[62] She says, "Even though women are excluded from the ordained ministry, in fact women are the true praxis of messiah-Jesus, in Korea."[63] For her, Jesus' messiahship comes from his suffering servantship. Therefore, she can recognize the praxis of new humanity most clearly through a female messiah who is in the suffering and struggle of Asian women. This female Christ is "the new humanity, siding with the oppressed, and liberating women from their suffering."[64]

Another female image of Jesus comes from the image of the shaman. Virginia Fabella shares her learning from Korean women in her article "Asian Women and Christology."[65] Under oppressive political and economic oppression, and under the added burden of the Confucian system of ethics which inculcates male domination, Korean women's life experience is *han* itself. The resentment, indignation, sense of defeat, resignation, and nothingness in *han* make many Korean women brokenhearted and physically sick. In this situation, what would be the significance of Jesus Christ for them? Fabella cites an answer from a Korean woman: "If Jesus Christ is to make sense to us, then Jesus Christ must be a priest of Han" for minjung women.[66] For the minjung women, salvation and redemption means being exorcised from their accumulated *han,* untangling of their many-layered *han.* Since Korean indigenous religion is shamanism, Korean women easily accept the Jesus of the synoptic gospels, who exorcised and healed the sick and possessed like a Korean shaman. As the Korean shaman has been a healer, comforter, and counselor for Korean women, Jesus Christ healed and comforted women in his ministry.

In Korea the majority of shamans are women. Shamanism is the only religion among the various Korean religious traditions where women have been the center all through its development. Women shamans have been "big sisters" to many deprived minjung women, untangling their *han* and helping them cope with life's tribulations.[67] When Korean women, therefore, see Jesus Christ as the priest of *han,* they connect with the female image of Jesus more than the male image of Jesus. They take Jesus as a big sister just as they take the shaman as a big sister in their community. . . .

Jesus as Worker and Grain

Female images of Jesus Christ enable Asian women to image Jesus on the earth. The revelation of God they have heard from the church is usually the revelation from above. Theology based on the revelation from above can easily be distorted into a theology of domination because this theology is based on the abstract thinking of the head and not on the concrete experience of the body. It is based on distant (and largely male) intellectualism and not on the everyday, experiential reality of Asian women. Some Asian women find Jesus in the most ordinary, everyday experience. They see the revelation of God from below, the bottom, the earth. They refuse any kind of heroism. They are not looking for great men and women to worship. Rather, they want to find God, the saving presence within their daily lives.

A witness of faith from a Korean factory worker shows the meaning of Jesus Christ among the ordinary poor people:

> I don't know how to live a Christ-like life. But I am discovering and awakening to the meaning of it little by little in my daily life. This is a cautious and mysterious process. . . .
>
> When I see workers, I feel the breath and heart-beat of history and the meaning of humanity and Christ in them. I think we will not be saved without workers because workers truly have the loving power and unbeatable endurance. I wonder how Jesus the Christ will look when he comes back again. When I was young, I dreamt about Jesus wearing silverly white clothing, accompanying many angels with bright light and great sounds of music. But now I wonder. If Jesus comes again, he may come to us wearing ragged clothing and give my tired mother, who even dozes off while she is standing, a bottle of *Bakas* [popular Korean drink] or he may come to me, working mindlessly in the noisy factory, and quietly help my work while wearing an oily worker's uniform. I think our *Christ is the ground of life, and my faith is in the midst of this working life and workers.*[68]

This factory worker sees her Christ in workers and their hard struggle for survival. She does not believe any longer in the image of a flamboyant Jesus who looks like one of the rich and famous people in her childhood. She finds Jesus in her fellow workers who endure despair, humiliation, and back-breaking hard work, yet share their love and resources with other workers. Jesus Christ does not descend from glorious-looking heaven; Christ emerges from the broken-body experience of workers when they affirm life and dare to love other human beings in spite of their brokenness. Workers become Christ to each other when they touch each other's wounds and heal each other through sharing food, work, and hope.

Another image of Jesus Christ which emerges from the earth is found in a poem from an Indian woman. She meets her Jesus Christ when she receives two hundred grams of gruel in a famine-stricken area. For her, Christ, God's beloved Son, is food for hungry people.

Every noon at twelve
In the blazing heat
God comes to me
in the form of
Two hundred grams of gruel.

I know Him in every grain
I taste Him in every lick.
I commune with Him as I gulp
For He keeps me alive, with
Two hundred grams of gruel.

I wait till next noon
and now know he'd come:
I can hope to live one day more
For you made God to come to me as
Two hundreds grams of gruel.

I know now that God loves me —
Not until you made it possible.
Now I know what you're speaking about
For God so loves this world
That He gives His beloved Son
Every noon through You.[69]

Without food, there is no life. When starving people eat the food, they experience God "in every grain." They "know" and "taste" God when they chew each grain. Food makes them alive. The greatest love of God for the starving people is food. When the grain from the earth sustains their life, they discover the meaning of the phrase, "For God so loves this world that He gives His beloved Son." When God gives them food through other concerned human beings, God gives them God's "beloved Son," Jesus Christ.

In conclusion, we have observed that there are *traditional* images of Jesus, which are being interpreted in fresh, creative ways by Asian women, largely based on their experiences of survival in the midst of oppression and on their efforts to liberate themselves. We also have observed *new* images of Jesus that offer a direct challenge to traditional Christologies. These new images of Jesus are also based on Asian women's experiences of survival and liberation.

NOTES

1. "Summary Statement from the Theological Study Group," paper presented at the Consultation on Asian Women's Theology on Christology, Singapore, Novem-

ber 20-29, 1987. This consultation was sponsored by *In God's Image.* For more information on the conference, see *IGI* (December 1987-March 1988). The documents from the consultation were published in *IGI* during 1988-1989. (Hereafter referred to as Consultation on Asian Women's Theology—1987.)

2. Ibid., p. 1.

3. Ibid., p. 2.

4. Ibid.

5. Choi Man Ja, "Feminist Christology," Consultation on Asian Women's Theology—1987, p. 3.

6. Komol Arayapraatep, "Christology," Consultation on Asian Women's Theology—1987, p. 6.

7. This is the common teaching Asian women receive from the institutional, male-dominated churches in Asia. When I was a Sunday school teacher at a Korean church in Orange County, California, in 1983, I witnessed a Korean woman, who was a Bible teacher for a college student group, share her experience of death and resurrection of self in front of the entire congregation. She confessed how sinful she was in relation to her husband. She said that she was not able to obey her husband because she thought he was not reasonable and fair. So she argued with him a lot. One day her husband, who was a medical doctor, threw a kitchen knife at her out of anger during an argument. Fortunately the knife missed her and stuck into the wall behind her. At that point, she said, she experienced the love of God through the judgment of her husband. She believed then that as a wife she had to obey her husband as God's will. She witnessed to the congregation that her old self was *dead* and her new self was born through her husband's *love.* This woman concluded her statement with: "There have been no arguments and only peace in my family after I nailed myself on the cross and followed God's will." After her talk, the entire congregation responded to her with a very loud "Hallelujah!" This is only one example of "woman hate" in Asian churches. I have heard countless examples of women's oppression in the church from other Asian women through various church women's gatherings.

8. For more information on the missionary history of China, see Kwok Pui-lan, "The Emergence of Asian Feminist Consciousness on Culture and Theology" (Hong Kong: unpublished paper, 1988).

9. I know that there are conflicting views on the role of the missionaries in Asia. Some people think that their role was destructive and others believe it was positive. My view is that their role was primarily, though not exclusively, negative.

10. Lydia Lascano, "Women and the Christ Event," in *Proceedings: Asian Women's Consultation* (Manila: EATWOT, 1985), pp. 121-29.

11. Ibid., p. 123.

12. Ibid., p. 125.

13. Ibid.

14. Virginia Fabella, "Asian Women and Christology," *IGI* (September 1987), p. 15.

15. Choi, p. 6.

16. Ibid.

17. Park Soon Kyung, *Hankook Minjok Kwa Yeosung shinhak eu Kwajae* [*The Korean Nation and the Task of Women's Theology*], p. 50.

18. See Jurgette Honclada, "Notes on Women & Christ in Philippines," *IGI,* October 1985, pp. 13-19.

19. See Mary John Mananzan, "The Philipino Woman: Before and After the Spanish Conquest of the Philippines," in Mary J. Mananzan, ed., *Essays on Women* (Manila: Woman's Studies Program, Saint Scholastica's College, 1987), pp. 7-36.

20. Ibid.

21. Park Soon Kyung, *Hankook Minjok Kwa Yeosung Shinhak eu Kwajae* [*The Korean Nation and the Task of Women's Theology*], p. 47.

22. Ibid.

23. Ibid., p. 48.

24. Ibid.

25. Ibid., p. 49.

26. Ibid., p. 47.

27. Consultation on Asian Women's Theology—1987, p. 2.

28. Monica Melanchton, "Christology and Women," Consultation on Asian Women's Theology—1987.

29. Ibid., p. 1.

30. Ibid.

31. Ibid., p. 2.

32. Ibid., p. 4.

33. Ibid., p. 6. Note the contradictory theological position on the appropriation of the Hindu notion of God in Christian theology.

34. Lee Oo Chung, "Korean Cultural and Feminist Theology," *IGI* (September 1987), p. 36.

35. Ibid.

36. Ibid., p. 37.

37. Ibid.

38. Ibid.

39. Ibid., p. 38.

40. Ibid.

41. "Women and the Christ Event," in *Proceedings: Asian Women's Consultation* (Manila: EATWOT, 1985), p. 131.

42. Ibid.

43. Pauline Hensman, "Women and the Christ Event," in *Proceedings: Asian Women's Consultation* (Manila: EATWOT, 1985), p. 116.

44. Lascano, p. 121.

45. Ibid., p. 125.

46. Ibid., p. 127.

47. Ibid.

48. Ibid., p. 128.

49. Ibid.

50. Ibid.

51. Kwok, "God Weeps with Our Pain," in John Pobee and Bärbel von Wartenberg-Potter, eds., *New Eyes for Reading* (Oak Park, IL: Meyer Stone Books, 1988), p. 92.

52. Lee Oo Chung, "One Woman's Confession of Faith," in Pobee and von Wartenberg-Potter, p. 19.

53. Ibid.

54. Ibid.

55. Ibid., pp. 19-20.

56. Ibid., p. 20.

57. Ibid.

58. Marianne Katoppo, "Mother Jesus," in Alison O'Grady, ed., *Voices of Women* (Singapore: Asian Christian Women's Conference, 1978), p. 12.

59. Marianne Katoppo, *Compassionate and Free* (Maryknoll, NY: Orbis Books, 1980), p. 79.

60. Katoppo, "Mother Jesus," in O'Grady, p. 12.

61. Park Soon Kyung, *The Korean Nation and the Task of Women's Theology*, p. 51. See also James Cone, *God of the Oppressed* (New York: Harper and Row, 1975). Cone makes a similar argument. For Cone, Jesus is black because if Jesus represents oppressed humanity, Jesus must be black in our historical situation where black people are constantly crucified.

62. Choi, p. 8.

63. Ibid., p. 7.

64. Ibid., p. 6.

65. See Virginia Fabella, "Asian Women and Christology."

66. Ibid.

67. Ibid.

68. Suh Nam Dong, *In Search of Minjung Theology* (Seoul, Korea: Kankil Sa, 1983), pp. 355-56. Translation and emphasis mine.

69. Anonymous, "From Jaini Bi—With Love," in O'Grady, p. 11. The editor explains that the Jaini Bi stands for all people who suffer extreme deprivation in a seemingly uncaring world but who receive a spark of hope from humanitarian concerns and actions.

10

Jesus Christ in Black Theology

JAMES H. CONE

Christian theology begins and ends with Jesus Christ. He is the point of departure for everything to be said about God, humankind, and the world. That is why christology is the starting point of Karl Barth's *Dogmatics* and why Wolfhart Pannenberg says that "theology can clarify its Christian self-understanding only by a thematic and comprehensive involvement with Christological problems."[1] To speak of the Christian gospel is to speak of Jesus Christ who is the content of its message and without whom Christianity ceases to be. Therefore the answer to the question "What is the essence of Christianity?" can be given in the two words: Jesus Christ.

Because Jesus Christ is the focal point for everything that is said about the Christian gospel, it is necessary to investigate the meaning of his person and work in light of the black perspective. It is one thing to assert that he is the essence of the Christian gospel, and quite another to specify the meaning of his existence in relation to the slave ships that appeared on American shores. Unless his existence is analyzed in light of the oppressed of the land, we are still left wondering what his presence means for the auction block, the Underground Railroad, and contemporary manifestations of black power. ... It is therefore the task of black theology to make theology relevant to the black reality, asking, "What does Jesus Christ mean for the oppressed blacks of the land?"

The task of explicating the existence of Jesus Christ for blacks is not easy in a white society that uses Christianity as an instrument of oppression. White conservatives and liberals alike present images of a white Jesus that are completely alien to the liberation of the black community. Their Jesus is a mild, easy-going white American who can afford to mouth the luxuries

From *A Black Theology of Liberation* (Philadelphia: Lippincott Co., 1970; Maryknoll, N.Y.: Orbis Books, 1986), pp. 110-128.

of "love," "mercy," "long-suffering," and other white irrelevancies, because he has a multi-billion-dollar military force to protect him from the encroachments of the ghetto and the "communist conspiracy." But black existence is existence in a hostile world without the protection of the law. If Jesus Christ is to have any meaning for us, he must leave the security of the suburbs by joining blacks in their condition. What need have we for a white Jesus when we are not white but black? If Jesus Christ is white and not black, he is an oppressor, and we must kill him. The appearance of black theology means that the black community is now ready to do something about the white Jesus, so that he cannot get in the way of our revolution. . . .

THE HISTORICAL JESUS AND BLACK THEOLOGY

Black theology takes seriously the historical Jesus. We want to know who Jesus *was* because we believe that that is the only way to assess who he *is*. If we have no historical information about the character and behavior of that particular Galilean in the first century, then it is impossible to determine the mode of his existence now. Without some continuity between the historical Jesus and the kerygmatic Christ, the Christian gospel becomes nothing but the subjective reflections of the early Christian community. And if that is what Christianity is all about, we not only separate it from history, but we also allow every community the possibility of interpreting the kerygma according to its own existential situation. Although the situation is important, it is not the gospel. The gospel speaks *to* the situation.

Christianity believes, as Paul Tillich has suggested, that it has the answer to the existential character of the human condition. It is the function of theology to analyze the changeless gospel in such a way that it can be related to changing situations. But theology must be careful not to confuse the two. If the situation becomes paramount (i.e., identified with the gospel), then there are no checks to the community's existential fancies. Black theology also sees this as the chief error of white American religious thought, which allows the white condition to determine the meaning of Jesus. The historical Jesus must be taken seriously if we intend to avoid making Jesus into our own images.

Taking seriously the New Testament Jesus, black theology believes that the historical kernel is the manifestation of Jesus as the Oppressed One whose earthly existence was bound up with the oppressed of the land. This is not to deny that other emphases are present. Rather it is to say that whatever is said about Jesus' conduct, about the manifestation of the expectant eschatological future in the deeds and words of Jesus, or about his resurrection as the "ultimate confirmation of Jesus' claim to authority" (Pannenberg), it must serve to illuminate Jesus' sole reason for existence: to bind the wounds of the afflicted and to liberate those who are in prison. To understand the historical Jesus without seeing his identification with the poor as decisive is to misunderstand him and thus distort his historical person. And a proper theological analysis of Jesus' historical identification with the helpless is indispensable for our interpretation of the gospel today. Unless the contemporary oppressed know that the kerygmatic Christ is the real Jesus, to the extent that he was completely identified with the oppressed of his earthly ministry, they cannot know that their liberation is a continuation of his work.

THE CHARACTER OF THE NEW TESTAMENT JESUS

What evidence is there that Jesus' identification with the oppressed is the distinctive historical kernel in the gospels? How do we know that black theology is not forcing an alien contemporary black situation on the biblical sources? These questions are important, and cannot be waved aside by black theologians. Unless we can clearly articulate an image of Jesus that is consistent with the essence of the biblical message and at the same time relate it to the struggle for black liberation, black theology loses its reason for being. It is thus incumbent upon us to demonstrate the relationship between the historical Jesus and the oppressed, showing that the equation of the contemporary Christ with black power arises out of a serious encounter with the biblical revelation.

Black theology must show that the Reverend Albert Cleage's description of Jesus as the Black Messiah[2] is not the product of minds "distorted" by their own oppressed condition, but is rather the most meaningful christological statement in our time. Any other statement about Jesus Christ is at best irrelevant and at worst blasphemous.

1. *Birth.* The appearance of Jesus as the Oppressed One whose existence is identified exclusively with the oppressed of the land is symbolically characterized in his birth. He was born in a stable and cradled in a manger (the equivalent of a beer case in a ghetto alley), "because there was no room for them in the inn" (Luke 2:7). Although most biblical scholars rightly question the historical validity of the birth narratives in Matthew and Luke, the mythic value of these stories is important theologically. They undoubtedly reflect the early Christian community's *historical* knowledge of Jesus as a man who defined the meaning of his existence as being one with the poor and outcasts. The visit of the shepherds, the journey of the wise men, Herod's killing of the babies, the economic, social, and political unimportance of Mary and Joseph—all these features reflect the early community's image of the man Jesus. For them Jesus is certainly a unique person, but the uniqueness of his appearance reveals the Holy One's concern for the lonely and downtrodden. They are not simply Matthew and Luke's explanation of the origin of Jesus' messiahship, but also a portrayal of the significance of his messiahship.

Jesus' messiahship means that he is one of the humiliated and the abused, even in his birth. His eating with tax collectors and sinners, therefore, was not an accident and neither was it a later invention of the early church; rather it is an expression of the very being of God and thus a part of Jesus' purpose for being born.

2. *Baptism and Temptation.* The baptism (affirmed by most scholars as historical) also reveals Jesus' identification with the oppressed. According to the synoptic Gospels, John's baptism was for repentant sinners, an act which he believed provided an escape from God's messianic judgment. For Jesus to submit to John's baptism not only connects his ministry with John's but, more importantly, separates him from John. By being baptized, Jesus defines his existence as one with sinners and thus conveys the meaning of the coming kingdom. The kingdom is for the poor, not the rich; and it comes as an expression of God's love, not judgment. In baptism Jesus embraces the condition of sinners, affirming their existence as his own. He is one of them! After the baptism, the saying "Thou art my beloved Son; with thee I am well pleased" (Mark 1:11) expresses God's approval of that very definition of Jesus' person and work.

The temptation is a continuation of the theme already expressed in the baptism. As with the birth narratives, it is difficult to recover the event as it happened, but it would be difficult to deny that the narrative is intimately related to Jesus' self-portrayal of the character of his existence. The tempter's concern is to divert Jesus from the reality of his mission with the poor. Jesus' refusal to turn the stone into bread, or to worship the tempter, or to throw himself from the pinnacle of the temple (Luke 4:3-12) may be interpreted as his refusal to identify himself with any of the available modes of oppressive or self-glorifying power. His being in the world is as one of the humiliated, suffering poor.

3. *Ministry.* The Galilean ministry is an actual working out of the decision already expressed in his birth and reaffirmed at the baptism and temptation. Mark describes the implication of this decision: "Now after John was arrested, Jesus came into Galilee, preaching the gospel of God, and saying, 'The time is fulfilled, and the kingdom of God is at hand; repent and believe in the gospel' " (Mark 1:14-15).

New Testament scholars have spent many hours debating the meaning of this passage, which sometimes gives the average person the impression that there is a hidden meaning discernible only by seminary graduates. But the meaning is clear enough for those who are prepared for a radical decision about their movement in the world. Jesus' proclamation of the kingdom is an announcement of God's decision about oppressed humankind. "The time is fulfilled, and the kingdom of God is at hand"—that is, slavery is about to end, because the reign of God displaces all false authorities. To "repent and believe in the gospel" is to recognize the importance of the hour at hand and to accept the reality of the new age by participating in it as it is revealed in the words and work of Jesus. The kingdom is Jesus, whose relationship to God and human beings is defined by his words and work.

From this it is clear that Jesus' restriction of the kingdom to the poor has far-reaching implications for our understanding of the gospel message. It is interesting, if not surprising, to watch white New Testament scholars explain away the real theological significance of Jesus' teachings on the kingdom and the poor. Nearly always they are at pains to emphasize that Jesus did not necessarily mean the economically poor but rather, as Matthew says, "the poor in spirit." Then they proceed to point out the exceptions: Joseph of Arimathea was a rich man (Matthew 27:57) and he was "a good and righteous man" (Luke 23:50). There are also instances of Jesus' association with the wealthy; and Zacchaeus did not promise to give up *all* his goods but only *half.* As one biblical scholar has put it:

> It was not so much the possession of riches as one's attitude towards them and the use one makes of them which was the special object of Jesus' teachings and this is true of the biblical teachings as a whole. Jesus does not condemn private property, nor is he a social reformer in any primary sense; he is concerned with men's motives and hearts.[3]

With all due respect to erudite New Testament scholars and the excellent work that has been done in this field, I cannot help but conclude that they are "straining out a gnat and swallowing a camel"! It is this kind of false interpretation that leads to the oppression of the poor. As long as oppressors can be sure that the gospel does not threaten their social, economic, and political security, they can enslave others in the name of Jesus Christ. The history of Christendom, at least from the time of Constantine, is a history of human enslavement; and even today, white "Christians" see little contradiction between wealth and the Christian gospel.

It seems clear that the overwhelming weight of biblical teaching, especially the prophetic tradition in which Jesus stood unambiguously, is upon God's unqualified identification with the poor precisely because they are poor. The kingdom of God is for the helpless, because they have no security in this world. We see this emphasis in the repeated condemnation of the rich, notably in the Sermon on the Mount, and in Jesus' exclusive identification of his ministry with sinners. The kingdom demands the surrender of one's whole life. How is it possible to be rich, seeing others in a state of economic deprivation, and at the same time insist that one has complete trust in God? Again, how can it be said that Jesus was not primarily a social reformer but "concerned with men's motives and hearts," when the kingdom itself strikes across all boundaries—social, economic, and political?

Jesus' teaching about the kingdom is the most radical, revolutionary aspect of his message. It involves the totality of a person's existence in the world and what that means in an oppressive society. To repent is to affirm the reality of the kingdom by refusing to live on the basis of any definition except according to the kingdom. Nothing else matters! The kingdom, then, is the rule of God breaking in like a ray of light, usurping the powers that enslave human lives. That is why exorcisms are so prominent in Jesus' ministry. They are a visible manifestation of the presence of the kingdom. "If it is by the finger of God that I cast out demons, then the kingdom of God has come upon you" (Luke 11:20).

Jesus is the Oppressed One whose work is that of liberating humanity from inhumanity. Through him the oppressed are set free to be what they are. This and this alone is the meaning of his *finality* which has been camouflaged in debates about his humanity and divinity.

4. *Death and Resurrection.* The death and resurrection of Jesus are the consummation of his earthly ministry with the poor. The Christian church rightly focuses on these events as decisive for an adequate theological interpretation of Jesus' historical ministry. Rudolf Bultmann pointed this out convincingly. Although post-Bultmannians generally do not agree with Bultmann's extreme skepticism regarding history, they do agree on his assessment of the importance of the death-resurrection event in shaping the Christian view of the earthly ministry of Jesus. The Jesus of history is not simply a figure of the past but the Christ of today as interpreted by the theological significance of the death-resurrection event.

Black theology certainly agrees with this emphasis on the cross and resurrection. The Gospels are not biographies of Jesus; they are *gospel* – that is, good news about what God has done in the life, death, and resurrection of Jesus. This must be the focus of christological thinking.

The theological significance of the cross and resurrection is what makes the life of Jesus more than just the life of a good man who happened to like the poor. *The finality of Jesus lies in the totality of his existence in complete freedom as the Oppressed One who reveals through his death and resurrection that God is present in all dimensions of human liberation.* His death is the revelation of the freedom of God, taking upon himself the totality of human oppression; his resurrection is the disclosure that God is not defeated by oppression but transforms it into the possibility of freedom.

For men and women who live in an oppressive society this means that they do not have to behave as if *death* is the ultimate. God in Christ has set us free from death, and we can now live without worrying about social ostracism, economic insecurity, or political tyranny. "In Christ the immortal God has tasted death and in so doing ... destroyed death"[4] (compare Hebrews 2:14ff.).

Christian freedom is the recognition that Christ has conquered death. Man no longer has to be afraid of dying. To live as if death has the last word is to be enslaved and thus controlled by the forces of destruction. The free are the oppressed who say no to an oppressor, in spite of the threat of death, because God has said yes to them, thereby placing them in a state of freedom. They can now deny any values that separate them from the reality of their new being.

Moltmann is correct when he speaks of the resurrection as the "symbol of protest":

To believe in the resurrection transforms faith from a deliverance from the world into an initiative that changes the world and makes those who believe into wordly, personal, social and political witnesses to God's righteousness and freedom in the midst of a repressive society and an unredeemed world. In this, faith comes to historical self-consciousness and to the recognition of its eschatological task within history.[5]

THE BLACK CHRIST

What is the significance of the historical and resurrected Jesus for our times? The answer to this question must focus on both the meaning of the historical Jesus and the contemporary significance of the resurrection. It is impossible to gloss over either one of these emphases and still retain the gospel message.

Focusing on the historical Jesus means that black theology recognizes *history* as an indispensable foundation of christology. We are not free to make Jesus what we wish him to be at certain moments of existence. He *is* who he *was,* and we know who he was through a critical, historical evaluation of the New Testament Jesus. Black theology takes seriously Pannenberg's comment that "faith primarily has to do with what Jesus was."[6]

To focus on the contemporary significance of the resurrection means that we do not take Pannenberg's comment on the historical Jesus as seriously as he does. No matter how seriously we take the carpenter from Nazareth, there is still the existential necessity to relate his person to black persons, asking, "What is his relevance to the black community today?" In this sense, unlike Pannenberg, we say that the soteriological value of Jesus' person must finally determine our christology. It is the oppressed community in the situation of liberation that determines the meaning and scope of Jesus. We know who Jesus *was* and *is* when we encounter the brutality of oppression in his community as it seeks to be what it is, in accordance with his resurrection.

The christological significance of Jesus is not an abstract question to be solved by intellectual debates among seminary professors. The meaning of Jesus is an existential question. We know who he is when our own lives are placed in a situation of oppression, and we thus have to make a decision for or against our condition. To say no to oppression and yes to liberation is to encounter the existential significance of the Resurrected One. He is the Liberator *par excellence* whose very presence makes persons sell all that they have and follow him.

Now what does this mean for blacks in America today? How are they to interpret the christological significance of the Resurrected One in such a way that his person will be existentially relevant to their oppressed condition? The black community is an oppressed community primarily because of its blackness; hence the christological importance of Jesus must be found in his blackness. If he is not black as we are, then the resurrection has little significance for our times. Indeed, if he cannot be what we are, we cannot be who he is. Our being with him is dependent on his being with us in the oppressed black condition, revealing to us what is necessary for our liberation.

The definition of Jesus as black is crucial for christology if we truly believe in his continued presence today. Taking our clue from the historical Jesus who is pictured in the New Testament as the Oppressed One, what else, except blackness, could adequately tell us the meaning of his presence today? Any statement about Jesus today that fails to consider blackness as the *decisive* factor about his person is a denial of the New Testament message. The life, death, and resurrection of Jesus reveal that he is the man for others, disclosing to them what is necessary for their liberation from oppression. If this is true, then Jesus Christ must be black so that blacks can know that their liberation is his liberation.

The black Jesus is also an important theological symbol for an analysis of Christ's presence today because we must make decisions about where he is at work in the world. Is his presence synonymous with the work of the oppressed or the oppressors, blacks or whites? Is he to be found among the wretched or among the rich?

Of course clever white theologians would say that it is not either/or. Rather he is to be found somewhere in between, a little black and a little white. Such an analysis is not only irrelevant for our times but also irrelevant for the time of the historical Jesus. Jesus was not for and against the poor, for and against the rich. He was for the poor and against the rich, for the weak and against the strong. Who can read the New Testament and fail to see that Jesus took sides and accepted freely the possibility of being misunderstood?

If the historical Jesus is any clue for an analysis of the contemporary Christ, then he must be where human beings are enslaved. To speak of him is to speak of the liberation of the oppressed. In a society that defines blackness as evil and whiteness as good, the theological significance of Jesus is found in the possibility of human liberation through blackness. Jesus is the black Christ!

Concretely, to speak of the presence of Christ today means focusing on the forces of liberation in the black community. Value perspectives must be reshaped in the light of what aids the self-determination of black persons. The definition of Christ as black means that he represents the complete opposite of the values of white culture. He is the center of a black Copernican revolution.

Black theology seeks to do in American theology what Copernicus did to thinking about the physical universe. Inasmuch as this country has achieved its sense of moral and religious idealism by oppressing blacks, the black Christ leads the warfare against the white assault on blackness by striking at white values and white religion. The black Copernican revolution means extolling as good what whites have ignored or regarded as evil.

The blackness of Christ clarifies the definition of him as the *Incarnate* One. In him God becomes oppressed humanity and thus reveals that the achievement of full humanity is consistent with divine being. The human being was not created to be a slave, and the appearance of God in Christ gives us the possibility of freedom. By becoming a black person, God discloses that blackness is not what the world says it is. Blackness is a manifestation of the being of God in that it reveals that neither divinity nor humanity reside in white definitions but in liberation from captivity.

The black Christ is he who threatens the structure of evil as seen in white society, rebelling against it, thereby becoming the embodiment of what the black community knows that it must become. Because he has become black as we are, we now know what black empowerment is. It is blacks determining the way they are going to behave in the world. It is refusing to allow white society to place strictures on black existence as if their having guns mean that blacks are supposed to cool it.

Black empowerment is the black community in defiance, knowing that he who has become one of them is far more important than threats from white officials. The black Christ is he who nourishes the rebellious impulse in blacks so that at the appointed time the black community can respond collectively to the white community as a corporate "bad nigger," lashing out at the enemy of humankind.

It is to be expected that some whites will resent the christological formulation of the black Christ, either by ignoring it or by viewing it as too narrow to include the universal note of the gospel. It will be difficult for whites to deny the whiteness of their existence and affirm the oppressed black Christ. But the concept of black, which includes both what the world means by oppression and what the gospel means by liberation, is the only concept that has any real significance today. If Christ is not black, then who is he? We could say that he is the son of God, son of Man, messiah, lord, son of David, and a host of other titles. The difficulty with these titles is not that they fail to describe the person of Christ, but they are first-century titles. To cling to them without asking, "What appropriate symbol do these titles refer to today?" is to miss the significance of them altogether.

What is striking about the New Testament names of Jesus is the dimension of liberation embedded in them. For example, Jesus Christ as Lord, a postresurrection title, emphasizes his complete authority over all creation. Everyone is subject to him. The Lord is the "ruler," "commander," he who has all authority. If "Jesus is Lord," as one of the earliest baptismal creeds of the church puts it, then what does this say about black and white relationships in America? The meaning is perhaps too obvious for comment. It means simply that whites do not have authority over blacks. Our loyalty belongs only to him who has become like us in everything, especially blackness. To take seriously the lordship of Christ or his sonship or messiahship is to see him as the sole criterion for authentic existence.

If Jesus is the Suffering Servant of God, he is an oppressed being who has taken on that very form of human existence that is responsible for human misery. What we need to ask is this: "What is the form of humanity that accounts for human suffering in our society? What is it, except blackness?" If Christ is truly the Suffering Servant of God who takes upon himself the suffering of his people, thereby reestablishing the covenant of God, then he must be black.

To get at the meaning of this and not get bogged down in racial emotionalism, we need only ask, "Is it possible to talk about suffering in America without talking about the meaning of blackness? Can we really believe that Christ is the Suffering Servant par excellence if he is not black?" Black theology contends that blackness is the only symbol that cannot be overlooked if we are going to take seriously the christological significance of Jesus Christ.

But some whites will ask, "Does black theology believe that Jesus was *really* black?" It seems to me that the *literal* color of Jesus is irrelevant, as are the different shades of blackness in America. Generally speaking, blacks are not oppressed on the basis of the depths of their blackness. "Light" blacks are oppressed just as much as "dark" blacks. But as it happens, *Jesus was not white* in any sense of the word, literally or theologically. Therefore, Albert Cleage is not too far wrong when he describes Jesus as a black Jew; and he is certainly on solid theological grounds when he describes Christ as the Black Messiah.

The importance of the concept of the black Christ is that it expresses the *concreteness* of Jesus' continued presence today. If we do not translate the first-century titles into symbols that are relevant today, then we run the danger that Bultmann is so concerned about: Jesus becomes merely a figure of past history. To make Jesus just a figure of yesterday is to deny the real importance of the preaching of the early church. He is not dead but resurrected and is alive in the world today. Like yesterday, he has taken upon himself the misery of his people, becoming for them what is needed for their liberation.

To be a disciple of the black Christ is to become black with him. Looting, burning, or the destruction of white property are not *primary* concerns. Such matters can only be decided by the oppressed themselves who are seeking to develop their images of the black Christ. What is primary is that blacks must refuse to let whites define what is appropriate for the black community. Just as white slaveholders in the nineteenth century said that questioning slavery was an invasion of their property rights, so today they use the same line of reasoning in reference to black self-determination. But Nat Turner had no scruples on this issue; and blacks today are beginning to see themselves in a new image. We believe in the manifestation of the black Christ, and our encounter with him defines our values. This means that blacks are *free* to do what they have to in order to affirm their humanity.

THE KINGDOM OF GOD AND THE BLACK CHRIST

The appearance of Jesus as the black Christ also means that the black revolution is God's kingdom becoming a reality in America. According to the New Testament, the kingdom is a historical event. It is what happens to persons when their being is confronted with the reality of God's historical liberation of the oppressed. To see the kingdom is to see a happening, and we are thus placed in a situation of decision—we say either yes or no to the liberation struggle.

The kingdom is not an attainment of material security, nor is it mystical communion with the divine. It has to do with the *quality* of one's existence in which a person realizes that *persons* are more important than property. When blacks behave as if the values of this world have no significance, it means that they perceive the irruption of God's kingdom. The kingdom of God is a *black* happening. It is black persons saying no to whitey, forming caucuses and advancing into white confrontation. It is a beautiful thing to see blacks shaking loose the chains of white approval, and it can only mean that they know that there is a way of living that does not involve the destruction of their personhood. This is the kingdom of God.

For Jesus, repentance is a precondition for entrance into the kingdom. But it should be pointed out that repentance has nothing to do with morality or religious piety in the white sense.

Günther Bornkamm's analysis of Jesus' call to repentance is relevant here. To repent, says Bornkamm, is "to lay hold on the salvation which is already at hand, and to give up everything for it."[7] It means recognizing the importance of the kingdom-event and casting one's lot with it. The kingdom is God's own event and inherent in its appearance is the invitation to renounce everything and join it. That is why Jesus said:

> If your hand or your foot causes you to sin, cut it off and throw it from you; it is better for you to enter life maimed or lame than with two hands or two feet to be thrown into eternal fire. And if your eye causes you to sin, pluck it out and throw it from you; it is better for you to enter life with one eye than with two eyes to be thrown into the hell of fire [Matthew 18:8-9].

According to Bornkamm:

> Repentance comes by means of grace. Those who sit at the table of the rich lord are the poor, the cripples, the blind and lame, not those who are already half-cured. The tax collectors and sinners with whom Jesus sits at meat are not asked first about the state of their moral improvement. . . . The extent to which all talk of the conditions which man must fulfill before grace is accorded him is here silenced, as

shown by the parables of the lost sheep and the lost coin, which tell only of the finding of what was lost, and in this very manner describe the joy in heaven "over one sinner who repents" (Luke 15:7, 10). So little is repentance a human action preparing the way for grace that it can be placed on the level of being found.[8]

The kingdom is what God does and repentance arises solely as a response to God's liberation.

The event of the kingdom today is the liberation struggle in the black community. It is where persons are suffering and dying for want of human dignity. It is thus incumbent upon all to see the event for what it is—God's kingdom. This is what conversion means. Blacks are being converted because they see in the events around them the coming of the Lord, and will not be scared into closing their eyes to it. Black identity is too important; it is like the pearl of great value, which a person buys only by selling all that he or she has (Matthew 13:44-46).

Of course, whites can say that they fail to see the significance of this black phenomenon. But loss of sight is characteristic of the appearance of the kingdom. Not everyone recognizes the person from Nazareth as the incarnate One who came to liberate the human race. Who could possibly imagine that the Holy One of Israel would condescend to the level of a carpenter? Only those with eyes of faith could see that in that person God was confronting the reality of the human condition. There is no other sign save the words and deeds of Jesus himself. If an encounter with him does not convince persons that God is present, then they will never know, except in that awful moment when perfect awareness is fatally bound up with irreversible judgment.

That is why Jesus compared the kingdom with a mustard seed and with yeast in dough. Both show a small, apparently insignificant beginning but a radical, revolutionary ending. The seed grows to a large tree, and the bread can feed many hungry persons. So it is with the kingdom; because of its small beginning, some viewers do not readily perceive what is actually happening.

The black revolution is a continuation of that small kingdom. Whites do not recognize what is happening, and they are thus unable to deal with it. For most whites in power, the black community is a nuisance—something to be considered only when the natives get restless. But what white America fails to realize is the explosive nature of the kingdom. Although its beginning is small, it will have far-reaching effects not only on the black community but on the white community as well. Now is the time to make decisions about loyalties, because soon it will be too late. Shall we or shall we not join the black revolutionary kingdom?

To enter the kingdom is to enter the state of salvation, the condition of blessedness. Historically it appears that "salvation" is Paul's translation of Jesus' phrase "kingdom of God." But, oh, how the word "salvation" has been beaten and battered in nineteen centuries of Christian verbiage! What can salvation possibly mean for oppressed blacks in America? Is it a kind of spiritual juice, squirted into the life of the dispirited that somehow enable them to withstand the brutality of oppressors because they know that heaven is waiting for them? Certainly, this is what rulers would like the oppressed to believe.

In most societies where political oppression is acute and religion is related to the state, salvation is interpreted always in ways that do not threaten the security of the existing government. Sometimes salvation takes the form of abstract, intellectual analysis or private mystical communion with the divine. The "hope" that is offered the oppressed is not the possibility of changing their earthly condition but a longing for the next life. With the poor counting on salvation in the next life, oppressors can humiliate and exploit without fear of reprisal. That is why Karl Marx called religion the opiate of the people. It is an open question whether he was right in his evaluation; but he was correct in identifying the intention of oppressors. They promote religion because it can be an effective tool for enslavement.

The history of the black church is a case in point. At first, white "Christian" slaveholders in America did not allow their slaves to be baptized, because Christianity supposedly enfranchised them. But because the white church was having few converts among blacks, it proceeded to assure slaveholders that baptism had nothing to do with civil freedom. In fact, many white ministers assured slave masters that Christianity would make for better slaves. With that assurance, the masters began to introduce Christianity to blacks, confident that it would make blacks more obedient. But many blacks were able to appropriate white Christianity to their own condition by turning it into a religion of liberation. The emergence of the "invisible institution" (secret church) among the slaves of the south, the organization of the African Methodist Episcopal Church (1816) and the African Methodist Episcopal Zion Church (1821), together with other black independent religious institutions, and their involvement in the antislavery movement, show that black religionists did see through the fake white Christianity of the period.

For the pre-Civil War black church, salvation involved more than longing for the next life. Being saved was also a present reality that placed persons in a dimension of freedom so that earthly injustice became intolerable. That was why Nat Turner, a Baptist preacher, had visions of God that involved his own election to be the Moses of his people, leading it from the house of bondage. After his insurrection black preachers were outlawed in many parts of the south.

Unfortunately, the post-Civil War black church fell into the white trick of interpreting salvation in terms similar to those of white oppressors. Salvation became white: an objective act of Christ in which God "washes" away our sins in order to prepare us for a new life in heaven. The resurgence of the black church in civil rights and the creation of a black theology represent an attempt of the black community to see salvation in the light of its own earthly liberation.

The interpretation of salvation as liberation from bondage is certainly consistent with the biblical view:

> In the Old Testament salvation is expressed by a word which has the root meaning of "to be wide" or "spacious," "to develop without hindrance" and thus ultimately "to have victory in battle" (I Sam. 14:45).[9]

To be saved meant that one's enemies have been conquered, and the savior is the one who has the power to gain victory:

> He who needs salvation is one who has been threatened or oppressed, and his salvation consists in deliverance from danger and tyranny or rescue from imminent peril (I Sam. 4:3, 7:8, 9:16). To save another is to communicate to him one's own prevailing strength (Job 26:2), to give him the power to maintain the necessary strength.[10]

In Israel, God is the Savior par excellence. Beginning with the exodus, God's righteousness is for those who are weak and helpless. "The mighty work of God, in which his righteousness is manifested, is in saving the humble ... the poor and the dispirited." The same is true in the New Testament. Salvation is release from slavery and admission to freedom (Galatians 5:1, II Corinthians 3 :17), saying no to the fear of principalities and yes to the powers of liberty (I John 4:18). This is not to deny that salvation is a future reality; but it is also hope that focuses on the present.

Today the oppressed are the inhabitants of black ghettos, Amerindian reservations, Hispanic barrios, and other places where whiteness has created misery. To participate in God's salvation is to cooperate with the black Christ as he liberates his people from bondage. Salvation, then, primarily has to do with earthly reality and the injustice inflicted on those who are helpless and poor. To see the salvation of God is to see this people rise up against its oppressors, demanding that justice become a reality *now,* not tomorrow. It is the oppressed serving warning that they "ain't gonna take no more of this bullshit, but a new day is coming and it ain't going to be like today." The new day is the presence of the black Christ as expressed in the liberation of the black community.

NOTES

1. Wolfhart Pannenberg, *Jesus — God and Man,* trans. by L. L. Wilkins and Duane A. Priebe (Philadelphia: The Westminster Press, 1968), p. 11.

2. See this book published by Sheed and Ward, 1968. I should point out that

my intention is not to suggest that my view of Christ is identical with Reverend Cleage's. Our perspectives do differ at points, but more importantly, we share in common the belief that *Christ is black.* It is also appropriate to express my indebtedness to his excellent work in this area.

3. Alan Richardson, "Poor," in Alan Richardson, ed., *Theological Word Book of the Bible* (New York: The Macmillan Co., 1960), pp. 168-69.

4. Richardson, "Death," in ibid., p. 60.

5. "Toward a Political Hermeneutic of the Gospel," *Union Theological Seminary Quarterly Review,* vol. 23, no. 4 (Summer 1968), pp. 211, 312.

6. Pannenberg, *Jesus,* p. 28.

7. Günther Bornkamm, *Jesus of Nazareth* (New York: Harper and Row, 1961), p. 82.

8. Ibid., pp. 83-84.

9. Ibid.

10. Ibid.

Questions for Discussion

1. Take a few minutes to think about the images of Jesus that you grew up with. Describe them. How do the images of Jesus presented in these articles compare with the images you grew up with?

2. Who do you recognize as poor in our world today? Who are the poor in the world of your daily life? Who are "those persecuted in the cause of right" today?

3. Liberation theologians argue that our relationship with God is expressed in our relationship with the poor. Can you remember any biblical passages that would suggest that they are right? Can we think of ourselves as being "close to God" if we are remote from those who suffer unjustly?

4. What is Jon Sobrino saying was of ultimate significance to Jesus? Do you agree? Do you think people tend to shape their image of Jesus by what is important to *them*? What if, in all honesty, what is of ultimate significance to you is quite different than what was significant to Jesus?

5. The articles by Chung Hyun Kyung and Anne Nasimiyu-Wasike point to some of the problems faced by Asian and African women at the bottom of the economic ladder and how these women experience Jesus. Do you think that groups of women in your own country who differ by race and/or economic background might have different images of Jesus?

6. Do you think that men and women's images of Jesus differ from one another?

7. How do you respond to the image of the Black Christ?

PART III

THE CHURCH IN SOLIDARITY: LIBERATION ECCLESIOLOGY

Introduction

MARILYN J. LEGGE

Christians today live in an ecumenical era, struggling to respond creatively to the issues and challenges of the modern world. The church has always sought to be faithful to the gospel in diverse contexts. Today the role or mission of the church is being increasingly redefined in relation to such issues as secularism, social justice, and the question of religious pluralism. Liberation theology, in its ecclesiology, or theological reflection on the church, is contributing to this process of rediscovery by relating the church both to the kingdom of God and to the world in a new and dynamic way.

Most biblical scholars in this century have accepted the judgment that the kingdom of God was the central theme of Jesus' preaching. But, as Albert Loisy remarked in a famous statement, if Jesus preached the kingdom, it was the church that came. This has posed a central problem for ecclesiology, namely, the relation between the church, the world, and Jesus' mission of inaugurating the reign of God. More broadly, what is the church and what is it for?

This introduction will look at the ways liberation theologians have addressed the question, beginning with a brief review of the origins and central images of the church as recorded in the New Testament before moving on to the emergence and ultimate crisis of "Christendom." We will then focus on the roots and location of the liberating church, the issue of pluralism, and finally on the question of ministry.

The readings that accompany this introduction to liberation ecclesiology reflect a wide range of contexts where the church has identified itself with those who are suffering and their struggles for full humanity—in Peru, Brazil, and Mexico, in Malaysia, in the Christian feminist community in the United States, and in South Africa. We will discover that distinctive ways of being a liberating church emerge wherever the church is oriented toward the kingdom of God. To be disciples of Jesus is to respond to the message that in Jesus God has come among us and that the kingdom has come near and been made concrete in the world. This does not mean that the church can be identified with the kingdom. Rather the church belongs "between the times," between the time when the kingdom of God was proclaimed and took form in Jesus, and the time to come, the fulfillment of that promise of abundant life at the end of all time. As an eschatological or ultimate symbol of liberated existence, the church comes into conflict with privatized faith, with oppressive power, and with exclusivistic theologies. Each essay raises the urgent question: What is the church and who does it stand with today? In dialogue with each voice we are invited and challenged to discern how we might engage that question in our own lives and contexts.

JESUS AND THE CHURCH'S MISSION

While Jesus did not intend to found a new religion called Christianity, the early church evolved as a necessary and appropriate development from Jesus' preaching of the reign of God. We turn to the New Testament to discover the origins of ecclesiology where the church was born at Pentecost with the gift of God's Spirit. The church always realizes itself in a twofold sense: as an event of God's grace and as an institution existing to minister in particular historical contexts. What was definitive in shaping the Jesus movement into a new community of faith was the experience of the living presence of the risen Christ after his crucifixion; Jesus had not left his disciples behind but was somehow present among them. What the disciples experienced was the reality Jesus embodied—the kingdom of God, a new way of being together in the world where love and mutual service, rather than hostility and alienation, reigned. As for the original Jesus movement, so for the church today: the criterion is the kingdom of God.

As a first-century Jew, Jesus clarified and embodied what it meant for people to live out their lives under conditions of the reign of God. He preached a radical, alternative understanding of what it meant to be "religious" or "spiritual." Religion for Jesus meant living in loyalty to God over against all other competing loyalties. God created the cosmos, including humanity as male and female in the image of God, and declared it good; nothing was outside the love of God. Jesus, therefore, came to save the whole world, not just the church. Thus the church is not to exist unto itself but to serve the world in realizing the promise of the kingdom as it is realized in "abundance of life" (Jn 10:11). When Jesus proclaimed the nearness of the kingdom of God, or the *basileia,* he offered an image that was basically communal and social. That is, God's rule called forth a new human community for the whole world based on love, liberation, inclusion, and gratitude.

Jesus gathered disciples who were to carry the good news of the inbreaking of the kingdom of God. In Greek *ekklesia* simply means "assembly," a word which New Testament writers used to designate "those called of God" or "the people or congregation of God." The kind of people Jesus called into table fellowship were mainly social outcasts. He initiated a kind of radical family life in which whoever does the will of God is a member (Mt 3:3–35). Thus Jesus refused to sanction a separate or restricted idea of the people of God. Rather, he showed that any divisions are between those who do God's will and those who oppose it. The new community is a people of God open to the presence and action of God—open to the poor, to women and children, to the disabled, to Jews, gentiles, and slaves.

Members of the early Christian community sought to live Jesus' radical commandment to love God and their neighbors as themselves. "The Way" that he recommended and embodied has been much disputed, but certain features are clearly recognized. Jesus invited people to change their lifestyles, their cultural ethos, and their communities to realize the peace offered by communion with God and neighbor. He spoke to those who were ill or physically maimed, people who saw themselves as invalids or outcasts, and offered them a healing that was social as well as physical or spiritual. To rich people who asked what his teaching meant for them he said they would have to turn their lives around, to change their entire way of relating to others if they were to enter the kingdom of God. Jesus called his closest followers friends. He taught them to honor God as they lived and cared for one another, and he sent them out to do as he did—calling on people to live in concert with the inbreaking of the kingdom of God.

BIBLICAL IMAGES OF CHURCH

An array of different images of the church can be found in the New Testament; scholars record nearly one hundred. Central among these are the church as the new creation, the body of Christ, and the people of God. These images reflect an understanding of the movement Jesus initiated as inclusive of everyone: lepers, women, tax collectors, prostitutes, the sick and injured, Samaritans, and other social and religious outcasts; all were included in his circle of friends and disciples. One joined this open-ended and inclusive circle by professing the radical commitment to follow Jesus, by being baptized in God's name, and by participating in the eucharist.

This authentically new creation is described by the apostle Paul as something that happens in history: "When anyone is united in Christ, there is a new act of creation; the old order has passed away, and a new order has begun" (2 Cor 5:17). The good news of being accepted as we are by God is envisioned in this understanding of church as new creation, a community of inclusive participation and effective purpose for the redemption of the world.

Another significant image used for the church in the New Testament period is the body of Christ: "For just as the body has many members, and all the members of the body, though many, are one body, so it is with Christ. For by one Spirit we were baptized into one body—Jews or Greeks, slaves or free ... Now you are Christ's body, and each of you a limb or organ of it" (1 Cor 12:12, 27). In other words, the community of Jesus' disciples is called into relationships of mutual honor and accountability— not a hierarchy based on power and domination, but a cooperative sharing of talents and spiritual gifts toward the creation of an integrated, healed, and whole body. This understanding speaks of the importance of diversity, of the way people at different stages of Christian faithfulness can contribute different gifts for the sake of the kingdom. Whether it was new creation, the body of Christ, or the people of God, the early church struggled to remain faithful to God and a vision of the whole world's salvation, praying "Thy Kingdom Come."

The church arises out of this proclamation and organizes itself in terms of the priorities of the kingdom. To participate in the cause of the kingdom, then, the church worships God and works for the historical liberation of the whole people of God. There will always be a tension between the church and the kingdom, because they can never be equated. This tension remains a source of prophetic critique within the church and a source of renewal, as each generation of Christians wrestles with the call to be a sign and instrument of the reign of God for the sake of the world.

CHRISTENDOM AND ITS CRISIS

Gradually, by the end of the first century, the church found its faith had shifted from proclaiming the coming of the kingdom to proclaiming Jesus as the Christ. The immediate expectations for the return of Christ were eventually projected onto Christ's future return. This shift in vision, combined with historical factors, led the way toward the era of Christendom. Here the church understood itself as the sole vehicle of the reign of God. The world, therefore, was to be christianized and contained by the church as the only means of salvation.

In the Nicene Creed of 325 C.E. we find the classic marks of the church: "We believe in the one, holy, catholic, and apostolic church." Within the mentality of Christendom, it was thought that there were only two kinds of people: those who had accepted faith in Christ and those who had rejected it. Because the church regarded itself as the exclusive mediator of salvation, it saw no problem in furthering its own life and teachings in alliance with civic power. It thus pursued a form of mission whereby the church, understood as a self-enclosed entity set apart from the world, was to incorporate the rest of society into its realm.

What gave force to this perspective was the conversion of the Roman Emperor Constantine and the edict of 381 C.E. which established Christianity as the official religion of the Roman Empire. As the church developed into a powerful institution over the next twelve centuries, the credal marks of true church were operative amidst diverse historical contexts. They functioned to safeguard *unity,* in the sense of uniformity, since there was "no salvation outside the church"; *catholicity,* as the proper name of the one and same official church identified as Roman Catholic and planted all over the (known) world; *holiness,* understood in terms of orthodox piety; and *apostolicity,* in the sense of the succession of bishops founded on a direct link with the first apostles.

While challenging the abuses of medieval Christianity, neither the Protestant Reformation of the sixteenth century nor the Counter-Reformation within the Catholic church, dislodged the premise of Christendom, namely, that the world lacked any autonomous or authentic reality outside its relationship to the church. Thus, despite the splitting of Christendom into many Christian groups, the ecclesiocentric perspective of Christendom remained intact: to be for or against the church meant to be for or against Christ. In the words of the famous formula, already cited, outside the church there was no salvation.

With the advent of the modern age, this mentality came under gradual assault. Secular philosophers of the Enlightenment began to explain the world in purely rational terms without reference to divine reality and they recommended remaking society in accordance with this rational principle. No longer was Christendom's message and means of salvation accepted as the only or best one; instead, the triumphalistic attitude of the church was challenged by the modern claim that autonomous reason, independent from the church's authority and applied to human problems in history, could emancipate society from its misery.

For the Catholic church, the most significant and creative response to the challenges of the modern age came with the Second Vatican Council convened by Pope John XXIII in 1962. The first general council in almost a century, and only the second since the Reformation, Vatican II gave profound new direction to the self-understanding of the church.

The Council significantly modified the traditional stance of the church toward the world and modernity. Abandoning the attitude of triumphalism and arrogance that had characterized previous church documents, the Council spoke warmly of such principles as freedom of conscience, democracy, and the presence of the Holy Spirit in the advance of justice and human rights in modern history. Holiness demanded participation in the constructive process of history; the identity of the church was to be redefined in terms of openness to the world for the healing of the total social order. Vatican II asked Christians to engage themselves in social action, and criticized purely individualistic responses. The Council recognized the emergence of a "new humanism" where human beings were called to a vocation of shared responsibility for history.

The biblical model of the church as People of God, emerged as a new image at the Council. This image, which highlighted the equality of all Christians in baptism, supplanted previous, more clerical and institutional models of the church, and made possible a deeper expression of solidarity with the entire human family, all called to be people of God. Instead of emphasis on the separation between the church and the world, one vocation was affirmed: the calling to all people to grow, unfold, and be self-determining under the influence of divine grace.

The Second Vatican Council has been described appropriately as opening up the windows and letting fresh air into the church. It clearly distinguished the church from the kingdom of God while at the same time identifying the church with the work of the kingdom in and for the world. This shift was new and exciting. At the same time, however, many of the Council's insights tended to reflect the values and perspectives of the dominant Western middle-class church. In its positive and optimistic view of history and modernity the Council was less successful in reflecting the experience and struggles of the world's poor.

One cause of the Council's limitations was the fact that it had left out too many voices, particularly those of women and the poor. Nevertheless, the direction established by Vatican II was toward a new global identity for the church. It was based on another new image of the church as *sacrament,* that is, a visible sign and instrument of salvation in Christ through the Holy Spirit. This image placed the church within the horizon of salvation but not as its sole vehicle. The image of the church as sacrament opened up the mission of the church to encountering God in history wherever people, whether Christian or non-Christian, were engaged in advancing the kingdom vision, characterized by communion with God and unity among men and women. This reality contributed a foundation to the emergence of liberation theology.

LOCATION OF THE LIBERATING CHURCH: SOLIDARITY WITH THE POOR

The church in liberation theology functions not at the center of the world but, as Gustavo Gutiérrez insists, "uncentered," in solidarity with all those who are marginalized. Recent decades have seen the rebirth of the church in its orientation to work with God for the healing and liberation of the world. Among the most compelling signs of the rebirth of the church are found today in Christian communities of the destitute, of indigenous, impoverished, black, and third world peoples, and also in ecumenical movements in solidarity with them. This liberating church encourages Christians to move away from Christendom's tendency to reduce salvific action to the church alone and thus to be preoccupied with the status and security of the church itself. Instead, the church must move out of the center of attention in order to immerse itself in the broader plan of salvation, the reign of God intended for the whole world.

A new idea of church has developed wherein Christian communities reform traditional church structures and forms of ministry on the basis of kingdom principles witnessed in the early Jesus movement. This model of church accepts that unity cannot be based simply on the structures themselves but on the basis of discipleship. In its commitment to continuing on the "Way" of radical discipleship, the church becomes the people of God, the people called to incarnate God's love for the world in history. Liberation theologies have built on the theological conviction that God is at work in the world, as well as in the church, and that the church's mandate is to recognize the kingdom of God both among us and before us, as both already and not yet fulfilled, already known and tasted, and yet still to come in fullness. It is in this "in-between" time that the church finds its mission.

The church in liberation theology is rooted in a faith in God and an option for the poor. The suffering of the poor is a sign of everything that contradicts the will of God in history, for their suffering is not simply a matter of accident. It is in large part due to the way the world's resources are controlled. A liberating church recognizes a network of domination and oppression that functions around the world to stifle freedom and keep the majority of human beings from meaningful work and participation in shaping their destinies according to God's good creation. Because the salvation present in Jesus Christ includes the liberation of people from every dehumanizing condition, social structures that promote domination by some at the expense of others is an injustice, a form of social sin.

Theologically, the church learns the meaning of the fact that God's covenant is with all God's people when it hears the cry of the poor. The Word of God is addressed to every human being and God's intention is for all to be co-creators in love of God and neighbor. No one is excluded from this kingdom vision. The presence of the poor is a sign of the inclusiveness of God's care. The poor, therefore, evangelize the whole world because God's approaching reign, offered especially to them, expresses most fully the meaning of God's love: those at the bottom of the social structure realize the grace of being accepted for who they are, not for what they own or possess. As the gospel proclaims God's judgment on human sin and God's promise of new life, so a church of the poor committed to the gospel of love and justice will stand against relations of domination, exploitation, and oppression. Thus, a church of the poor does not offer a vague universal approach to helping the poor with aid while ignoring poverty. It is not a church *for* the poor. Nor is it merely a part of the wider church which co-exists with equal rights within it. Rather, it is a church whose life, identity, and mission are radically determined by the presence of the poor, and their struggles, anxieties, and hopes.

For middle-class Christians the call to the church becomes in a new way a call to conversion and solidarity. For a liberating church follows a double commitment to the poor: to look at society from the perspective of the victims and to express solidarity with them in public action. The operative vision of this model of church is the promise of "a land flowing with milk and honey" wherein God's kingdom will come, God's will of redemption will be done, including the liberation of people from conditions of oppression. In this way the church's solidarity is with the entire human community, but particularly with the poor and marginalized, as God calls it into the world as friend and servant.

THE CHURCH IN A PLURALISTIC WORLD

The church in liberation theology embraces a mission to oppose sin and celebrate the gift of life in both church and world. That the gospel is intended for everyone, however, does not imply that everyone is meant to belong to the Christian church. It does mean that we are called to become a people of God and that as we come to define our own identity in relation to the poor we must simultaneously make room for the self-defining identities of others with whom we share the world. A liberating church repents of its long history of treating other faiths and ideologies as the enemy, as inferior, as unworthy of dialogue. The ecumenical movement of the twentieth century has awakened the church to define itself differently, this time in dialogue with the ecumenical aspirations of other faith communities.

As we have seen, the church in our time lives in a post-Christendom world. That is, the church can no longer assume its position as the "sacred canopy" of the social order. In the midst of religious pluralism, the church can become "holy" to the extent that it actualizes through worship and action the reconciliation of humanity with God. It can become "one" by embracing its true ecumenical mission to transform dehumanizing social systems and relations into ones that reflect dignity, friendship, and justice as the fullest expressions of love. It can become "apostolic" by empowering the laity and entering into solidarity with suffering humanity. It can become "catholic" by giving up any imperialistic tendencies and cooperating with respect for religious differences, especially in the struggles for social justice.

The church which pursues a liberating option around the world may indeed be a minority, but the Bible offers abundant witness to the power of things that are seemingly small and insignificant. The community of faithful, according to the parables of Jesus in Matthew 5:13-16 and Luke 13:18-21, is compared to yeast or salt or light in the world. The kingdom of God is like a mustard seed, tenacious, productive, vulnerable. These images encourage the church to honor the mystery of God as well as the multiplicity of cultures and communities, to envision a church that is called by God to be open to the Spirit that blows where it wills (Jn 3:8).

The criterion for identifying the "true" church remains the kingdom of God. The church arises out of this proclamation and organizes itself in that direction, uncentered in relation to the world and human history. The task of a church which seeks liberation is to bear the burden of suffering with other people, to struggle with others, whether Christian or not, for greater justice, and to strengthen the bonds that unite people, despite differences in religion, culture, and racial origin, and in doing so to become a sign of God's grace in the world.

All of this has profound implications for the understanding of ministry in the church. Traditionally, the understanding of Christian ministry in the church has been defined by Jesus' three designations as prophet, priest, and king. Maria Harris, in her book, *Fashion Me a People,* puts an interesting spin on these different vocations. She suggests that the church has a *prophetic* vocation in the ministries of justice and concern for others. It has a *priestly* vocation in the ministries of healing, blessing, teaching, and remembering. And it has a *political* vocation to shape and reshape the forms of church and public life so that all are welcome. Shared among a church with a popular base, these ministries function together for pastoral empowerment, to develop a fresh awareness of the people's own resources for ministry, and to create a whole people of God at work to incarnate God's love and justice in a suffering world.

PREVIEW OF OUR TEXTS

The following readings have been chosen to illustrate a range of the ecclesial struggles and signs of hope in our world. The first selection by Peruvian priest Gustavo Gutiérrez describes the "uncentering" of the church as the process of recognizing the church as a sacrament of salvation, the efficacious sign and instrument of God's grace in the world. The idea of church as sacrament, heralded at Vatican II, indicates also that the church exists for the world, and not the world for the church, as in Christendom. Gutiérrez shows how this has ushered in a radically new understanding of church, one that firmly grounds the eschatological vision of the coming kingdom in history.

A global movement in the church is discovering anew what it means to be church, how to be the place where God's purposes for freedom and love become visible in history. For Gutiérrez the church is, therefore, a "sacrament of history." As a sign of God's saving presence in the world, the church must denounce and withdraw its support from all social systems of oppressive power, while simultaneously announcing and orienting itself toward the coming of God's reign, where community, justice, and freedom manifest in history God's love and purpose for the world.

The second selection by Dominique Barbé from Brazil describes the elements that have created the church base communities. These groups are essentially the church of poor people in rural areas and in marginal districts of urban centers. Throughout Brazil there are some 80,000 base Christian communities. Barbé outlines how a church base community is formed and what its tasks are, especially in a situation of oppression.

The roles of priests and the laity in this context are related to the scriptural understanding of Jesus' followers as agents of the kingdom of God. The base communities have nurtured thousands of ministries over the years in building up the mission of the church. In this essay, stages of creating a base Christian community are discussed: living together by sharing in a common community as friends; joining together in prayer; restoring a voice to the people by having them tell stories of their deepest needs and hopes; moving toward collective action for freedom, in the neighborhood, in popular movements, and in broader actions designed to create participatory social structures. Barbé affirms the nature of base Christian communities as places for celebrating the faith and strengthening communal resolve to transform the world.

In our next selection, Maria Pilar Aquino comments on the contributions of women to the base Christian community movement. A Roman Catholic theologian originally from Mexico and now working in Hispanic ministries in California, she adds a much needed voice to the struggle of the church for justice. In light of the presence of the poor that has renewed the church's mission and identity, Pilar Aquino discusses specific needs and demands of oppressed women. Because women are the backbone of the church, the option for the poor is an option for women. This essay describes how women in base Christian communities enable the church to be an authentic agent of life for the poor, the majority of whom are women. In particular, the church is challenged by women to repent of its sexism, which thwarts women's gifts and wisdom, and to function as a sanctuary for those in need of protection under conditions of repression and persecution.

The fourth selection is by a Malaysian Protestant, Yong Ting Jin, who has worked in Hong Kong as the Asia-Pacific Regional Secretary of the World Student Christian Movement. This essay is written from the perspective of women and challenges the church to consider how the church has lost its true essence. She deals not only with the oppressive features of the church, but also with how it is liberating for women when it responds to their challenges and contributions. She urges the church to be faithful by practicing inclusiveness—in new lifestyles, ecumenical work, a new exercise of power, and a new way of doing theological reflection amidst church involvement in the various dimensions of the people's struggle.

In our fifth essay Mary Hunt, a Catholic theologian and co-director of Women's Alliance for Theology, Ethics and Ritual in Washington, D.C., continues with the theme of women and the church. Hunt describes the nature of the movement known as "women-church." Women-church initially developed in North America and Europe as Christian women have struggled for self-identity, survival, and liberation in a patriarchal society and church. When women confront the inequality and rejection they experience on the basis of their gender, and when they experience God's sustaining grace and liberating presence in the midst of their struggles for justice, freedom, and wholeness for all, women-church is born. Hunt discusses women-church as global, ecumenical, feminist base communities of justice-seeking friends who engage in ritual, sacrament, and solidarity.

The sixth and final selection comes from Charles Villa-Vicencio, a white anti-apartheid activist and professor of religious studies at the University of Cape Town, South Africa. Villa-Vicencio was interviewed by Jim Wallis, the editor of *Sojourners* magazine, about the reality of the church in South Africa. In the past some churches endorsed apartheid, the majority adopted a reformist stance, with only a minority of others actively siding with the anti-apartheid struggle. Villa-Vicencio believes that the church will not really confront the state until such time as the church has rediscovered itself.

At the time of the essay's publication, the author was acutely aware that the churches were divided. Since then, significant developments have taken place in South Africa, including the release of Nelson Mandela and the establishment of multi-racial coalitions and consultations to move toward reconstruction. However, Villa-Vicencio criticizes the churches that protest but do not translate church statements into political action. Like all churches in contexts of poverty and oppression, the situation of conflict is generating a transformation of the church. Hope for the church in South Africa lies in its becoming a liberating church, "not only in solidarity with the poor, but a church of the poor—allowing, enabling, and empowering the poor to take control of the church and to be church, giving it identity, giving it a program, and giving it direction. That's the challenge facing the churches."

The following essays introduce a range of images appropriate for a liberative ecclesiology: the church as sign and sacrament of God's grace in the world, as church base community, as sanctuary, as a redemptive community, as women-church, and as agent of God's liberation. In a pluralistic and struggling world, we badly need such an abundance of images.

11

The Church: Sacrament of History

GUSTAVO GUTIÉRREZ

Because the Church has inherited its structures and its lifestyle from the past, it finds itself today somewhat out of step with the history which confronts it. But what is called for is not simply a renewal and adaptation of pastoral methods. It is rather a question of a new ecclesial consciousness and a redefinition of the task of the Church in a world in which it is not only *present,* but of which it *forms a part* more than it suspected in the past. In this new consciousness and redefinition, intraecclesial problems take a second place.

UNIVERSAL SACRAMENT OF SALVATION

The unqualified affirmation of the universal will of salvation has radically changed the way of conceiving the mission of the Church in the world. It seems clear today that the purpose of the Church is not to save in the sense of "guaranteeing heaven."[1] The work of salvation is a reality which occurs in history. This work gives to the historical becoming of humankind its profound unity and its deepest meaning. It is only by starting from this unity and meaning that we can establish the distinctions and clarifications which can lead us to a new understanding of the mission of the Church. The Lord is the Sower who arises at dawn to sow the field of historical reality before we establish our distinctions. Distinctions can be useful for what Liégé calls "the new initiatives of God in the history of men," but as he himself says, "Too great a use of them, however, threatens to destroy the sense of a vocation to a single fulfillment toward which God has not ceased to lead the world, whose source he is."[2] The meaning and the fruit-

From *A Theology of Liberation*, 15th Anniv. Edition (Maryknoll, N.Y.: 1988), pp. 143–48, 150–56. Translated by Sister Caridad Inda and John Eagleson.

fulness of the ecclesial task will be clear only when they are situated within the context of the plan of salvation. In doing this we must avoid reducing the salvific work to the action of the Church. All our ecclesiology will depend on the kind of relationship that we establish between the two.

A New Ecclesiological Perspective

The perspective we have indicated presupposes an "uncentering" of the Church, for the Church must cease considering itself as the exclusive place of salvation and orient itself towards a new and radical service of people. It also presupposes a new awareness that the action of Christ and his Spirit is the true hinge of the plan of salvation.

Indeed, the Church of the *first centuries* lived spontaneously in this way. Its minority status in society and the consequent pressure that the proximity of the non-Christian world exercised on it made it quite sensitive to the action of Christ beyond its frontiers, that is, to the totality of his redemptive work. This explains why, for example, the great Christian authors of that time affirmed without qualification human liberty in religious matters as a natural and human right and declared that the state is incompetent to intervene in this area. Because they had confidence in the possibility of salvation at work in everyone, they saw liberty not so much as a risk of wandering from the path as the necessary condition for finding the path and arriving at a genuine encounter with the Lord.

The situation of the Christian community changed in *the fourth century.* Instead of being marginated and attacked, Christianity was now tolerated (Edict of Milan, A.D. 313) and quickly became the religion of the Roman state (Decree of Thessalonica, A.D. 381). The proclamation of the gospel message was then protected by the support of political authority, and the Christianization of the world of that time received a powerful impulse. This rapid advance of Christianity brought about a change in the manner of conceiving the relationship of humankind to salvation. It began to be thought that there were only two kinds of people: those who have accepted faith in Christ and those who have culpably rejected it. The Fathers continued to teach the doctrine of the universal will of salvation and held that this could not occur without free acceptance on the part of human beings. But they asserted that there was no longer any excuse for ignorance of the Savior, for thanks to the ministry of the Church, the voice of the Gospel had come in one way or another to all humans. Neither Jews nor gentiles had any excuse. These ideas, which were presented with hesitation and even anguish in the fourth and fifth centuries, gradually gained ground. By the Middle Ages, when the Church was coextensive with the known world of that time and deeply pervaded it, Christians had the vital experience of security and tranquility that "outside the Church there is no salvation." *To be for or against Christ came to be fully identified with being for or against the Church.* Therefore it is not strange that there was no longer any mention of bits of truth which could be found beyond the frontiers of the Church; there was no longer any world outside the Church. The Church was regarded as the sole repository of religious truth. In a spontaneous and inevitable fashion there arose an ecclesiocentric perspective which centered more and more on the life and reflection of the Church—and continues to do so even up to the present time.

From that time on, therefore, there was a subtle displacement of religious liberty as "a human and natural right" of all humans by "the liberty of the act of faith"; henceforth, the right of liberty in religious matters would be synonymous with the right not to be coerced by the forced imposition of the Christian faith. In a parallel fashion there occurred another important displacement: no longer was it a question of the "incompetence" of political power in religious matters; rather it was a question of the state's "tolerance"—which presupposed an "option" for the truth—toward religious error. The reason for these two displacements is the same: the position of strength of a Church which had begun to focus on itself, to ally itself with civil power, and to consider itself as the exclusive repository of salvific truth.

This condition of the Church began to change in the *modern period,* with the internal rupture of Christendom and the discovery of new peoples. But at the beginning of this period the ecclesiocentric perspective persisted, with a few exceptions. In the matter of religious liberty, which we have focused on here, it was the period of "religious tolerance": what Thomas Aquinas considered valid for the Jews was extended to the descendants of Christians who had "culpably" separated themselves from the Church. In the nineteenth century religious toleration gave rise to the by-product of the theory of the thesis and the hypothesis; this theory sought to respond to the ideas born in the French Revolution by giving a new impulse to the development of toleration. But fundamentally the condition continued being the same: salvific truth could be found only in the Church. It is for this reason that "modern freedoms" endangered the eternal destiny of humankind.

The effects of the new historical situation in which the Church found itself began to be felt more strongly in the nineteenth century and even more so in recent decades. Vatican II did not hesitate to place itself in the line of a full affirmation of the universal will of salvation and to put an end to the anachronistic theological and pastoral consequences deduced from the ecclesiocentrism which we have already mentioned. This explains the change of attitude regarding religious liberty. The declaration dedicated to this subject tried to achieve a consensus by placing itself simply on the level of the dignity of the human person. But this position implies a change of position with regard to deep theological questions having to do with the role of the Church in the encounter between God and humankind.

We might speak here of a return to the posture of the Church in the first centuries. Without being inexact, however, this affirmation tends to schematize the process. There is never a pure and simple regression. The process which began in the fourth century was not simply an "accident." It was a long and laborious learning experience. And that experience forms part of the contemporary ecclesial consciousness; it is a factor which explains many phenomena today. It also cautions us against what might happen again. What was spontaneously and intuitively expressed in the first centuries must manifest itself today in a more reflective and critical fashion.

Sacrament and Sign

Thanks to the process which we have just reviewed, Vatican II was able to set forth the outlines of a new ecclesiological perspective. And it did this almost surprisingly by speaking of the Church as a sacrament.[3] This is undoubtedly one of the most important and permanent contributions of the Council. The notion of sacrament enables us to think of the Church within the horizon of salvific work and in terms radically different from those of the ecclesiocentric emphasis. The Council itself did not place itself totally in this line of thinking. Many of the texts still reveal the burden of a heavy heritage; they timidly point to a way out from this turning in of the Church on itself, without always accomplishing this. But what must be emphasized is that in the midst of the Council itself, over which hovered an ecclesiocentric perspective, new elements arose which allowed for a reflection which broke with this perspective and was more in accord with the real challenges to the Christian faith of today.

In theology the term *sacramentum* has two closely related meanings. Initially it was used to translate the Greek work *misterion*. According to Paul, *mystery* means *the fulfillment and the manifestation of the salvific plan:* "the secret hidden for long ages and through many generations, but now disclosed" (Col. 1:26). The Gospel is, therefore, "that divine secret kept in silence for long ages but now disclosed . . . made known to all nations, to bring them to faith and obedience" (Rom. 16:25-26). This mystery is the love of the Father, who "loved the world so much that he gave his only Son" (John 3:16) in order to call all humans, in the Spirit, to communion with God. Human beings are called together, as a community and not as separate individuals, to participate in the life of the Trinitarian community, to enter into the circuit of love that unites the persons of the Trinity.[4] This is a love which "builds up human society in history."[5] The fulfillment and the manifestation of the will of the Father occur in a privileged fashion in Christ, who is called therefore the "mystery of God" (Col. 2:22; see also Col. 1:27; 4:3; Eph. 3:3; 1 Tim. 3:16).[6] For the same reason Sacred Scripture, the Church, and the liturgical rites were designated by the first Christian generations by the term *mystery,* and by its Latin translation, *sacrament.* In the sacrament the salvific plan is fulfilled and revealed; that is, it is made present among humans and for humans. But at the same time, it is through the sacrament that humans encounter God. This is an encounter *in* history, not because God comes *from* history, but because history comes from God. The sacrament is thus the efficacious revelation of the call to communion with God and to the unity of all humankind.

This is the primordial meaning of the term *sacrament* and it is in this way that it is used in the first centuries of the Church. At the beginning of the third century, however, Tertullian introduced a nuance which gradually gave rise to a second meaning derived from the first. This African Father began to use the term *sacrament* to designate the rites of Baptism and the Eucharist. Gradually the two terms, *mystery* and *sacrament,* became distinct. The first referred more to the doctrinal mysteries; the second designated what we commonly call sacraments today. The theology of the Middle Ages recovered the meaning of sacrament, in the strict sense, in the formula *efficacious sign of grace.* The sign marks the character of visibility of the sacrament, by means of which there occurs an effective personal encounter of God and the human person. But the sign transmits a reality from beyond itself, in this case the grace of communion, which is the reason for and the result of this encounter. This communion is also an intrahistorical reality.

To call the Church the "visible sacrament of this saving unity" (*Lumen gentium,* no. 9) is to define it in relation to the plan of salvation, whose fulfillment in history the Church reveals and signifies to the human race. A visible sign, the Church imparts to reality "union with God" and "the unity of all humankind" (*Lumen gentium,* no. 1). The Church can be understood only in relation to the reality which it announces to humankind. Its existence is not "for itself," but rather "for others." Its center is outside itself, it is in the work of Christ and his Spirit. It is constituted by the Spirit as "the universal sacrament of salvation" (*Lumen gentium,* no. 48); outside of the action of the Spirit which leads the universe and history towards its fullness in Christ, the Church is nothing. Even more, the Church does not authentically attain consciousness of itself except in the perception of this total presence of Christ and his Spirit in humanity. The mediation of the consciousness of the "other" — of the world in which this presence occurs — is the indispensable precondition of its own consciousness as community-sign. Any attempt to avoid this mediation can only lead the Church to a false perception of itself — to an ecclesiocentric consciousness.

Through the persons who explicitly accept his Word, the Lord reveals the world to itself. He rescues it from anonymity and enables it to know the ultimate meaning of its historical future and the value of every human act. But by the same token the Church must turn to the world, in which Christ and his Spirit are present and active; the Church must allow itself to be inhabited and evangelized by the world. It has been said for this reason that a theology of the Church in the world should be complemented by "a theology of the world in the Church."[7] This dialectical relationship is implied in the emphasis on the Church as sacrament. This puts us on the track of a new way of conceiving the relationship between the historical Church and the world. The Church is not a non-world; it is humanity itself attentive to the Word. It is the People of God which lives in history and is orientated toward the future promised by the Lord. It is, as Teilhard de Chardin said, the "reflectively Christified portion of the world." The Church-world relationship thus should be seen not in spacial terms, but rather in dynamic and temporal ones.

As a sacramental community, the Church should signify in its own internal structure the salvation whose fulfillment it announces. Its organization ought to serve this task. As a sign of the liberation of humankind and history, the Church itself in its concrete existence ought to be a place of liberation. A sign should be clear and understandable. If we conceive of the Church as a sacrament of the salvation of the world, then it has all the more obligation to manifest in its visible structures the message that it bears. Since the Church is not an end in itself, it finds its meaning in its capacity to signify the reality in function of which it exists. Outside of this reality the Church is nothing; because of it the Church is always provisional; and it is towards the fulfillment of this reality that the Church is oriented: this reality is the Kingdom of God which has already begun in history.[8] The break with an unjust social order and the search for new ecclesial structures—in which the most dynamic sectors of the Christian community are engaged—have their basis in this ecclesiological perspective. We are moving towards forms of presence and structure of the Church the radical newness of which can barely be discerned on the basis of our present experience. This trend, at its best and healthiest, is not a fad; nor is it due to professional nonconformists. Rather it has its roots in a profound fidelity to the Church as sacrament of the unity and salvation of humankind and in the conviction that its only support should be the Word which liberates.

We must recognize, nevertheless, that the ecclesiocentric point of view is abandoned more rapidly in the realm of a certain theological reflection than in the concrete attitudes of the majority of the Christian community. This presents not a few difficulties, for what is most important is what happens at this second level. To dedicate oneself to intraecclesial problems—as is often done in certain forms of protest in the Church, especially in the developed countries—is to miss the point regarding a true renewal of the Church. For this renewal cannot be achieved in any deep sense except on the basis of an effective awareness of the world and a real commitment to it. Changes in the Church will be made on the basis of such awareness and commitment. To seek anxiously after changes themselves is to pose the question in terms of survival. But this is not the question. The point is not to survive, but to serve. The rest will be given.

In Latin America the world in which the Christian community must live and celebrate its eschatological hope is the world of social revolution; the Church's task must be defined in relation to this. Its fidelity to the Gospel leaves it no alternative: the Church must be the visible sign of the presence of the Lord within the aspiration for liberation and the struggle for a more human and just society. Only in this way will the message of love which the Church bears be made credible and efficacious. . . .

DENUNCIATION AND ANNUNCIATION

The primary task of the Church, as we have said, is to celebrate with joy the salvific action of the Lord in history. In the creation of fellowship implied and signified by this celebration, the Church—taken as a whole— plays a role which is unique, but varies according to historical circumstances.

In Latin America to be Church today means to take a clear position regarding both the present state of social injustice and the revolutionary process which is attempting to abolish that injustice and build a more human order. The first step is to recognize that in reality a stand has already been taken: the Church is tied to the prevailing social system. In many places the Church contributes to creating "a Christian order" and to giving a kind of sacred character to a situation which is not only alienating but is the worst kind of violence—a situation which pits the powerful against the weak. The protection which the Church receives from the social class which is the beneficiary and the defender of the prevailing capitalist society in Latin America has made the institutional Church into a part of the system and the Christian message into a part of the dominant ideology. Any claim to noninvolvement in politics—a banner recently hoisted by conservative sectors—is nothing but a subterfuge to keep things as they are. The mission of the Church cannot be defined in the abstract. Its historical and social coordinates, its here and now, have a bearing not only on the adequacy of its pastoral methods. They also should be at the very heart of theological reflection.

The Church—with variations according to different countries—has an obvious social influence in Latin America. Without overestimating it, we must recognize that numerous facts have demonstrated this influence, even up to the present day. This influence has contributed, and continues to contribute to supporting the established order. But this is no longer the entire picture. The situation has begun to change. The change is slow and still very fragile, but in this change are involved growing and active minorities of the Latin American Christian community. The process is not irreversible, but it is gradually gaining strength. It is still afflicted with many ambiguities, but the initial experiences are beginning to provide the criteria by which these ambiguities can be resolved. Within these groups—as might have been expected—there has arisen a question; on its answer will depend to a large degree the concrete path to be followed. The question is: Should the change consist in the Church's using its social influence to effect the necessary transformations? Some fear a kind of "Constantinianism of the Left," and believe that the Church should divest itself of every vestige of political power. This fear is opportune because it points out a genuine risk which we must keep in mind. But we believe that the best way to achieve this divestment of power is precisely by resolutely casting our lot with the oppressed and the exploited in the struggle for a more just society. The groups that control economic and political power will not forgive the Church for this. They will withdraw their support, which is the principal source of the ambiguous social prestige which the Church enjoys in Latin America today. Indeed, this has already begun. Moreover, formulated in this way the question is somewhat artificial. How can the Church preach the Word, incarnated where the pulse of Latin American history throbs, without putting this social influence at stake? How can it perform a disappearing act with the situation which—with all its ambiguities—is the Church's own? How can it denounce the unjust order of the continent and announce the Gospel outside of the concrete position which it has today in Latin American society? Indeed, it is not a question of whether the Church should or should not use its influence in the Latin American revolutionary process. Rather, the question is in what direction and for what purpose is it going to use its influence: for or against the established order, to preserve the social prestige which comes with its ties to the groups in power or to free itself from that prestige with a break from these groups and with genuine service to the oppressed? It is a question of social realism, of becoming aware of an already given situation, to start from it, and to modify it; it is not a question of creating that situation. The situation is already there and is the concrete, historical framework for the task of the Latin American Church.

Within this framework the Latin American Church must make the prophetic *denunciation* of every dehumanizing situation, which is contrary to fellowship, justice, and liberty. At the same time it must criticize every sacralization of oppressive structures to which the Church itself might have contributed. Its denunciation must be public, for its position in Latin American society is public. This denunciation may be one of the few voices— and at times the only one—which can be raised in the midst of a country submitted to repression. In this critical and creative confrontation of its faith with historical realities—a task whose roots must be in the hope in the future promised by God—the Church must go to the very causes of the situation and not be content with pointing out and attending to certain of its consequences. . . . In Latin America this denunciation must represent a radical critique of the present order, which means that the Church must also criticize itself as an integral part of this order. This horizon will allow the Church to break out of its narrow enclosure of intraecclesial problems by placing these problems in their true context—the total society and the broad perspective of commitment in a world of revolutionary turmoil. . . .

The denunciation, however, is achieved by confronting a given situation with the reality which is *announced*: the love of the Father which calls all persons in Christ and through the action of the Spirit to union among themselves and communion with him. To announce the Gospel is to pro-

claim that the love of God is present in the historical becoming of humankind. It is to make known that there is no human act which cannot in the
last instance be defined in relation to Christ. To preach the Good News is
for the Church to be a sacrament of history, to fulfill its role as community —
a sign of the convocation of all humankind by God. It is to announce the
coming of the Kingdom. The Gospel message reveals, without any evasions,
what is at the root of social injustice: the rupture of the fellowship based
on our being offspring of the Father; the Gospel reveals the fundamental
alienation which lies below every other human alienation. In this way, evangelization is a powerful factor in personalization. Because of it persons
become aware of the profound meaning of their historical existence and
live an active and creative hope in the fulfillment of the fellowship that
they seek with all their strength.

Moreover, the personalization stimulated by the annunciation of the
Gospel can take on — in cases like Latin America — very particular and
demanding forms. If a situation of injustice and exploitation is incompatible
with the coming of the Kingdom, the Word which announces this coming
ought normally to point out this incompatibility. This means that the people
who hear this message and live in these conditions by the mere fact of
hearing it should perceive themselves as oppressed and feel impelled to
seek their own liberation. Very concretely, they should "feel their hunger"
and become aware that this hunger is due to a situation which the Gospel
repudiates. The annunciation of the Gospel thus has a conscienticizing
function, or in other words, a politicizing function. But this is made real
and meaningful only by living and announcing the Gospel from within a
commitment to liberation, only in concrete, effective solidarity with people
and exploited social classes. Only by participating in their struggles can we
understand the implications of the gospel message and make it have an
impact on history. The preaching of the Word will be empty and ahistorical
if it tries to avoid this dimension. . . .

The concrete measures for effecting the denunciation and the annunciation will be discerned little by little. It will be necessary to study carefully
in a *permanent* fashion the signs of the times (*Gaudium et spes,* no. 4),
responding to specific situations without claiming to adopt at every step
positions valid for all eternity. There are moments in which we will advance
only by trial and error. It is difficult to establish ahead of time — as we have
perhaps tried to do for a long time — the specific guidelines which ought to
determine the behavior of the Church, taken as a whole, in these questions.
The Church should rise to the demands of the moment with whatever lights
it has at that moment and with the will to be faithful to the Gospel. Some
chapters of theology can be written only afterwards.

But the incertitude and apprenticeship involved in this task should not
lead us to disregard the urgency and necessity of taking stands or to forget
what is permanent — that the Gospel annunciation opens human history to
the future promised by God and reveals God's present work. On the one

hand, this annunciation will indicate that in every achievement of fellowship and justice among humans there is a step toward total communion. By the same token, it will indicate the incomplete and provisional character of any and every human achievement. The Gospel will fulfill this function based on a comprehensive vision of humankind and history and not on partial focuses, which have their own proper and effective instruments of criticism. The prophetic character of the Christian message "always works from an eschatological option and affirmation. According to it, history—as long as it has not achieved its eschatological end—will not achieve its total maturity. Therefore every historical period always has new possibilities before it."[9] On the other hand, by affirming that human fellowship is possible and that it will indeed be achieved, the annunciation of the Gospel will inspire and radicalize the commitment of the Christian in history. In history and only in history is the gift of the love of God believed, loved, and hoped for. Every attempt to evade the struggle against alienation and the violence of the powerful and for a more just and more human world is the greatest infidelity to God. To know God is to work for justice. There is no other path to reach God.

NOTES

1. The theme has been studied especially in missionary circles. See the provocative article of Joseph Comblin, "Le but de la mission: sauver l'homme," *Spiritus* 9, no. 34 (May 1968): 171-79.

2. "Church of the World," in the work written in collaboration with Nikos A. Nissiotis and Philip Maury, *Discerning the Times: The Church in Today's World*, trans. Sister Agnes Cunningham, SSCM (Techny, Illinois: Divine Word Publications, 1968), p. 150.

3. In this regard the most important texts are *Lumen gentium*, nos. 1 and 48; see also nos. 9 and 59; *Gaudium et spes*, no. 45; *Sacrosanctum concillium*, nos. 5 and 26; and *Ad gentes*, no. 9.

4. The decree *Ad gentes*, in one of the texts of greatest theological importance of Vatican II, links closely the plan of salvation and the Church's task in that plan to the Trinitarian missions (nos. 1-5).

5. Juan Luis Segundo, *Nuestra idea de Dios* (Buenos Aires: Lohlé, 1970), p. 91; English version, *Our Idea of God*, 1974, was published by Orbis Books as one in the series entitled *A Theology for Artisans of a New Humanity*.

6. See Edward Schillebeeckx, *Christ, The Sacrament of the Encounter with God* (New York: Sheed and Ward, 1963).

7. Clement, "Ensayo de lectura," *Iglesia en el mundo*, p. 663.

8. "The Church, of only she be rightly understood, is living always on the proclamation of her own provisional status and of her historically advancing elimination in the coming Kingdom of God" (Karl Rahner, "The Church and the Parousia of Christ"; in *Theological Investigations*, vol. 6 [Baltimore: Helicon Press, 1969], p. 298).

9. Lucio Gera, "Reflexión teológica," *Sacerdotes para el Tercer Mundo* (Buenos Aires: Ed. del Movimiento, 1970), p. 141. Later he writes, "Prophecy not only

desacralizes every place, temple, race, or nation; it also desacralizes every time. It does not set up as the final and definitive goal any empire that supplants another, any level of civilization—no matter how Jewish or Christian it might be—or any political, economic, or social system" (p. 142).

12

Church Base Communities

DOMINIQUE BARBÉ

THE CONCEPT OF CHURCH BASE COMMUNITY

Although church base communities exist on other continents, it is in Latin America that they have acquired their key status in the contemporary church. These communities are defined by the three parts of the name.

As *communities,* church base communities are groups of human size, that is, of a size wherein one can learn the name and the history of each member (generally numbering between 20 and 150 persons). In the countryside, the communities average more members than in the city. In the city, the poor, over and above their economic poverty, are uprooted persons, from every corner of the country, who do not know each other. Furthermore, in the city the working schedules are so inhuman that the time available for meeting is much less. In the countryside often, though not always, the misery is greater, but more *time* is available; the church is the sole place for meeting.

The life of a base community is intense. In it the members jointly take on the essential struggles for survival or for the improvement of living — the struggle for water, for clinics, for sewers. Above all is the struggle for land, in the city as well as in the countryside; for in the city, land on which to build a house or squatters' land on which to establish a *barraco* are the objects of ceaseless fighting. There are struggles for job training, for daycare centers, in opposition to police violence, for the rehabilitation of young people on drugs or in armed gangs, on behalf of families who arrive destitute from the interior of the country, for the defense of local traditions and popular festivals, against the increase of the cost of living in support of strikes. The list goes on and on. It should be understood that these base

From *Grace and Power: Base Communities and Nonviolence in Brazil* (Maryknoll, N.Y.: Orbis Books, 1987), pp. 88-106. Translated by John Pairman Brown.

communities are not "communes": they hardly ever reach the point of a
full sharing of goods or of common meals.

Still there exists a minimum of community structures: a coordination
team elected or chosen, usually renewable; a common fund; a yearly and
monthly program; regular general assemblies; several gatherings each week.
The intra-church tasks (assisting at the sacraments, liturgical celebrations,
catechesis, biblical groups) and the extra-church tasks (people's struggles
in the *bairro* or factories) are taken by laypeople. The same persons may
take responsibility both for tasks called "religious" and for tasks designated
as human or political betterment; the same one who gives the Bible instruc-
tion or who preaches at the Mass may also be the chief union activist.
Theologically, we call these "charisma" or "ministries": a particular gift
from God to one of God's children (a charism) corresponds to a task (a
ministry), which is taken on for the good of the collectivity. There is no
"division of tasks" properly speaking, even though much time is spent in
organizational meetings. It is practice that reveals the gifts of each one,
and there is no delegation of power as such from the community. Whoever
is able to do so takes responsibility for the community meeting by taking
account of each one's competence and putting order into the gifts. If certain
ones are not in the right place, they leave their jobs under pressure of
events: people, without saying anything about it, no longer come to the
meeting, the liturgy, the activity that no longer is able to attract their interest. In general there is no official recognition of these ministries except in
more difficult situations where it is necessary to reinforce the authority of
somebody who has taken on a task with competence.

Finally, the base community is a community and not a group, because
all the generations are represented in it: children, young people, adults,
old people. There are families; the unmarried; and frequently, visiting
guests.

As *church-oriented*, the principle motivation of base communities is religious. Practically speaking, all are built around the urban parish in the poor
quarters or around the country chapel. They are strongly connected with
the bishop; whereas in Europe the base communities, often having a different social origin and being communes rather than communities, are mis-
trusted by the hierarchy, and vice versa. These are communities of faith,
hope, and charity, which are gathered together around the word of God
and the Eucharist, and receive the energy to change the world through the
celebration of their faith. They represent a church revolution to the extent
that they correspond to a gigantic *restructuring* of the Catholic community
on the Latin American continent. It is estimated that in Brazil there are
80,000 base communities of this type, meeting in the local parish churches.

As *base communities,* these communities are overwhelmingly made up of
people who work with their hands: mothers of families, domestic servants,
workers in industry, the unemployed, those who have retired from work
(often at a young age, because of sickness), peasants occupying the land

without title for generations, agricultural laborers, small farmers, bricklayers, workers on big public projects or with urban contractors building the homes of the rich, migrant laborers, and so forth. The community members are mostly people with three to four times the legal minimum monthly income. They live in rented buildings on the outskirts of the big cities, or in places they themselves have built during weekends on sites that they are buying through long-term mortgages in the face of rampant real-estate speculation, or in shantytowns *(favelas)* on land that does not belong to them and on which they have simply squatted.

In the countryside they live either in little villages or on the outskirts of small towns where they are picked up each morning in trucks to be employed as agricultural laborers by the day or week. Such are called *boia-fria* ("cold dish"), for they have no way of heating food at the workplace. Whether in the city or in the country, they are illiterate or only marginally literate; some can recognize the alphabet letter by letter, but cannot grasp the sense of something they have just read. Some can read, but without retaining much of what is written, and can only write with the greatest difficulty.

Carlos Mesters, a Dutch Carmelite who has lived and worked in Brazil for many years, has learned how to study the Bible with the people and make it accessible to them. He says that the base communities have received a triple mission from Jesus (Mk. 3:14): to be with Jesus; to proclaim the good news; and to have authority to cast out the numerous demons that fill our society. Correspondingly, Mesters says, these communities must remain faithful (Acts 2:42): to the teaching of the apostles (through the biblical circles); to fraternal communion (through mutual aid and sharing); and to the breaking of bread (in the Eucharist).

There is no doubt that the guiding model in the Spirit for these communities, once again, has been the community of the Acts of the Apostles (Acts 2:42-47; 4:32-35), as it always has been in the ages of church renewal. . . .

PEDAGOGY OF THE CHURCH BASE COMMUNITY: ONE WAY TO GO ABOUT IT

We shall speak here about our personal experience with a base community in a big city, more exactly in the miserable outskirts of the big Latin American cities. We are aware that roads different from those that we have followed are possible.

May we start by making a general observation. Church base communities nearly always have at their beginnings a priest or a sister. These are movements of clerical origin, even though their evolution right from the beginning leads to a state of affairs where the clergy no longer concentrate all the power in their own person. . . . It was on the whole normal that the church base communities should have been the responsibility of pastors;

for in the end, what was going on if not the *restructuring of the Catholic community?* And this is properly the bishops' task: to supervise the growth of love within communities and the good order of Christian assemblies, as well as their multiplication and their mutual relations. . . .

Here is the method that we have followed in the creation of church-based communities. It falls into six stages: living together; prayer; restoring a voice to the people; restoring action to the people; the expansion of ministries; toward collective action.

Living Together

A beautiful Portuguese word defines this stage: *convivência,* living together. Friendship takes time. Jesus lived thirty years at Nazareth before acting and speaking. The "wretched of the earth"—those who from their ancestors onward suffer oppression, descendants of black slaves, of Indians who have been the objects of veritable acts of genocide, of those poor European immigrants—are very suspicious: they have been deceived so many times! . . . So there is no shortcut, no recipe. One must embrace the cause of the oppressed, break with one's position in the ruling class, "live with" even in material circumstances if in any way possible as regards one's quarters, daily work, and so on.

Prayer

Always start from people's traditions, above all their religious traditions. For my own part I always began my base communities with prayer, even with reciting the Rosary! There are two reasons for that.

First, these migrants who come to live in the big city do not know each other. They are uprooted people who come from all states of Brazil, especially from the northeast and Minas Gerais. Only a slender thread still holds them together: popular devotions. If the padre calls a novena, a Rosary, a *casa em casa* (a progressive novena from house to house in the neighborhood), everybody comes, and it is a chance for the neighbors in the same street to meet each other or to deepen a passing acquaintance. Second, prayer or, rather, the activities of prayer create the anticipation of a new world within societies in the process of change, which must not be underestimated.

Restoring a Voice to the People

Another essential stage, which can begin very early, is that of bringing down the word to those without their own voice. Everybody knows that before taking the Bastille, it is necessary to take the word. What does that mean?

It arises from the situation where, as the Bible says, the word of the poor has no worth. The person speaks and nobody listens; "they say, who is this fellow?" (Sir. 13:22-23). Among themselves the poor have got into the habit of self-depreciation. What a laborer says has no weight besides the word of an engineer or a priest. "At least they have studied. You are like us, you know nothing." How can the world be changed through a people as discouraged as this? That is why each base community is founded through a gentle and gradual pedagogy, which teaches the humble once again to listen to each other and speak to each other *in community;* to *give worth* to what they have to say as they express themselves to each other. It is really the miracle of the healing of the deaf-mute once again. Later in this stage we begin to read the Scripture together.

Telling What Happened Today: It is evening at a gathering of the base community, or a study day. Each one describes his or her day from morning till evening. Very often at the beginning we hear something like this: "Who, me? Nothing interesting. As usual. Washing the laundry. Cooking. . . . " She has let the word slip out: nothing interesting. It is important for a mother of a family to be able to tell what time she got up; how many times she got up during the night or at dawn to give the bottle to the baby, to heat the coffee for her husband who is going off to the factory, to fix the lunch-box for her oldest son who leaves later, to get the children ready for school. We go around the table and each one is able to describe the day that has just finished.

Introducing Family or Friends: In the course of the gathering each one presents the family: how many children they have, their names, where they work. It must be done with discretion and some brevity; it should not sound like a police interrogation. Sometimes we use the old method of the Catholic Worker Youth, the *"diagram of relations,"* to present one's most basic relations to the participants in the community gathering. It is a piece of paper with the name of the one speaking in the center; that person writes down the names of the people that he or she *regularly* meets at work, at the bus stop, in the street, at the church, at home, or elsewhere. Very often in this way the participants discover mutual friends or acquaintances.

Telling One's Story, the Past: In the end, during these gatherings, the fundamental needs of every human being are reached. After family, the past; origins. Where do you come from? These are very emotional meetings; friendship and mutual confidence are presupposed, because in the end each one is describing his or her misfortunes. What a way of the cross has been traveled by these lives that come from the very depths of the country's interior and that, from misery to misery, end up in the big city! We must listen to the young mother of a family tell how at the age of thirteen she was placed as a domestic in the city, in a household where her patron took advantage of her, and how she did not dare tell her mother, because she was the family's source of income. Or the young man who has become a specialized worker tells how, when he was a child traveling to São Paulo with his family, they all had to interrupt their train trip because they did not have enough money left to buy a loaf of bread: "And my father and I would not look at each other, because he knew that I was hungry, and I knew that he didn't have any money."

Certainly these exercises of recalling the past and the communal discovery of each one's history can be used differently. The best can be lifted up along with the worst. In it a Christian can see the narrative of each one's sacred history: like that of the people of God, it is made of weal and woe, of horrors and beauties. Also constantly present for whoever can see through appearances and read the signs of the times is grace: that is, the presence of the good that triumphs over evil; the faith that helps overcome every wish to abandon the struggle; the intervention of friends who, like the prophets, come in to condemn evil, to warn of dangers, to console; the "miracles." It is a religious reading of each one's history, done in a setting of prayer, during these gatherings.

There can also be a scientific reading of the past: the important events in each one's history are written down in a column. In a parallel column are noted important events in the life of the country or of the world, which happened at the same time. Thus the very poor learn to find their place in general history; historical memory is amplified.

Evoking the Future: After the past, the future: "If you had the chance, what would you want to get before everything else for yourself and your children?" In one column is written down the wishes, the "Project Hope" of each one. In the second column, the obstacles in the way of this "dream." In a third column, there can be proposed the first embryonic solutions. That is action. Note that here we are using the old method: see, judge, act. In a fourth column could be evoked the eschatological dimension of the kingdom, that is, citations of scriptural texts, parables, words of Jesus or of the prophets, which show how the kingdom is to be realized. It is good to have a political reading of the hoped-for future, but also a theological reading.

Additional topics that work well in getting people to talk are the following (always based on fundamental human needs):

The Bairro: *Its greatest needs:* We proceed in the same way as before, by a system of parallel columns: "If you could, how would you change the *bairro?*"

The Factory and Workplace: Narrate a day at the factory from beginning to end. On the blackboard draw a plan of your work area and of the other parts of the factory. Explain how it operates. "If you could, how would you reorganize your work area, the whole factory . . . ?"

Clearly this is a simple method. For people to be able to recover their power of speech, they must be able once again to express themselves about time and space: their personal time (their own story, past and future) and their personal space (family, friends, workplace, home).

During this stage, as we noted, we begin to read the gospel, to read about the things that happened to Jesus and his friends. Generally each meeting has a substantial time reserved for reading and explaining the word of God. We have already stressed the fact that the biblical text is in a certain sense the ideal mediation: it allows all those who live in oppressive situations to find themselves in a character of the Bible who lives the same reality, and thereupon to see how grace operates its salvation in them and in us—a true liberation of the whole being, individual and social. ("Zaccheus, that's me!" "I am Magdalen!" Etc.)

The meeting of the base community can proceed in many other ways. The following is typical: (1) song or initial prayer, after the usual greeting; (2) reading a text from the Bible; (3) storytelling by the participants on one of the general themes listed above (obviously not all the themes or all the participants can be included in a single meeting); (4) discussion of problems that have been discovered during the meeting, or an effort to solve an urgent question that has come up in the *bairro*; (5) prayer and final song.

It will be seen that all this is flexible and that not all the items need to be covered each time: perhaps the group will concentrate on just one. The essential thing is that life should never be separated from faith, acting from seeing.

Restoring Action to the People

Now we arrive at the decisive moment in the birth of a church base community. Everything we have said until now is preliminary. A group does not become a community until the day it decides to *act together*, to pass to action. Mission creates unity. Action permits a verification of whether or not the word has truly taken on flesh. We must leave Egypt in order to journey toward the Promised Land; the exodus of action is always necessary.

As for us, our community took form the day when the group, which had been talking together and studying the Bible, decided to reconstruct the *barraco* of a widow with ten children and expecting the eleventh. Her husband had been killed some days earlier on the highway that passes not far from us. So it was decided that one Sunday morning all the volunteers would show up with saws, hammer and nails, and axes at seven in the morning to work on the widow's house. What happened was what has been happening since human beings appeared on earth.

Initially there was laziness or fatigue. A person who has worked hard all week long, on an impossible schedule, never wants to lose Sunday rest. And so a certain number of the biblical circle were not there at the hour agreed on. The rest waited for them, in vain, all day long. No doubt each one had a valid excuse.

And throughout there was the usual difficulty that people have working together. Nobody wants to be ordered around by somebody else, especially when the task is one of benevolence. "I know how to build a *barraco* at least as well as you do." "I don't need to take orders from you." Each one has a different idea how to proceed. And a third part of the volunteer army disappears into the woods on one pretext or another. It looks very much like the story of Gideon's army: the force that was to confront Midian shrank from 20,000 to 300! It was with 300 courageous men, chosen by God, that Gideon confronted the enemies of his people—a remnant fighting against a much more powerful enemy (Judg. 7:1-8). It is the same way with base communities. In the case we describe, those who stuck it out to the end at the widow's house, who overcame the obstacles to action, still today, after six years, make up the cadre of the community!

Surprises were not lacking all during this little event. Inspectors from the town council came to tear down the hut, which although only partially built was already being lived in, and the widow had to pretend to go into labor—she was so frightened that she almost lost the baby. The next week we had to employ a ruse. The walls of the hut were to be constructed separately, at a distance, and then assembled in an instant the next Sunday. We had barely finished when the officials appeared again on the horizon. The widow barely had time to install herself in her new lodging, still unfinished, with a bundle of clothes; for a municipal decree provides that no dwelling whatever may be demolished if it is actually occupied by the person who takes shelter there. So that was a victory.

Still today, as in the age of Gideon, we have to destroy the altars of false gods where human energies are destroyed under Satan's sun: namely, the unjust laws and social structures that turn the human being into a machine for production, instead of being a creature in the image of God made to love and be loved. It is certain that prayer, the celebration of the faith, biblical and theological study, and nourishment by the sacraments are indispensable to gospel energy, as we have insisted. But we must never forget that only action can verify whether or not prayer is authentic: "Not those who say 'Lord, Lord' ... " (Mt. 7:21). People can pray together for twenty years side by side in the same church and never have a disagreement. But on the day when they begin to act together, everything starts to change. That is when we see whether the charity that "bears all things, hopes all things, believes all things, endures all things" (1 Cor. 13:7) will win out over our egotism and allow us to work together.

That is the decisive moment when a base community is born. Afterward we need simply continue in the same direction: in the name of the love of human beings that animates us, because God by the Holy Spirit has poured divine love into us, that we may throw ourselves into action in order to rescue our brothers and sisters, to love them. Let me set down a parable told me by Jean-Claude Barreau. Every Christian life, every human life, is like an airplane flight in which each passenger enjoys the usual comforts but also has a parachute on his or her back. At a certain moment during the flight, the captain's voice is heard: "Ladies and gentlemen, those who wish are invited to present themselves at the rear of the craft to make a parachute jump!" Only the minority take the risk; the others prefer to continue their flight carried by the plane's wings, and arrive uneventfully at the airport, perhaps joyfully. But for those who jump, it is an extraordinary experience; they enter another dimension of reality. Plunged into the void, with the impression of hurtling toward an earth suddenly become hostile, they put their trust in their parachutes and in the word of the men and women that have already passed that way. For, an extraordinary surprise: the bags on their backs open, expand; and they discover a power that holds them up, sustains them, allows them to slide gently toward the earth they must rejoin.

So with the power of God. If, in the name of faith in Jesus' word, we throw ourselves into actions that are apparently impossible, out of love for our brothers and sisters and toward the construction of the kingdom, God in divine omnipotence will be with us and sustain us. We shall not destroy ourselves, we shall not be destroyed, even if the event leads us to the sacrifice of the cross. It is not an affair of throwing oneself from a pinnacle of the temple to astonish the crowds; it is an affair of doing what is commanded by love, of discerning together whether or not it is love that is speaking—and then of going at it. Only those who take a risk in the name of the faith will experience the faith, that is, the presence of the living God in their lives. The others are not bad people, but their uneventful flight will leave them nearly insensible of the divine. They will be cold.

The Expansion of Ministries

Ministries appear and are differentiated at the heart of action. That is easy to understand: gifts are revealed when one is put to the test during a struggle. Those gifts are charismata—gifts of the Holy Spirit, grace accorded, in view of service to brothers and sisters for the common good of the collectivity. In struggle one person reveals gifts as head, as organizer; another is shown able to speak, express things clearly; a third discovers qualities as a strategist. Also there appears the person to handle money and plan the budget. Certain men or women reveal awareness of the theological aspects of the struggle, others of the political aspects. Also required are wise ones who can keep in balance different aspects of the struggle of the people of God—family life, the life of activism. . . .

Toward Collective Action

A base community evolves very slowly. In our opinion, it takes ten years for it to arrive at maturity. Does it not take about the same time to train a priest, a doctor, an engineer? Priests have at least six years of seminary, not counting periods of review and supplementary studies. It is at least as difficult to shape a Christian community as to train its members—at least if we really want it to hold together.

At the end of five or six years, certain ones discover that creating a civilization of love is not all that easy. Structures must be thought about. The spontaneous mutual assistance of the *bairro* is no longer adequate.

THE PHASES OF A BASE COMMUNITY

In general, a base community passes through four phases regarding its social and political involvements.

First, a base community is in search of itself as a community: it is centered on the religious activities for which it was originally founded. It is looking in the gospel for answers to its everyday problems.

Second, a base community participates in broader movements, where it meets not only Catholics but non-Catholics, not only believers but also nonbelievers. These are called "popular movements" because they are oriented toward the most numerous strata of the population, those that are trying to organize themselves in the *bairros,* or on a nationwide level, to improve their existence. To strive for a clinic, sewers, a day-care center by uniting several *bairros* is to create a popular movement.

Third, a base community, so to speak, passes from the *bairro* to the factory. The people's base little by little is woven into a web of small organizations—of the *bairro,* of the factory, of farm workers who have learned to act together. From these have emerged the activists (*militantes*) who are working to regain control of their trade unions. Thus there has reappeared an autonomous workers' movement, in the city and in the countryside, in industry and in the fields, whose strands are composed for the most part of members of the church base communities.

Fourth, a base community raises the political question. It becomes necessary to build political parties in order to gain access to the political bodies that govern the nation: the Senate, the Chamber of Deputies, the state governors, the mayors, the municipal councils, and so on. This step is much debated. The church base communities as such do not endorse any political party. But many of their members, including those who make up specialized pastorates (workers' pastorate, agricultural pastorate, and so on), frequently support the Workers' party. That raises questions.

But all this is *consequence,* however inevitable. The *essence* of the church base community is not in the political but in the religious realm. (However, what we have previously said about the relation between those two realms must not be forgotten.) The church base community, like the workers' pastorate and the agricultural pastorate, is not a political body but a body for the celebration of the faith and the overall education of the human being. It is the place where those gospel energies are awakened and strengthened that aim to transform the world so that charity may be possible in it and God may reveal the divine Name. If political instruments are created to get a firmer grip on reality, that is a consequence, one that should not be confused with the normative activity of the communities. That is why the communities, like the pastorates, are distinguished without separation from the trade union and the party. They are not separated, because many of their members belong to a union or a party, as we have noted. But union and party must forge themselves in an autonomous manner, "outside" the community, so to speak, not identifying themselves with it, which would be a catastrophe no less theological than political: the community would lose the religious character that constitutes its energy and raison d'être, and the trade union or party would become an instrument of a new Christendom.

13

Women's Participation in the Church

MARIA PILAR AQUINO

INTRODUCTION

The theme of women and the church in Latin America today must locate itself within the context of a reality marked by oppression, dependence, and the conflict of opposing interests. Within this context a struggle exists to eradicate oppression by changing the conditions that foster dependence and by affirming the right of the poor to *life*. The struggle itself is being translated and expressed in the process of the liberation of Latin America.

The struggle for liberation occurs as a reaction to oppression; thus both liberation and oppression are two aspects of an unjust society. There are those who benefit from injustice and look to maintain it. There are those who seek to escape it and thereby combat it. The church in Latin America is involved in both oppression and liberation.

The church reproduces at its center the situations and relationships of oppression. This is because faith, religious expressions, spiritual experience, the relationships of men and women—all express the same interests of the dominant sector of society. And these are interests of class, race, and gender. Yet we cannot oversimplify. The church also embodies the dreams, defeats, successes, and interests of the oppressed. This has its impact on the church itself, as well as on society.

Therefore, to recognize the role of the church as an agent of oppression should not weaken our recognition of the church as the community of the poor who are loved by God. This church continues to liberate itself in history as it grows in discernment of the path of the community of faith,

From *With Passion and Compassion: Third World Women Doing Theology,* Virginia Fabella, Mercy Amba Oduyoye, eds. (Maryknoll, N.Y.: Orbis Books, 1988), pp. 159-64. Translated by Louise Bernstein, C.S.J.

hope, and love. The followers of Jesus, who are the church, remain the sign and saving instrument of the God of life in the course of history.

It is true that, within the church, processes exist that encourage domination and that consider irrelevant the needs and demands of women. At the same time, processes exist that diminish the action of the powerful and act in favor of the oppressed. The active and dynamic presence of women in the church is proof of this.

THE OPTION FOR THE POOR IS AN OPTION FOR WOMEN

Historically, the church has served as a vehicle transmitting cultural patterns of patriarchy as well as religious traditions with respect to women, which sought to keep them both domestic and private. Yet in the bold relief of history we see the presence of women who stood in opposition to domination.

Since the late 1960s, the church in Latin America has seen itself in a serious process of renewal. The renewal deals with the invasion of the poor into the heart of the church. The massive number of these poor presents varied questions and solutions in each country and region in terms of conscience, strength, impact, and organization.

The presence of the poor has generated within the church a rediscovery of its own mission and identity. Their presence has led the church to new official positions, such as that of the preferential option for the poor. This option has opened new perspectives in relation to oppressed groups. In the case of women, in particular, it should be noted that the church made explicit recognition of a situation of double oppression in the Puebla Document of 1979. In addition, women have actively participated in the formation and advancement of the basic ecclesial communities.

The church as a whole has not proposed a deliberate, organized, and voluntary action in favor of women. However, to the degree that the Latin American church insists upon meeting the needs, the aspirations, and the interests of the poor, it promotes the participation of women.

The presence of women in the church is necessary in order to deepen and enrich the church's own identity and mission as a community of equals called to serve as sacramental sign of the humanity of Christ. As long as only the masculine presence is seen by the church as the exclusive means of salvation, the church fragments and delegitimizes its unity, holiness, and catholicity.

The question of women, therefore, has to be recognized by the church, because their presence in the church conforms to evangelical thinking and because it contributes to the forging of a more integrated conscience—a bright, new presence of church in the heart of oppressed peoples.

Identification with the oppressed and participation in their struggles of liberation have permitted the reformulation of the vocation and mission of the church in Latin America. This experience finds its best expression in the basic ecclesial communities.

These communities propose a living-out of communitarian values. They assume that evangelization is an integral part of their identity. They are liberating areas of faith. They are also democratic spaces of learning and sharing, spaces where God has something to say. In these communities life and faith find profound articulation, and those who experience this life and faith find that one cannot exist without the other. The basic ecclesial communities generate social and ecclesial practices that recapture a more evangelical meaning of church, precisely because of their commitment to the poor and to the struggle for liberation.

In the genesis of the basic ecclesial communities, the growing participation of women in new and freeing evangelization works has appeared. Women are involved in radiophonic schools, popular catechetics, celebration of the Word, the establishment of new communities, and the creation of para-liturgies.

This incorporation of women into liberating evangelizing tasks has followed diverse rhythms according to country and region. But women's quantitative and qualitative presence is a fact. Their presence is expressed in ecclesial practices that are bound specifically to the new expression of church, which takes its faith as stemming from the practice of liberating the oppressed.

In the case of grassroots catechesis and celebration of the Word, women have received an official church mandate to exercise the ministries. Women now participate in various services that educate in the faith, form conscience and ethical values, and project the symbolic/liturgical Word from a liberating perspective.

However, in the formation of new ministries, there remains a question. Are the cultural traditions of Latin America, in which the woman is assigned the role of protagonist, influencing the direction that creativity in the ministries assumes? The future will answer this question.

As for the debate over priesthood for women, the question is posed in different terms in Latin America than in other latitudes. In many areas of Latin America, priesthood for women is simply not seen in terms of righting a massive wrong. In other areas, where priesthood for women is a goal, it is most concerned with priesthood as a presence, service, and option for the aspirations and struggles of the poor.

The basic ecclesial communities provide a space in which women participate in the basic, primary needs of the community. This participation makes it possible to form a conscience in two dimensions of oppression: as poor and as woman. Involvement brings the realization that the struggle for justice for the poor is a challenge and a task reaching beyond the single community.

The emergence of women as equals in the struggle for justice poses the requirement for a more humanized understanding, rather than a man/

woman understanding, of the process of liberation. The new humanity requires a more integrating, more global, more unified face, because it has brought a feminized face into the struggle.

The church is enriched by the quality that women bring to their ministerial, evangelizing, pastoral, and sacramental tasks. But the enrichment reaches beyond that level into theological expression. That expression is altered when the life of faith is celebrated through the eyes of women, because that celebration requires a rethinking of the theological task, freed from the macho culture that has molded both the men and the women of Latin America.

In this dynamic and conflicted state of the new presence of women in the church, many aspects need work in the future. There must be more specific reflection on the themes of gender, on the questions of responsibility in leadership, on the recognition of women's presence, on the recognition of women's theological work, and on the new theological reflection their presence inspires.

OTHER CONTRIBUTIONS TOWARD THE AFFIRMATION OF LIFE

We tend to see in the traditional religious expressions of the poor Latin American woman a sense of resignation and defeat because her church is one that shares with the world a vision of domination. Yet we must see, existing alongside this resignation and defeat, an attitude of resistance to oppression. There exists in Latin American history a long trajectory of practices and a symbolic world that has helped the subjugated woman persist as capable of dreaming and creating.

One example can be seen in devotion to the Virgin. Our Lady of Guadalupe has been expressly linked to the processes of independence and a struggle for the land, a struggle always on the side of the poor.

There has been a deeply consistent devotion to the saints and to the dead as intercessors. There has been a conceptualization of God as a God who saves, and of suffering that will be redeemed in the beyond. All contain elements of criticism and resistance to oppression. All indicate dreams of a new and different society, either before or after death. Yet as an ethical indignation toward the actual situation, it is a timid rebellion, a silent rejection of the status quo.

This divided world, this negation of women as human beings and as agents and subjects in history—these do not correspond to God's plan. Women do not voluntarily identify with the interests and the values of actual society. The opposite is true. There is continually present in the church communities the heartbreaking "why?" of hunger, poverty, lack of work, and repression.

Though the grass-roots woman cannot identify the actual state of society as "good," she remains capable of celebration. Life is affirmed, but not life as the powerful say that it is. The woman as dominated sufferer is not the reality, because that reality has been invaded by a new process in which women take the initiative. They create projects. They enliven celebrations. They multiply communities. Life and hope are affirmed against death. The new society in which men and women drink together of the wine of rights and are the sacrament of Christ in history has already arrived.

The presence of women in the church of Latin America is a presence of tension. The rest of the church and its leaders are pressured by that presence to move toward an option for the poor and to take as their own the question of women.

Like the poor, women are objects of suspicion. In the basic ecclesial communities, women become aware of their dual oppression as poor and as woman. They begin to view themselves as creators of a new alternative. They become dangerous when they question the powerful and masculine model of the internal structures of the church. Once this questioning begins, the process is irreversible. There is posed the urgent matter of power and, what is more, of sacred power.

From the massive presence of women in the church, there can surge a transformation of the church. The transformation will occur in the measure that women affirm the creation of ecclesiality, organize anew, and take the evangelization initiative. It will occur through the building of communities in which power does not flow from an ecclesiastical masculine body, but from the necessities of the community itself.

The institution of marriage, particularly, requires attention in order that it support the dignity of women, in spite of the patriarchal context in which it exists. The medieval church, in fact, recognized the right of women to determine the establishment of the marriage bond. But practice has not upheld this recognition.

Another area of concern is the right of sanctuary. This has to do with the protection and defense of the foreigner or the persecuted. Sanctuary has its roots as much in the Old Testament (Num. 35:10ff.; Dt. 9:1ff.) as in the Middle Ages. Today we continue its tradition.

The church in Latin America is a place of encounter, recognition, expression, communication, celebration, organization, and the strengthening of the oppressed. Conditions such as these have, in all revolutionary times, called forth from the church the protection of sanctuary. In sanctuary, combatants have rebuilt their strength to return to the battle.

In various countries, under conditions of repression and persecution, it is in the church that the persecuted find asylum and protection. Here they are recognized as children of God, they are nourished, they can criticize themselves and grow. In situations of sanctuary, in church, chapel, and convent, women play the dominant role.

The Latin American church has been torn and enriched by martyrdom. This has moved it to a reappropriation of the living God as a God of the poor, the defender of widows, the nurturer of the impoverished. The church has assumed a faith in a greater God, in a Lord of history who, by the fact of the violent and early deaths of its children, has taken sides in favor of the poor against the powerful.

Women, wives, widows, sisters, and mothers raise the cry on every front in defense of human rights. The potential of women is expressed with painful vehemence when parts of the body are wounded. Mothers transcend the limits of fear and take on a warlike struggle to find the son or daughter who has disappeared through the forces of destruction and death.

There emerges, then, as a fruit of the presence of women in the Latin American church, a clearer understanding of love. Or, said in another way, women are now translating with new emphasis what love really means in its strictest theological and social sense. Love means:

— to participate actively in the building of new structures;

— to collaborate for a better quality of life for all;

— to affirm woman's being as woman who complements and broadens the totality of human life;

— to articulate woman's cause as the cause of the innocent, the oppressed of the earth;

— to sustain a persistent battle against an order contrary to the practice of Jesus and the Kingdom of God;

— to verify the original design of God, promoting life from its primary base;

— to reaffirm woman's right to be church, to make church, to build church, creating participation, service, commitment, and celebration.

Women spread love as a dynamism of life and for life.

14

New Ways of Being Church

YONG TING JIN

THEOLOGICAL REFLECTIONS ON WOMEN IN THE CHURCH

At the Asian Women's Consultation on Total Liberation from the Perspective of Asian Women, held in Manila (Nov. 21-30, 1985), varied expressions were given to reflect theologically on women in society, and church in particular, as found in the statement below:

> Oppression of women is SINFUL. This systemic sin is rooted in organized and established economic, political, and cultural structures with PATRIARCHY as an overarching and all-pervading reality that oppresses women.
>
> As church people, we have come to realize that the highly patriarchal churches have definitely contributed to the subjugation and marginalization of women. Thus we see an urgent need to reexamine our church structures, traditions, and practices in order to remedy injustices and to correct misinterpretations and distortions that have crippled us.[1]

Such is the existing reality of the church! Apparently the church has become an institution, with all its goods, services, laws, doctrines, liturgies, rites, ministries, structures, and traditions. The entire mechanism developed gradually, resulting in a pyramidal hierarchy. This form of domination is typical of the patriarchal system, pervading all spheres of life. Particularly in the arena of church politics, the power game ranks high, breeding corruption, cultivating and securing superiority, exhibiting abuses of power for

From *With Passion and Compassion: Third World Women Doing Theology,* Virginia Fabella and Mercy Oduyoye, eds. (Maryknoll, N.Y.: Orbis Books, 1988), pp. 100-107.

political motives and vested interests. Yet this is the leadership model we are given to follow. The image and marks of the church as *ecclesia* are scarred.

Leonardo Boff[2] made a most provocative critique of the Roman Catholic Church and the ways in which power, sacred power, is manipulated and abused. This is in no way any less true of the Protestant church. His contention was that since the fourth century the church has become prey to the forces, the dynamics, of power, which have nothing to do with the power of the gospel. Again, this historical reality is confirmed repeatedly in our experiences of the institutional church today.

These are the old ways of being church—full of distortions, plagued by corruption and high-powered lip service, glaringly unjust practices. Even the so-called renewed community of the supposedly progressive ecumenical movement of men and women is not spared from this critique, as long as we too fall prey to tendencies and practices of the "old"!

The church has lost its real essence, meaning, and effects. Though there have been serious attempts and prolific theological reflections/writings to redefine the meaning of *ecclesia,* it remains an important priority for us to return yet again to an understanding of the church as *ecclesia* and faith community.

While confirming the effects of the present realities of the church and the hurts upon our lives and those of other women, the participants at the Manila Consultation experienced yet again the liberating gospel and spirit of Christ. By Jesus' breakthroughs with a tradition that would diminish one-half of humanity, we felt affirmed and empowered to persevere in our painful struggle for full humanity. Jesus demonstrated this full humanity by his own life; and the teaching of God's kingdom was one with his deeds.

In the light of the gospel truth, Jesus is GOOD NEWS to all women! We have every reason to rejoice, to be hopeful, and to order our lives after the model of the New Creation in Jesus Christ.

WOMEN AND NEW WAYS OF BEING CHURCH

The original Greek meaning of *ekklesia* (a gathering; church) refers to a gathering of people belonging to a community. It has a common history, founded on an event and sharing a common experience. In a theological sense, the *ekklesia* history began when a few women acted together by paying respect to their dead friend Jesus at the tomb on the Sabbath day, during which they were forbidden to do any work. Already they were doing something "new" and profound, though it was treated as an insignificant, small job! And later, as enlightened first witnesses to the (cross-) resurrection-event and a new personal experience of Jesus the risen Christ, their "storytelling" of the Good News was ridiculed and passed over as unsound. Yet this was how the *ecclesia* emerged. It was a new birth with a new identity.

Swept by the unique experience of the Spirit and its charisms at the Pentecost, the faithful believers of men and women were moved to assemble in one place, celebrating and sharing their resources and life in common. Daily they deepened their faith by examining the Scriptures and breaking bread. Care, love, and concern for one another prevailed and increased in the community—a distinctive *koinonia* indeed. The Spirit led and shaped the faith community. It bore a new, distinguishing mark and vision patterned after the life and mission of Jesus. In building up a community, the believers grew in character, individually and corporately—one and all responding to and professing the power of the gospel in the living out of their life together.

We can find, as conceived in the New Testament writings, a host of theological thinking, terms, and expressions used and described to put new meaning and content into this gathering of faithful women and men. Looking at the epistles of Peter and Paul, the *ecclesia* is characterized as the "people of God," the "body of Christ."

In fact, the term "people of God" has its deep historical roots tracing back to Old Testament times. Related to its cultural and sociological terms, the "people of God" also refers to a chosen race, a royal priesthood, a holy nation. In I Peter 2:5-10, they are a community called to proclaim God's saving act for all humanity.

Paul described *ecclesia* with reference to the "body of Christ" as a corporate unit. A plurality of gifts is evidenced by the members of the body. Each person has a unique and creative role to play as inspired and sustained by the Spirit. Everyone is charismatic, no one is useless. As such, each member has a decisive place in the community, but all serving one another, all having and enjoying equal dignity. There is no room for any part of the body to despise, oppress, or dominate the other: "The eye cannot say to the hand, 'I do not need you,' nor can the head say to the feet, 'I do not need you' " (I Cor. 12:21). All charisms that God bestows upon each person, man and woman, young and old, must be used and shared in service and humility to the whole community.

Going back to the gospel accounts, one finds that the nature and character of *ecclesia* was initially enacted in Jesus' ministry. The great following of the "Jesus community" was a dynamic presence in the midst of the sociocultural and political setting of Palestine in the time of Jesus. However, the birth of this "Jesus community" came into being when Jesus announced the Good News of God's kingdom *(baseleia)* as the vision of the new creation. Precisely in this context the *ecclesia,* or the then "Jesus community," was understood to be a visible and dynamic sign of the kingdom vision directed toward a holistic transformation of society. This was the most radical new way of being church in the widest ecumenical sense of the word.

When Jesus sought to communicate a vision of the new era, his core message was leveled against the social, cultural, political, and economic situation of the time. In favor of bringing about a total liberation to each human person and to society as a new way of life as well as a new order of society, Jesus spoke in parables. They depict pictures and scenes of life in a community where old and new values are contrasted. The story of the banquet portrays a scene of the sharing community, where an invitation is extended to people from the streets and lanes—poor, blind, and lame— until the house is full! In Jesus' understanding, a sharing community does not seek to establish its own exclusive social class, as the Pharisees were doing, separate from those we regard as inferior or subordinate. On the contrary, it seeks for inclusiveness as a definite value and way of life, doing away with social division and all forms of discrimination.

The story of the meal, and how people rush for positions of honor and power, is also far from the way of life in a community. Instead, humility— a lifestyle of servanthood and self-denial, or self-emptying—is needed. Jesus taught that all power and authority must be exercised in deepest humility for the love and service of others. This is something that demands a transcendence of old attitudes and mentality; indeed, a very costly new way to discipleship!

Baseleia is good news for women! Women were the most oppressed and powerless of all, but Jesus associated with them and restored the dignity due them regardless of their social status or stigma. He affirmed the full personhood in women as being created in God's image, a concept that culture and traditions may distort and so cause women to be seen as less than human. Unlike the rabbinic tradition, Jesus taught women openly. Women were among the band of disciples following Jesus because he included women in his teaching and practice of God's kingdom. In historical reality, as the Gospels have it, women were in fact the first in faith, in terms of both their coming to faith and their quality of faith. When Jesus appeared and reached out to them at the tomb, he sent them to carry the Good News of his resurrection to the other disciples. Thus women must today redis- cover their original and distinctive role in the Gospel. Precisely because of the primacy of women's faith, women played a decisive role in the disclosing of God's liberation history, as recounted, in Matthew's and Luke's Gospels, in the birth stories of Jesus.

Women were active participants in all areas of the life and mission of the early Christian communities. They were apostles, teachers, prophet- esses, providers, workers, preachers, each according to her potential and God-given talents. Indeed, they were full-time partners alongside men in the Gospel of Christ.

Today, women must become fully aware and take confidence in Christ to rediscover their original and distinctive role in the Gospel. In realizing their potential they ought to reclaim their rightful place in the kingdom and God's New Creation through Jesus Christ. They must receive with faith the salvation of God by grace and begin to experience anew the power of the Gospel, which sets free every person from all forms of bondage and oppression. With this faith and hope, women can, with new minds, assume in new ways the role of leaders, decision-makers, pastors, educators, teachers, prophetesses, peacemakers, theologians, and so forth. Women in the New Creation must set aflame their lives and be followed in the order of faith.

The new ways of being church are modeled and implied, based on the values, characteristics, and qualities of the new as embodied in the person, life, and value system of Jesus. Every person, female and male, is summoned to participate in the building processes of the new. When the new era comes, it cannot leave the old structures and lifestyles intact. The new wine will burst the old wineskins, calling for a new creation (Mk. 2:21-22). Likewise, a piece of new cloth does not match the old one. Behold, the old is passing away, and the new has come!

IMPLICATIONS OF THE WOMAN'S ROLE AND CONTRIBUTION IN THE NEW CREATION

In the light of the new-woman consciousness and of women reclaiming power in their significant role, they are empowered to play a creative role and to make positive contributions in new ways of being church. A host of things come to mind calling for a reconstruction of the old and an innovative creation of the new. The challenge is waged at all levels and dimensions of life. It goes further than the verbal, analytical perspective by expanding frontiers of action as well as involving a fuller integration of both personal and corporate lives together in a human community of women and men.

A New Lifestyle

Being a new woman in the new creation, she has to participate in the new, making it relevant by living out a lifestyle that is Christ-like. Right at the start, when Jesus announced and summoned people to the kingdom and its vision, he called for repentance. Living out the life of the kingdom, therefore, requires continuous repentance and faith in the Good News. It calls for a total change of heart, mind, and spirit—at the personal level as well as at the social, in the structures of the heart no less than in the structures of economics, politics, culture, and all other spheres of life and systems of society. Repentance is required of any new person in Christ, without bias or distinction of race, sex, and class. Here the process of repentance causes one to seek first God's *baseleia* and righteousness. Without constant repentance and search on the personal and the corporate levels, a total transformation of society will not be realized. Therefore, women too need to enter into the process of repentance and search in order to remain responsible agents in the building of a new faith community or church. While submitting herself to the spirit of God in this process, the woman must see herself playing the role of educator and preacher promoting new ways of being church as envisioned by Jesus. This is primary, prior to any concrete actions, role, and contribution.

An Ecumenical Role

The woman's role and contribution in new ways of being church must be approached in the widest ecumenical sense, taking into account the realities of social and religious institutions such as the church, home, and society at large. Today, increasingly, women in the church are addressing themselves to the twin tasks of total transformation in the church and in the society.

A New Exercise of Power

In the institutional church, women are faced with confronting and challenging patriarchal structures and traditions. Alternative models are needed to shape and build up a new faith community of women and men. New meanings and definitions of the leadership, power, and authority concepts must be given. In the biblical sense, Jesus speaks of being a leader and handling power in the most unworldly manner. Jesus rejected and opposed strongly the kind of power, position, status quo, and glory offered by Satan in the story of the three temptations. As a leader, Jesus washed the feet of his friends. This power is the blessing for one to live in love, in peace with justice, in community. This power is never violent or destructive, ego-centered or domineering. This power is understood, motivated, and exercised by one's set of values as patterned after the vision of God's new creation. It serves to foster, enhance, and nurture all of life. This power is dynamic and constructive because it has to do with caring, inclusiveness, peace with justice as against racism, sexism, classism, and militarism.

Today, women having past and present experiences of powerlessness may treat this as a special calling to sing of power in a new key. They are capable of exploring ways to move beyond powerlessness into new visions and meanings of power.

The new exercise of power goes with a new approach to leadership. The old model is hierarchical, bureaucratic, and exclusive. It is also based on a one-man heroic show highly motivated by a spirit of competition and a male-macho image. To be followed in the order of faith, women have to show themselves as leaders different from the male style. In Jesus' words, to be a leader, one must be a servant — a suffering servant. Women are presently practicing and sharing collective leadership. This proves a better alternative as they adopt a creative and cooperative process of decision-making, of mutuality and trust based on consensus.

A New Theological Reflection

In the present total life and mission of the church, women have a vital role to play. They are the renewing force. A primary task may be creating an educational program on a rereading of the Bible from the women's perspective. Thus women's contribution to doing theology from their lived experiences in a relevant context is crucial in the order of faith. This too leads to the formulation of worship, its content and form of liturgies; the use of language and new symbols that are inclusive of all people without distinction of gender, race, and class.

While reaching out to women in the church, some kind of creative and regular dialogue is needed between women and men, and among women themselves. This helps to build up and nurture a new community of women and men who are already engaged in struggle for total human liberation, including the women's struggle against oppression.

Among women theologians and women making theological reflections, the need for a partnership of women and men in contributing to the total life and mission of the church is becoming more recognized. This contribution is essential, particularly in terms of maximizing women's participation in all areas and sharing in all forms of ministries, theological dialogue, and education toward partnership.

The New Faith Community

In the broadest ecumenical view, new ways of being church extends to and embraces all of creation and humanity in the whole inhabited world. The church as a faith and human community is located in the midst of the current global realities. Perhaps women find that their role is more than double as they assume the task of analyzing the situation at all levels — global, regional, and local — by translating the Good News of God's kingdom relevant to the social realities. Women become the prophetic voice as they pose challenges to other women and men to repent and live the new order of life.

The woman's role and contribution goes further than merely engaging at the level of social analysis. In the light of the greater human struggle for total liberation and social transformation, more women are moving to the forefront in the people's movement, in the peace movement, and also in consolidating their own movement.

Women in the new faith community can play a part in enabling other women to participate in women's movements around the world. Concrete concerns of the women's situation in the national or local context should be brought to the attention and care of the faith community. This is an important area of contribution by women for and with other women who are among the poorest and most oppressed of all. It can become a new missionary venture, an evangelization on new frontiers. Women in the faith community then can take a leading role in interpreting the church's mission to women who are oppressed in all sectors of the society. Issues, problems, and concerns may vary from country to country in Asia. However, these may be classified under the following broad categories:

militarization and nuclearization, and their effects on women;
prostitution and exploitation of women's bodies;
exploitation of women workers;
customs, traditions, and religious practices oppressive to women;
racism and racial minorities;
women in politics and people's struggles.

Concerted actions will have to be taken in response to the conditions of women listed above. Women in the church can enter into a joint endeavor with women's organizations already existing in their locality that are working with women of various sectors for consciousness-raising and toward mobilization for change.

A New Pattern of Relationship

The home-and-family tends to be a forgotten place even though it is a basic institution of education within the larger society. However, it is a place where patriarchal attitudes, ideas, and values are reinforced daily in all aspects of family life. Children grow up with stereotyped roles defined for their lives as male and female. The pattern of relationship between man and woman, husband and wife is one of a superior and a subordinate, as perpetuated and accepted by social and cultural conditionings. The home, being a most basic social and educational institution, must be transformed. The woman's role and contribution in new ways of being church should also consider educating the young, especially in the formation of minds and hearts, inculcating new values following the vision of the new order where equality, love, justice, and peace will reign.

The need for creating a new form and pattern of relationship between man and woman, husband and wife must be approached on a more personal level. It may be seen as unimportant, but in order to be fully integrated in the new, the old model and pattern of relationship must also go. New ones must be created. Women together with men will have to break through traditions and cultural practices that keep them in their respective gender roles. This involves a long and painful process. Women will have to help themselves, first of all, to break out of the roles defined for them, the image and the position that restrict them from creativity and freedom. By working through this at the personal level, half the job is already done when men and women enter consciously into an equal and mutual partnership in the total life and mission of the church.

CONCLUSION

Women, church, and new ways of being church are viewed in the perspective of God's kingdom and the new creation. It is in the light of this perspective that the woman's role and contribution are discussed. However, it is felt that this is a limited discussion. Nevertheless, the task is very demanding of all of us at all levels of change.

In obedience to our faith, let us in solidarity struggle together as members of the people of God, the body of Christ, new citizens of the kingdom, new creation made in God's image toward the vision of the New Heaven and New Earth where God's spirit, justice, peace, and love will reign and prevail in the order of life.

NOTES

1. Quoted from the statement "Asian Church Women Speak," drafted at the EATWOT Manila Consultation, Nov. 21-30, 1985.
2. Leonardo Boff, *Church: Charism and Power* (New York: Crossroad Publishing Co., 1985).

15

Defining "Women-Church"

MARY HUNT

The growing movement called "women-church" throughout the world conjures up various images. In Dutch the words convey something like a ladies' sewing circle; in Spanish the "church" part is hard for feminists to swallow. Definitions of women-church emerge from various women's experiences. I offer one which I was asked for at the Swiss meeting at Interlaken, where over one thousand women gathered for celebration and discussion. It comes from my experience as a white, middle-class, Catholic woman in the United States. I invite readers to shape their own, using my remarks as a springboard.

Women-church refers to the various expressions of women's religious agency in a patriarchal world. It is a phrase that describes our efforts to believe in the values of love and justice even though we receive contrary evidence from our churches. It is an affirmation of the need to act as people who have a significant contribution to make even though as women we have been told that we are at best assistants in the work of the religious world. Women-church is a statement of our humanity as women and our share in divinity as church.

Defining women-church in the negatives, saying what women-church is not, will help to clarify what I mean. Women-church is not an organization with members, elected officials, even with its own clergy. It is not a club from which men are excluded and in which children are tolerated if they keep quiet. It is not the women's auxiliary of the larger church. Nor is it simply a place where women who have been wounded by patriarchy can find comfort.

My definition of women-church is a *global, ecumenical movement made up of local feminist base communities of justice-seeking friends who engage in*

From *Waterwheel*, vol. 3, no. 2, Summer 1990.

sacrament and solidarity. I will explain each element of this definition to provide an overview of women-church.

Women-church is a global ecumenical movement. While it is true that, like blue jeans and rock music, women-church was first articulated in the United States, it would be a mistake to confine the definition to that reality. Women-church is a religious expression of the historical stirring of feminism and womanism (feminism coming from white women's struggle for rights, and womanism emerging from Afro-American women's struggle for survival) throughout the world. For example, women-church meets in Seoul, Korea where the Reverend Young Kim, an ordained Methodist minister, leads weekly worship and reflection on scripture.

Women-church is ecumenical. For Catholic women it is a clear alternative to a church which is not a church for us. For Protestant women it is a way to challenge and expand the efforts of institutional churches, as in the case of the World Council of Churches' Decade in Solidarity with Women. It is a way for women who have no previous affiliation with church to join with other women in search of meaning and value.

Most of all, women-church is a movement, a growing, uncontrollable, unpredictable, spontaneous, faith-filled movement by those who have traditionally been the heart and soul of virtually every church. As such there is no headquarters, no president, no pope. There are simply many people who are sparking the spiritual creativity of women, plumbing the often hidden history of ourselves and our sisters, and organizing events which gather our communities.

Women-church is made up of local feminist base communities. While the expression of women-church differs according to cultures, there are certain common elements. There are local groups in which one participates; one cannot be women-church simply in one's imagination. Of course, a group may not be available, but periodically one needs to gather with the community.

These groups are composed of individuals who form a movement, not simply as individuals coming together but as groups. Women-church is a relational reality, not a characteristic of a person. It is not that *I am* women-church but that we together are trying to be women-church.

Such groups are feminist. Of course, "feminist" has many definitions, but at least, they are feminist insofar as they recognize the historical and contemporary oppression of women, especially poor women and women of color and their dependent children. They seek to change social structures and personal attitudes to stop this oppression.

Women-church is made up of local base communities. The term base community has a Latin American ring to it for a reason. These are groups in which the deep unity of reflection and action, prayer and politics, or what I call sacrament and solidarity, is taken seriously. These groups gather regularly, usually with food and drink, to deepen ties and to work and worship as church. The worship varies but sources include chants, songs, poetry. Goddess materials, eucharist, dance and many other creative expressions of women's spirits.

Women-church is made up of justice-seeking friends. While this is perhaps the most controversial aspect of the definition, it is for me the most compelling. Those of us who make up the women-church movement want to bring up our children with the values of love, justice and community. We do this best as justice-seeking friends.

In a patriarchal culture friendship has received a bad name. It has been privatized into a one to one relationship that makes us feel good without necessarily making change. I reject this notion as a pitiful projection of male experience. To the contrary, as women-church grows it becomes more and more obvious that the revolutionary power of women's friendship is at its heart. The political and theo-political call to go and make friends in all nations is an imperative. On that Israeli and Palestinian women can become friends and make peace, for example.

Our love for one another as women, something that we have been taught not to take seriously especially in its physical dimensions, is precisely the model of a "discipleship of equals" that Elisabeth Schüssler Fiorenza envisions as a model of church. To be friends is the ultimate political act. It is the deepest affirmation of human community. It is the foundation of women-church.

Women-church groups engage in sacrament and solidarity. Groups act according to their own culture and the urgency of their own situations but the actions may be characterized as sacrament and solidarity if we wrest those concepts, à la Mary Daly, from their patriarchal context. Sacrament is a church word if ever there was one, a word that has served to divide life into the sacred and the profane. From a feminist perspective a sacrament is an act of lifting to public expression the everyday life of people because it is holy. This is what prayer is — momentary attention to the presence of the divine. Attention does not make the divine present, it simply recognizes what is so. This sense of sacrament comes, admittedly, from the Catholic experience. It is key because it breaks down the barriers between those who can celebrate and those who cannot, namely, women. It emphasizes the importance of music, silence, incense, drums, gongs, chants, dance, oil, flowers, touch, candles and all the creative rituals that enhance the word traditions.

Solidarity needs to be expanded in meaning in much the same way. It must be taken from its linear patriarchal meaning and given a new richness in women-church. Political work for those of us in the north and west is at the heart of our responsibility for a just world. But it need not be guilt-induced, the product of a purely political agenda, nor humorless and militant.

Solidarity work that emerges from justice-seeking friendship is solidarity work with a human face, letting the most deeply affected set the agenda, telling the rest of us how we can be helpful and humane. It is work that includes hugs as well as legislation, watching one another's children grow as well as stopping nuclear war, attending to the environment as well as ending global conflict. Solidarity is just as spiritual as sacrament is political in women-church.

This four-part definition of women-church is not meant to limit other expressions but to encourage them. Two central problems abound which need to be addressed as such new definitions come forth.

First, what is the relationship of women-church to the larger church? Is women-church a schismatic movement, a new church, a new denomination? I say no to all of these options not because I am afraid of heresy, too timid to found a new church nor so uncreative as to imagine only a new denomination. Rather, I say no because women's infinite creativity and cleverness permit us to be many things at once. We can and do participate simultaneously in our churches of origin as well as in women-church. We even use the money of those churches to make women-church happen; we use the buildings of the larger community for our worship.

We do not demand unilateral allegiance to women-church. Nor do we make it a practice of criticizing other churches. We are church. Our primary attention is on being church. The rest is detail. Women-church is not schismatic; it is a spiral expression of the deepest aspects of the Christian tradition.

Second, what is the theology of women-church? We do not seek a creed nor a set of dogmas. Such are meant to exclude and create a certain elite. Rather, with our feminist brothers and our children we seek to live out a theology of "mutual relation" (as Carter Heyward has called it) and a praxis of radical love.

Of course, we need to articulate beliefs and a framework for action, but that will take place in local groups according to local needs. It comes later, after we have lived a little more in this new reality called women-church. It comes only when many can speak, when more can sing, when all can dance. It must be done by theologians and non-theologians alike.

Moving toward that day as women-church is the task ahead. As women-church we are well accompanied by one another in our local groups and around the world. This accompaniment is the source of our power. Blessed be.

16

A Struggle for the Church's Soul

AN INTERVIEW WITH CHARLES VILLA-VICENCIO

What are your impressions of the current status of the church-state conflict in South Africa?

Charles Villa-Vicencio: I would certainly say that we are experiencing a church-state confrontation in the present situation. I would also want to introduce a word of caution with regards to this, inasmuch as there is not a direct confrontation between state per se and church per se.

What I'm pleading for is an understanding that when we talk about the church, we are not talking about a homogeneous group of people. The churches are divided. Every conceivable division that one discerns within society as a whole in this country one discerns within the life of the churches.

Second, there is, in fact, a yawning gap between the church as it is—as a social institution—and the church as it theologically ought to be. It ought to be an agent of God. However, the church is not that in practice.

We recognize that this God who has called the church into being is a God who is decidedly on the side of the poor and the oppressed rather than the rich and the powerful. We recognize very clearly that the church is not where it ought to be. The church historically and institutionally in this country, since the time of its birth with the arrival of the missionaries in the nineteenth century, has been on the side of the status quo. There have been groups within the church who have sought to locate themselves on the side of the poor and the oppressed, but the church as institution has been on the side of the status quo.

The so-called English-speaking churches, which means loosely those

From *Crucible of Fire: The Church Confronts Apartheid,* Jim Wallis, Joyce Hollyday, eds. (Maryknoll, N.Y.: Orbis Books and Washington, D.C.: Sojourners, 1989), pp. 81-91. The interview occurred in March 1988.

churches that belong to the South African Council of Churches, have a marvelous track record. They have protested consistently and persistently against apartheid and against the introduction of every conceivable new form of oppression over the years. In recent times they've even gone so far as to declare the government to be illegitimate.

These same churches, however, have failed when it comes to translating that protest into resistance. When it comes to translating their resolutions that have gone through synods and conferences and general assemblies into political programs, they are weak. The churches have protested without becoming an inherent part of the political struggle for the duration.

Institutionally, the churches have allowed themselves to be domesticated by the dominant forces within society. They've allowed themselves to be forced to live in a little ghetto, where the emphasis is on other-worldly theology rather than a theology that engages them in struggle.

The churches have accepted the formula which has been prescribed over the years by a succession of rulers, both within and without the church. It is a formula which says theology and politics don't mix. The church has suppressed and ignored that dimension of its own tradition which emphasized social engagement. It has been said that the best-kept secret in the theology of the church is that theology which requires the church to be engaged in social, political, and economic issues. . . .

What I perceive happening in South Africa is a conflict not only between church on the one hand and state on the other. I see a conflict within the church between those reactionary forces that continue to seek to domesticate the church and those forces within the church which requires people to live in a certain way both spiritually and in terms of social action. It is a struggle, in other words, for the soul of the church.

It's very important for us to ask, if Desmond Tutu and Allan Boesak and Frank Chikane [church leaders in the struggle against apartheid] do not represent the entire church, why is it that they are perceived as such a significant danger to the status quo and to the state? [President] P. W. Botha is absolutely right. He's not having bad dreams; he's right—they are a danger to the state. Why? For three reasons.

First, they are articulating a message that is instinctively understood and responded to by the majority of the oppressed people, who make up the majority of the church. They recognize that message to be the message of the residual gospel of liberation which has been suppressed for so long within the life of the church.

It's the gospel they read about in the New Testament, even if it's not proclaimed in their pulpits. They know it is the gospel of Jesus Christ, and they respond instinctively to it. P. W. Botha—when he hears those people preach, and when he notes the response—must have, and ought to have, sleepless nights.

Second, what we are experiencing within the life of the church today is an organization, a mobilization, of the church of the poor and the oppressed in a way that we've never seen before. As I look back on the history of the church in this country, this is the first time that there is an overt and explicit attempt by significant and recognized church leaders to mobilize the poor and the oppressed within the churches to be on the side of the broad liberation struggle.

Third, for the first time in the history of this church, we have seen a new breed of church leadership emerge—a breed of leadership which is representative of the majority who are oppressed. A breed of leadership who articulate the values, the aspirations, the hopes and the fears, the determination, and the commitment of the oppressed.

That is a significant shift. That is where my hope lies for the church—that we have leaders articulating a message that is understood to be the gospel. We are seeing through their urgency, and the urgency of others, the mobilization of the poor within the church. We are seeing a group in leadership who are prepared to act ecumenically and corporately to oppose the state. That is good news, no question about it.

What, then, is the confrontation? I would say the confrontation is between the state and that group within the church who are seeking to affirm the radical gospel of Jesus Christ—that residual gospel which has been suppressed, which has been covered by layers of piety and all kinds of other theology to the point that it's hardly recognizable.

That gospel, sometimes referred to as a dangerous memory within the church that is being reawakened within this period of time, is being rearticulated by these people. Thus the church, as institution, is not very well-equipped to deal with this new phase of renewal. The people within the church who are oppressed are beginning to rise up almost instinctively, and certainly passionately, in response to this articulation of the gospel. It constitutes the hope of the church.

As we see this initiative to organize and mobilize the church of the poor—and it is a significant threat to the state—we would be very, very wrong if we for one moment forgot that the forces of oppression within this country are going to act to counter that move. They are going to act not only through the intensification of repression and oppression, but also by seeking to counter it through right-wing movements within the church, by spending a great deal of money there.

We ought also to recognize that this process of transformation, this process of renewal which we are witnessing within the life of the church, is a process that has come about as a result of forces very often outside of the church, as a result of the broad liberation struggle within the country spilling back into the church. These extra-parliamentary groups outside of the church are now restricted; so people are looking to the church to engage themselves, as a vehicle through which to pursue the struggle.

That's not bad news, or a misuse of the church. It's good news. The church is offering a home to the poor and the oppressed, which is a basic message of the New Testament. As oppression is penetrating the life of the church, so the world, interestingly enough, is reactivating within the church a latent and almost forgotten gospel of resistance and commitment to a totally transformed social order. That is what I see happening in South Africa; the struggle is on.

Is the church making any headway in the black townships? How do the comrades and the youth feel about the churches?

The impression I get as I speak with people in the townships is that many of these people in recent years drifted out of the churches. They turned their backs on the institutional churches per se, because what they experienced happening in those churches was totally divorced from, and indifferent to, what was happening in the world of their daily lives. They "voted with their feet" — an expression I think Americans have used. They left.

What one has seen in recent days, as the church has taken a more explicit stand, is that many of these comrades are looking at the church and saying, "Hey! What's going on here?" They are beginning to see that the church is not that homogeneous group on the side of the status quo. If they look carefully, they discern a struggle for the life of the church, and they begin to show interest.

We go into the townships to pray for the downfall of the government. I've often said to my colleagues in these situations, "I would love to do a census right here to determine how many of these people go to church on Sunday."

The comrades, and others who are opposed to the system and struggling to transform it, are very excited. They are interested, at least, in what is happening in this alternative church. It is to those issues that the comrades respond, not necessarily to the institutional churches. We would be wrong if we overestimated the influence of the institutional church.

You have spoken of the domesticated church that has lost the memory of the gospel. There is another church in this land, which has been more than domesticated; it has been the bulwark, the theological justifier, of the state. What is the role of the Dutch Reformed Church in the current situation?

I have never for one moment thought that the white Dutch Reformed churches were in the process of undergoing change. The Dutch Reformed Church now talks the language of P. W. Botha, and so-called reformism and pragmatism. But the fundamentals are exactly the same as they always were. These guys have now been revealed for who they are and where they are: firmly on the side of, and in the pocket of, the government.

It's a little difficult to discern whether they in fact control the government, or whether the government controls them; but they are hand in glove. There's no question about it. No question about it whatsoever.

What frightens me, when it comes to looking at some of the statements that are made by some of the leaders of the white Dutch Reformed Church, is that there are far too many liberal church leaders in this country who actually get taken in by them. Our analysis has to be far, far better than that. We've got to be as wise as serpents; otherwise, we are going to be misled.

When P. W. Botha writes a letter attacking the church leaders, the letter is replete with theological language, biblical quotations, references to Jesus, and religious challenges. Does the state president have the theological capacity to write those letters himself, or does he have advisers writing his letters for him or with him?

I have absolutely no doubt in my mind that P. W. Botha is incapable of writing those letters and many things that he says in them. Just who those unknown scribes are, I don't know.

We listen to President Botha's attacks on the church. They are the words of a very angry, bad-tempered old man. We all know that Botha has a very bad temper; I think we should just ignore it. I think we should talk about the mandate of the church—to be obedient to the gospel of Jesus Christ.

It's as if there's a church that is not only in the pocket of the state, but is almost synonymous with the state. The state president boasts about his being a Christian and a member of the Dutch Reformed Church. And so you have the state claiming a primary sort of ecclesial legitimacy over and against those who would challenge the state.

Then you have the church that you call the liberal church, which has pro-tested but has not resisted. And the church which you are calling the alternative church, which is taking the lead and now includes the institutional leaders, in many cases, of at least the English-speaking churches. So this church is expand-ing and moving into more places. If what the church leaders are talking about and hoping for—a mobilization in the streets of the masses of Christians from many churches—comes to be, do you think the state will treat that response any differently than it has treated various challenges to its power before?

Contrary to what P. W. Botha has said, I would find it hard to accept that the strategists in the government could be counseling the government to go for the confrontation between church and state. I don't think it's in the interest of the state.

If the churches begin to be a vehicle for mobilizing the poor and the oppressed in resistance against the system—if the churches begin to become a threat to the security of the state—I have no doubt that the state will act against them in the most ruthless way possible. They will do it in such a way as to try to convince large sections of the white community in this country that this is not the church per se, because what happens in the church is what happens on a Sunday morning inside a church building.

To them, when people take to the streets, we're no longer talking about Christian worship. We're now talking about something else. They will say to the white populace that the communists are using the church for devious ends. They will act against it in the most gruesome way.

It is very difficult for the state to act against the obvious leaders such as Boesak and Tutu and Chikane. That must be a headache for them. If they try to formally restrict any of them, I have no doubt that those people would believe that, in obedience to God, they are obliged to disobey those restrictions.

If they put them in prison, if they detain them, there's going to be a major uprising. So what happens then? How do they get rid of them? I don't know. I'm not suggesting anything. All I want to say is that other prominent leaders within this country have disappeared; they have encountered their death in a very mysterious way. At whose hands? Through what agencies? I don't know.

But I don't think it is an overstatement when we read in the newspaper that Allan Boesak fears assassination. There are enough cranks running around. There are enough right-wing agencies that would be ready and willing to do it.

So for the church to rediscover the dangerous memory of the gospel in South Africa, it needs to enter into not only a period of confrontation between church and state, but also into the experience of suffering on the part of the people of God?

I believe that the church will not really confront the state until such time as the church has rediscovered itself. Judgment begins with the household of God. We have got to discover what it means to be a church not only in solidarity with the poor, but a church *of* the poor—allowing, enabling, and empowering the poor to take control of the church and to be the church, giving it identity, giving it a program, and giving it direction. That's the challenge facing the churches.

It is important for church leaders to march. We will all march from time to time. Yet, more important is for the church to go into the squatter camps, and to be a part of the poor and the oppressed in the sense of empowering the poor and the oppressed.

If the confrontation between church and state is going to happen, let it happen there. Let the state move in and prevent us from being the church when we are about God's business of uplifting the poor and the oppressed. That is a costly presence.

If the church does respond, it will suffer. What do you as an African church person have to say to the church in the United States and elsewhere? What kind of solidarity, what kind of symbolic and concrete support, are going to be required in this period?

Solidarity is very important. When you are sitting in prison, when you are being convinced by your interrogators that you've been forgotten, and then you come out and know that there were a whole lot of Christians both at home and abroad doing what they could to support you, and to support your family, that's very important. Don't let anybody ever underestimate the importance of simple support and solidarity.

Second, there are a number of programs in which we are engaged in this country, in which the churches are deeply involved both here and abroad—the disinvestment campaign, pressure on embassies, especially of Western governments. In that area, many of the churches have been very responsive. And also in the area of providing needed funds and resources.

When you say to me, "What about the churches in the United States or anywhere else?" I would want to say to my sisters and my brothers over there—and this is the most important point—that you have to discover what it means to be the church of the poor and the oppressed in your own country. When I look at the socio-economic and racial divisions in churches in this country, and then I go abroad and visit your country, I've got a strange, uneasy feeling that I'm right at home. That's what disturbs me. I don't think that Christians in the United States or in other parts of the world are really in a position to minister to us until they have dealt with the fundamental issues of racism and economic injustice within their own countries.

One of the major reasons why the present regime in South Africa continues to exist is because of the good services rendered to this regime by the United States. We are what we are—we have the resources we have—because the multinationals in your country sustain our economy, and develop our economy, and get rich off our economy. Until the churches take on those demonic forces within your country, those churches aren't really coming to grips with the issue of this country. If Christians in your country are going to live with all the comforts and all the prosperities of a Western capitalist, so-called free enterprise First World nation, one that oppresses Third World nations, and at the same time make nice liberal noises about suffering in South Africa, then I get the impression that they are making those noises to ease their own consciences rather than addressing the fundamental problem that we have in this country. That's the way I see it.

The division that you have in the world between a First World nation, such as the United States, and Third World nations, you also have in Washington, D.C., and New York. The division between First World and Third World nations is what we are experiencing in South Africa.

What one can witness in South Africa is not some sort of strange society, an aberration. It is in fact a microcosm of what is happening globally. As First World nations are wealthy and prosperous as a result of the poverty of Third World nations, so it is in South Africa. We have one nation—mainly the wealth of the whites, the wealth of the establishment—that is a direct consequence of the poverty and oppression of blacks in the country.

We are seeing here in a very explicit and grotesque way—a diabolical way—what the world is experiencing in a less obvious, less explicit, and less concentrated way. But that does not make it any less evil in other places.

I think we should be saying to Christians around the world that we all need to join the struggle. We need to disturb you, you need to disturb us. In solving your problem, you will help us solve ours. We need to join together globally in transforming the social and economic order.

Questions for Discussion

1. One author states that "authentic mission is not worship or catechesis, but transformation of the world so that love is possible" (Barbé). In your view, what is the significance of this statement for the church?

2. Why do you think basic ecclesial communities are growing in certain third world countries? What factors impede their growth? Do you think it is possible to form basic Christian communities in North America? What are the dangers and promise of this model of church and for its growth?

3. How can the poor effectively participate in the life of the church (parishes, congregations, church structures)?

4. On the basis of the selections and your experience, what might be some "marks" or defining characteristics of the church today? What are some ways you and your church are called to live out the priestly, prophetic, and pastoral vocations?

PART IV

Spirituality and Liberation

Introduction

MARY HEMBROW SNYDER

From a Western Christian perspective spirituality can mean different things to different people. To certain fundamentalist Christians it implies a life predicated on a literal interpretation of the Word of God as it is found in the Bible and an intense commitment to a specific church community. To many traditional Catholics it involves attendance at Mass on Sunday, frequent prayer, devotion to the saints and the Blessed Virgin Mary, meditation, ascetical disciplines such as fasting periodically, the practice of charity, and adherence to the Ten Commandments. To many other Protestants and Catholics spirituality has come to extend beyond prayer, meditation, and liturgical participation, to also include an active commitment to peace and justice.

For these Christians spirituality has come to be understood primarily as "relationship" — not only with God, but also with other human beings and nature itself. Irish theologian Donal Dorr presents such a perspective when he suggests that spirituality has three dimensions: personal, interpersonal, and public. Integral to these dimensions is ecological sensitivity which Dorr maintains can lead us to a deeper awareness of God's presence in creation.[1] Thus, much contemporary spirituality among mainline Protestants and Roman Catholics is understood in a multidimensional way. Consequently, spirituality is perceived as a way of life which flows from our relationship with God; at the same time, however, this relationship shapes and is shaped by the quality of our relationships with human beings and the earth. In other words, spirituality is not a question of a purely personal relationship with the Divine, but rather the lived expression of how we understand ourselves, other persons, the world, and ultimately God.

221

Jesus Christ is the paradigmatic embodiment of this "relational" spiri-tuality in the Western Christian tradition. During his lifetime Jesus prayed and worshipped regularly. Most of us have little trouble modeling this aspect of Jesus' behavior in our own spirituality. However, Jesus also reg-ularly championed the cause of the poor and oppressed. He reached out, particularly, to the economically poor, people who were ill, and those clas-sified as sinners, such as tax collectors and prostitutes. He ate with them, prayed with them, healed them, and forgave their sins. He also criticized those in positions of power and privilege, whether politicians or religious leaders, who looked down upon people they considered inferior and made their lives miserable. Further, he treated women with respect and dignity thereby contradicting the patriarchal biases of his religious culture. He lived trying to bring forth the Reign or Kingdom of God and, in his own person, embodied what that reign was all about: namely, respect, equality, hospi-tality, justice, and peace. Those who claim to be disciples of Jesus are called to live as he did. This means that in regard to our personal relationship with God, we must pray and worship regularly. Interpersonally and publicly, it also means we must reach out in compassion toward the poor and oppressed and become one with them in their struggle for justice. Only then will our spirituality be an authentic reflection of Jesus' life and mes-sage.

The majority of Jesus' disciples in the world today are extremely poor. Most do not live in the Western hemisphere, but in Africa, Asia, Central and Latin America. Some conservative statistics will illustrate the magni-tude of their poverty:

> Five-hundred million persons are starving; one billion, six-hundred million persons whose life expectancy is less than sixty years (when a person in one of the developed countries reaches the age of forty-five, he or she is reaching middle age; in most of Africa or Latin America, a person has little hope of living to that age); one billion persons living in absolute poverty; one billion, five-hundred million persons with no access to the most basic medical care; five-hundred million with no work or only occasional work and a per capita income of less than $150 a year; eight-hundred-fourteen million who are illit-erate; two billion with no regular, dependable water supply.[2]

No doubt such conditions do not reflect Jesus' vision of the Reign of God; no doubt such conditions require profound transformation for those who take Jesus' vision and life seriously. In light of this situation committed Christians are challenged to ask themselves what it means to claim belief in Jesus as the savior of the world. For if Christian belief is not coupled with action on behalf of justice for those suffering in our world today, it betrays Jesus' values and his vision of the Reign of God.

LIBERATION SPIRITUALITY

Many poor Christians in Africa, Asia, Latin America, and the slums of developed nations, practice "liberation spirituality." Such a spirituality is both like and different from some of the practices of spirituality traditionally found in the Western world. For example, like most Christians in developed countries, Christians in developing countries who practice a liberation spirituality revere the Bible as the Word of God, although they do not believe it is inerrant. They recognize the complexity of the Bible and the way it has been shaped by its human authors. It is the message of scripture that they emphasize, rather than the literal words used to convey that message. They also worship God regularly in small groups; in Spanish they are called *comunidades eclesiales de base*, or base Christian communities. Prayer is very important to them as are the Ten Commandments and concrete charitable action. However, unlike many Catholic and Protestant Christians in developed nations, Christians in developing countries who practice a liberation spirituality are deeply committed to transforming their societies through political action. Following the example of Jesus as they see it in the gospels, they do whatever they can to transform their communities to resemble more fully the Reign of God. Thus, wherever there is misery and oppression, be it social, economic, cultural, or political, they attempt to bring about justice, peace, and love. They do not see any split between their love of God and their love of neighbor. They believe that truly spiritual persons must live as Jesus did by trying to insure that every human being has a dignified life. For them, today, this means trying to create just social, political, and economic structures so that all people have the opportunity to receive a decent job, enough food, adequate health care, and proper education. They also want to create societies in which people can live free from fear of violent oppression because of their class, race, culture, or gender. Tragically such oppression is the daily experience of millions of people today.

The liberation spirituality of these people displays four main characteristics. It is a spirituality which is biblical, historical, christocentric, and ecological.

The biblical basis for liberation spirituality is found in the book of Exodus, the prophetic texts of the Hebrew Bible, and in Jesus' own message and praxis as it is found in the four gospels. The image of God which emerges in these books, and in Jesus' own teaching, is that of a God who takes sides with those who suffer unjustly at the hands of the wealthy and powerful. This God delivered the Israelites from slavery and dehumanization under Pharaoh in Egypt. This God raised up prophets like Micah, Isaiah, Jeremiah and others to denounce individuals and societies who victimized the poor. This God's vision of a just world was made visible in Jesus who enabled the blind to see, the lame to walk, and captives to be free. This God remains in steadfast solidarity with the forgotten ones of history. And it is this image of God, revealed in the scriptures, that represents the biblical basis of liberation spirituality.

Liberation spirituality is also historical. This means it arises from the real, concrete experiences of suffering humanity that characterize so much of Asia, Africa, Latin America and those pockets of poverty hidden away in the affluent countries of the developed world. Unlike some forms of spirituality which admonish the poor to accept their suffering passively in this life and hope for their reward in the next, liberation spirituality seeks to change the circumstances and institutions which are responsible for that suffering. It envisions God's reign being realized more fully on earth wherever steps are taken to restore dignity and freedom to the victims of injustice. Conscious that these steps are partial and incomplete, people who practice liberation spirituality do not despair. The fullness of God's Reign will come in God's good time. For now, the task is to contribute to that coming as their historical circumstances and their faithfulness to the spirit of Jesus demand.

The third characteristic of liberation spirituality is that it is christocentric, that is, centered in Jesus' life and ministry.

> The Christ of history is the one who defined his mission as a mission of liberation. There is a consensus that in the text of Luke 4:18-19 Jesus presents the content of this liberation: "The spirit of the Lord is upon me," he says, "for he has anointed me to announce good news to the poor. He has sent me to proclaim liberation to the captives and to the blind, the restoration of their sight, to set the oppressed free, to proclaim a year of favor for the Lord." The liberation Jesus brings is thus a total liberation.[3]

Looking at the synoptic gospels of Matthew, Mark, and Luke, we see a portrait of Jesus as someone who deeply cared about the poor and oppressed. His profound compassion led him to act very tenderly toward them. Jesus did everything in his power to heal their pain and suffering. He touched these people both literally and metaphorically, and by doing so, gave them new life and hope. At the same time, he also challenged the social leaders of his day when he called them to recognize how their misuse of political and religious power caused so much of the pain and oppression he was trying to ameliorate. Jesus' spirituality, then, led him to take provocative action against social injustice which ultimately resulted in his death on the cross. It was Jesus' "praxis of liberation," that is, Jesus' thoughtful action on behalf of those who were suffering in first-century Palestine, that enables people in Asia, Africa, Latin America, and black and Hispanic ghettos to see him as their liberator today. They realize there is a connection between his life and spirituality and their own.

What does Jesus' thoughtful action or "praxis of liberation" look like in the synoptic gospels? When we read them we see Jesus portrayed as one who thought deeply about the world in which he lived. He was very conscious of the political unrest his people were experiencing due to the Roman occupation of Palestine. He was aware that his religious tradition, orthodox Judaism, was interpreted and lived differently by many groups such as the Sadducees, the Pharisees, and the Essenes. He realized there were "haves and have-nots" in his society and that the economically poor, sinners, and those who were ill were treated with contempt and disdain by many people, particularly those with social and religious power. Reflecting upon all of this seems to have led him to act quite radically on behalf of those who were suffering. For example, he had tablefellowship with them. This scandalized religious people who believed Jesus' practice of eating with such people was a violation of ritual laws. Jesus did it anyway. Also, he healed sick people who were considered ritually unclean and who were ostracized because their illnesses were believed by many people to be a punishment from God. Further, he socialized with tax collectors and prostitutes despite the bad reputation it gave him. Jesus consistently refused to discriminate against these people because he felt they deserved to be treated with dignity and respect.

Another major aspect of Jesus' "praxis of liberation" was his attitude and actions toward women. In the culture of first-century Palestine women were considered inferior to men. Among other things, they were not allowed to study the Hebrew scriptures, they were subservient to men in marriage, could not testify in a court of law, and were considered "unclean" whenever they were menstruating. Given such cultural prejudice no respectable Jewish male would speak to a woman in public. Jesus, however, did not support such biases against women. They were his friends; he ate with them, talked with them, and healed them. He always gave women the same respect he gave men. Again, this scandalized many people who considered him in violation of religious laws for doing so.

These few examples briefly illustrate the "praxis of liberation" Jesus exercised toward the poor and oppressed of his society. His compassionate actions and attitude toward them demonstrate his "option for the poor," that is, his deliberate choice to be in solidarity with the victims of his society, to be a voice for them and to defend them whenever necessary.

Jesus' praxis of liberation and option for the poor called into question the status quo. Through his ministry to the marginalized he challenged the classism, racism, and sexism that prevailed in first-century Palestine. Jesus had an alternative vision of what life could be like — a vision of the Reign of God. It was this vision that impelled him to act so compassionately toward those who suffered. It was also this vision of God's Kingdom that empowered him to liberate all who suffered unjustly at the hands of the wealthy and powerful. Today, it is this vision of Jesus as liberator which energizes the poor and oppressed and those in solidarity with them. It inspires them to continue to struggle to renew the face of the earth so that justice and peace may prevail. It is faith in this Christ and his vision that constitutes the heart of liberation spirituality.

Finally, liberation spirituality, especially in the last decade, is profoundly concerned with ecological issues. It recognizes that justice for those who suffer from oppression must also include justice for the earth. Christian theologians all over the globe, conscious of the devastation wreaked on the earth in the name of "progress," are calling for an end to ecological destruction. Many are denouncing the anthropocentric, mechanistic worldview that has characterized Western Christian theology for the last several centuries. In its place they seek a more cosmocentric perspective rooted in a renewed understanding that God is the Creator and Sustainer of the entire cosmos, not just human life. Such a view presupposes that organic and non-organic life is interconnected and interdependent; liberation for either cannot be achieved at the expense of the other. Consequently, the emerging ecological sensitivities within a liberation spirituality are marked by calls for harmonious and respectful communion with the earth, as well as its human inhabitants. In today's world, such an approach to spirituality demands justice and well-being for all life on this planet.

A PREVIEW OF OUR TEXTS

The first article in this section is taken from a book entitled *The Gospel of Solentiname*. Solentiname is an archipelago of thirty-eight islands on Lake Nicaragua in Central America. The people who live and work in Solentiname are *campesinos*, that is, poor peasants. They are members of a base Christian community called Our Lady of Solentiname. Each Sunday the members of this community come to Mass. Instead of hearing a sermon preached by a priest, most of the people, including their pastor, Fr. Ernesto Cardenal, have a conversation about the meaning of the Gospel reading for that Sunday. In this text, the conversation is based on Mark 12:28-34 and is entitled "The Most Important Commandment." Keep in mind that these conversations took place a few years before the Sandinista Revolution of 1979. The people whose comments you read had been victimized for decades by an unjust government headed by the Somoza family. They longed for an end to the misery and exploitation they had experienced at the hands of this government. In simple but powerful language they discuss the radical demands of Christian discipleship and spirituality. They know their beliefs must lead them to take action against oppression which, in their circumstances, is a dangerous option. Yet, their fidelity to the gospel leaves them little choice.

"Spiritually and Politics: To Be a Contemplative in Liberation," by Leonardo Boff, is the second article included in this section. The author is a Franciscan priest who has spent many years of his life working with the poor in Brazil, where he is also a professor of theology.

In this article Boff presents a vision a "new kind of Christian," one who is deeply committed to both heaven *and* earth, prayer *and* action, faith *and* liberation. According to Boff, such a Christian is a person who has experienced the reality of God in the suffering of the poor and oppressed. This spiritual experience, in turn, propels the authentic Christian to struggle with the poor for justice, and to embrace their dreams and desires for the fullness of life promised by Jesus Christ.

Concretely this means that this new kind of Christian recognizes, not only the centrality of prayer in the Christian life, but the centrality of action for justice as well. She or he knows that faith in Jesus Christ must find expression in deeds that promote the Reign of God on this earth. For such Christians, faith in God and action on behalf of justice issue from a sacramental and contemplative attitude toward the world which enables them to acknowledge the omnipresence of God, especially in the suffering poor.

Further, Boff outlines several characteristics of the spirituality this new kind of Christian upholds. Some of these include understanding prayer as a vehicle for critical reflection on one's actions individually and communally; using liturgical worship as a means to unite faith and life, spirituality and politics; recognizing different forms of holiness today; naming "courage and historical patience" as signs of a contemplative vision; and accepting the paschal mystery as key to the struggle for justice.

Deeply rooted in a revelation of God experienced in the suffering poor and oppressed, this spirituality is the heart of the Latin American liberation process — a process wedded to the integral liberation of all.

The third article in this section, "Emerging Spirituality of Asian Women," is written by Mary John Mananzan, a Benedictine Sister from the Philippines who has a Ph.D. in philosophy, and Sun Ai Park, an ordained minister of the Disciples of Christ who is editor of *In God's Image*, an Asian women's theological journal. They approach the issue of liberation spirituality from the perspective of Asian women. The authors raise several key questions from this perspective: namely, what is spirituality and how does it relate to the actual lives of Asian women?

Women in Asia are seeking a more integrated spirituality, one that will lead them, as well as men, to the fullness of life. This must be understood as the core out of which their spirituality emerges. Like their sisters all over the world, Asian women are domestically, economically, politically, and religiously oppressed. At the same time, the authors indict those Asian women who yield to tokenism and those who refuse to be open to conversion. Asian women have sinned, they insist, against themselves and other women by cooperating with the patriarchal values that dehumanize them. Women committed to liberation spirituality in Asia seek to transform these situations so that the structures of their societies will promote the well-being of all women in full partnership with men.

In addition, the authors examine the framework and nature of Asian women's spirituality, as well as its ecumenical dimension. Patriarchal domination exacerbates the political, economic, religious, and domestic oppression of Asian women. Asian women's spirituality seeks to change this situation so that all women, men, and children can live with dignity and self-determination. Furthermore, Asian Christians are a minority in every Asian country except the Philippines. Their cultural context is predominantly Hindu, Buddhist, or Muslim. Asian women have had to acknowledge the oppressive historical legacy of Christianity as it has been preached by many European and North American missionaries in developing nations. Often such missionaries uncritically espoused colonial and neocolonial values that they erroneously conflated with the gospel. Given the mistakes of the past, Asian Christian women today are committed to forging a new path of dialogue with their non-Christian sisters and brothers who are also searching for a new and more wholesome way of life—one that includes an appreciation of Asian culture as containing deep insights into the human condition.

The fourth article in this section on liberation spirituality is entitled, "The Eucharist in Contemporary Society." Its author is an Asian theologian and priest from Sri Lanka named Tissa Balasuriya. In the article he acknowledges the central importance of the eucharist in the life and spirituality of the Christian community. At the same time he cites several key issues modern Christians are faced with and how often such issues are not connected in any way to the celebration of the eucharist. Such issues include peoples' search for meaning and inner fulfillment, their desire for community, global and national concerns for justice and human rights, women's liberation, interreligious dialogue, and the role of the priesthood. He further argues that the celebration of the Mass is sometimes little more than a formal ritual that lacks any substantial connection to the issues mentioned above.

Balasuriya's discussion of the eucharist and the role it plays in the development of Christian spirituality is very challenging to Christians everywhere. Among other things, he points out that, "it should lead us to a deep conversion of hearts and to action for the reformation of society." For too long now, he insists, the eucharist has been stripped of its potential to challenge and transform unjust communities.

The final article in this section on liberation spirituality is entitled, "Imaging a Theology of Nature: The World as God's Body." It is written by one of the foremost ecological theologians of our time, Sallie McFague. Ecological concerns have emerged in recent years as a further dimension of all liberation theologies. Sensitive to this, McFague is seeking to develop a holistic theology of nature and challenges us to replace our anthropocentric worldview with one that reflects more theocentric, life-centered, and cosmocentric sensibilities.

The author's approach is an imaginative, searching effort to reconceptualize the way we think about God and God's relationship to the world. The model for the relationship that has dominated most Western Christian thought up to the present is monarchical, picturing God as a king in relation to his realm and subjects. God in this model appears as a cold, detached, distant observer of creation. Such an image, McFague contends, has become the model for human behavior in relation to the earth and has led to the wanton destruction of the environment. Therefore, McFague proposes an incarnational model of God and God's relationship to the world. Here the world is perceived as God's body, and God is seen as a caring, embodied presence in this world. Such a view has profound consequences for human behavior — consequences that could radically alter the way we care for the earth. In suggesting such a perspective, McFague hopes this will lead us to recognize the interdependence of all human and non-human life, and impel us to assume a sense of responsibility for preserving the planet and cosmos we inhabit. What McFague does not say in this text, but has said elsewhere is that we must come to understand that the earth itself is among the oppressed. Hence a liberation theology perspective should include concern for the earth, God's body suffering again in our own times.

NOTES

1. See Donal Dorr's two most recent works: *Integral Spirituality: Integral Spirituality for Community, Peace, Justice and the Earth*, 1990 and *The Social Justice Agenda: Justice, Ecology, Power, and the Church*, 1991. Both are published by Orbis Books, Maryknoll, New York.

2. Leonardo Boff and Clodovis Boff, *Introducing Liberation Theology*, translated by Paul Burns (Maryknoll, New York: Orbis Books, 1987), pages 2-3.

3. Louise Tappa, "The Christ-Event from the Viewpoint of African Women," in *With Passion and Compassion: Third World Women Doing Theology*, eds. Virginia Fabella, M.M. and Mercy Amba Oduyoye (Maryknoll, New York: Orbis Books, 1988), pages 31-32.

17

The Most Important Commandment

(Mark 12:28-34)

ERNESTO CARDENAL

> *Then came also one of the teachers of the law,*
> *who had heard them discussing,*
> *and as he knew that Jesus had answered them well,*
> *he asked him: "Which is the first of all the*
> *commandments?"*

I: "The teachers of the law, also called doctors of the law, or scribes, almost always appear in the Gospels as evil people. They are frequently compared with the Pharisees. They were like the theologians or the moralists; and with the priests they were the religious leaders. (In the Gospels there is mention of a scribe who wanted to follow Jesus, but that isn't said of any priest.) This teacher, it seems that he approached with good intentions because he saw that Jesus, in the discussion on the resurrection that he had with the Sadducees, a very conservative, aristocratic, and priestly group, had 'answered them well.' This scribe's question, about which commandment is most important, was of great interest, for the Jews had more than six hundred religious commandments."

> *Jesus answered:*
> *"The first commandment of all is:*
> *'Listen, Israel,*
> *the Lord our God is the only Lord.*
> *So love the Lord your God with all your heart,*

From *The Gospel of Solentiname* vol 4 (Maryknoll, N.Y.: Orbis Books, 1982), pp. 111-120. Translated by Donald D. Walsh.

with all your soul, with all your mind,
and with all your strength.'
This is the first commandment.
And the second is like it, and it is:
'Love your neighbor as yourself.'
There is no other commandment
more important than these."

ELVIS: "To love the poor, the oppressed, is to be loving God. And that is the commandment we must obey."

I: "But why does he talk, then, about loving God? He could just have said love your neighbor."

ELVIS: "Well, God is your neighbor; God's the people."

FELIPE: "I think he's saying that you have to love your neighbor like you love God."

I: "Yes, but in any case he talks about loving God. And he considers it so important that he puts it together with love of neighbor, and even ahead of it."

We thought awhile. Then I said: "God appears before the people of Israel freeing them from the slavery of Egypt. And he gives them some laws so that they would be a just society and so that they wouldn't oppress one another as they were formerly oppressed by the Egyptians. And he wants the people to be faithful to him and not to recognize other gods of other societies, which do not represent any liberation. So to love him is to love liberation and justice and that's the same thing as to love your neighbor. To love God, then, is to love love. And therefore it's logical that the second commandment should be very similar to the first one. I also note that phrase that God is 'the only Lord': I see that that commandment is not to have other gods, not to have idols. The commandment is that there is no other God than love. And that is why we must love God with all our hearts, with all our souls, with all our minds, with all our strength. And the second commandment is the same, because if it weren't the same, with what love are you going to love your neighbor if you're loving God with all the love you have?"

FELIPE: "To love your neighbor then is to love God. You can't love God without practicing justice. And you can't love your neighbor without practicing that justice that God commands."

GLORIA: "I think Jesus made him see that if we love God and don't love our neighbor, we're really not loving God."

I: "The two commandments were in the Bible; in the Bible it also said you have to love your neighbor like yourself, including foreigners among your neighbors. What was original in Jesus, and what was very revolutionary and what must have scandalized a lot of people, was joining the two things and saying that one was similar to the other."

ELVIS: "We agree, then, that loving your neighbor is already loving God, right?"

LAUREANO: "Because God is humanity. They are equal. (Some of us believe, then, that they are the same thing. Or that it's God, that humanity is God.)"

I: "No, I believe that what we should say is that God is love among people. That God does exist, but that God doesn't exist in another way, separated from love among people, as God is usually imagined. God exists, but God exists among us only in that form: as mutual love."

FELIPE: "I think that's why Christ says that to that teacher of the law, because they used to be confused and thought that God was a God separated from the people. That you could commit injustices and then light a bunch of candles to God. At that time they thought God was a personage separated from people."

I went on: "I believe we cannot say that God is people. That would mean that Hitler or Pinochet are God because they are people."

LAUREANO: "Humanity loving each other and united, that's what God is. Just societies are the ones that can see God. Not those sons of bitches. Those bastards are outside of God."

ELVIS: "Where there's a community and everybody's united and lives in community, that's the real God, right?"

I: "That's why I said that God is the love that unites people."

ELVIS: "If that's clear, everything's clear."

DOÑA NATALIA, Elvis's mother: "I don't know, but it seems to me that, as I'm a bit ill I can say something crazy. I believe that love between husband and wife is love of God."

I: "Jesus says the second is very much like the first. You can say, then, that those that obey the second, it's as if they're obeying the first. Those who don't love God, for example, because they don't believe in God, but love their neighbor, according to Christ it's as if they're obeying the first commandment. Since one is similar to the other, it's like saying that it's equal. And he stresses this equality when he says, putting them on the same plane, that 'there is no other commandment more important than these.' I also think that to love God above all things is not to make anything into God, or not to make a thing of God, and from that comes the ban on making images of God. The only image of God is a human being, according to the Bible. And as God is love, to love God 'above all things' is like loving humans, and therefore the first commandment is like the second."

> Then the teacher of the law said:
> "Well said, Master.
> It is true what you say that there is only one God,
> and that there is no other except God.
> And that to love God with all one's heart,
> with all one's understanding,

with all one's soul and with all one's strength,
and to love one's neighbor as oneself
is worth more than all the sacrifices
and all the offerings that are burned on the altar."

I: "The teacher of the law repeats what Christ said, with the addition that there is only one God and there is no *other*. Maybe this is a little like what Laureano was saying, that we can't imagine a false God, a God that is not love. God *is* love, justice, and there is no other. And this man adds also something more radical, which Jesus hadn't said: that this love is worth more than religion. That's what he means by the things that he mentions: 'all the sacrifices and all the offerings that are burned on the altar.' He got the idea. And Jesus agrees with him. And another interesting thing: he has understood that love of God and of others is a single thing, when he joins them in a single phrase and says that that is superior to religion."

IVAN: "He's saying that it's better to give your life for the people than to give money to build a temple."

MANUEL: "That's very good. Because what the rich do is give some money to the bishop to build a baptismal font and the people are starving to death."

FELIPE: "That teacher was seeing that those sacrifices and those offerings were false rites, because they were a bunch of exploiters, hypocrites."

I: "But here he's not talking only about false rites but true rites. He says that love is worth more than all religious rites."

MANUEL: "This doesn't mean we should abandon all the rest."

I: "What rest?"

MANUEL: "Well, church and all that."

I: "But isn't that what you were saying?"

MANUEL: "Not about myself, but about others who burn candles."

I: "And is there any value in that?"

MANUEL (laughing): "Maybe God likes smoke."

I: "And this Gospel, what does it say?"

MANUEL: "Well, yes, here it says the opposite. But if I'm really loving my neighbor, I can be doing those things even if they're secondary."

I: "Here it doesn't say you mustn't do them. It says the other is more important."

MANUEL: "Yes, I agree."

FELIPE: "And it's not a sin to fail to do them."

I: "And that you can also have no religion, right? Even when it talks here about 'all the sacrifices and all the offerings that are burned on the altar,' it seems to me that the tone is a little contemptuous."

MARIITA: "Yes, of course, religion must serve for love of our neighbor. That's worth more than anything."

LAUREANO: "Religion is the opium of the people."

Then, when Jesus saw that he had answered wisely,
he said to him: "You are not far from the kingdom of
God."

MANUEL: "Well, he wasn't far from love; he was getting to love. Maybe he wasn't loving yet, but he was getting there."

OLIVIA: "At other times we've seen that people are saved by people. Whether people are saved depends on their relationships with people. We see it in that business about the Last Judgment: 'For I was hungry and they fed me.' It means then that everything is related to people. Forgetting that is what has harmed us, and that's why there's so much injustice, so much hunger. We've lived through a traditional religion of baptismal fonts, as Manuel says, of candles, and we forget love, which is what can save us. Love of our neighbor is what saves us. And meanwhile there have been people who don't even mention God and they've sacrificed themselves and died for the love of neighbors. It means that that is fundamental and that it's been useless, that religion full of lies that we've had and that they have in many countries."

I: "So Christ shows us here, then, what the kingdom of heaven is: love among neighbors. And he tells that teacher of the law that he is not far from it, with what he has said."

And no one dared ask him more questions.

OLIVIA: "Maybe because they had understood everything, and they saw that that was an awkward situation for them, and if Jesus went on talking to them the situation would get worse. They didn't want to go on hearing that kind of thing."

I: "They probably didn't like what was being said about sacrifices, offerings, something like what Laureano has said — right? — about religion being the opium of the people, and they didn't want to question him any more."

GUSTAVO, the Colombian: "Yes, I agree with what Laureano says, and they must have been startled at those new ideas, right? That all their rites, the animals they sacrificed, the incense they burned, and all that was valueless. Then they didn't want to ask him any more questions because they were afraid; what Christ was saying was too revolutionary."

I: "And possibly because they didn't know what to answer. He was talking here about the Bible; this was the thought of the Bible, the teacher of the law understood it very well, and the others must have understood. Many Christians also understand this, and they don't like to hear it.

"But we mustn't blame people that live in this traditional religion because this is what they've been taught. I'm thinking of my parents, who are very good people, but they've been taught this and they've known nothing else."

ALEJANDRO: "Many Jews used to go to make their sacrifices to the temple in good faith. Mary and Joseph also took Jesus to the temple, to make those sacrifices, when he got lost on them."

LAUREANO: "Don Tomás hasn't said anything."

Old DON TOMÁS: "I was paying attention to what was being said. What you've been saying is very good, and I didn't have anything to say, so I'd better be quiet. (after a pause) As for that business about the offerings: I don't think they had the offerings in those times that we have now. We used to do what we were told; we'd come with candles and this or that and we didn't understand, right? And as our parents taught us that, we had to do what they did. Now we've discovered a new law. I understand all that. I see that the old law that our parents had, we had to follow, because it was the one our parents taught. But now a law has come that is quite different, so now we have to obey another law. Not keep the same one, because that's wrong. That's why we come to church, to Mass. Instead of staying in the hammock listening to the radio. Because we have to listen and seek and see what the new one is like."

I: "In the Bible the opponent of God isn't atheism; it's the idols. The fact that 'there is only one God,' which we've seen here, means that we must not adore idols. And that was because all pagan religions were alienating. Only Yahweh liberates. In Psalm 82 God appears rebuking the gods because they are on the side of the oppressors, because they have not been just to the weak and orphaned, because they do not liberate the poor and the needy. The first commandment, says Christ, is like the second; it really *is* the second. Not to serve other gods means to love your neighbor, because it means to love only God, and love of God is achieved only through love of your neighbor. And it's a betrayal of the thought of Jesus to try to make two commandments and not one. It's not a question of loving God and loving your neighbor, but rather of loving God-in-neighbor as a single thing, because God can be loved only in your neighbor. What is said here is that love of God-in-neighbor is worth more than any worship of God."

18

Spirituality and Politics

LEONARDO BOFF

TO BE A CONTEMPLATIVE IN LIBERATION

The outstanding characteristic of Latin American church life in recent years has been an increasing awareness of the Christian responsibility in faith to help create social changes, to help society move in the direction of more justice and societal participation for the masses of the poor in our countries.

Spiritual Shock: Encounter with God in the Class of the Poor

In the light of faith, in evangelical solidarity with the very neediest, increasing numbers of groups within the Church, including entire national episcopates, now seek to live and teach the Christian faith in such a way that it will be a motivating force for the integral liberation of the human being. Thus a vast, systematic liberation process, sprung from the unity of faith and life, is under way at the heart of our Christian communities.

Simultaneously, the corresponding critical discourse has developed. The theology of liberation is practiced in the interests of integral liberation, especially that of the most oppressed members of society. But what sustains both the practice and the theory (the theology) of liberation is a spiritual experience of encounter with the Lord of the poor. Underlying any innovative practice in the Church—including, and especially, any genuine and genuinely new theology—is a latent religious experience. This total existential experience, this "word," is the source from which all else springs.

From the essay, "Spirituality and Politics" in *Faith on the Edge: Religion and Marginalized Existence* (New York: Harper & Row, 1989; Maryknoll, N.Y.: Orbis Books, 1991), pp. 80-91. Translated by Robert R. Barr.

The rest is an effort to translate this word into the framework of a historically limited reality. Only from such a starting point can the great syntheses of the theologians of the past be explained.

Any spiritual experience means an encounter with a new, challenging face of God, emerging from the great challenges of historical reality. Great social and historical changes are charged with an ultimate meaning, a supreme demand, which religious minds recognize as having proceeded from the mystery of God. God has meaning only when appearing as the only radically important piece of a given reality, blazing away amid the lights and shadows of the rest of that reality. Here God is seen not as a closely defined, limited category in a religious framework but as an event of meaning, of hope, of absolute future for men and women and their history. This experience breeds a peculiar, typical experience of the mystery of God.

This, then, is the subjective moment of the experience of which we speak. But we can enunciate the same phenomenon in strictly theological language. Let us put it this way: God, in a will to self-communication, inserts a concrete self-revelation into history. Human beings grasp a new face of God because God's self-revelation actually contains this new face. It is God who posits the sacramental signs, chooses the emissaries, inspires the creation of an adequate discourse, and stimulates the practices consistent with the revelation in question. There will always be attentive spirits, who will identify this new divine voice and be faithful to its challenges.

In recent years, it seems to us, God has burst upon our continent like an erupting volcano. The divine will has prioritized the poor as the sacrament of this self-communication. The ruler of the universe assures us that our poor hear the divine call for solidarity, identification, justice, and dignity. And the particular churches have obeyed that call (Latin *ob-edire*, from *audire*, "to hear"). In the face of the scandal of poverty, God urges us all to act in behalf of the poor against poverty, to the end that we may all enjoy the fruits of justice. The required activity holds a clear liberation dimension sprung from the incarnation of a Christian faith that now seeks to cling to the Lord present in the poor. To struggle at the side of the poor, to be enfleshed in their longings, to commune with Christ present in the poor is to live in Christ's discipleship.

Holding to the Christ of the poor means being a "contemplative in liberation": *contemplativus in liberatione*. It implies a new way of seeking holiness and mystical union with God. A spiritual collision with God's new manifestation has produced specific new traits in the spirituality lived and practiced by so many Christians committed to the integral liberation of their sisters and brothers. This spiritual collision is the basis of the theology of liberation.

Before describing this new spirituality, however, let us briefly examine the great spiritual tradition of the Church, underscoring the original contribution of each major stage in its development. The problem in the contemporary stage is how to be a contemplative in liberation, how—in our pastoral practices, in our contact with the people—we may live a vital, concrete encounter with God. Perhaps by reflecting on this topic against a background of the Christian spiritual tradition we may more easily locate the specific difference of this new Latin American spirituality. . . .

Synthesis of Prayer and Liberation

The synthesis that must be developed, and the one that is being developed in Latin America, is a synthesis of prayer *in* action, prayer *within* activity, prayer *with* the deed. What must be eliminated is a divorce between prayer on one side and action on the other—prayer severed from a lived commitment to the liberation of the oppressed. The correct relationship of prayer and action consists of prayer offered in the very process of liberation, when we experience an encounter with God *in* our sisters and brothers. Every great saint in history has managed this vital, concrete synthesis, and it has always constituted the secret of an authentically Christian life.

In Latin America, however, we are in something of a new situation, or at least one with particular accents. The problem is not simply that of the relationship between prayer and activity. The problem is the relationship between prayer and liberation precisely—between prayer and political, social, historical, transforming action. In its correct formulation, the question must be posed in terms of *spirituality and politics.* How is one to make a radical commitment to the liberation of the oppressed and at the same time a commitment to the source of all liberation, God? How can passion for God, the characteristic of any genuinely religious human being, be steeped in a passion for the people and for justice to the people, which is the distinctive note of the political activist? . . .

The synthesis constituting the object of our quest is not a verbal one. The problem is not how to manage a correct correlation of terms. The problem is how to *live* a Christian practice imbued with prayer and commitment. How can commitment spring from prayer and prayer well up from the heart of commitment?

Passion for God in a Passion for the Impoverished

The experience of a vital, authentic faith effects a unity of prayer and liberation. But the experience of faith must be correctly understood. As we have said many times, faith is first of all a vital experience of all things in the light of God. Faith defines the *whence* and the *whither* of our very existence, which is God and God's design of love communicated and realized in all things. For the person of faith, reality is not primarily profane or sacred. It is simply sacramental. Creaturely reality reveals God, evokes God, comes steeped in the divine reality. Thus the experience of faith unifies life, for it contemplates reality as unified by the fact that God is the origin and destiny of its every part and parcel. A living faith is a way of life. It therefore carries a contemplative attitude toward the world. It sees tokens, traces of God on all sides. But it is not enough that faith be alive. It must also be true. And faith is only true when it becomes love and justice. To be pleasing to God, it is not enough to accept God. One must build the Reign of God, which is a Reign of truth, love, and justice. Only a committed faith is salvific faith and therefore true. "The faith that does nothing in practice . . . is thoroughly lifeless. . . . Without works faith is idle. . . . Faith without works is as dead as a body without breath" (James 2:17, 20, 26). Sheer belief is of no avail. "Do you believe that God is one? You are quite right. The demons believe that, and shudder" (James 2:19).

Christian faith knows that Christ is in the poor in an especially concentrated sacramental way. Not only do the poor have needs that must be alleviated; they possess a singular wealth of their own. They are the chosen vessels of the Lord, the prime addressees of the Reign of God, the potential evangelizers of the Church and of the whole human race. The believer has a view of the poor that is more than socioanalytic. Over and above identifying the passion of the poor and the causes of the mechanisms of their impoverishment, the believer gazes upon the class of the impoverished with the eyes of faith and sees the suffering face of the Servant of Yahweh. Nor is this gaze satiated with the moment of contemplation, as if the believer were merely using the poor as a means to union with the Lord. Christ identifies with the poor in order to be served and welcomed *precisely in them.* Their miserable condition provokes a movement of the heart: "I was hungry . . . " (Matt. 25:35). We are truly with the Lord in the poor, then, when we commit ourselves to struggle against the poverty that demeans persons and contravenes the will of God, to struggle against the fruit of a relationship of sin and exploitation. The true faith itself, precisely by virtue of its truth, implies and demands a commitment to liberation: ". . . and you gave me food . . ." (Matt. 25:35). If we undertake no liberating action, then not only do we not love our neighbor, we do not love God (1 John 3:17). "Let us love in deed and in truth and not merely talk about it" (1 John 3:18).

This spiritual experience bestows unity on the relationship between faith and life, between spirituality and politics. But just how do we maintain this unity? How are we to foster it in the face of so many forces of decay and dissolution? The vision at once contemplative and liberating does not emerge spontaneously. It is the most significant expression of a living, true faith. But how are we to establish this consistency between contemplation and liberation?

Here two poles emerge: prayer and practice. The question cannot, however, be answered by way of either a polarization or a juxtaposition. . . . We must create a dialectical articulation of the poles. We must regard them as two reciprocally open, mutually involved spaces. However, one pole will have priority: prayer.

Through prayer, human beings express what is noblest and most profound in their existence. Through prayer they rise above themselves, transcend all the grandeurs of creation and history, assume an "ecstatic" position by which they "stand out" from themselves, strike up a dialogue with the supreme mystery, and cry, "Father!" Not that they leave the universe behind. On the contrary, they sweep it up and transform it into an offering to God. But they do deliver themselves from all bonds of earth: they denounce all historical absolutes, relativize them, and stand naked and alone with the Absolute, with whom they then proceed to create history. Here God is discovered as the Holy. With God we are before the supremely momentous, the Definitive. And yet this God, so holy, so absolutely momentous, is revealed as an engaged God, a God who wants to "get involved," a God sensitive to the sobs of the oppressed, a God who can say, "I have witnessed the affliction of my people . . . and have heard their cry of complaint against their slave drivers, so I know well what they are suffering. Therefore I have come down to rescue them . . . " (Exod. 3:7-8). Thus the God who says to us in our prayer, "Come," also says in the same prayer, "Go." The God who calls us to the divine union also calls us to make a commitment to liberation. God commands that our passion for God in Jesus Christ be lived in a passion for our suffering, needy brothers and sisters.

The activity of service to our sisters and brothers, in solidarity with their struggles for liberation, springs from the depths of the prayer that reaches the heart of God. Prayer fosters the outlook by which the believer sees in the poor, in an entire class of exploited persons, the sacramental presence of the Lord. Without a prayer born of faith, our eyesight would grow dim, seeing only the surface of things, failing to descend to the mystical depths in which we enter into communion with a Lord present in the condemned, awaiting us all in the humiliated and wronged of history.

Conversely, the pole of liberating practice refers us to the pole of prayer, that nourishing, supportive wellspring of strength for the struggle. Prayer guarantees the maintenance of Christian identity throughout the liberating process. For a Christian, liberation, in order to be genuine, must anticipate the Reign of God. It must render Jesus' redemption a matter of concrete history. Faith and prayer permit us to see our own human effort, which so often seems to have so little lasting value, as an integral part of the historical construction of the Reign.

Social practice has its concrete, this-worldly solidity, and this in itself would have sufficed to justify it. But in fact, the meaning of social practice is not exhausted here. Our human efforts have a transcendent value, a salvific meaning as well, and faith reveals this dimension of transcendence. For a person of faith, then, a service of liberation in behalf of one's sister or brother constitutes a genuine *diakonia* to the Lord, an association to his work of redemption and liberation, and therefore a genuine *leitourgia* in the Spirit. This is what it means to be a *contemplativa in liberatione.* Contemplation is not reserved to the sacred space of prayer or to the sacrosanct enclosure of church or monastery; it finds its place also in a social and political practice watered, cultivated, and fertilized by a faith living and true.

It is the noble heritage of the Latin American Church that the bishops, priests, religious, and laity most committed to the cause of the poor (the cause of their justice, their rights, their dignity) are also the most prayerful. They join together God and their neediest neighbor in one and the same movement of love and dedication.

A NEW SPIRITUALITY: PRINCIPAL CHARACTERISTICS AND CHALLENGES

What are some of the more significant traits of this new spirituality, this contemplation lived in a context of liberation?

1. Prayer Materialized in Action

The prayer of liberation gathers up all the material of the committed life – the struggles, the collective efforts, the mistakes, the defeats, and the victories of that life – returns thanks for the steps already taken, and makes its petitions not individualistically but with a view to the whole spiritual pilgrimage of a *contemplativus in liberatione*. The prayer of liberation is a prayer for those who suffer and for those who inflict the suffering. The conflict of the liberation process finds a special echo in prayer. To confess one's sins becomes a spontaneous, joint concern of the entire community, where no one hides behind ethereal words but all open their hearts, revealing matters of the utmost intimacy. Here is a prayer that reflects the liberation of the heart. We especially notice and confess any inconsistencies between what we profess and how we live – any lack of solidarity and commitment by which our Christian lives may be impaired.

2. Prayer as a Self-Expression of the Liberation Community

Private prayer has its permanent, unquestionable value. But in our committed groups, prayer is essentially a sharing of experiences and practices, enlightened by the light of faith and the gospel and criticized in that light. The experience of prayer is not limited to the splendid intimacy of the soul alone with the Alone. Here is a prayer that opens the praying subject out to others. Here is a prayer heard not only by God but by our neighbor, for it communicates to that neighbor. We word our prayer in such a way as to comfort and encourage one another. We talk aloud to God about someone's problems – just before rushing to that person's assistance. No "holy shame," no false modesty conceals our divine visitations and illuminations. For most of us, our soul is an open book. This in itself is a manifestation of the process of personal liberation transpiring at the very heart of the community.

3. Liturgy as Celebration of Life

The canonical liturgy has the power to unite. It expresses the catholicity of our faith. But the more closely our communities wed faith to life, spirituality to politics, the more they express this shared celebration of life in liturgy. And a rich creativity appears whose worth and sacred nature are assured by the people's refined sense of the sacred and exalted. The people avail themselves of symbols of special meaning for their group. For example, they choreograph their own dances and use them in plays to be presented to others of their group. The resulting spiritual dramas, performed to the accompaniment of bodily expressions having a special meaning and importance for the people, are frequently rich and moving.

4. Critical Prayer

Liberation prayer frequently becomes a vehicle for critically examining the practices and attitudes of community members. Our people are able to listen to criticism from one another without undue sensitivity or personal offense. The important thing here is to be sure we use objective criteria: the Reign of God, liberation, and respect for the pilgrimage of the people. We simply confront the practices of our lay ministers with these criteria. True conversions emerge from this sort of sincerity and loyalty, affording us a great deal of help in our evangelization.

5. Political Holiness

Christian tradition is peopled with saints who were ascetics—who overcame their passions and faithfully observed the laws of God and the Church. It knows almost no saints who were politicians or activists. But the liberation process has created the matrix of another type of holiness. Christians must continue to battle their own passions. This is clear. But now they battle the mechanisms of exploitation and destruction of the community as well. New virtues emerge, difficult but genuine: solidarity with one's sisters and brothers, the members of the impoverished class; participation in community decisions, and fidelity to these decisions once they are made; victory over one's hatred of the agents of the mechanisms of impoverishment; an ability to see beyond the obvious and work for a future society not yet in sight and perhaps never to be enjoyed at all. This new type of asceticism makes its own demands and calls for particular sacrifices if one is to remain pure of heart and celebrate the spirit of the Beatitudes.

6. *Prophetic Courage and "Historical Patience"*

From their faith and their prayer many committed Christians have drawn the courage to confront the powers of this world in a struggle for the cause of the people and their trampled dignity. In this they show their apostolic *parrhesia* — the courage to "speak up" to someone of higher rank — oblivious to the risk of persecution, imprisonment, loss of employment, torture, even physical annihilation. And paradoxically, along with this evangelical courage, they have the "historical patience" to bear up under the hardships of a long, slow journey in the company of the people they love. They have acquired a sensitivity to the measured pace of a people accustomed to repression. They have confidence in these people, in their courage, their capacity to struggle despite their limitations, mistakes, and intellectual backwardness. They have a keen belief in the power of the Spirit, who acts in the lowly and the suffering. They believe in the victory of their cause and the rightness of their struggle. This attitude springs from a contemplative vision of history, whose only sovereign is God.

7. *An Attitude of Easter*

Liberation always comes at a price. Death and resurrection are to be accepted with evangelical joviality and serenity. Sacrifices, threats, even martyrdoms inspire no fear. Hardship of any sort is accepted as part of following Jesus. Our communities have a powerful sense of the cross. They look on it as a necessary step along the road to victory. When justice triumphs, when the people win their struggle and life is worth living, they experience resurrection. Historical liberation is a share in Jesus' resurrection. It is experienced as the temporal anticipation of the fullness of eschatological triumph. And it is celebrated as it is experienced, for it is the power of the presence of the Spirit at the heart of history.

We could list other characteristics of this kind of prayer, which is coming to be more and more frequently practiced in communities committed to the liberation of the very neediest. Our communities maintain a union of prayer and action, faith and liberation, a passion for God expressed in a passion for the people. New possibilities are constantly being created for the emergence of this new kind of Christian, the Christian deeply committed to the cities of earth and heaven alike, convinced that the latter depends on how we shall have busied ourselves in the creation of the former. Heaven is not the enemy of earth. It actually begins on earth. Both realms of existence are under the rainbow of grace, of God's deed of liberation in Jesus Christ.

This is not mere theology. This is the life and spirituality of a great many Christians.

19

Emerging Spirituality of Asian Women

MARY JOHN MANANZAN AND SUN AI PARK

WHAT IS SPIRITUALITY?

Spirituality is not a simple concept. It is used to describe different realities that have converging elements. The totality of the elements may differ from one understanding to another. Christians or theistic people, for example, may not be able to understand how nonbelievers could have a spirituality. And yet self-proclaimed atheists may be deeply spiritual people.

What then is spirituality? In Christian theology and practice, an old understanding of spirituality would more or less describe it as theology applied to daily life — to one's personal life of prayer and asceticism, to be more precise. There is, however, an emerging understanding of spirituality as the inner core made up of all the experiences and encounters one has had in one's life and out of which come the motivations, inspirations, and commitment that make one live and decide in a particular way. One might say, it is the shape in which the Holy Spirit has molded herself into one's life.

Donal Dorr[1] writes about the center in a person, which is partly influenced by one's genetic heritage and environment but is largely shaped by one's gut-level experiences and major options in life. It is also this center that is the focus of our "experience of God." It is here we allow the Holy Spirit to move us, to act in us, to assimilate the major experiences we encounter in our lives, especially the new and unpredictable that might totally contradict the accumulated experiences that through the years have shaped our core. This is where the phenomenon of conversion, metanoia, may be realized. Meditation, prayer, and asceticism enable individuals to

From *With Passion and Compassion: Third World Women Doing Theology*, Virginia Fabella, Mercy Amba Oduyoye, eds. (Maryknoll, N.Y.: Orbis Books, 1988), pp. 77-88.

integrate these experiences into their inner core or to revise it partially or completely.

Modern-day prophetic theologians, especially Latin American liberation theologians and feminist theologians, come out boldly on the holistic liberation message that the Judeo-Christian religion has in its core, and point out errors and misunderstandings that traditional church theology has woven into the Christian understanding of spirituality. One of the most serious errors is the dualism that separates the spiritual from the bodily and material realm, intellectual from emotional expressions, concerns of the other world from those of this world, and that subsequently divides men from women. Feminist theologians attribute the last division to patriarchy.

Gustavo Gutiérrez expresses the holistic nature of spirituality in a rather pointed way: "When one is concerned with one's own stomach, it is materialism, but when one is concerned with other people's stomachs it is spirituality."[2] Both are concerned with the stomach, but one is called materialism and the other spirituality. Christian spirituality deals with this fine distinction, which can be summed up as the unity of self and others, the material and the spiritual, love and justice, community and individuals, religions and politics, peace and struggle toward holistic salvation.

Women's struggle is part and parcel of the historical struggle for the holistic salvation of all humanity. Women can make a unique contribution toward this goal based on their spirituality, which is formulated throughout their concrete pro-life way of living and experiences. All the disastrous dimension of patriarchal culture is typically exemplified in its demeaning, ignoring, and despising the very spirituality of women that is oriented toward and sustaining life in love. The spirituality affirming womanhood, reaching out for liberation of all women and all humanity, is emerging in all parts of the world, and Asia is not exempt.

ASIAN WOMEN'S REALITY

The spirituality of women has its context in the situation of oppression in which they live. It is therefore necessary to describe the Asian situation in order to understand the emerging spirituality of women in the continent.

Asian women share the domestic, economic, political, and religious oppression that their sisters all over the world suffer. However, the concretization of the oppression varies. The image of the subservient, servile Asian woman is behind the varied forms of trafficking of Asian women ranging from mail-order brides to prostitution. Because of the economic crisis, women in Asia suffer a double burden in the work situation (low wages and sexual harassment) and a triple burden in the case of rural women (field work, domestic work, and marketing of goods). Because of political repression, Asian women have also been raped, tortured, imprisoned, and killed for their political beliefs.

Specifically, Malaysian women suffer the resurgence of religious fundamentalism and worsening communal relations; Korean women suffer from the division of their country into North and South and from the oppressive Confucian family law; Indian women suffer from the caste system and the dowry system—and Muslim women in some Asian countries have to submit to female genital mutilation. Sri Lankan women are torn by the ethnic struggle. Although Japanese women belong to a First World society, they also suffer from the male-oriented emperor system, the tragic experience of the nuclear bomb, and the hazards of a highly technological society.

In Asia, as well as in other parts of the world, there is the problem of "tokenism." Some women are given a status of equality and privilege as an excuse to perpetuate the general structure and patterns of society. "Token" women are not oriented into the new vision of human relationship and community that the alternative feminist ideology offers; therefore, they are not committed to the work of renewal. Instead they ape the old pattern of individualism and dogged competition for self-glory. That is the reason why this present dialogue on Asian women's spirituality provides a very important groundwork. If Eve is as equally responsible as Adam for "the fall," she also needs repentance and conversion to be accepted into the reign of God. This honest admission of shared responsibility in sin, but with hope and faith in the grace of God, which brings wonders and new creation, is the starting point of an emerging Asian women's spirituality that motivates their actions and reflections. Aggravating the situation is the division and misunderstanding among women because of differences in perception regarding oppression. In fact, in Asia there is a real oppression of women by other women, evident in the caste system and in the practice of having domestic servants.

It is these complex and varied forms of oppression that Asian women are struggling against, and in the process of the struggle they are giving birth to a spirituality that is particularly woman's and specifically Asian.

FRAMEWORK AND NATURE OF ASIAN WOMEN'S SPIRITUALITY

External and internal exploitation and oppression in the sphere of politics and economics do not exclude women. On the contrary, in their powerlessness they are more severely victimized than their male partners in their particular class, race, and caste. This is the result of patriarchal domination. Women's oppression comes in different combinations of political, economic, and religio-cultural oppression within the underlying patriarchal domination. Therefore, in Third World countries, dealing only with women's issues cannot uproot all the problems women face in their societies. It is obvious that the emerging Asian women's spirituality longs for freedom from exploitation—a free society for themselves as well as for the men and children. The liberation framework of Asian women includes, and is included in, the overall people's movement to be free. It brings a qualitatively different vision and interpersonal relationship from the traditional male ways of constructing communities.

In the Philippines, women are involved in national liberation struggles; they were alongside the men in the anti-Marcos-dictatorial-regime movement. Filipino women are still committed to the struggle of the people in the economic, political, and cultural movements of liberation, which have not ceased even after the February 1986 event [overthrow of the dictator Ferdinand Marcos—eds.]. They see this struggle toward societal transformation as a necessary though not sufficient condition for their own liberation. As they go through the crucible of suffering, they experience significant changes in their understanding and practice of religion and in the manifestation of their religiosity. We see that the spirit of protest against domination, whether it be the social, political, economic, ecclesial, or domestic order, has correlation with the spirituality of the Asian women's overall struggle for liberation. The general tendency of this spirituality is the search for human dignity and self-determination toward holistic liberation.

The February 1986 event in the Philippines—the demonstration of people power that negated the dictatorial oppression of Ferdinand Marcos—has not solved the basic problems of the country. There is still the unequal distribution of land and capital, with 2 percent of the population owning and controlling 70 percent of the resources; and the Philippines continues to be exploited by the United States through the International Monetary Fund/World Bank and the transnational corporations. Thus massive poverty is still widespread, and prostitution remains a very big problem.

As the women take up the prostitution issue in the Philippines and in other countries like Thailand, Korea, India, and Sri Lanka, they are dealing with the question of the human dignity and self-determination of these innumerable victims who are pushed into the degrading situation by force of circumstance. And they are fully aware that the problems are structural and systemic. Asian people everywhere are coming to this realization and various types of protest movements are occurring. They are protesting against the control of the big powers and their own exploitation, which deprives them of their right to self-determination and human dignity. A few examples are Korea, India, and Sri Lanka.

Let us turn to Korea. The division of the country was decided by the superpowers at the end of World War II. This decision was imposed on the Korean people by the two competing ideologies that exist in today's world. Did Koreans have the time or the opportunity to make their own choice? See what has happened there ever since.

These two tiny countries are used as buffer zones by the two ideological powers and are the frontline of their warfare. The Korean War in 1950-53 was an example. At the expense of millions of lives, and grave human and economic casualties, the war gained nothing but deep-rooted enmity and increasing militarism. It is said that the two Koreas now rank as fifth and sixth in military might in the world, with nuclear weapons in stock to be used at any time.

The intellectuals and workers in South Korea see clearly the foreign and local exploitation that accompanies political oppression. The protest demonstrations have continued ever since student power toppled the American-backed dictatorial regime in 1960. Thousands of students have been tortured and imprisoned. What do they want, risking so much? They want to have a truly independent and unified democratic country where the rights of the people for self-determination, and their participation in building a political and economic system for the people and of the people, will be a reality and not mere lipservice.

If Koreans are protesting against the arbitrary division of the nation and its consequences, in the Indian subcontinent the protest is against the colonial policy or the arbitrary bringing together of different ethnic, linguistic, and religious groups to form a nation. The communal conflict in Sri Lanka and India has this factor. Of course, other factors such as the discriminatory economic and educational policies of the two governments are also responsible. The struggle of the Tamils in Sri Lanka, the Punjabs in India, the ethnic minorities in Japan — all have the same spiritual traits. They all want equal and just treatment and a full share of human dignity. And in all these, the women are the most affected and are therefore correspondingly militant in the struggle for the liberation of their people.

In an atelier of Japanese women artists, Tomiyama Daeko has a large picture depicting her eschatological vision. As in Isaiah, babies are playing with wild beasts, and flowers and plants are all around, growing in peace. In the center is a house in which a woman is giving birth to a child.

For Ms. Tomiyama, female sexuality is sacred. It is in the center of the universe. For her, depicting it in a meaningful way is important so that it does not become pornographic. It is reminiscent of the fertility cult of ancient times where birthing was the center of worship, and goddesses and priestesses were the free expressions of matriarchal ideology.

Modern-day feminist theologians give new interpretations to female sexuality. For example, Phyllis Trible explores the original Hebrew meaning of the word "womb" and associates it with compassionate spirituality.[3] Carol Ochs develops the spirituality of women in their motherhood function.[4] Dorothee Sölle emphasizes the life-giving aspect of women to choose life amid the nuclear devastation threatening today's world.[5]

The experience of motherhood must be incorporated in the process of marching toward a new society, which feminist women and men envision. The nature of this new society is feminist. Feminism promotes the equality of all human beings, and the ideology is derived from the experiences of women giving birth, and caring, and nurturing their children and family to the extent of denying themselves in the highest spirituality of love. The women do this in order to give life and to provide for others so that all may live. Here the self and the community are one. The extreme individualism we see in the Western societies cannot have its way.

However, there can be a danger of condoning the traditional self-effacing masochism of women reinforced in the glorification of motherhood, keeping them in the depth of despair and resignation. This is so if motherhood is used for exploitation, by an individual man, of one or more women where nothing is questioned and no meaning is given. However, when conscientized women and men act and live out this supreme spirituality toward the goal of a new heaven and new earth in concrete models, it is liberational.

A woman worker in Korea, Soon Ock Lee (pseudonym) was trained in the urban and rural mission program when she worked for a textile company in Seoul. She organized a workers' union and faced police violence. After a year in prison, her name was put on the list of people not to be hired by any other company. She had to struggle for survival. After several desperate attempts for a job she was hired by a bus company as a ticket girl, using her relative's identity card. It was a very tough job.

About seventy girls working for the company lived in a longhouse, which was fenced with barbed wire to prevent any of them from running away. They were awakened at 4 A.M. to get ready to go to work at 5 A.M. The day's work was tiring and heavy. They had to swallow insulting words from customers and had to face occasional bodily search on suspicion of embezzling bus fares. When they returned to the house after 11 P.M., everybody was tired and cross. They had to queue up for the shower. There was only one running-water faucet. They had to sleep in indescribable conditions.

Soon Ock hated the whole situation. But eventually she thought of the reasons why the girls were the way they were and decided to help them. When everybody went to sleep she collected all the handkerchiefs and socks, which were thrown about everywhere in the room. She washed all of them and tidied them when they were dry. For the first couple of days, the girls did not notice, but eventually they began to appreciate and trust Soon Ock. When she won their confidence, she organized a strike to demand better working conditions, humane treatment, and overtime pay (which was not provided for). She booked a motel room, which was several miles away from the house. She woke up all the girls one night and took them out of the house and to her motel room. The next morning, the bus company found no ticket girls. The authorities started to investigate. Soon the police were mobilized in the vicinity of the motel, but the girls refused to come out for three days, until their demand was considered. The girls' working conditions improved a bit, but Soon Ock was again dismissed and her name continued to be on the list.

In this story we see a similarity to the Exodus-event. The women, coming from different situations, the mother, the sister, the midwives, and the Pharaoh's daughter, all acted in saving and preserving a life, which became the mighty undercurrent of the historical liberation of the exploited and oppressed Hebrew people. Soon Ock's action for justice was motivated by the love of neighbor. Her sacrificial act of protest against injustice and dehumanization of her sister workers made them experience a glimpse of liberation and solidarity of sisterhood. The individuality of Soon Ock is unified with the collective destiny of her colleagues, culminating in a perfect unity of love and justice, self-assertion and service for others, a quality of spirituality blended with spontaneous actions, where the material concerns became transformed into purified spirituality.

As women, we experience regular and everyday discrimination: the limiting experiences of housewives confined to the home, as society assigns them, the despair of the wives who are beaten but who cannot separate from their husbands "because of the children" or because of social disapproval or because of their own emotional and psychological dependence on their husbands. We defy the exploitation and discrimination and sexual harassment of our sisters who work either in the rural areas as an invisible contribution to agricultural production or in the urban setting as factory workers. We defy the continuous insult to our womanhood in the mass media and advertisements and the more blatant exploitation of our sisters through prostitution, mail-order brides, and so forth.

But aside from these regular, day-to-day experiences, we have our own private hell, which we experience at crisis points of our lives as women and to which each one of us could relate with poignancy and anguish and from which we emerge either triumphantly with inner liberation or with bitterness and resentment, crushed and mortally wounded in the depth of our being.

A Filipino prostitute, who was a guest in an alternative tourism seminar, is still struggling to find meaning in her life of prostitution that began when she lost her virginity at the age of fifteen to get money to pay the hospital bills of her tubercular mother. She struggles with the hate that wells up within her as she tells of how a policeman, Mang Apeng, threatened to arrest her and her American companion. After being paid 150 pesos (approximately $7) by the American, Mang Apeng still waited for her at the hotel to rob her of the 200 pesos that she earned after the exhausting and degrading evening with her companion. In despair, she shared with us the fact that she is two months pregnant, and exclaimed, "Lord, forgive me, I have to abort it if I have to continue earning my living."

We feel there is a growing awareness among Asian women of the ramifications of the women's question. The personal and social experiences of women as well as their common struggle have shaped the particular form of spirituality that is emerging among them. This spirituality is nourished by their growing understanding of their self-image, which has been obscured by the roles that have been assigned to them by patriarchal society. It in turn influences not only their interpersonal relationships with the significant people in their lives, like their husbands, but also their relationship with men in general. This also forms the collective consciousness that is growing among women as they struggle against the exploitation and discrimination against them, and as they experience the triumph and victory they have achieved in this struggle. It is therefore not just a vertical relationship with God but an integral spirituality that is shaped by prayer and also by relational experiences and struggle—personal, interpersonal, and societal.

The emerging spirituality of women is characterized by an inner liberation from the internal and external slaveries they have struggled to break. Militant women are one in the experience of this sense of liberation coming from their development in self-knowledge and self-acceptance and in their growth in self-esteem.

Christian women involved in national struggles have begun questioning the traditional teachings of the church, especially those that justify the subordination of women. They are slowly getting a clearer self-image and are experiencing a process of inner liberation from the abiding guilt feelings induced by religious doctrines and ethical teachings of the church. Women are less and less inclined to pattern their life after the impossible model of virgin-mother of the domesticating Mary-cult imposed by foreign missionaries. They are questioning the interpretation of St. Paul's "wives, obey your husbands" when it comes to the use of their body in the frequency of pregnancy or in submitting to their husbands every time the latter claim their marital rights. Although the Catholic church has never budged from its insistence on the natural method of birth control, about 90 percent[6] of Catholic Filipino women quietly contravene this Catholic position and use other forms of contraceptives. Not a few have had themselves ligated after the birth of their third or fourth child.

Among middle-class women, who more than their lower-class sisters are devastated by broken relationships with men, there has been an acceptance of single parenthood. Women are learning to face life alone, conquering their emotional and psychological dependency, finding a meaning in life apart from their estranged male partners. The growing organization of women among the urban poor and in labor unions has resulted in a sense of sisterly solidarity that strengthens the women in their struggle against the discrimination and oppression they experience both in their homes and in their work places.

INTERFAITH DIALOGUE AND ASIAN WOMEN

Interfaith dialogue is an important part of the discussion of the emerging Asian women's spirituality. Ecumenical spirituality seeks unity of humankind in humility and reverence toward all life and all belief systems. Christian triumphalism, which is the spirituality of colonialism and neocolonialism, is judged here. A Hindu has this to say regarding Christian missionary endeavor:

Look at what Christian civilization has done to the life in the world. There is merciless exploitation of natural and human resources, which has brought ecological crisis and suffering and the misery of millions

of workers and peasants in Asia. There is the nuclear threat, which
can annihilate more than twenty times over the total life on the planet.
And still you want to make us Christians?[7]

How are we going to face this accusation of non-Christians who are
seriously concerned with the well-being of all humanity? As Christian
women, can we condone all the structural and systemic evils Christian civilization has brought, and concentrate only on securing privileged posts in
a rotten structure? While it is important to fight for power positions when
one is discriminated against for being a woman, it is as important to be
committed to bringing about radically new values that are people-oriented,
concerned for life and for a truly humane community. This goal is a double
task for a better society with women leaders. But if we women claim to be
the hope, we must carry out this task. There is no easy way out. The story
of Esther has a profound message. Esther went through a highly competitive
screening test, but she hid her identity until it was time to reveal it. She
used strategic actions, all carefully planned in order to save her people
from imminent schemes of peril. Her action was founded on total commitment. She said: "If I must perish, I must perish!" (Esther 4:17). She was
ready to give her own life for the many; Christian women leaders must be
accountable for the faith of their sisters and brothers. For this, a consciousness-raising education that would awaken the awareness of Christian
women to this task is of utmost importance.

This search for the wholeness of life that is the core of the emerging
women's spirituality is further underlined in the statement of the Urban
and Rural Mission of the Christian Conference of Asia on the occasion of
the Bhopal, India, tragedy in 1986:

Christian: Biblical faith, spirituality and religion have centered on
liberation/salvation. Salvation means wholeness ... meaning whole,
entire, complete or uninjured, unimpaired, unbroken. ... Wholeness
suggests all that the Hebrew word *Shalom* conveys. *Shalom* is a comprehensive word for prosperity and well-being, peace, harmony, happiness of the people of God in [God's] presence and company.
SHALOM.

Buddhist: The key word for the affirmation of wholeness of life is to
walk on. When one is a weakling, one is afraid of death and suffering
and cannot walk on. Once we understand the Dharma, then we can
adjust our inner condition to have a detached view of the world, less
greed, hatred and delusion.

Muslim: All creation and humankind is one single whole, living
through genesis, leading to the perfection of the person, i.e., the complete expression of one's creativity in terms of reaching towards two

essential arms *(a)* the relation between person and environment, and *(b)* the relation between person and God, i.e., the inner being.

Hindu: That which holds is Dharma, i.e., the order. It is a totality, a holistic point of view towards life. . . . It is a question of an order, a complete, total view of things in which things have to fall in place. . . . When we talk of the so-called Hindu, in fact, we are talking of civilization and not of religion or faith.

This statement represents the common views of these four major religions in Asia as they seek the holistic salvation of humanity. However, knowing that deep-rooted misogynous ideologies and practices are the reality in all the existing major religions and cultures in Asia, one cannot help but raise a burning question. No matter how beautiful the idea of wholeness might be, can a patriarchal culture be inclusive of women's aspirations?

What Elisabeth Schüssler Fiorenza says about feminist suspicion in hermeneutics[8] is echoed by Asian women as we open our eyes to the reality of discrimination against women in the name of respect for the traditional culture and religions. Women find themselves very often excluded even by the ideology of wholeness and holistic salvation. It is because patriarchy can never be holistic. Patriarchy is basically androcentric, and it can never include women and children in the center of its world as equals. Even love for women and children is for men's own selfish needs. That is the reason why women and children are put perpetually on the periphery even if mechanisms of make-believe are woven into their emotional and financial dependency.

In the coming reign of God, Christ will put children in the center (Mt. 19:1315). In Jesus' life and mission of counterculture, he befriended all the downtrodden, including women. If a growing people's movement all over Asia is a sign of our times, demands made in the various women's movements are the torch lighting the way toward the true wholeness of life.

Having pointed out the need for feminist critics, what do we do with our traditional culture? On the one hand, the women of Asia are rediscovering their history and are resurrecting their women leaders, heroines, and saints of their particular tradition as sources of cooperation and strength for their struggle. The Filipinos enshrine Princess Urduja and Gabriela Silang, the Indians Mira Bai, Panditta Rama Bai, and so forth. Realizing that the Bible, in spite of all reinterpretations, remains a book written in a particular society, and fully aware of a necessary cultural critique, Asian women are delving into their own traditions, myths, and legends to provide them with the insights, values, and inspiration in their effort toward the full flowering of their womanhood. On the other hand, there is also need for women to undertake a critique of culture. They must actively participate in the interfaith dialogue to give feminist input, sorting out what are the really liberating elements and what are the oppressive elements in them. This kind of cultural analysis in the search for an alternative culture from the feminist perspective is another aspect of the emerging spirituality.

CONCLUSION

From the foregoing reflection we can glean the characteristics of the emerging spirituality we have appropriated as "feminist." In this spirituality, God is one who unites — not one who divides people by creedal dogmas. This spirituality discloses a very liberating portrait of Jesus. The image of the human being transcends the dualistic body-and-soul relationship and has an optimistic view of the possibilities of personhood. Faith is not a security in being saved because of legalistic obedience but is an exciting dimension of radical openness. Salvation has a communal historical and cosmic dimension and is integral and total. The emerging spirituality is active rather than passive, expansive rather than limiting. It celebrates rather than fasts, it surrenders rather than controls. It is an Easter rather than a Good Friday spirituality. It is creative rather than conservative.

Our understanding of salvation that emerges is one worked out by a God of history with the people, and results in a liberation that is total and concrete: total in the sense of the whole person being saved, body and soul, in the context of a social milieu; and concrete in the sense of being a liberation from concrete evils such as slavery, as well as bringing about concrete blessings like land. Throughout salvation history, this was the experience of the people of God. The emerging spirituality of women shows the characteristics of the original meaning of salvation, namely, its totality and concreteness. The release of women's creative energy and new insights have resulted in a refocusing of the different elements of spirituality, which tend to converge in a certain trend that draws its vitality from creation as contrasted with the traditional spirituality that focuses on the fall and redemption.

Spirituality is a process. It is not achieved once and for all. It does not become congealed. It is not even a smooth, continuous growth. There can be retrogression or quantum leaps. It has peaks and abysses. It has its agonies and its ecstasies. The emerging spirituality of women promises to be vibrant, liberating, and colorful. Its direction and tendencies seem to open up to greater possibilities of life and freedom, and therefore to more and more opportunities to be truly, intensely, and wholly alive!

NOTES

1. Donal Dorr, *Spirituality and Justice* (Maryknoll, N.Y.: Orbis Books, 1984), p. 20.

2. In a conversation Sun Ai Park had with Gustavo Gutiérrez when she visited him in his parish house in Lima, Peru, in 1980.

3. Phyllis Trible, *God and the Rhetoric of Sexuality* (Philadelphia, Pa.: Fortress Press, 1978).

4. Carol Ochs, *Women and Spirituality* (Totowa, N.J.: Rowman & Allanheld, 1983).

5. Dorothee Sölle, *Choosing Life* (London: SCM Press, 1981).

6. As reported in a random study made in a women's studies course in a leading women's college in the Philippines.

7. From a conversation Sun Ai Park had with Dr. Stanley Samartha when he was in Singapore to prepare an Interfaith Dialogue Consultation in 1986.

8. Elisabeth Schüssler Fiorenza, "The Will to Choose or to Reject: Continuing Our Critical Work," *Feminist Interpretation of the Bible*, ed. Letty Russell (Philadelphia, Pa.: Westminster Press, 1985), p. 130.

20

The Eucharist in Contemporary Society

TISSA BALASURIYA

Contemporary society has many characteristics which present serious problems to the churches concerning the Eucharist. Some are new issues, others are old questions seen with a new insight and urgency. Some such problems are the quest for meaning and inner fulfillment, the search for community, the concern for justice and human rights in a divided society and world, the emancipation of women, the dialogue of world religions and cultures, and the role of the priesthood. We offer some comments on these issues.

THE QUEST FOR PERSONAL MEANING

Almost everywhere in the world human beings are going through a phase in which they seek to know more clearly the meaning of their lives and of what they do. This is partly due to a disillusionment with the world as it is. They feel deceived by different leaders who have brought them to the present mess. The very power of the control over their lives by modern technology makes their spirit search elsewhere for fulfillment. Even the practices of the traditional religions do not measure up to this requirement. They sense the relative emptiness of much external ritual or conformity without inner meaning or conversion.

The widespread interest in Yoga and the meditative practices of the other oriental religions is an indication of the nature of this search. That western society is discovering the value of Yoga is indicative of both the spiritual quest of many in those countries and of their sense of the inadequacy of the spiritual practices of traditional Christianity. The attraction for Buddhism, Hinduism, Yoga, and meditation is fairly widespread in

From *The Eucharist and Human Liberation* (Maryknoll, N.Y.: Orbis Books, 1979), pp. 42-63.

Europe and North America. This cannot be lightly dismissed as some passing phase, or a fanciful taste for the exotic. It indicates that one dimension of the search of contemporary persons is for interiority, quiet, and meaning. ...

It is not our present intention to develop the theme of Yoga and of meditation in other religions. Rather, we wish to indicate the need for Christian spirituality to relate to the issues posed to contemporary persons by modern society. In this the oriental practices of meditation may teach us how to relate the training of the body and mind to being attuned to the divine and the neighbor.

Since the Eucharist is central to the Christian community and to its spirituality, we have to ask ourselves: Has the Eucharist been able to meet this need, to respond to this dimension of human fulfillment? A deeper problem concerns the meditative practices of the Christian tradition of spirituality: Have these been inadequate and restricted to the religious and clergy? The Mass, especially as celebrated on Sundays in parishes, has been generally very much an externalized ceremony. There is little possibility of quiet meditation at it; or at least it is not fashioned to foster the meditative spirit. There is too much of a concern with externals. The congregation's interest is drawn to different things by the readings, the sermon, the gestures, and also the collections. All these may have a value if they relate to real human concerns. But from the point of view of the need for quiet reflection they can be a distraction. In this sense the Mass does not meet this need. It is hardly a school of spirituality as Yoga and the meditative practices are. It may of course be argued that the practice of the adoration of the Eucharist could provide this need for reflection. This is true. But here too there has been very little development of a method and practice of meditation for lay persons.

The finer inspiration of Christianity concerning the human body as the temple of the Holy Spirit is not actuated in the Eucharist as presently celebrated in the parishes. Christian revelation has an understanding of the human body that includes several aspects. It is spoken of as weak and a source of temptation. The body is also the agent of much good. The care for the corporal needs of others is a criterion of eternal salvation. The body is to rise again at the resurrection of the dead to everlasting happiness. For this the body needs disciplining and training. In the Eucharist all these are given a more specific and deeper meaning when Jesus says "This is my body" which is offered for all. His offering of his body is sacrificial, redemptive, exemplative. It is the will of the Father that in his contestation of the public evils of the day his body should be tortured and crucified.

The Christian tradition had in the Middle Ages an accent on meditation on the body of Christ. There were practices of corporal asceticism. Monastic meditation was related to the rhythm of the day and hence of the human body too. The Gregorian chant, especially of the psalms, provided a background for a meditative reflection on the word of God. It also gave time for the sense of the words to penetrate the inner being of the person. It had a deep meditative mood and potential.

But the present way of celebrating the Eucharist, especially in big churches, does not really harness its potential for meditation, for the education and formation of the body and for giving meaning to life integrally. It is not interior in the better sense of the word: of being deep, personal, reflective, and formative. Nor is it external in the good sense of being active, committed, and transformative of persons and society. It is externalized and rather ritualistic, but does not have much social commitment. Some confuse spiritual with being passive, and communitarian with being merely externalized. Hence they cannot easily see the spiritual dimension of sociopolitical commitment to justice. Nor can they appreciate the social demands of personal holiness. On the other hand, Jesus bears witness to both and to their interrelation in the Eucharist. His offering of his body is real and definitive. It is the ultimate sacrifice offered in deep prayer and personal reflection. He is conscious of the weight of his cross: "My soul is very sorrowful even unto death; remain here and watch with me. . . . My Father, if it be possible, let this cup pass from me . . ." (Matt. 26:38-39). He does not contest the Jewish high priests and the Roman authorities without serious thinking about it. He is intensively active in his exterior life too. This is linked to his profound personal thought, prayer, and convictions. In prayer he decides to go ahead: "Behold the hour is at hand and the Son of man is betrayed into the hands of sinners. Rise, let us be going; see my betrayer is at hand" (Matt. 26:45-46).

The liturgy of the Word can be a powerful help toward both interior reflection and social commitment. For this there must be a fundamental change in the approach toward the Eucharist. There should be a closer relationship to the public life of Jesus, the Last Supper, and his crucifixion — all of which are intimately linked. It is a pity that those who legislate for the renewal of the liturgy do not pay serious attention to this total relationship. On the other hand, much of the concern of the central church authorities is with a rigid conformity to the rubrics and a quantitative fulfillment of the Sunday obligation. Even the reports required by the Roman Sacred Congregations from local bishops ask for data concerning the number of those who attend Mass or receive Communion. There is much less emphasis, if any at all, on the qualitative and deeper personal and social dimensions of the Eucharist.

THE SEARCH FOR COMMUNITY

Corresponding to the quest for a personal identity as against the alienation of human persons from themselves is the search for being in harmony with others. The desire for community is a strong urge in our day too. Human solidarity is seen as an urgent need. The media bring us news of the lack of brotherliness and sisterliness in the relationships among persons and nations. The world spends about U.S. $300 billion on armaments. When this is taken in the background of the $4 billion a year which the United States offers as "aid" to the world (most of it is military aid and investment) we can try to grasp something of the enormous waste involved in the production of these brutal weapons.

This is only one aspect of the lack of community today. Similar waste can be seen at national levels. The inequalities in the world and within countries make the search for community even more challenging. Within a small group such as a parish, an action group, or a religious community also there is a desire for understanding among persons. To be accepted by others, to be cared for, to be able to love and care for others are basic human needs. They are intensified as needs because of today's widespread isolation and individualism.

Modern "civilization," while being technologically extraordinarily advanced, is utterly inhuman in its concern for others and for nature. We are highly civilized barbarians. We have conquered nature in many aspects. We can communicate to and from other celestial bodies. We can move mountains, cause rain, and overcome many diseases. Humanity was never so skilled as now. We are civilized in that sense. We are also refined in some of our manners of behavior. We know how to talk suavely; we can be polished and diplomatic in our relationships. We have developed the sciences as well as the arts.

Yet we are also barbarians. We can destroy nature, and we do so. We pollute the earth. We kill lakes and seas. We erode mountainsides and plains. We destroy trees, exterminate animals. We produce super-powerful lethal weapons. We trade them. We improve them systematically; we use them for genocide.

We are selfish, greedy, and gluttonous. We have enough food for all men, women, and children on the earth; yet a few of us grab this food for ourselves, our animals, and our garbage cans. We feast while others starve to death. We see this on our television screens and we pass pious resolutions about an ambiguous "aid" to those from whom we steal the food. We go to church on Sunday; we say, "Give us this day our daily bread," but our social and economic options deprive the hungry of food, the multitudes of remunerative work.

We are barbarians, for we steal from the hungry, we rob the famine-stricken. If two out of ten children ate the food of the eight others and gave knives to the half-starved eight to fight each other, we would condemn the children as barbarians. This is the position of the human race today. We the rich countries and the rich of the poor countries are "civilized" but we are barbarians.

Thus, while everywhere in the world society is deeply divided, especially between the rich and the poor, the powerful and the weak, the exploiting and the exploited, the Eucharist as a sacrament of unity should build togetherness or at least tend toward it. It is the sacrament for the nourishment of the spiritual life of those baptized and, hence, must tend to create the values of the kingdom of Christ in which there will be no discrimination as between rich and poor, Jew and gentile, and man and woman. It is also a sacrament of repentance and conversion. In the presence of disunity and discrimination, it should lead us to a deep conversion of hearts and to action for the reformation of society. In this way, the Eucharist is a remedy against selfishness both individual and social and a help in the struggle for building the new human society on earth. Thus the healing power of the blood of Christ is to take effect in society.

Unfortunately, the Eucharist itself has very often been the means of perpetuating injustice and divisions. Different places have been built for worship by different communities, such as different Christian groups, churches, and racial groups. There are different Masses in the same city meant for persons of different social classes. The Masses offered on occasions like weddings and funerals, with the graded charges, are also another means of catering to social divisions. Instead of turning toward repentance, reform, and conversion of heart, these encourage disunity, discrimination, and sometimes exploitation. In certain countries like South Africa there are parishes and services which are meant only for whites and others only for blacks. These are maintained by some without an effort to combat the inequalities and discrimination in the system of apartheid. But what is true of South Africa is often true of the rest of the world even though the situation may not be so blatantly revolting. Further, the Eucharist has the disadvantage of several centuries of linkage with colonial exploitation and its brutality.

Such divisions and injustices are an obstacle to the truthfulness of the celebration of the Eucharist. Often, as a eucharistic community, people are not even aware of the division in their society. This is because eucharistic communities seldom reflect together on the type of society in which they live. There is not much social analysis taking place among participants in the Sunday Eucharist in the parishes. They come there almost as a matter of obligation or by routine. On the other hand, before Jesus celebrated the Eucharist he prepared the apostles, for three years, to understand their mission so that when the Eucharist was offered they were aware of its grave significance. They were even frightened of it. At the end of the eucharistic meal Jesus told the apostles, "Let us now go to the Garden of Olives," and he went afterward to Calvary. Whereas we at our eucharistic gatherings try to finish as early as possible in order to be able to go to our Sunday relaxation and the activities of the rest of the week.

THE LIBERATION OF WOMEN

The Eucharist has been involved in several unfortunate circumstances. It has been associated with Roman imperialism in its latter days, with feudalism, with the rise of capitalism and the spread of colonialism. There is another circumstance to which perhaps not adequate attention is given. The Eucharist, like the rest of religion, has been largely conditioned by male domination of society both among the Jews and in countries that controlled Christianity. Much of what society accepts as normal and even just in the attitudes toward women can thus pass into the practice and teaching concerning the Eucharist with almost a divine sanction by Jesus himself. We see an exclusion of women from responsible action concerning the Eucharist in most Christian churches. How far is this justifiable? Should such a situation be continued until the end of time, all over the globe?

Contemporary emancipation of women has fortunately brought these questions to the fore. The churches, especially the Catholic church, have consequently to face serious issues concerning the Eucharist also. It is noteworthy that the movement for the emancipation of women has emerged and developed without much direct support from the churches. The churches have tended to be the last refuge of male dominance. They have given male chauvinism not only a practical expression, but also a theological and even a quasi-divine legitimation. The Catholic church, once again, can claim to be the most rigid and uncompromising in this respect too.

Women have traditionally been the most faithful supporters of the church and of the eucharistic devotions. Even when the working class was largely dechristianized in Europe and refrained from attending the Sunday Eucharist, the women were much more numerous than the men at the eucharistic services. Without the women many churches would hardly have a congregation. The children are also generally brought by them. Young women often persuade their husbands to return to the sacraments. Women contribute generously to the mainstay of the clergy and of church activities. Women religious are most assiduous in the care of the altar. They give long hours to prayer and work in connection with the eucharistic services.

While women have thus given so much to the cult of the Eucharist, most churches have excluded them from the priesthood or from any serious responsibility concerning the eucharistic celebration. They are or were considered unsuitable due to their sex. Till recently they could not even read the Scriptures at the services. Girls could not serve at the altar. Any little boy was preferable to any female. A certain sense of inferiority or unworthiness concerning the Eucharist was thus ingrained in the women from their earliest days.

Today, however, the situation is changing. Women are asserting their rights as human beings. They have advanced in all spheres of life. They are in almost all the professions in most countries. There are women prime ministers and cosmonauts. They drive tractors and manage industry. The question is therefore raised as to their position in the church. Why can they not be priests? Why can they not preside at the eucharistic sacrifice? Why should these be male preserves? What in their sex disqualifies them from these functions in the church? They feel insulted in their very being when

they are thus excluded merely because of their way of being human—
namely, as a female.

Many women still accept the traditional position of the priestly role being
confined to males. They have been conditioned to think and act in that
way. Some may even feel more at ease with a male performing some of
these functions than another female. Even if the majority of women are
not conscious of these issues, the more alert and dynamic among the women
dedicated to the cause of Christ feel that there is here a definite discrimination of a sexist nature. They are thus hurt in their deepest being. They
are torn between a respect for the church and their inability to accept such
a treatment from a community which should foster human equality and
solidarity. Due to a sense of loyalty and religiosity they love and accept the
church. On the other hand, their convictions concerning feminism and their
need to combat male chauvinism in its different ramifications make them
somewhat lose their confidence in the church. Their self-respect makes it
difficult for them to accept the church attitudes with complacency. Yet
many do not leave the church or the Eucharist. But as they grow in awareness of the problem they are ill at ease within themselves and in the eucharistic gatherings.

The question arises: Is the discipline of the church unchangeable? Is it
merely a matter of a certain social conditioning of the church? Or is it from
Christ? If so, was Christ a misogynist? Does God also favor males? Is sexism
in the church an incurable evil? If so what is the nature of the church?
Should its sexism be combated from within or should feminists leave the
church?

One of the difficulties in this regard is the argument put forward by
some churchmen that they are only following the example of Jesus. The
saying of Paul concerning women being silent is added for good measure.
The history of the churches is adduced as further corroboration of the thesis
that the priesthood should be confined to males. While the facts of the case
seem to be true, there are many loopholes in this line of argument.

First of all, it is not clear that Jesus established the priesthood. The
priesthood as it is presently known began later on in the life of the church.
If it is argued that he gave the power over the Eucharist to his apostles,
and that they are the predecessors of the bishops, then should not the
bishops be the ones to preside over the Eucharist? Why can bishops confer
this power to other males who are priests and not to any women? Is the
male traitor better than the faithful women who stood by Jesus at the foot
of the cross? Is it not to them that Jesus first revealed himself after his
resurrection? One could further argue that since the apostles were Jews,
all bishops should still be Jews, and circumcised. Could the argumentation
be continued further to say that the chief of the bishops should be married,
as Peter was? We ask these questions in order to ask: Where do we draw
the line in following the example of Jesus? Could it not be possible that
the line was drawn on a sex basis due to the tradition of male domination,

rather than due to any divine inspiration? Even if Jesus chose males as apostles (not priests) how much was this due to the social conditions of the times?

Recently the Vatican Congregation for the Doctrine of the Faith declared that priests should be males in order to be like Jesus. It presupposes that Jesus was an ordained priest of the Christian (or Catholic) church. Jesus was not an ordained minister of the Christian religion. He was a rabbi, a lay teacher among the Jews. Nor did he begin the Christian ordained priesthood. Insofar as he is called the unique high priest of the New Testament, there are to be no other priests like him. He teaches that we can go directly to the Father without any intercessors. Therefore it does not seem to be a valid conclusion from the maleness of Jesus of Nazareth to argue that women cannot be priests in the Catholic church. If this were a valid argument, once again can we not ask whether all priests should not be Jews, circumcised, poor, vagrant . . . like Jesus? And that only males should be at the Eucharist, as at the Last Supper?

Not only is this case rather poor, it is adding insult to injury to women. It is bad enough that women are thus treated in the church; but when the sex characteristics of Jesus are adduced in favor of a male priesthood one can see to what extent male domination can go to suit its own purposes. But this type of argument raises further christological questions. In what sense is Jesus the Christ? Is God a male? Is the Christ, in whom all things are to be resumed on earth and in heaven, a male? Are females a lower species in relation to the divinity?

On the other hand, it could be maintained that very much of the practice and teaching of the Christian churches concerning the priesthood and the male presidency over the Eucharist are the consequence of a male-dominated social system. Jesus himself had to face a similar or even worse situation than we or those of past centuries have had to. There was little respect for women in Jewish society. They were to live as far as possible withdrawn from public life. Men were to converse little with them in public. Men of religion were to be particularly reserved in their dealings with women. In the temple, too, there was discrimination against women; they had access only to the women's forecourt. They were treated in the same way as slaves regarding the obligation of prayer. Men could divorce women easily by simply issuing a writ of divorce.

Jesus was extraordinary in going against these taboos and inhibitions. We do not argue that he foresaw or forestalled all that the Women's Liberation movement of today would do or want. But he was far ahead of his time. He set an example of contesting such male domination. Jesus got away from the custom of having no contact with women. He was friendly to them. He moved freely with them. There were men and women in the company of his followers. Even persons of ill repute of both sexes, public sinners, were among his followers. This was an accusation against him. He loved them and was loved by them. They were loyal to him in life and in death. Women were among the principal witnesses to his message and to his resurrection. The Samaritan woman with five husbands and Mary Magdalene were among the first to evangelize others—to proclaim Jesus and his message. (Strangely enough, women could not preach in churches—at least till recent times.) His injunction against divorce was a defense of the rights of women, who could earlier be repudiated easily by their husbands. In that context this too was a progressive step. In all this Jesus was living up to his program of "liberating the captives and setting the downtrodden free."

In this sense it would be more valid to argue that Jesus was in favor of the liberation of women, rather than their domestication forever. He was far in advance of his day. If the church had continued his approach, the emancipation of women might have come much sooner in history. This is similar to the case of slavery. Jesus did not preach the immediate abolition of slavery as we understand it today. But his life and teaching were a rejection of the bases on which slavery was founded. The insistence on human dignity, on authority as service, on personal freedom, were quite contrary to the practices and legitimations of slavery in Jewish and Roman society.

It is important that the churches recognize this radical stance of Jesus concerning women too. We can then draw our conclusions with a dynamic view of history and not merely argue for the selective continuance of the status quo of Jewish society or of some of the practices of Jesus. In any case, this is one of the aspects in which the Eucharist has to be renewed today.

If women are not accepted as equal persons before the Eucharist, in the long term the churches will perhaps suffer much more than the women. For it is not likely that adult women will tolerate male chauvinism even in the religious sphere for many more decades. This is, however, not just a question of opportunism for the churches, but a matter of justice to all persons.

Women are being gradually liberated from the hard lot which has been theirs for generations. Even the dangers and difficulties of child-bearing are being reduced. Almost everywhere in the world the processes of family planning are reducing the number of years when women have to stay at home looking after the children. They are gaining more control over their own bodies and the functions of reproduction. They can give much more of their time to work outside the homes. The home chores are being increasingly reduced due to scientific advances and the better preparation of husbands to share them.

Women claim equality in every sphere of life as a right. In this they are right. The very consciousness of being oppressed is a dynamic to liberative action. We can regard these as a process of maturation of humanity. Women and men are being better respected as persons. The liberation of women, well understood, is also an opportunity for the humanization of man. Man can thus be less an exploiter of others.

In all this what is to be the role of the churches? Are they going to be in the vanguard of this process? Or will they be an obstacle to be overcome? The attitude of the churches toward the role of women concerning the Eucharist is important in this regard. It is also symbolic of the entire attitude of Christians toward women.

THE EUCHARIST AND OPPRESSED PEOPLES

As mentioned earlier, the history of the Eucharist is one of very close association with oppression. After Christianity became the religion of the Roman Empire, the celebration of the Eucharist was absorbed by the social establishment as a special expression of its triumph. It gave divine legitimation to power. Prior to that, catacombs and private houses were the meeting places of the eucharistic community. The Christians lived a rather underground existence, especially during times of persecution. With the conversion of Christianity and the Roman Empire to each other, the big imperial basilicas were made available to the churches. Thus during feudal times the lords of the manors had their own churches. The ecclesiastical and civil lords were closely linked in relationships of power and wealth.

There were naturally occasional conflicts between the secular and religious powers; but the millennium of feudalism was one in which by and large the power elite of the church was on the side of the feudal nobles and kings. It is important that this be remembered and reflected on when we try to understand this tradition of the Eucharist as subservient to power. It is only a few centuries ago that Europe left feudalism behind. And what are a few centuries for those who think of "eternal Rome" and its mission to rule the Christian world? Medieval Christianity tried to evolve some social norms concerning the just ruler, just price, and fair wages. These were good and useful. But there was no idea of changing the relationships of domination and dependence that feudalism implied. Today we should not blame the past. But neither can we afford to ignore it; for it lives with us as a permanent legacy. We have to ask ourselves how the church was able to integrate itself and the Eucharist within feudalism. This implied a fundamental acceptance of the social system with its good and bad. Further, it meant in practice that the powerful in the church were able to benefit from the operation of the system. They found a sacral niche within the feudal hierarchy of power and privilege. A reflection on this can be a lesson for us concerning alliances between power and the eucharistic celebration in our times.

We referred earlier to the intimate connection between the Eucharist and the colonial expansion of Europe. Here too it is enlightening to ask ourselves how and why it was possible for the Christian conscience to be so conditioned that the celebration of the Eucharist could go hand in hand with history's worst plunder and genocide. It is the peoples who have suffered such oppression who are able to understand the heinousness of these crimes. Whereas Jesus gave his life for others, and the Eucharist is a memorial of that self-sacrifice, in the colonial expansion the roles were reversed. The "Christians" were the robbers and plunderers. They murdered in the name of the expansion of western civilization and of the religion of Christ. Entire populations and civilizations were wiped out from the face of the earth. The pope in Rome, who is considered the guardian of the eucharistic message and mystique, presided over this division of the then known world between the two major Catholic powers of the day: Spain and Portugal.

We are not repeating these things to retell their gruesome details. We wish, however, that the lessons of history be learned. We see that at each phase the eucharistic community was in the main oblivious to its obligation of love of neighbor. Rather, we should say more. The Christian community had even developed a theology and a spirituality that legitimized this cruel phase of European history. The authorities of the church who claimed to be God's special representatives and Christ's vicars did not really side with the people who were being exterminated. A few voices of protest were heard here and there. But these were exceptions. They were marginal to the main thrust of the "holy people of God." They were "eccentrics" who tried to identify with the oppressed. In fact they were even considered disobedient children who had to be watched by the local church and Christian civil rulers, so that the most worthy cause of the expansion of the kingdom of Christ might not be impeded.

The tragedy is that the peoples who have suffered thus either are no more as a people, or are unable to communicate their thinking to the church powers. We have to ask ourselves how theology was evolved in that day. How did theologians come to support such exploitation and suppress dissent? Why were the groans and squeals of the oppressed millions unable to penetrate to the ears and hearts of the successors of the apostles? Even more important is to ask ourselves whether or not the system has yet changed within the church. Is theology evolved very differently in the centers of church power? Do they have experience of suffering oppression?

An important theological conclusion is that when the "controllers" of theology and church discipline have no live experience of oppression, they are not likely to understand or even listen to the cries of the oppressed masses. Further, where the power elite of the church is ensconced within the exploiting group, they are likely to develop a theology which is in effect an ideology of conquest and domination. For this would suit their own interests. We are saying this as a conclusion of historical experience, and not as an ideological conclusion. It is a pity that many European thinkers and church authorities do not reflect adequately on this aspect of the history of theology and of church discipline. We have still to await a history of the church written from the point of view of the oppressed and marginated peoples of the world. Instead we have generally church histories written by the victors in the process of western expansion. The intercommunication between secular events and the ecclesiastical adaptations to them are not critically examined.

An important conclusion is that where ecclesiastical authorities and law-makers are part of the ruling social establishment, the church law itself tends to be corrupted in favor of the powerful. Then the eucharistic norms are made to fit into the needs of an exploiting system. Another way of saying this is to ask: Who makes the church laws? Who decides the theology that is considered orthodox by church authorities? Ever since the Constantinian compromise, the oppressed have generally been at the receiving end of theology and spirituality. Even today, how far can workers influence the theology of Canterbury, Geneva, New York, Rome, or for that matter even Moscow? Where are the women theologians—except at the margins of churches, if they are present at all? The youth are not accepted as initiators and much less as determinants of theological thought.

Perhaps even more significant is the fact that the peoples of Asia, Africa, and Latin America have not been listened to in this historical process. It is not enough to have a few yellow, brown, or black faces in the ecclesiastical high courts. The voices of the oppressed masses, their sufferings and experiences, must be the subject matter of theology and spirituality. The Eucharist must take into account what is happening to these peoples and the causes of their worsening situations. We can at least hope that these considerations will make the present lawgivers of churches a little less cocksure of themselves. They should reflect on the situation that, for thousands of years, they and their predecessors have been on the exploiting side of history. This might have a salutary effect on them. They may then begin to question their present assumptions. They may not then come to conclusions so facilely. If ever they really suffer with the oppressed they may be able to give a new direction to the eucharistic practices too.

A repentant meditation on the colossal insensitivity of the eucharistic communities and especially of their lawgivers to plunder, enslavement, and murder by Christians may be the beginning of wisdom for the eucharistic groups of today. There was a certain repentance in the attitude of Vatican Council II toward the other Christians and the modern world of Western Europe and North America. This was salutary. It was a sign of hope. But it should only be a beginning. For there is much more for which the churches have to repent. This is especially true with reference to the working classes of the world and the peoples of Latin America, Asia, and Africa.

The Eucharist is in captivity. It is dominated by persons who do not experience oppression in their own selves. Even within the poor countries, the church leaders generally belong to and side with the affluent elite. The Eucharist will not be liberated to be true to its mission so long as the churches are captive within the world's power establishments. The Eucharist has to be liberative; it should lead to sharing and genuine love. But in its social impact it fails to do so. It has been interpreted conservatively, rigidly, and formally. If, on the other hand, it were to become the ferment of contemporary Christianity, the churches would change radically. It is when Christians make a fundamental option against oppression, and struggle against it, that the Eucharist itself will be liberated. Already this is happening among certain groups committed to integral human liberation in the perspective of Jesus Christ.

Even with reference to interchurch ecumenism this is an important consideration. The Christian churches have differed and divided over their eucharistic teaching and practices also. But the more important point for the future getting together of the churches is not the exact doctrinal resolution of their divergences concerning the Eucharist or other issues of dogma. It is the option of the churches concerning the present struggle against oppression all over the world that will be the dividing line. Perhaps the churches as a whole will not make such options. They have not been able to express themselves unequivocally even about the Vietnam war or apartheid. Those who opt to struggle with the oppressed, the weak, the excluded, and the marginalized will be on one side, whatever their church denomination. Today the major division among Christians cuts across the frontiers of churches. Communion in the liberation struggle is increasingly becoming a more uniting factor than affiliation to ecclesiastical groups. When these issues are taken seriously communion within the same church becomes difficult unless it involves at least a desire for human liberation from oppression. Interclass communion is likely to be increasingly under question.

These are issues which Christians and the churches have to face in the coming years. Ecumenism in the sense of exchange of pulpits, visits by church leaders to each other, and beating of breasts for the evils of the Reformation will soon achieve its limited objectives. Repentance by Christians together for their whole historical complicity in the exploitation of the oppressed nations, classes, and sex is a more urgent and deeper requirement. As it takes place the Eucharist will be progressively liberated. The Eucharist, well celebrated, can also help raise this new consciousness and sensitivity among followers of Jesus Christ of all denominations.

21

Imaging a Theology of Nature:
The World as God's Body

SALLIE McFAGUE

I spent my last sabbatical in England, and I think all will agree that England is a green and pleasant land. I recall an early morning trip to Coventry on the bus: the lovely, gently rolling hills, quaint villages with thatched-roofed cottages—very pastoral, idyllic. There were sheep dotting the hills, but also something else: huge, concrete towers of nuclear plants rising up through the morning mist. It seemed a strange juxtaposition: sheep and nuclear towers—life and potential death. Our cruise missiles also dotted the countryside, though I did not see them. These towers and missiles symbolize a situation unique to our time. We are the first generation of human beings out of all the billions of humans who have ever lived who have the responsibility of nuclear knowledge. In perverse imitation of God, the creator of life, we have become potential uncreators. We have the knowledge and the power to destroy ourselves and much of the rest of life. And we will *always* have this knowledge—regardless of nuclear disarmament. Jonathan Schell in his book *The Fate of the Earth* speaks of the "second death"—the death of life (Schell, 99ff.). The first death is our own individual one and difficult as that is to face, we at least know that birth will follow and others will take our place. But the death of birth is the extinction of life and that is too horrendous to contemplate, especially when we know *we would be responsible for it.*

Our nuclear knowledge brings to the surface a fundamental fact about human existence. We are part and parcel of the web of life and exist in interdependence with all other beings, both human and nonhuman. As

From *Liberating Life: Contemporary Approaches to Ecological Theology,* Charles Birch, William Eakin, Jay B. McDaniel, eds. (Maryknoll, N.Y.: Orbis Books, 1990), pp. 201-27. The original essay included a scholarly dialogue carried on through footnotes, which are omitted here.

Pierre Teilhard de Chardin puts it in a moment of insight: "I realized that my own poor trifling existence was one with the immensity of all that is and all that is in process of becoming" (Teilhard 1968a, 25). Or, as the poet Wallace Stevens says, "Nothing is itself taken alone. Things are because of interrelations and interconnections" (Stevens, 163). The evolutionary, ecological perspective insists that we are, in the most profound way, "not our own": we belong, from the cells of our bodies to the finest creations of our minds, to the intricate, ever-changing cosmos. We both depend on that web of life for our own continued existence and in a special way we are responsible for it, for we *alone know* that life is interrelated and we *alone know* how to destroy it. It is an awesome—and unsettling—thought.

As we near the close of the twentieth century we have become increasingly conscious of the fragility of our world. We have also become aware that the anthropocentrism that characterizes much of the Judeo-Christian tradition has often fed a sensibility insensitive to our proper place in the universe. The ecological crisis, epitomized in the possibility of a nuclear holocaust, has brought home to many the need for a new mode of consciousness on the part of human beings, for what Rosemary Ruether calls a "conversion" to the earth, a cosmocentric sensibility (Ruether, 89).

What does all this mean for theology, especially for a theology of nature? Theology, I believe, has special responsibility for the symbols, images, the language, used for expressing the relationship between God and the world in every age. The sciences are also concerned with interpreting reality—the universe or universes, if you will—although cosmology means different things to scientists than it does to theologians. Nonetheless, here is a meeting place, a place of common interest, to scientists and theologians. David Tracy and Nicholas Lash have called recently for a "collaborative" relationship between science and theology in order to "help establish plausible 'mutually critical correlations' not only to interpret the world but to help change it" (Tracy and Lash, 91). They note that relations between science and theology are not only those posed by a recognition of analogies between the two areas on methodological issues but, more pressingly, by a common concern with the cosmos. Thus, a focus on the cosmos with the intent both to understand it better—and to orient our praxis within it more appropriately—is one collaborative effort for science and theology in our time.

While cosmology may mean several different things, the theologian's contribution is concerned with "accounts of the world as God's creation," and, within that broad compass, one specific enterprise especially needed in our time involves "imaginative perceptions of how the world seems and where we stand in it" (Tracy and Lash, vii). In other words, I propose that one theological task is an experimental one with metaphors and models for the relationship between God and the world that will help bring about a theocentric, life-centered, cosmocentric sensibility in place of our anthropocentric one.

This exercise would take place at the juncture between a theology of nature and a theocentric or life-centered ethic. That is, an analysis in some detail of one model of the God/world relationship—that of the world or universe as God's body—would mediate between concepts and praxis, between a theoretical and a practical orientation.

As we begin this task we must keep in mind some criteria for any theology of nature pertinent to the closing years of the twentieth century. First, it must be informed by and commensurate with contemporary scientific accounts of what nature is. Second, it needs to see human life as profoundly interrelated with all other forms of life, refusing the traditional absolute separation of human beings from other creatures as well as of God from the world. Third, it will be a kind of theology that is creation-centered, in contrast to the almost total concern with redemption in some Christian theologies. It will be a theology that focuses, in the broadest and deepest sense, on the incarnational presence of God in the world. Finally, it will acknowledge and press the interconnectedness of peace, justice, and ecological issues, aware that there can be no peace or justice unless the fabric of our ecosystem is intact. What this means, I believe, is that for the first time in the history of the human race, we see the necessity of thinking responsibly and deeply about *everything that is*. That is a tall order, but once the scales fall from the eyes and one understands the profound relationships between issues of peace and war, justice to the oppressed, and concern for our home—the earth—there is no possibility of going back to piecemeal thinking. In other words, a theology of nature must be holistic.

One task that needs to be done within this overarching assignment is to *imagine* in some detail and depth the relationship between God and the world in a way not only consonant with these criteria, but in a fashion that would help it to come alive in people's minds and hearts. Human behavior appears to be profoundly influenced by the imagistic, symbolical, narrative powers of human reflection. How would we, for instance, act differently if we imagined the world to be the body of God rather than considering it to be, as the tradition has, the realm of the Almighty King? That question is the basic one I want to consider in this paper.

The kind of theology I will be engaged in here, by no means the only kind, could be called heuristic theology; in analogy with some similar activities in the sciences, it "plays" with possibilities in order to find out, to discover, new fruitful ways to interpret the universe. In the case of an heuristic theology focused on cosmology, the discovery would be oriented toward "remythologizing" creation as dependent upon God. More specifically, I propose as a modest contribution to the contemporary understanding of a theological cosmology for our time an elaboration of the model of the world as God's body, both as a critique of and substitute for the dominant model of the world as the realm of God the king.

The following, therefore, will be a "case study," with a theological model for reenvisioning the relationship between God and the universe. Before turning to this study, however, we will make some preliminary comments on the method employed in this kind of theology as well as on metaphors and models, their character and status.

IMAGINATION AND THEOLOGY

Christian faith is, it seems to me, most basically a claim that the universe is neither indifferent nor malevolent, but that there is a power (and a personal power at that) that is on the side of life and its fulfillment. Moreover, the Christian believes that we have some clues for fleshing out this claim in the life, death, and appearances of Jesus of Nazareth. Nevertheless, each generation must venture, through an analysis of what fulfillment could and must mean for its own time, the best way to express that claim. A critical dimension of this expression is the imaginative picture, the metaphors and models, that underlie the conceptual systems of theology. One cannot hope to interpret Christian faith for one's own time if one remains indifferent to the basic images that are the lifeblood of interpretation and that greatly influence people's perceptions and behavior.

Many of the major models for the relationship between God and the world in the Judeo-Christian tradition are ones that emphasize the transcendence of God and the distance between God and the world: God as king with the world as his realm, God as potter who creates the cosmos by molding it, God as speaker who with a word brings the world to be out of nothing. One has to ask whether these models are adequate ones for our time, our ecological, nuclear age, in which the radical interdependence and interrelationship of all forms of life must be underscored. Quite apart from that crisis, however, responsible theology ought to be done in the context of contemporary science and were it to take that context seriously, models underscoring the closeness, not the distance, of God and the world would emerge. A. R. Peacocke makes this point well when he says,

> There is increasing awareness not only among Christian theologians, but even more among ordinary believers that, if God is in fact the all-encompassing Reality that Christian faith proclaims, then that Reality is to be experienced in and through our actual lives as biological organisms who are persons, part of nature and living in society (Peacocke, 16-17).

For a number of reasons, therefore, experimentation with models underscoring the intimacy of God and creation may be in order and it is this task, with one model, that I will undertake. I have characterized the theological method operative here as heuristic and concerned with metaphors and models. Let us look briefly at these matters. Heuristic theology is distinct from theology as hermeneutics or as construction but has similarities with both. The *Shorter Oxford English Dictionary* defines *heuristic* adjectivally as "serving to find out" and, when employed as a noun related to learning, as "a system of education under which pupils are trained to find out for themselves." Thus heuristic theology will be one that experiments and tests, that thinks in an as-if fashion, that imagines possibilities that are novel, that dares to think differently. It will not accept solely on the basis of authority but will search for what it finds convincing and persuasive; it will not, however, be fantasy or mere play but will assume that there is something to find out and that if some imagined possibilities fail, others may succeed. The mention of failure and success, and of the persuasive and the convincing, indicates that although I wish to distinguish heuristic theology from both hermeneutical and constructive theology, it bears similarities to both.

If the characteristic mark of hermeneutical theology is its interpretive stance, especially in regard to texts—both the classic text of the Judeo-Christian tradition (the Hebrew Scriptures and the New Testament) and the exemplary theologies that build on the classic text—then heuristic theology is also interpretive, for it claims that its successful unconventional metaphors are not only in continuity with the paradigmatic events and their significance expressed in this classic text but are also appropriate expressions of these matters for the present time. Heuristic theology, though not bound to the images and concepts in scripture, is constrained to show that its proposed models are an appropriate, persuasive expression of Christian faith for our time. Hence, while heuristic theology is not limited to interpreting texts, it is concerned with the same "matter" as the classic texts, namely, the salvific power of God.

If, on the other hand, the distinctive mark of constructive theology is that it does not rely principally on classical sources but attempts its articulation of the concepts of God, world, and human being with the help of a variety of sources, including material from the natural, physical, and social sciences as well as from philosophy, literature, and the arts, then heuristic theology is also constructive in that it claims that a valid understanding of God and world for a particular time is an imaginative construal built up from a variety of sources, many of them outside religious traditions. Like theology as construction, theology as heuristics supports the assertion that our concept of God is precisely that—*our concept* of God—and not God. Yet, while heuristic theology has some similarities to constructive theology, it has a distinctive emphasis: it will be more experimental, imagistic, and pluralistic.

Its experimental character means it is a kind of theology well suited for times of uncertainty and change, when systematic, comprehensive construction seems inappropriate if not impossible. It could be called "free theology,"[1] for it must be willing to play with possibilities and, as a consequence, not take itself too seriously, accepting its tentative, relative, partial, and hypothetical character.

Its imagistic character means it stands as a corrective to the bias of much constructive theology toward conceptual clarity, often at the price of imagistic richness. Although it would be insufficient to rest in new images and to refuse to spell out conceptually their implications in as comprehensive a way as possible, the more critical task is to propose what Dennis Nineham calls a "lively imaginative picture" of the way God and the world as we know it are related (Nineham, 201-2). It is no coincidence that most religious traditions turn to personal and public human relationships to serve as metaphors and models of the relationship between God and the world: God as father, mother, lover, friend, king, lord, governor. These metaphors give a precision and persuasive power to the construct of God that concepts alone cannot. Because religions, including Christianity, are not incidentally imagistic but centrally and necessarily so, theology must also be an affair of the imagination.

To say that heuristic theology is pluralistic is to insist that since no metaphor or model refers properly or directly to God, many are necessary. All are inappropriate, partial, and inadequate; the most that can be said is that some aspect or aspects of the God-world relationship are illuminated by this or that model in a fashion relevant to a particular time and place. Models of God are not definitions of God but likely accounts of experiences of relating to God with the help of relationships we know and understand. If one accepts that metaphors (and all language about God) are principally adverbial, having to do with how we relate to God rather than defining the nature of God, then no metaphors or models can be reified, petrified, or expanded so as to exclude all others. One can, for instance, include many possibilities: We can envision relating to God as to a father and a mother, to a healer and a liberator, to the sun and a mountain. As definitions of God, these possibilities are mutually exclusive; as models expressing experiences of relating to God, they are mutually enriching.

In summary, the theology I am proposing is a kind of heuristic construction that in focusing on the imaginative construal of the God-world relationship, attempts to remythologize Christian faith through metaphors and models appropriate for our time.

What, however, is the character and status of the metaphors and models that are the central concern of heuristic theology? A metaphor is a word or phrase used *in*appropriately. It belongs in one context but is being used in another: the arm of the chair, war as a chess game, God the father. From Aristotle until recently, metaphor was seen mainly as a poetic device to embellish or decorate. Increasingly, however, the idea of metaphor as unsubstitutable is winning acceptance; what a metaphor expresses cannot be said directly or apart from it, for if it could, one would have said it directly. Here, metaphor is a strategy of desperation, not decoration; it is an attempt to say something about the unfamiliar in terms of the familiar, an attempt to speak about what we do not know in terms of what we do know.

Metaphor always has the character of *is* and *is not*: an assertion is made but as a likely account rather than a definition.[2] The point that metaphor underscores is that in certain matters there can be no direct description. It used to be the case that poetry and religion were thought to be distinctive in their reliance on metaphor, but more recently the use of metaphors and models in the natural and social sciences has widened the scope of metaphorical thinking considerably and linked science and theology methodologically in ways inconceivable twenty years ago.

The difference between a metaphor and a model can be expressed in a number of ways, but most simply, a model is a metaphor with "staying power," that is, a model is a metaphor that has gained sufficient stability and scope so as to present a pattern for relatively comprehensive and coherent explanation. The metaphor of God the father is an excellent example of this. In becoming a model, it has engendered wide-ranging interpretation of the relationship between God and human beings; if God is seen as father, human beings become children, sin can be seen as rebellious behavior, and redemption can be thought of as restoration to the status of favored offspring.

It should be evident that a theology that describes itself as metaphorical is a theology at risk. Jacques Derrida, in defining metaphor, writes, "if metaphor, which is mimesis trying its chance, mimesis at risk, may always fail to attain truth, this is because it has to reckon with a definite absence" (Derrida, 42). As Derrida puts it, metaphor lies somewhere between "nonsense" and "truth," and a theology based on metaphor will be open to the charge that it is closer to the first than the second. This is, I believe, a risk that theology in our time must be willing to run. Theology has usually had a high stake in truth, so high that it has refused all play of the imagination: through creedal control and the formulations of orthodoxy, it has refused all attempts at new metaphors "trying their chance." But a heuristic theology insists that new metaphors and models be given a chance, be tried out as likely accounts of the God-world relationship, be allowed to make a case for themselves. A heuristic theology is, therefore, destabilizing. Since no language about God is adequate and all of it is improper, new metaphors are not necessarily less inadequate or improper than old ones. All are in the same situation and no authority—not scriptural status, liturgical longevity, or ecclesiastical fiat—can decree that some types of language, or some images, refer literally to God while others do not. None do. Hence, the criteria for preferring some to others must be other than authority, however defined.

We come, then, finally, to the issue of the status of language about God. R. W. Hepburn has posed it directly:

> The question which should be of the greatest concern to the theologian is . . . whether or not the circle of myth, metaphor, and symbol is a closed one: and if closed then in what way propositions about God manage to refer (Hepburn, 23).

The "truth" of a construal of the God-world relationship is a mixture of belief (Ricoeur calls it a "wager"), pragmatic criteria, and what Philip Wheelwright terms a "shy ontological claim," or, as in Mary Hesse's striking remark, "God is more like gravitation than embarrassment" (Arbib and Hesse, 5). Belief in God is not taken to be purely a social construct. At least this is what a critical realist would claim. Thus, metaphors and models of God are understood to be discovered as well as created, to relate to God's reality not in the sense of being literally in correspondence with it, but as versions or hypotheses of it that the community (in this case, the church) accepts as relatively adequate. Hence, models of God are not simply heuristic fictions; the critical realist does not accept the Feuerbachian critique that language about God is nothing but human projection. On the other hand, any particular metaphor or model is not the only, appropriate, true one.

How does one come to accept a model as true? We live *within* the model, testing our wager by its consequences. These consequences are both theoretical and practical. An adequate model will be illuminating, fruitful, have relatively comprehensive explanatory ability, be relatively consistent, be able to deal with anomalies, and so on. This largely, though not totally, functional, pragmatic view of truth stresses heavily the implications of certain models for the quality of human and nonhuman life. A praxis orientation does not deny the possibility of the "shy ontological claim," but it does acknowledge both the mystery of God and the importance of truth as practical wisdom. Thus it acknowledges with the apophatic tradition that we really do not *know* the inner being of divine reality; the hints and clues we have of the way things are, whether we call them religious experiences, revelation, or whatever, are too fragile, too little (and often too negative) for heavy metaphysical claims. Rather, in the tradition of Aristotle, truth means constructing the good life for the *polis*, though for our time this must mean for the cosmos. A "true" model of God will be one that is a powerful, persuasive construal of God as being on the side of life and its fulfillment in our time.

GOD AND THE WORLD

We turn now to consider models for the relationship between God and the world. The dominant model has been monarchical; the classical picture employs royalist, triumphalist metaphors, depicting God as king, lord, and patriarch, who rules over and cares for the world and human beings. Ian Barbour, theologian and philosopher of science, says of this model:

The *monarchical model* of God as King was developed systematically, both in Jewish thought (God as Lord and King of the Universe), in medieval Christian thought (with its emphasis on divine omnipotence), and in the Reformation (especially in Calvin's insistence on

God's sovereignty). In the portrayal of God's relation to the world, the dominant western historical model has been that of the absolute monarch ruling over his kingdom (Barbour, 156).

This imaginative picture is so prevalent in mainstream Christianity that it is often not recognized as a picture. It is a powerful imaginative picture and a very dangerous one. As Gordon Kaufman points out in *Theology for a Nuclear Age*, divine sovereignty is the issue with which theologians in the nuclear age must deal. In its cruder versions, God is the king who fights on the side of his chosen ones to bring their enemies down; in more refined versions God is the father who will not let his children suffer. The first view supports militarism; the second supports escapism. As Kaufman states, two groups of American Christians currently rely on these images of God in their responses to the nuclear situation: one group claims that if a nuclear holocaust comes, it will be God's will—the Armageddon—and America should arm itself to fight the devil's agent, Communist Russia; the other passively relies on the all-powerful father to take care of the situation. Is divine sovereignty the appropriate imagery for our time? It may have been for some ages, but in *our* time, when the interdependence of all life and our special responsibility for it needs to be emphasized, is it *for ours*?

As Kaufman points out, the monarchical model results in a pattern of "asymmetrical dualism" between God and the world, in which God and the world are only distantly related and all power, either as domination or benevolence, is on God's side (Kaufman, 39). It supports conceiving of God as a being existing somewhere apart from the world and ruling it externally either directly through divine intervention or indirectly through controlling the wills of his subjects. It creates feelings of awe in the hearts of loyal subjects and thus supports the "godness" of God, but these feelings are balanced by others of abject fear and humiliation: in this picture, God can be God only if we are nothing.

Very briefly, let me summarize a few major problems with this model as an imaginative framework for understanding God's saving love as an inclusive one of fulfillment for all of creation. In the monarchical model, God is distant from the world, relates only to the human world, and controls that world through domination and benevolence. On the first point: the relationship of a king to his subjects is necessarily a distant one for royalty is "untouchable." It is the distance, the difference, the otherness of God, that is underscored with this imagery. God as king is in his kingdom—which is not of this earth—and we remain in another place, far from his dwelling. In this picture God is worldless and the world is Godless: the world is empty of God's presence. Whatever one does for the world is not finally important in this model, for its ruler does not inhabit it as his primary residence, and his subjects are well advised not to become too enamored of it either.

Although these comments may at first seem like a caricature rather than a fair description of the classical Western monarchical model, they are the direct implications of its imagery. If metaphors matter, then one must take them seriously at the level at which they function, that is, at the level of the imaginative picture of God and the world they project. And one of the direct implications is distance and at best only external involvement. To be sure, kings want their subjects to be loyal and their realms peaceful, but that does not mean internal, intrinsic involvement. Kings do not have to, and usually do not, love their subjects or realms; at most, one hopes they will be benevolent.

But such benevolence extends only to human subjects: in the monarchical model there is no concern for the cosmos, for the nonhuman world. Here is our second objection to this model. It is simply blank in terms of what lies outside the human sphere. As a political model focused on governing human beings, it leaves out most of reality. One could say at this point that, as with all models, it has limitations and needs to be balanced by other models. Such a comment does not address the seriousness of the monarchical model's power, for as the dominant Western model, it has not allowed competing models to arise. The tendency, rather, has been to draw other models into its orbit, as is evident with the model of God as father. This model could have gone in the direction of parent (and that is clearly its New Testament course), with associations of nurture, care, guidance, and responsibility, but under the powerful influence of the monarchical model, the parent becomes the patriarch, and patriarchs act more like kings than like fathers: They rule their children and they demand obedience.

The monarchical model is not only highly anthropocentric, but it supports a kind of anthropocentricism characterized by dualistic hierarchies. We not only imagine God in our image, but those images we use for imaging God also become standards for human behavior. Dualistic, triumphalistic thinking fuels many forms of oppression. While the monarchical model may not be responsible alone for hierarchical dualism, it has supported it: the dualisms of male/female, spirit/nature, human/nonhuman, Christian/non-Christian, rich/poor, white/colored, and so forth. The hierarchical, dualistic pattern is so widespread in Western thought that it is often not perceived to be a pattern, but is felt to be simply the way things are. It appears natural to many that whites, males, the rich, and Christians are superior to other human beings, and that human beings are more valuable in all respects than other forms of life.

We come, then, to the third criticism of the monarchical model: God rules either through domination or benevolence, thus undercutting human responsibility for the world. It is simplistic to blame the Judeo-Christian tradition for the ecological crisis, as some have done, on the grounds that Genesis instructs human beings to have dominion over nature; nonetheless, the imagery of sovereignty supports attitudes of control and use toward the nonhuman world. Although the might of the natural world when unleashed is fearsome, as is evident in earthquakes, tornadoes, and volcanic eruptions, the power balance has shifted from nature to us, and an essential aspect of the new sensibility is to recognize and accept this. Nature can and does destroy many, but it is not in the position to destroy all, as we can. Extinction of species by nature is in a different dimension from extinction by design, which only we can bring about. This chilling thought adds a new importance to the images we use to characterize our relationship to others and to the nonhuman world. If we are capable of extinguishing ourselves and most, if not all, other life, metaphors that support attitudes of distance from, and domination of, other human beings and nonhuman life must be recognized as dangerous. No matter how ancient a metaphorical tradition may be and regardless of its credentials in scripture, liturgy, and creedal statements, it still must be discarded if it threatens the continuation of life itself. If the heart of the Christian gospel is the salvific power of God, triumphalist metaphors cannot express that reality *in our time*, whatever their appropriateness may have been in the past.

And this is so even if God's power is seen as benevolence rather than domination. For if God's rule is understood benevolently, it will be assumed that all is well — that the world will be cared for with no help from us. The king as dominating sovereign encourages attitudes of militarism and destruction; the king as benevolent patriarch encourages attitudes of passivity and escape from responsibility. The monarchical model is dangerous in our time. It encourages a sense of distance from the world; it attends only to the human dimension of the world; and it supports attitudes of either domination of the world or passivity toward it. As an alternative model I suggest considering the world as God's body.

In what ways would we think of the relationship between God and the world were we to experiment with the metaphor of the universe as God's body, God's palpable presence in all space and time? If the entire universe is expressive of God's very being — *the* incarnation, if you will — do we not have the beginnings of an imaginative picture of the relationship between God and the world peculiarly appropriate as a context for interpreting the salvific love of God *for our time*? If what is needed in our ecological, nuclear age is an imaginative vision of the relationship between God and the world that underscores their interdependence and mutuality, empowering a sensibility of care and responsibility toward all life, how would it help to see the world as the body of God?

This image, radical as it may seem (in light of the dominant metaphor of a king to his realm) for imagining the relationship between God and the world, is a very old one with roots in Stoicism and elliptically in the Hebrew Scriptures. The notion has tantalized many, including Tertullian and Irenaeus, and though it received little assistance from either Platonism or Aristotelianism because of their denigration of matter and the body (and hence did not enter the mainstream of either Augustinian or Thomistic theology), it surfaced powerfully in Hegel as well as in twentieth-century process theologies. The mystical tradition within Christianity has carried the notion implicitly, even though the metaphor of body may not appear: "The world is charged with the grandeur of God" (Gerard Manley Hopkins, 27). "There is communion with God, and a communion with the earth, and a communion with God through the earth" (Teilhard 1968a, 14).

As we begin this experiment with the model of the world as God's body, we must once again recall that a metaphor or model is not a description. We are trying to think in an as-if fashion about the God-world relationship, because we have no other way of thinking about it. No metaphor fits in all ways, and some are more nonsense than sense. The king-realm kind of thinking about the God-world relationship sounds like sense because we are used to it, but reflection shows that in our world it is nonsense. For a metaphor to be acceptable, it need not, cannot, apply in all ways; if it did, it would be a description. The metaphor of the world as God's body has the opposite problem to the metaphor of the world as the king's realm; if the latter puts too great a distance between God and the world, the former verges on too great a proximity. Since neither metaphor fits exactly, we have to ask which one is better in our time and to qualify it with other metaphors and models. Is it better to accept an imaginative picture of God as the distant ruler controlling his realm through external and benevolent power or one of God so intimately related to the world that the world can be imagined as God's body? Which is better in terms of our and the world's preservation and fulfillment? Which is better in terms of coherence, comprehensibility, and illumination? Which is better in terms of expressing the Christian understanding of the relationship between God and the world? All these criteria are relevant, for a metaphor that is all or mostly nonsense has tried and failed.

Therefore, a heuristic, metaphorical theology, though hospitable initially to nonsense, is constrained as well to search for sense. Christians should, given their tradition, be inclined to find sense in body language, not only because of the resurrection of the body but also because of the bread and wine of the eucharist as the body and blood of Christ, and the church as the body with Christ as its head. Christians have a surprisingly "bodily" tradition. Nonetheless, there is a difference between the traditional uses of body and seeing the world as God's body: when the world is viewed as God's body, that body includes more than just Christians, and more than just human beings. It is possible to speculate that if Christianity had begun in a culture less dualistic and antiphysical than that of the first-century Mediterranean world, it might have been willing, given the more holistic anthropology and theology of its Hebraic roots, to extend its body metaphor to God. At any rate, in view of the contemporary holistic understanding of personhood, in which embodiment is the *sine qua non*, the thought of an embodied divine person is not more incredible than that of a disembodied one; in fact, it is less so. In a dualistic culture where mind and body, spirit and flesh, are separable, a disembodied, personal God is more credible, but not in ours. This is only to suggest that the idea of God's embodiment—

the idea as such, quite apart from particulars—should not be seen as nonsense; it is less nonsense than the idea of a disembodied personal God.

We are imagining the world to be God's body. The body of God, then, would be nothing less than all that is—the universe or universes and everything they contain of which cosmologists speak. The body of God, as theologians would say, is creation, understood as God's self-expression; it is formed in God's own reality, bodied forth in the eons of evolutionary time, and supplied with the means to nurture and sustain billions of different forms of life. *We* give life only to others of our own species, but God gives life to *all* that is, all species of life and all forms of matter. In a monotheistic, panentheistic theology, if one is to understand God in some sense as physical and not just spiritual, then the entire "body" of the universe is "in" God and is God's visible self-expression. This body, albeit a strange one if we take ours as the model, is nothing less than all that exists.

Would God, then, be reduced to the world or the universe? The metaphor does come far closer to pantheism than the king-realm model, which verges on deism, but it does not identify God totally with the world any more than we identify ourselves totally with our bodies. Other animals may be said to be bodies that have spirits; we may be said to be spirits that possess bodies. This is not to introduce a new dualism but only to recognize that, although our bodies are expressions of us both unconsciously and consciously, we can reflect about them and distance ourselves from them. The very fact that we can speak about our bodies is evidence that we are not totally one with them. On this model God is not reduced to the world if the world is God's body. Without the use of personal, agential metaphors, however, including among others God as mother, father, healer, lover, friend, judge, and liberator, the metaphor of the world as God's body would be pantheistic, for the body would be all there were. Nonetheless, the model is most precisely designated as panentheistic; that is, it is a view of the God-world relationship in which all things have their origins in God and nothing exists outside God, though this does not mean that God is reduced to these things.

Nevertheless, though God is not reduced to the world, the metaphor of the world as God's body puts God "at risk." If we follow out the implications of the metaphor, we see that God becomes dependent through being bodily in a way that a totally invisible, distant God would never be. Just as we care about our bodies, are made vulnerable by them, and must attend to their well-being, God will be liable to bodily contingencies. The world as God's body may be poorly cared for, ravaged, and as we are becoming well-aware, essentially destroyed, in spite of God's own loving attention to it, because of one creature, ourselves, who can choose or not choose to join with God in conscious care of the world. Presumably, were our tiny corner of this body destroyed, another could be formed; hence, God need not be seen to be as dependent on us or on any particular body as we are on our bodies. But in the metaphor of the universe as the self-expression of God—

God's incarnation—the notions of vulnerability, shared responsibility, and risk are inevitable. This is a markedly different basic understanding of the God-world relationship than in the monarch-realm metaphor, for it emphasizes God's willingness to suffer for and with the world, even to the point of personal risk. The world as God's body, then, may be seen as a way to remythologize the inclusive, suffering love of the cross of Jesus of Nazareth. In both instances God is at risk in human hands: just as once upon a time in a bygone mythology human beings killed their God in the body of a man, so now we once again have that power, but in a mythology more appropriate to our time; we would kill our God in the body of the world. Could we actually do this? To believe in the resurrection means we could not. God is not in our power to destroy, but the incarnate God is at risk; we have been given central responsibility to care for God's body, our world.

If God, though at risk and dependent on others, is not reduced to the world in the metaphor of the world as God's body, what more can we say about the meaning of this model? How does God know the world, act in it, and love it? How does one speak of evil in this metaphor? In the monarchical model, God knows the world externally, acts on it either by direct intervention or indirectly through human subjects, and loves it benevolently, in a charitable way. God's knowledge, action, and love are markedly different in the metaphor of the world as God's body. God knows the world immediately just as we know our bodies immediately. God could be said to be in touch with all parts of the world through interior understanding. Moreover, this knowledge is empathetic, intimate, sympathetic knowledge, closer to feeling than to rationality. It is knowledge "by acquaintance"; it is not "information about." Just as we are internally related to our bodies, so God is internally related to all that is—the most radically relational Thou. God relates sympathetically to the world, just as we relate sympathetically to our bodies. This implies, of course, an immediacy and concern in God's knowledge of the world impossible in the king-realm model.

Moreover, it implies that the action of God in the world is similarly interior and caring. If the entire universe, all that is and has been, is God's body, then God acts in and through the incredibly complex physical and historical-cultural evolutionary process that began eons ago. This does not mean that God is reduced to the evolutionary process, for God remains as the agent, the self, whose intentions are expressed in the universe. Nevertheless, the manner in which these intentions are expressed is internal and, by implication, providential—that is, reflective of a "caring" relationship. God does not, as in the royal model, intervene in the natural or historical process *deus ex machina* fashion, nor does God feel merely charitable toward the world. The suggestion, however, that God cares about the world as one cares about one's own body, that is, with a high degree of sympathic concern, does not imply that all is well or the future assured, for with the body metaphor, God is at risk. It does suggest, however, that to trust in a God whose body is the world is to trust in a God who cares profoundly about the world.

Furthermore, the model of the world as God's body suggests that God loves bodies: in loving the world, God loves a body. Such a notion is a sharp challenge to the long antibody, antiphysical, antimatter tradition within Christianity. This tradition has repressed healthy sexuality, oppressed women as sexual tempters, and defined Christian redemption in spiritualistic ways, thus denying that basic social and economic needs of embodied beings are relevant to salvation. To say that God loves bodies is to redress the balance toward a more holistic understanding of fulfillment. It is to say that bodies are worth loving, sexually and otherwise, that passionate love as well as attention to the needs of bodily existence are part of fulfillment. It is to say further that the basic necessities of bodily existence — adequate food and shelter, for example — are central aspects of God's love for all bodily creatures and therefore should be central concerns for us, God's co-workers. In a holistic sensibility there can be no spirit/body split: if neither we nor God is disembodied, then denigration of the body, the physical, and matter should end. Such a split makes no sense in our world: spirit and body or matter are on a continuum, for matter is not inanimate substance but throbs of energy, essentially in continuity with spirit. To love bodies, then, is to love not what is opposed to spirit but what is one with it — which the model of the world as God's body fully expresses.

The immanence of God in the world implied in our metaphor raises the question of God's involvement with evil. Is God responsible for evil, both natural and humanly willed evil? The pictures of the king and his realm and of God and the world as God's body obviously suggest very different replies to these enormously difficult and complex questions. In the monarchical construct, God is implicitly in contest with evil powers, either as victorious king, who crushes them or as sacrificial servant, who (momentarily) assumes a worldly mien in order to free his subjects from evil's control. The implication of ontological dualism, of opposing good and evil powers, is the price paid for separating God from evil, and it is a high price indeed, for it suggests that the place of evil is the world (and ourselves) and that to escape evil's clutches, we need to free ourselves from "the world, the flesh, and the devil." In this construct God is not responsible for evil, but neither does God identify with the suffering caused by evil.

That identification does occur in the metaphor of the world as God's body. The evil in the world, all kinds of evil, occurs in and to God as well as to us and the rest of creation. Evil is not a power over against God; in a sense, it is God's "responsibility," part of God's being, if you will. A monistic, panentheistic position cannot avoid this conclusion. In a physical, biological, historico-cultural evolutionary process as complex as the universe, much that is evil from various perspectives will occur, and if one sees this process as God's self-expression, then God is involved in evil. But the other side of this is that God is also involved, profoundly, palpably, personally involved, in suffering, in the suffering caused by evil. The evil occurs in and to God's body; the pain that those parts of creation affected by evil feel God also feels and feels bodily. All pain to all creatures is felt immediately and bodily by God: one does not suffer alone. In this sense God's suffering on the cross was not for a mere few hours, as in the old mythology, but it is present and permanent. As the body of the world, God is forever "nailed to the cross," for as this body suffers, so God suffers.

Is this to suggest that God is helpless in relation to evil and that God knows no joy? No, for the way of the cross, the way of inclusive, radical love, is a kind of power, though a very different kind from kingly might. It does imply, however, that unlike God the king, the God who suffers with the world cannot wipe out evil; evil is not only part of the process but its power also depends on us, God's partners in the way of inclusive, radical love. And what holds for suffering can be said of joy as well. Wherever in the universe there is new life, ecstasy, tranquility, and fulfillment, God experiences these pleasures and rejoices with each creature in its joy.

When we turn to our side of this picture of the world as God's body, we have to ask whether we are reduced to being mere parts of the body. What is our freedom? How is sin understood here? How would we behave in this model? The model did not fit God's side in every way, and it does not fit ours in every way either. It seems especially problematic at the point of our individuality and freedom. At least in the king-realm model, human beings appear to have some freedom since they are controlled only externally, not internally. The problem emerges because of the nature of bodies. If we are parts of God's body—if the model is totally organic—are we not totally immersed, along with all other creatures, in the evolutionary process, with no transcendence or freedom? It appears, however, at least to us, that we are a special part. We think of ourselves as *imago dei*, as not only possessing bodies but being agents. We view ourselves as embodied spirits in the larger body of the world which influences us and which we influence. That is, we are the part molded on the model: self:body::God:world. We are agents, and God possesses a body: both sides of the model pertain to both God and ourselves. This implies that we are not mere submerged parts of the body of God but related to God as to another Thou. The presence of God to us in and through God's body is the experience of encounter, not of submersion. For the saving love of God to be present to human beings it would have to be so in a way different from how it is present to other aspects of the body of the world—in a way in keeping with the peculiar kind of creatures we are, namely, creatures with a special kind of freedom, able to participate self-consciously (as well as be influenced unconsciously) in an evolutionary process. This gives us a special status and a special responsibility: We are the ones like God; we are selves that possess bodies, and that is our glory. It is also our responsibility, for we alone can choose to become partners with God in care of the world; we alone can—like God—love, heal, befriend, and liberate the world, the body, that God has made available to us as both the divine presence and our home.

Our special status and responsibility, however, are not limited to consciousness of our own personal bodies, or even of the human world, but extend to all embodied reality, for we are that part of the cosmos where the cosmos itself has come to consciousness. If we become extinct, then the cosmos will lose its human, although presumably not its divine, consciousness. As Jonathan Schell remarks, "In extinction a darkness falls over the world not because the lights have gone out but because the eyes that behold the light have been closed" (Schell, 128).[3]

It is obvious, then, what sin is in this metaphor of the world as God's body: it is refusal to be part of the body, the special part we are as *imago dei*. In contrast to the king-realm model, where sin is against *God*, here it is against the world. To sin is not to refuse loyalty to the king, but to refuse to take responsibility for nurturing, loving, and befriending the body and all its parts. Sin is the refusal to realize one's radical interdependence with all that lives; it is the desire to set oneself apart from all others as not needing them or being needed by them. Sin is the refusal to be the eyes, the consciousness, of the cosmos.

What this experiment with the world as God's body comes to, finally, is an awareness, both chilling and breathtaking, that we, as worldly, bodily beings, are in God's presence. We do not have to go to some special place — a church, for instance — or to another world, to find God, for God is present with us here and now. We have a basis for a revived sacramentalism, that is, a perception of the divine as visible, as present, palpably present in the world. But it is a kind of sacramentalism that is painfully conscious of the world's vulnerability, its preciousness, its uniqueness. The beauty of the world and its ability to sustain the vast multitude of species it supports is not there for the taking. The world is a body that must be carefully tended, that must be nurtured, protected, guided, loved, and befriended both as valuable in itself — for like us, it is an expression of God — and as necessary to the continuation of life. We meet the world as a Thou, as the body of God where God is present to us always in all times and in all places. In the metaphor of the world as God's body the resurrection is remythologized as a worldly, present, inclusive event — the offering of the world, God's body, to all: "This is my body." As is true of all bodies, however, this body, in its beauty and precariousness, is vulnerable and at risk — it will delight the eye only if we care for it; it will nourish us only if we nurture it. Needless to say, then, were this metaphor to enter our consciousness as thoroughly as the royal, triumphalist one has entered, it would result in a different way of being in the world. There would be no way we could any longer see God as worldless or the world as Godless. Nor could we expect God to take care of everything, either through domination or through benevolence.

We see through pictures. We do not see directly. The pictures of a king and his realm and of the world as God's body are ways of speaking, ways of imagining the God-world relationship. The one pictures a vast distance between God and the world; the other imagines them as intrinsically related. At the close of day one asks which distortion (assuming that all pictures are false in some respects) is better by asking what attitudes each encourages. This is not the first question to ask, but it may well be the last. The monarchical model encourages attitudes of militarism, dualism, and escapism; it condones control through violence and oppression; it has nothing to say about the nonhuman world. The model of the world as God's body encourages holistic attitudes of responsibility for and care of the vulnerable and oppressed; it is nonhierarchical and acts through persuasion and attraction; it has a great deal to say about the body and nature. Both are pictures. Which distortion is more true to the world in which we live and to the good news of Christianity?

It may be, of course, that neither picture is appropriate to our time and to Christian faith; if so, others should be proposed. Our profound need for a powerful, attractive, imaginative picture of the way God is related to our world demands that we not only deconstruct but reconstruct our metaphors, letting the ones that seem promising try their chance.

The model of the universe as God's body is admittedly an immanental one, significant in part because it redresses the heavily transcendent imagery for God in the Judeo-Christian tradition. But it also suggests, in its own way, a model of transcendence—what one might call cosmocentric transcendence—that is awe-inspiring. The common "creation story" emerging from the fields of astrophysics, biology, and scientific cosmology makes small any myth of creation from the various religious traditions: some ten billion or so years ago the universe began from a big bang exploding the "matter," which was infinitesimally small and infinitely dense, outward to create the untold number of galaxies of which our tiny planet is but one blip on the screen. From this beginning came all that followed, so everything that is is related, woven into a seamless network, with life gradually emerging after billions of years on this planet (and perhaps on others) and resulting in the incredibly complex, intricate universe we see today. To think of God as the creator and continuing creator/sustainer of this massive, breathtaking cosmic fact dwarfs all our traditional images of divine transcendence—whether political or metaphysical. And yet, to think of the transcendence of God this way would not contradict the immanental body image. Rather, the two would come together in a cosmocentric, immanental model of transcendence: God the creator of the evolving, incredibly vast and complex universe understood as the divine "body."

What I am suggesting is that we learn to think differently about what the saving love of God must mean in our time if it is to be really *for our time*, addressing the question of the possible end of existence raised by ecological deterioration and nuclear escalation—and that we do this by thinking in *different images*. The one I have suggested is just that: *one* image—many others are needed. We must be careful, very careful, of the imagistic glasses through which we interpret God and the world. As Erich

Heller, the German philosopher and literary critic, said: "Be careful how you interpret the world. It is like that."

Some treatments attempting to raise consciousness on the ecological, nuclear situation paint a picture of nuclear winter or the extent of death and destruction that will occur after such an event. But it is even more telling in terms of our perception of the world, of how wondrous it is and how much we do in fact care for it, to think small. Almost anything will do—sheep on the English hills, a child's first steps, the smell of rain on a spring day, whatever, as long as it is some particular, cherished aspect of the world—and then dwell on its specialness, its distinctiveness, its value, until the pain of contemplating its permanent loss, not just to you or me, but to all for all time, becomes unbearable. This is a form of prayer for the world as the body of God that we, as lovers and friends of the world, are summoned to practice. This prayer, while not the only one in an ecological, nuclear age, is a necessary and permanent one. It is a form of meditation to help us think differently about the world, to enable us to work together with God to save our beleaguered planet, our beautiful, vulnerable earth, our blue and green marble in a universe of silent rock and fire.

NOTES

1. Robert P. Scharlemann uses this phrase to describe the kind of theology that constructs theological models, and he sees it as an alternative to other kinds of theology, confessional, metaphysical, biblicistic, religious thought. "It is free theology in the sense that it can make use of any of these materials—confessional, metaphysical, biblical, religious, and secular—without being bound to them" (Scharlemann, 82-83).

2. My position here is very close to that of Ricoeur, as found in *The Rule of Metaphor* and elsewhere.

3. I am indebted to Rosemary Radford Ruether for the import of this paragraph.

WORKS CITED

Arbib, Michael, and Mary Hesse. *The Construction of Reality*. Cambridge: Cambridge University Press, 1986.

Barbour, Ian. *Myths, Models and Paradigms: A Comparative Study in Science and Religion*. New York: Harper & Row, 1974.

Black, Max. *Models and Metaphors*. Ithaca, NY: Cornell University Press, 1962.

Booth, Wayne. "Metaphor as Rhetoric: The Problem of Evaluation." In *On Metaphor*. Ed. Sheldon Sacks. Chicago: University of Chicago Press, 1978.

Chopp, Rebecca. *The Praxis of Suffering: An Interpretation of Liberation and Political Theologies*. Maryknoll, NY: Orbis Books, 1986.

Cobb, John. "Feminism and Process Thought." In *Feminism and Process Thought*. Ed. Sheila Greene Daveney. New York: Edwin Mellen Press, 1981.

Cobb, John B., and David R. Griffin. *Process Theology: An Introductory Exposition*. Philadelphia: Westminster Press, 1976.

Daecke, Sigurd. "Profane and Sacramental Views of Nature." In *The Sciences and Theology in the Twentieth Century*. Ed. A.R. Peacocke. Notre Dame, IN: University of Notre Dame Press, 1986.

Derrida, Jacques. "White Mythology: Metaphor in the Text of Philosophy," In *New Literary History* 6 (1974):5-73.

Farley, Edward. *Ecclesial Reflection: An Anatomy of Theological Method*. Philadelphia: Fortress Press, 1982.

Farley, Edward, and Peter C. Hodgson. "Scripture and Tradition." In *Christian Theology: An Introduction to Its Traditions and Tasks*, rev. ed. Ed. Peter C. Hodgson and Robert H. King. Philadelphia: Fortress Press, 1985.

Goodman, Nelson. *Languages of Art: An Approach to a Theory of Symbols*. Indianapolis: Bobbs-Merrill, 1968.

Gustafson, James M. *Ethics from a Theocentric Perspective*. Chicago: University of Chicago Press, 1981.

Hartshorne, Charles. "Philosophical and Religious Uses of 'God.' " In *Process Theology: Basic Writings*. Ed. Ewert H. Cousins. New York: Newman Press, 1977.

Hepburn, R. W. "Demythologizing and the Problem of Validity." In *New Essays in Philosophical Theology*. Eds. Antony Flew and Alasdair MacIntyre. London: SCM Press, 1955.

Hesse, Mary. "Cosmology as Myth." In *Cosmology and Theology*. Ed. David Tracy and Nicholas Lash. Edinburgh and New York: T. & T. Clark and Seabury Press, 1983.

Hopkins, Gerard Manley. *Poems and Prose of Gerard Manley Hopkins*. London: Penguin Books, 1953.

Jantzen, Grace. *God's World, God's Body*. Philadelphia: Westminster Press, 1984.

Julian of Norwich. *Showings*. Trans. Edmund Colledge and James Walsh. New York: Paulist Press, 1978.

Kaufman, Gordon. *God the Problem*. Cambridge: Harvard University Press, 1979.

———. *The Theological Imagination: Constructing the Concept of God*. Philadelphia: Westminster Press, 1981.

———. *Theology for a Nuclear Age*. Philadelphia: Westminster Press, 1985.

Lash, Nicholas. *Theology on the Road to Emmaus*. London: SCM Press, 1986.

Lewis, C. S. *The Four Loves*. New York: Harcourt, Brace & Co., 1960.

McDaniel, Jay. "God and Pelicans." In *Church and Society, Report and Background Papers*. Meeting of the Working Group. Glion, Switzerland: World Council of Churches, 1987.

McFague, Sallie. *Metaphorical Theology: Models of God in Religious Language*. Philadelphia: Fortress Press, 1982.

———. *Models of God: Theology for an Ecological, Nuclear Age*. Philadelphia: Fortress Press, 1987.

McMullin, Ernan. "How Should Cosmology Relate to Theology?" In *The Sciences and Theology in the Twentieth Century*. Ed. Arthur Peacocke. Notre Dame, IN: University of Notre Dame Press, 1982.

Moltmann, Jürgen. *The Trinity and the Kingdom of God*. San Francisco: Harper and Row, 1981.

Nineham, Dennis. *The Myth of God Incarnate*. Ed. John Hick. Philadelphia: Westminster Press, 1977.

Peacocke, Arthur. *Creation and the World of Science*. Oxford: Clarendon Press, 1979.

Pippard, Sir Brian. "Instability and Chaos: Physical Models of Everyday Life." In *Interdisciplinary Science Reviews* (1982): 91-102.

Rahner, Karl, and Herbert Vorgrimler. *Kleines theologishches Wortenbuchen*. Freiberg: Herder & Herder, 1961.

Ricoeur, Paul. "Biblical Hermeneutics," *Semeia* 4 (1975):29-145.

————. *The Rule of Metaphor: Multi-disciplinary Studies of the Creation of Meaning in Language*. Study 8. Trans. Robert Czerny. Toronto: University of Toronto Press, 1977.

Ruether, Rosemary. *Sexism and God-Talk: Toward a Feminist Theology*. Boston: Beacon Press, 1983.

Scharlemann, Robert P. "Theological Models and Their Construction." In *Journal of Religion* 53 (1973): 65-82.

Schell, Jonathan. *The Fate of the Earth*. New York: Avon Books, 1982.

Soelle, Dorothee. *The Strength of the Weak: Toward a Christian Feminist Identity*. Trans. Robert and Rita Kimber. Philadelphia: Westminster Press, 1984.

Soskice, Janet Martin. *Metaphor and Religious Language*. Oxford: Clarendon Press, 1985.

Stevens, Wallace. *Opus Posthumous*. Ed. S.F. Morris. New York: Alfred A. Knopf, 1957.

Stewart, Claude. *Nature in Grace: A Study in the Theology of Nature*. Macon, GA: Mercer University Press, 1983.

Teilhard de Chardin, Pierre (a). *Writings in Time of War*. Trans. Rene Hague. London: William Collins, 1968.

———— (b). *Divine Milieu*. New York: Harper and Row, 1968.

Tillich, Paul. *Systematic Theology*. Vol. 1. Chicago: University of Chicago Press, 1963.

Toulmin, Stephen. *The Return to Cosmology: Postmodern Science and the Theology of Nature*. Berkeley: University of California Press, 1982.

Tracy, David. *The Analogical Imagination: Christian Theology and the Culture of Pluralism*. New York: Crossroad; London: SCM Press, 1981.

Tracy, David, and Nicholas Lash, eds. *Cosmology and Theology*. Edinburgh and New York: T. & T. Clark and Seabury Press, 1983.

Trible, Phyllis. *God and the Rhetoric of Sexuality*. Philadelphia: Fortress Press, 1978.

White, Lynn. "The Historical Roots of Our Ecologic Crisis." In *Ecology and Religion in History*. Ed. David and Eileen Spring. New York: Harper & Row, 1974.

Questions for Discussion

1. Does your interpretation of "the greatest commandment" coincide with or differ from how the *campesinos* in Solentiname interpret it? For what reasons?

2. What can women and men in North America learn about the meaning and practice of spirituality from Asian women?

3. Has your usual experience of the eucharist challenged you to work for justice in society as Balasuriya says it should? Why or why not? If not, what can be done to change this?

4. Examine your own view of God's relationship to the world. How has it affected the way you relate to nature? Is McFague's model of the world as God's body a promising catalyst for ecological sensitivity? If so, how? If not, why not?

5. How can North American Christians develop their own "liberation spirituality"? What would be some of its characteristics?

Contributors

Maria Pilar Aquino, was born in Mexico, received her doctorate from the Pontifical University of Salamanca (Spain), and currently lives in Los Angeles, where she is director of the Hispanic Ministry Program at Mount St. Mary's College. Her book, *Our Cry for Life: Latin American Theology from the Perspective of Women* is forthcoming from Orbis Books.

Tissa Balasuriya is a Sri Lankan theologian with degrees from Oxford, the Gregorian University in Rome, and the University of Paris. A former president of the Aquinas University College in Sri Lanka, he now works at the Centre for Society and Religion in Colombo. His books include *The Eucharist and Human Liberation* (Orbis Books, 1979) and *Planetary Theology* (Orbis, 1984).

Dominique Barbé was a French priest who lived and worked among the base communities of São Paulo, Brazil from 1968 until his death in 1988. His writings were largely devoted to nonviolence and the means of struggle for social justice. Two of his books were translated into English: *Grace and Power: Base Communities and Nonviolence in Brazil* (Orbis Books, 1987) and *A Theology of Conflict and Other Writings on Nonviolence* (Orbis, 1989).

Clodovis Boff is a Brazilian priest of the Servite Order, who divides his time between teaching at the Catholic University of São Paulo and working as a theological consultant to base communities. His books include *Theology and Praxis: Epistemological Foundations* (Orbis Books, 1987) and *Feet-on-the-Ground Theology* (Orbis, 1987). He is co-author (with George V. Pixley) of *The Bible, the Church, and the Poor* (Orbis, 1989), and (with his brother Leonardo) *Introducing Liberation Theology* (Orbis, 1987).

Leonardo Boff is a Franciscan theologian from Brazil, and one of the most influential and prolific exponents of liberation theology. His many books include *Jesus Christ Liberator* (Orbis Books, 1978), *Ecclesiogenesis* (Orbis, 1986), *Passion of Christ, Passion of the World* (Orbis, 1987), *Trinity and Society* (Orbis, 1988), and *Faith on the Edge* (Orbis, 1991). His work has been subject to public review and criticism by the Vatican Congregation for the Doctrine of the Faith. As a result of questions based on his book *Church: Charism and Power* (Crossroad, 1985), he was ordered to maintain a year of silence. His most recent book in English is *New Evangelization* (Orbis, 1992).

Curt Cadorette is a Maryknoll priest who has worked among the Aymara people of Peru. He received his doctorate in theology from St. Michael's College,

Toronto, and has taught at the Maryknoll School of Theology and Marist College. He is the author of *From the Heart of the People: The Theology of Gustavo Gutiérrez* (Meyer-Stone, 1988).

Ernesto Cardenal is a Nicaraguan poet and priest, a founder of the peasant/artisan community of Solentiname in Nicaragua (suppressed by the National Guard of Anastasio Somoza), who served as Minister of Culture in the revolutionary Sandinista government from 1979-89. Because of his service in a government position, he was deprived of his priestly faculties, an order that has not been lifted. Internationally known for his poetry, his many books include the four-volume series, *The Gospel of Solentiname* (Orbis Books, 1976, 1978, 1979, 1982). He currently lives in Managua.

Chung Hyun Kyung is a Korean theologian who teaches systematic theology at Ewha Women's University in Seoul, Korea. She received her doctorate from Union Theological Seminary in New York. She is the author of *Struggle To Be the Sun Again: Introducing Asian Women's Theology* (Orbis Books, 1990). Her plenary address before the 1990 Canberra Conference of the World Council of Churches under the theme "Come Holy Spirit" attracted international attention as a result of her integration of symbols and themes from non-Western and non-Christian religious traditions.

James H. Cone is Charles A. Briggs Distinguished Professor of Systematic Theology at Union Theological Seminary. One of the pioneers of black theology, he has been an important figure in the international dialogue among third world theologians. His books include *A Black Theology of Liberation* (Twentieth Anniversary Edition, Orbis Books, 1990), *For My People* (Orbis, 1984), *The Spirituals and the Blues* (1972; Orbis, 1991), and *Martin & Malcolm & America: A Dream or a Nightmare* (Orbis, 1991). With Gayraud Wilmore he has edited *Black Theology: A Documentary History* (Orbis, 1979). A second volume of this history will appear in 1993.

Jean-Marc Éla is a Cameroonian theologian who has worked among peasants in north Cameroon. He holds doctorates in theology and sociology from the University of Strasbourg. Since 1985 he has been teaching at the University of Yaoundé. His books include *African Cry* (Orbis Books, 1986) and *My Faith as an African* (Orbis, 1988).

Ivone Gebara, a religious sister and theologian, is Professor of Philosophy and Theology at the Theological Institute of Recife, Brazil. She is the author (with Maria Clara Bingemer) of *Mary: Mother of God, Mother of the Poor* (Orbis Books, 1989).

Marie Giblin received her Ph.D. in Christian ethics from Union Theological Seminary in New York City. She worked for nine years in Tanzania and continues research on Africa, with special interest in women's issues, health and economic development, and U.S. policy in that region. Currently she teaches at the Maryknoll School of Theology.

Gustavo Gutiérrez is a Peruvian priest and theologian who lives in Lima. His book, *A Theology of Liberation,* (Orbis Books, 1973) published in 1971, has become the classic statement of liberation theology. Apart from his theological research, he lives and works among the poor of Rimac, a Lima slum. His other books include *We Drink from Our Own Wells* (Orbis, 1984), *On Job: God-Talk and the Suffering of the Innocent* (Orbis, 1987), *The Truth Shall Make You Free* (Orbis, 1990), *The God of Life* (Orbis, 1991), and *Las Casas: In Search of the Poor of Jesus Christ* (Orbis, 1992).

Mary Hunt is co-director of the Women's Alliance for Theology, Ethics and Ritual (WATER) in Washington, D.C.

Marilyn J. Legge received her doctorate from Union Theological Seminary. Currently, she teaches at St. Andrew's College in Saskatoon, Canada.

Sallie McFague, Carpenter Professor of Theology at Vanderbilt Divinity School in Nashville, Tennesee, is the author of many books, including *Metaphorical Theology* and *Models of God: Theology in an Ecological, Nuclear Age* (both Fortress Press).

Mary John Mananzan, a Missionary Benedictine Sister from the Philippines, has a Ph.D. in philosophy and is dean of St. Scholastica's College in Manila.

Carlos Mesters is a Dutch Carmelite priest who has worked for more than twenty years among base Christian communities in Brazil. Best known for his popular biblical commentaries, he is also the author of *Defenseless Flower: A New Reading of the Bible* (Orbis Books, 1989), which elaborates his work on the interpretation of the Bible in base communities.

Anne Nasimiyu-Wasike is a religious sister and theologian who teaches at Kenyatta University in Nairobi, Kenya.

Sun Ai Park is a Korean minister of the Disciples of Christ, Asian Coordinator of the Women's Commission of the Ecumenical Association of Third World Theologians, and Coordinator of the Asian Women's Resource Centre for Culture and Theology. She is co-editor of *We Dare to Dream: Doing Theology as Asian Women* (Orbis Books, 1990).

Mary Hembrow Snyder received her doctorate from St. Michael's College of Toronto. Currently she is associate professor of theology and religious studies at Mercyhurst College, PA. She is author of *The Christology of Rosemary Radford Ruether: A Critical Introduction.*

Jon Sobrino is a Spanish-born Jesuit priest and theologian who has worked for over twenty years in El Salvador. His books include *Christology at the Crossroads* (Orbis Books, 1978), *The True Church and the Poor* (Orbis, 1984), *Jesus in Latin America* (1987), and *Spirituality of Liberation* (Orbis, 1988). Drawing on his perspective as a theological advisor to the martyred archbishop of San Salvador,

Oscar Romero, he has published a collection of essays entitled *Archbishop Romero: Memories and Reflections* (Orbis, 1990). Sobrino was a surviving member of the Jesuit community of the University of San Salvador, massacred in 1989 by the Salvadoran armed forces. His reflections on this event appear in *Companions of Jesus: The Jesuit Martyrs of El Salvador* (Orbis, 1990).

Charles Villa-Vicencio is Associate Professor and Head of the Department of Religious Studies at the University of Cape Town, South Africa. He is author of *Trapped in Apartheid* (Orbis Books, 1988), *Theology and Violence* (Eerdmans, 1988), and co-editor of *Apartheid Is a Heresy* (Eerdmans, 1983).

Yong Ting Jin, a member of the Basel Christian Church of Malaysia, is the Asian-Pacific regional secretary of the World Student Christian Federation, based in Hong Kong.

Glossary

Anthropocentric: a perspective on life in which human beings are perceived as the high point of creation, sometimes in opposition to nature. Such a viewpoint, if unchecked, can lead to ecological irresponsibility and even violence against the environment since human beings see themselves as the sole beneficiaries of the natural world with an inherent right to use it as they alone see fit.

Apartheid: a political and social term, used in South Africa, to designate and legitimize the segregation of people according to race. An English rendering of the term might be "apartness." According to this concept, racial groups are meant to be separate because they are inherently different. Implicit in the idea of *apartheid* is the notion that certain racial groups are inherently superior or inferior to others, thus justifying separation and even the oppression of one group by another.

Apocalyptic Thought: a worldview ranging from about the third century before Christ until the third century after. According to this perspective i) human history is seen in terms of struggle between good (divine) and evil; ii) the dominance of evil in human history is only apparent, for in the larger picture God controls the outcome of events; iii) history is moving toward the final triumph of good over evil, in fact it may be already underway though the signs are only apparent to certain individuals/prophets. This approach was a break from other views of history which considered political catastrophe a sign of God's judgment on human beings.

Base Christian Community: These small groups of poor and believing people are found in many countries today. Their structure and underlying ideas are quite varied, but they all strive to generate close spiritual ties between members, an air of mutual support, and a stronger faith that makes sense in the contemporary world. (Also *basic Christian community, basic ecclesial community.*)

Black Power: a term that in the 1960s began to replace "integration" as the goal of civil rights activists.

Bourgeois: This French word basically refers to the middle-class and a pro-capitalist worldview. The bourgeois outlook on life is characterized by a concern with individuality and material comfort.

Capitalism: This economic concept is essentially synonymous with the contemporary "free market system." It is based on the law of supply and demand. For most liberation theologians, this system produces massive inequality, and is one of the key reasons for the poverty of millions of people in the world today.

Casuistic: refers to the method of deciding morality on a case to case method by bringing principles to bear on the cases; casuistry and casuistic (the adjective) can also refer to the abuse of this kind of method which sometimes develops into overly fine-tuned arguments about small details rather a more humanistic probing of a case.

Christological: having to do with Jesus Christ, especially concerned with his person and identity.

Colonialism: a political or economic condition prevalent in the developing world characterized by the systematic material and cultural oppression of less powerful peoples by European or North American nations. Colonial powers have generally exploited less powerful countries for the sake of cheap natural resources. In the late twentieth century, few countries still possess colonies. Colonialism, however, is still a sociopolitical reality exercised through indirect but effective means which provide access to natural resources in the developing world. This new, somewhat more refined mode of exploitation is sometimes referred to as *neo-colonialism*.

EATWOT: acronym for the Ecumenical Association of Third World Theologians founded in 1976.

Ecclesiology: theological reflection on the church.

Epistemology: study of the nature and grounds of knowledge.

Eschatology (eschatological): ideas about the end-times or things of the end-times; traditionally the branch of theology concerned with the final events in the history of the world. In contemporary theology the notion holds in tension the importance and value of the present historical moment seen in light of the ultimate end of history. Two important categories of eschatology (both present in the New Testament) are *realized eschatology* (which considers the end-times to have already arrived in Christ (e.g. Gospel of John) and *future eschatology,* especially apocalyptic eschatology.

Essenes: a sect of Judaism in Palestine from the second century before Christ until the war with Rome in 66-70 C.E. They were critical of temple leadership and members were forbidden to participate in temple ritual. They had a rigorous ethics, maintained ritual purity, and kept themselves spiritually ready for the intervention of God to destroy evil. They were apocalyptic in their thought and orientation.

Exegetical (exegesis, exegete): having to do with the scientific study of biblical texts through biblical research, analysis, and commentary. The work itself is called exegesis; the person doing the analysis is the exegete.

Existentialism: refers to a way of looking at our human existence that highlights the tension between our freedom and our finitude, i.e. between our sense of infinite potential and the concrete limitations of our factual existence as we experience it.

Exordium: [of the Gospel of Mark]: the beginning of the gospel, its introduction.

Favelas: This Portuguese word refers to an urban slum area. Large Brazilian cities have immense favelas in which the working poor are packed together. Such slums, however, exist throughout the world.

Fundamentalism: This term refers to the tendency of certain Christians to read the text of the Bible in a literal way, with little or no reference to the background of the text or the human author who wrote it. Furthermore, fundamentalists take little stock of the way their own context and worldview influences their interpretation of biblical materials.

Gratuity of the Kingdom: the kingdom as gift from God rather than the result of human work.

Han: a Korean word that on the one hand refers to feelings of resentment, indignation, and the will to overcome, and on the one hand, a sense of defeat, resignation, and nothingness.

Hegemony: the domination of a social, economic, or even intellectual system by another. For example, the United States is a hegemonic power in relationship to most Latin American countries. It shapes their social policies and values in ways that repress autonomous decisions and thought.

Hermeneutics: the study of the principles of interpretation (here, of the Bible); concerned with how we can understand today the sense of texts whose worldview we no longer share.

Ideology: This term, which is used in the social sciences and liberation theology with great regularity, is very difficult to explain, since people use it in different ways. Some scholars understand ideology to be nothing more than a worldview, or set of values, that hold a society together. Drawing on Karl Marx, however, many writers use the term in a negative sense. For them it connotes a false and distorted notion of reality imposed by people in power. Their understanding of reality, which is based on their own class interests, is made normative for everyone else.

Indigenization: in theological terms, an attempt to make Christianity more compatible and consonant with a particular cultural system, particularly one that is non-Western.

Kerygma: a New Testament term for the "good news" of God's saving activity in the life, death, and resurrection of Jesus. The term literally means preaching, but the content of the preaching is also intended.

Kerygmatic Christ: Jesus Christ as he has been preached by the church, in contrast to the historical Jesus. See *kerygma* (above).

Machismo: This Spanish word refers to a society or culture in which males are considered superior to females. In "machistic" societies men are often allowed to live more freely, and sometimes more irresponsibly, than women. Social expectations and gender rules are rigidly enforced. The result is the culturally-sanctioned oppression of women by men.

Minjung: a Korean word that means those who are oppressed and denied their basic rights.

National Security, Doctrine of: During the 1960s many countries in the so-called developing world were ruled by military governments. This phenomenon was not something spontaneous. It was the result of a calculated political doctrine and strategy. Convinced that their countries were threatened by Marxist groups, members of the military took over governments from civilian politicians and attempted to eradicate groups that they deemed dangerous. They often resorted to mass executions and torture to achieve their ends. Although this phenomenon began to abate in the 1980s with the resurgence of democratically elected governments, the military is still a powerful political force in many nations.

Neo-colonialism: see Colonialism.

Parousia: a Greek word that means "presence" or "arrival"; it refers to the second coming of Jesus Christ at the end of time.

Patriarchal: This adjective describes male domination over virtually every aspect of women's lives (political, economic, social, sexual, religious, etc.) in a given culture.

Patriarchy: social organization characterized by the supremacy of males and the subordination of women.

Personalism: a philosophical approach that is concerned with persons and considers self-conscious experience to be the key to reality; personality is the fundamental explanatory principle. Liberation theologians are critical because of the lack of attention to historical context. Its use in Sobrino: "Therefore any hermeneutical presupposition, conscious or unconscious, along the lines of a pure personalism is a serious obstacle to understanding what the kingdom of God was for Jesus."

Pharisees: one of several Jewish sects in the first century (see also Essenes); they emphasized synagogue worship and ritual observances of various kinds in contrast to the Sadducees who emphasized the rituals associated with the Jerusalem temple.

Politicization: This term, which is found in the writings of many liberation theologians, refers to the process whereby poor people become critically aware of their political environment and committed to changing it in a more just way.

Popular Movement: The term popular movement, like that of popular religion, comes from the Latin word *populus* which refers to the ordinary people of a society. The popular movement and popular religion, therefore, are political or religious currents of thought which ordinary people identify with, sometimes in distinction from official political parties or the institutional church.

Praxis: a Greek word, praxis is understood by liberation theologians in the sense of the combination of theory and action. When, for example, base communities decide to build a school or clinic for their neighborhood, they are involved in praxis. Their action on behalf of the community is informed and motivated by their Christian values. Their combined ideas and energies produce what is called liberative praxis.

Preferential Option for the Poor: This concept, which is central to liberation theology, was first articulated by the bishops of Latin America in 1968 in a meeting held in Medellín, Colombia. First of all, the preferential option for the poor refers to God's special concern and compassion for oppressed people. In many ways, this concept is modeled after Jesus' own life and action since he paid particular attention to the needy people of his day. As the bishops stated in 1968, it is also the duty of the Christian church to opt for the cause of the poor as well. This is especially true in a continent marked by injustice and grinding poverty.

Second Vatican Council: This great event in the life of the Catholic church, often called Vatican II, took place from 1962 until 1965. It was called by Pope John XXIII who felt that the church should open itself up to the modern world after a long period of defensiveness. He assembled the bishops of the church to study ways and means to make the church more responsive to its historical environment. The fruits of their labors are known as the Vatican Documents. These texts continue to exert a profound influence on the self-understanding of Catholic Christians and the daily practice of the institutional church.

Shamanism: belief in an unseen world of gods, demons, and ancestral spirits who are responsive to priests called shamans. Shamans sometimes enter trances in which they act as the spokespersons for spiritual forces. In a trance shamans often provide answers meant to solve a crisis or point out a course of future action.

Soteriology: section of theology that deals with salvation; in Christian theology the study of the redemptive work of Jesus Christ.

Syncretism: When two cultures or religious systems begin to blend together, the result is a new reality which is often described as "syncretistic." For example, when black Africans were brought to the western hemisphere as slaves, they came with their own cultures and religions. They were also exposed to the cultures and religions of their captors which they gradually began to understand and assimilate. Yet they still retained much of their old worldview which became part of their new cultural and religious universe. In short, they created a syncretistic culture and religion which met their needs and expressed their understanding of reality.

Synoptic: literally, "with one eye"; the gospels of Mark, Matthew, and Luke are known as the synoptic gospels because they share many of the same sources.

Theophany of God: disclosure, unveiling, or manifestation of God.

Transcendence: that which is separate from, exalted above, the physical universe. Its use in Sobrino: "In Jesus, the ultimate is presented in a unity of transcendence and history."

Zealots: the name associated with persons who opposed the Roman occupation of Palestine at the time of Jesus. There is scholarly controversy over whether the Zealots can be considered a nationalist resistance movement at the time of Jesus or became so only later.

Index

Eucharist and, 265-68; political, 248; of the poor, 58; sin of, 115; wealth and, 115; of women, 58, 193, 195-97, 208, 246
Orthodoxy, 85
Orthopraxis, 85, 90
Pannenberg, Wolfhart, 142, 148
Pantheism, 281
Park, Sun Ai, 227, 293
Park Soon Kyung, 127-29, 135
Parousia, 297
Patience, historical, 243
Patriarchy, 132, 209, 246, 250, 253: the Church and, 198-99; cultural patterns of, 193; definition of, 297; the home and, 205; power and, 203; women-church and, 207; women's spirituality and, 245
Pentecost, 160
People of God, the, 162, 175, 200
Personalism, 106, 297
Personal meaning, the quest for, 256-58
Pharisees, the, 83, 107, 113, 115, 201, 225, 230, 298
Pluralism, 3, 166-67
Poetry, 48-49, 61
Politicization, 298
Politics, 16-17, 190-91, 209-10, 212
Poor, the: the Bible and, 52-53; the church of, 212-13; God and, 237; irruption of, 66-68; Jesus and, 112-13, 240; justice and, 119; the Kingdom of God and, 109, 111, 112, 146; oppression of, 58; solidarity and, 68, 72; the voice of, 184-87; the Word of God and, 67-68
Populorum Progressio, 38
Power, 199, 203, 265-66
Praxis: definition, 298; of liberation, 224, 225; liberative, 78; of love, 119
Prayer, 33, 223, 240-42: Church base communities and, 184; liberation and, 238; practice and, 239
Preferential option for the poor, 165, 193-95, 196, 225, 298
Priests, the, 115, 230
Priesthood, the, women and, 194, 262-63

Prophecy, 58
Prophets, the, 110, 111
Prophetical traditions, 105
Prophetico-apocalyptic tradition, 107
Prostitution, 247, 250
Protestant Reformation, the, 4, 79, 163
Rabbis, the, 107
Racism, 6, 217
Rahner, Karl, 5, 11, 81
Reality, 44, 60-61, 109
Reconciliation, 111
Reign of God, the, 82-84, 225, 239. See also Kingdom of God
Renewal, of the Church, 175, 193
Repentance, 66, 152, 153, 202, 260
Resurrection, the, 84, 147-48
Revelation, 2, 5, 41, 137
Roman Empire, the, 83
Rosary, the, 27-28
Ruether, Rosemary Radford, 92, 270
Sabbath, the, 116
Sacrament, 173-74, 209
Sacramentalism, 285
Sacrament and sign, the Church as, 173-76, 193
Sadducees, the, 225
Salvation: holistic, 253; as liberation, 155, 254; oppressed blacks and, 153-55; privatization of, 81; sacrament of, 170-76
Schell, Jonathan, 285: *The Fate of the Earth,* 269
Schüssler Fiorenza, Elisabeth 209, 253
Science and technology, 1, 2, 270
Scribes, the, 115, 230
Second Vatican Council, the, 4-5, 81, 163-64, 172-73, 267, 298
Sermon on the Mount, the, 105, 146
Sexuality, female, 248-49
Shamanism, 136, 298
Sin, 114-15, 119: against the world, 285; forgiveness of, 24; history of, 107; liberation and, 20; liberation from, 84; social, 165; suffering and, 7
Snyder, Mary Hembrow, 221-29, 293
Sobrino, Jon, 85, 293-94: "Jesus and the Kingdom of God," 104-22